▼▼

A COOK'S TOUR OF SONOMA

A COOK'S TOUR

OF

SONOMA

MICHELE ANNA JORDAN

ILLUSTRATIONS BY MARSHA SERAFIN

ARIS BOOKS

ADDISON-WESLEY PUBLISHING COMPANY, INC.

READING, MASSACHUSETTS   MENLO PARK, CALIFORNIA   NEW YORK

DON MILLS, ONTARIO   WOKINGHAM, ENGLAND   AMSTERDAM   BONN

SYDNEY   SINGAPORE   TOKYO   MADRID   SAN JUAN

The recipe "Fiesta Sonoma Grilled Chicken" originally appeared in *Season by Season: The Sonoma County Farmers Market Cookbook* by Hilda Swartz, editor. Copyright © 1988 by the Sonoma County and Sonoma Valley Farmers Markets.

The recipe "Blueberry and Chicken Liver Salad with Blueberry Vinaigrette" originally appeared in *Women Chefs* by Jim Burns and Betty Ann Brown. Copyright © 1987 by Jim Burns and Betty Ann Brown. Reprinted by permission of Addison-Wesley Publishing Co., Inc., Reading, MA.

Many of the designations used by manufacturers and sellers to distinguish their products are claimed as trademarks. Where those designations appear in this book and Addison-Wesley was aware of a trademark claim, the designations have been printed in initial capital letters (e.g., Bear Flag brand).

Library of Congress Cataloging-in-Publication Data

Jordan, Michele Anna.
    A cook's tour of Sonoma / Michele Anna Jordan.
      p. cm.
    ISBN 0-201-52356-6
    1. Cookery. 2. Grocery trade—California—Sonoma County—Guide-
books. 3. Sonoma County (Calif.)—Description and travel—Guide-
books. I. Title.
TX714.J67   1990
641.5—dc20   90-332
                                              CIP

Text design by Beth Tondreau Design/Jane Treuhaft
Set in 11-point Electra by G&S Typesetters, Inc., Austin, TX

A B C D E F G H I J-VB-943210
First printing, September 1990

▼▼▼

FOR DECLAN MACMANUS
aka Elvis Costello,
whose phenomenal talent as a singer and songwriter
and compassion and conscience as a thinking human
have enriched my life immeasurably.

CONTENTS

LIST OF RECIPES

FOREWORD

I fell in love with Sonoma County in the late sixties. I worked in San Francisco then for a large corporate food producer and used to make the trip across the Golden Gate as often as I could both to revitalize my soul and to search out new, fresh products for my table. It came to me that what I was witnessing then was a rebirth of the family farm. Here were all these agrarian artists (many of them refugees from the back-to-the-land idealism of the sixties) who had decided that being close to the earth was the only way to make sense of a crazy world. Many found out that agriculture was a very hard way to make a living and left. But others remained and were joined by more to form a community that is now producing an incredible bounty of fresh and unusual foods.

Part of what has made Sonoma County so unique is that the population is small enough and isolated enough from the anonymity of the big city that cooks and farmers can influence one another personally and directly. I love knowing the people who grow my lettuce, for example. It truly is a cook's paradise!

I do not think that what is happening here is another "precious" food trend but rather the birth of a unique regional cuisine keyed to its environment. Michele has been a devoted mother and advocate in bringing this culinary baby to adulthood. She has been outspoken in her commitment to preserve the fragile ecology in which it grows. I think you will find this book not only a useful reference but also a passionate statement of Michele's love of food. Savor it. I think you will enjoy it as much as I do.

John Ash
January 1990

ACKNOWLEDGMENTS

So many people have helped make this book a reality, some in subtly supportive ways they may not even realize, some by practically holding my hand through the difficult times when the book seemed an unreachable dream or an unwieldy adolescent. All of their contributions deserve my acknowledgment and thanks, which I offer here to:

My wonderful daughters, Gina and Nicolle, with love; Ginny Stanford, for her constant, unwavering support, for her undyingly enthusiastic appreciation of my cooking, and for her invaluable criticism and contributions to the manuscript; David Browne, whose constant belief that I could do it made it possible; M. F. K. Fisher, with great affection, from one bat lover to another; Rico Traverso and Louis Traverso, their sons George and Bill, their families, and their wonderful Italian market and delicatessen, Traverso's; Mary and Guy Duryee for their incredibly enthusiastic support of my writing and my cooking, and for providing me with the beautiful home where the book was written; Rob Cole, also known as Dr. Music, my friend and muse, for the inspired soundtrack; Nick Topolos, for simply being himself; to my editor and friend, John Harris, whose enthusiasm and faith in me have been a source of inspiration when I most needed it, and whose creative contributions to the book have been invaluable; Peter Reinhardt of Brother Juniper's Bakery, for his warmth, emotional generosity, and encouragement, and for his delicious bread; Bruce Robinson, for forcing me to take the first step back in 1986; Julieta Leal, for the comic relief and gossip, and for providing the most interesting editing jobs any writer has ever had; Jill Wattles, Gabrielle Mazura-Hartan, Ulli Posey, and Maggie O'Brien, for their efforts and support of The Jaded Palate, and for their friendship; John Ash, for the interest and support he offered me, and for sharing his talents so generously; all the contributing chefs; all of my recipe testers and enthusiastic tasters who provided inval-

xviii

uable comments and reactions; Mathilda, Mario, and little Olive, my three cats, for their intense interest in and scrutiny of the manuscript; Bruce Corson and Doug Hoff, for easing my way into the modern world; Marcus Schmidt, Ron Magee, and Kathy Trombley for taking such good care of me; Richard Gossett, Bob Sala, Scott Murray, and Scott Kinzy for playing my requests; Anna Cherney, Mary Rich, Tony Mountain, and J. J. Wilson, for the years of kindness, support, friendship, and love they've offered; and A. J. DiMauro, who knows why.

INTRODUCTION

The purpose of this book, besides being a collection of what I hope you find to be delicious recipes, is twofold: To provide a source, a gateway, into the sometimes exotic pantry of Sonoma County and to demystify it. The culinary explosion of the last fifteen years has made such items as shiitake mushrooms and raspberry vinegar quite familiar to the ear and to some degree, familiar to our palates as well, but to the majority of home cooks, they are still somewhat mysterious. Sonoma County wines are perhaps the most well known of all our products, but are just one of the important elements in Sonoma's culinary equation, being inseparable from the kaleidoscope of foods grown and produced here. Do you know, for example, that it takes exactly the same conditions to grow shiitake mushrooms as it does to grow Gravenstein apples, and that Sebastopol, in western Sonoma County, is one of the world's largest producers of both?

Kozlowski Farms in Forestville produces the best version of raspberry vinegar I have ever found. What a delicious and varied ingredient it can be. A grilled chicken sandwich with raspberry mayonnaise is one delicious way to enjoy it; tender stalks of steamed asparagus smothered in Raspberry Hollandaise is another; and these are just two examples. A *Cook's Tour of Sonoma* will, I hope, open the doors to Sonoma's wondrous pantry and allow you not merely access but also the opportunity to fill your own pantry with Sonoma's best.

I also hope that my book encourages cooks to turn to their own communities and harvest the varied richness they find. This is indeed a book about Sonoma County, but it is also a book about gleaning the best of what is at hand, wherever you may find yourself. Many ingredients, in fact, most of the ingredients I use are common to us all and provide, say, the grammar of our cooking. The spirit of Sonoma, and its vast, varied abundance, provides for an enticing cuisine, but when you want to try the Tomato-Cilantro Soup on page 100 you will not, in all likelihood, be using a tomato grown in Sonoma. You will have two choices when you gather ingredients for that recipe. You can go to your local supermarket and get a cardboard tomato, the same mealy, tasteless, but perfectly round and red tomato that you will find there all year, or you can find the farmer or the fruit stand or the farm market in your area and buy locally grown, real tomatoes when they are in season. I find no gastronomic joy greater than that of a perfectly grown, ripe tomato and, if I achieve my purpose, this book will motivate you to seek out that local, in-season tomato.

In this sense, you could say that my purpose is political as well as gastronomic. There is a growing trend everywhere including here in Sonoma for large corporations to take over the most minute details of our daily lives. With alarming frequency shopping centers replace the corner market. From the radio stations we listen to, to the newspapers we read and the stores where we buy our food and clothing, there is an increasing trend towards homogenization, towards the generic. Some supermarket chains even have their own cable radio stations that pipe in the exact same messages to shoppers throughout the country. It is a frightening trend, one that seriously threatens our individuality and our diversity. At the same time, however, there is another movement in the opposite direction towards the original, the regional, the local. The discovery that American cooking, American cuisine, if you prefer, is really a vast collection of re-gional cuisines, influenced by the immigrants who originally settled the area, the natives who lived there, the climate, and the geography, is yielding a crop of regional cookbooks. Sonoma County reveals the influences of the many different countries whose people came to build their lives on our fertile ground. It is just that diversity of culture, the Indian, the Russian, the Italian, the Spanish, the Portuguese, that has resulted in the richness of this enclave sandwiched between the Pacific Ocean and the dry inland valley of Napa. A Big Mac may be the national dish of corporate America, but it is the cranberries of the northeast, the oysters of the northwest, our farmstead cheeses, Louisiana gumbos, Tex-Mex barbecue, and the myriad regional foods and styles of preparing them, that really make up American food.

Farm markets are springing up all over the country, and there is a growing awareness of the value of the local family farm and its products. A network of regional, organic, thoughtfully produced foods, if properly nurtured, can compete with the agribusiness conglomerates that offer us only cardboard tomatoes nourished not by nature's nutrients, but by a frightening menu of poisonous petroleum-based fertilizers. Sonoma County is an example of the success of this effort. 1989 was the year in which the general public embraced the concept of organic food, long considered the domain of the health nut or fanatic or, more recently, of back-to-the-earth hippies. Organic produce is now the common, easily available alternative to the pesticide-ridden foods offered us by agribusiness. We discovered that protecting our families from toxic residues was not just the healthier choice to make, but resulted in a richer, tastier, more diverse diet as well. In Sonoma County, an ever-increasing number of farms is in the transitional process of converting to all-organic farming, returning to the soil the natural richness that years of chemicals have leached out. The battle has by no means been won, but if public awareness and demand continues to increase, nutritious, wholesome, natural food will eventually prevail.

Sonoma County has changed a great deal since I arrived in 1972 to attend the university and to raise my two young daughters in the country. It seemed to be the best of all possible worlds then, like a well-kept secret, which in retrospect, I realize it truly was. Less than forty-five minutes from the Golden Gate Bridge, life in Sonoma County seemed hours away from the fast-paced urban life that was actually so near. We lived in a small farm house surrounded by the low dairylands outside Petaluma and were nourished by the eggs my landlady's chickens left in our backyard and by milk from her cow, Mulie. The days seemed longer then, with plenty of time for leisurely trips to Bodega Bay for some fresh fish, a stop along the way at one of the many roadside blackberry patches, with plenty of time left over to stop at fruit stands, the Organic Grocery, the raw milk drive-in. I could go for weeks without ever seeing the inside of a major supermarket. It is hard to imagine now, but I even managed to cut my own

firewood in those days. You could drive to Santa Rosa at any time without worrying about commuter traffic or gridlock. You can still do all of these things, except drive to Santa Rosa at any time without gridlock, and no longer at the same leisurely pace. Stories of our farms and vineyards and cheesemakers and chefs appear in the national press with somewhat alarming yet satisfying frequency. Sonoma has been discovered.

My own part in this development is probably small, but undeniable. In January of 1986, Bruce Robinson, then the editor of *The Sebastopol Times and News* asked me to write a column on food for the paper. "Include some recipes," he said, "and a bit of narrative." I loved the idea, but did not respond to his request; it seemed too good to be true, and I was overwhelmed by the thought of appearing in print. In March, Bruce asked again, this time much more specifically. "Have something to me by Friday," he urged, "and make it about Easter." Thus began my opportunity to combine two of my great loves, food and the written word. As a graduate student of English Literature, I had frequently supported myself and my daughters by working in restaurants and found that I loved the world of food and food service. Apparently a cook by instinct, I could work with food with a confidence I never felt when I stood before a classroom attempting to convey a grammatical concept or a nuance of meaning. After extended periods of working in the restaurant business, however, I found myself longing for that other world, the world of words, and books, and ideas. To have had the opportunity to bring these worlds together and to make them the focus of my career is the realization of a dream I dared not dream, so impossible did it once seem. *A Cook's Tour of Sonoma* is that dream in tangible form. Yet, I view it with ambivalence: What effect will it have on the world that nourished it?

One of the problems with discovery by the media is that once the ball is rolling, it is hard to get it to change direction. The same names, the same farms, the same ingredients appear over and over again, and then visitors come and look only for those things, frequently with blinders on that keep the best of the county hidden from their sight. The bigger businesses, the chains, the hotels, the investment restaurateurs who have set up shop to take advantage of the discovery of Sonoma often have the budgets to create highly visible profiles, but they are not the heart or the best of the county. To find that heart in the midst of the ever-escalating growth takes increasing effort. I have tried to include here not just those products that have made it to national stardom or those that are most visible, but the little gems I have discovered away from the crowds and the limelight. Sonoma is not just a wine-tasting, goat-cheese-and-flower-petal place. We may have pioneered many of the newer foods available, but Sonoma is a rich amalgam of cultures, soils, climates, micro-climates, and temperaments, all working together to give shape to our own complex dreams and desires. Sometimes the disparate elements collide; sometimes they all work together in sweet harmony. Always they express themselves interestingly.

A word about how to use this book. Just as I have gleaned what I have found best in Sonoma and presented it to you here, so, too, should you adopt that which appeals to you most in this book and make it your own. Perhaps the ingredients will become some of your favorites and sun-dried tomatoes or blueberry vinegar or Bear Flag Dry Jack cheese standard items in your own pantry. Maybe you will be inspired to pay us a visit sometime, searching out your own favorites from what Luther Burbank called the chosen spot of all of nature, making your own discoveries. If you try my recipes and like them, then perhaps it will be my cooking style that stays with you, my love of spicy food, my consistent use of larger than usual amounts of garlic, my passion for olive oil. Remember, though, that a recipe is a road map of sorts, but is not the only way to get to your destination. A recipe begins as an idea, a vision of taste, a dream of perfect harmony among many ingredients. A professional cook then combines the ingredients using the knowledge accumulated through years of cooking, along with a healthy dose of instinct and intuition, and finally writes it down, where all too often it seems cast in stone. Let my recipes guide you, but get to know the ingredients on your own, separate from the constraints I have, out of the simple necessity of the written word, subjected them to. Enjoy them. I cook because I love to cook and I use Sonoma County products because I love them, and because they are an intimate part of my daily life in so many ways. I love knowing I will eat the apples from the orchards I see flowering in the spring; I love knowing I will one day drink the wine from the vineyards I see daily. It enriches my life to speak to the farmers, the cheesemakers, the bakers, whose wonderful products nour-

ish me. I offer you my book in the same spirit, and hope that it will become your book as well.

DISCOVERING SONOMA'S DIVERSITY

What wond'rous life is this I lead!
Ripe apples drop about my head;
The luscious clusters of the vine
Upon my mouth do crush their wine;
The nectarine and curious peach,
Into my hands themselves do reach;
Stumbling on melons, as I pass,
Insnar'd with flow'rs, I fall on grass

Meanwhile, the mind, from pleasure less,
withdraws into its happiness.

Annihilating all that's made
To a green thought in a green shade.

ANDREW MARVELL
"In the Garden"

Sonoma's Bountiful Pantry

Using Sonoma County products has been second nature to me since I first arrived here and was given eggs, cream, milk, and butter from the farm where I rented a small house. There were no designer vegetables then, no fresh pasta, and the flowers that now appear on our salad plates graced our tables in vases. It was a simpler time. But many of our cheese factories had already been established for several decades, as had our wineries, and the farmers were working their land, coaxing from it their particular specialty. The gourmet revolution of the seventies had a great effect on Sonoma County, as such pioneers as Alice Waters of Chez Panisse came to our fertile soil seeking the high-quality ingredients for which her restaurant is famous and bringing to the attention of the world what Luther Burbank had proven generations ago, that this is richly blessed agricultural country.

Luther Burbank arrived in Santa Rosa in 1875 and, by the time he died, fifty-one years later, he had made horticultural history, developing more than eight hundred new plants and helping to transform exhausted soil and a depressed economy into a booming agricultural industry in an area that became the eighth richest farming county in the country. You cannot bite into a succulent, juicy plum, nor prick a fragrant, steaming baked potato, nor grace your table with Shasta daisies without partaking of Burbank's vast influence. Today in Sonoma, we see Burbank's influence not only in the foods we grow and the foods we eat, but also in the many businesses, streets, and festivals that bear his name. The largest event, the Luther Burbank Rose Parade and Festival, with its floats full of thousands of roses, begins at his home in downtown Santa Rosa, where he is buried. In The Luther Burbank Center for the Performing Arts, we hold concerts, conferences, and weddings, as well as many celebrations of our abundance, including The Symphony of Food and Wine and the Celebrate Sonoma festival. The legacy of Luther Burbank, beyond the cornucopia of his discoveries and creations, has been our knowledge and our appreciation of how nature has blessed this land; the legacy of the gourmet revolution has been that the rest of the country now knows it.

How did I decide what foods, what products, would be included in this book? It seemed that every time I thought I had assembled all of them, new ones, good new ones, would appear on the scene, or small, out-of-the-way growers or producers that I had yet to discover would suddenly take the limelight, or I would discover some new, wonderful way to use a product I had not worked with before. And the process continues. This is a book that I could write forever, just as I could continue to discover the richness of Sonoma forever, or at least for the finite number of years allotted one small life. The fertile soil, the mild yet seasonal climate, the diversity of talent, continue to draw people to the area and continue to inspire experimentation and creation, just as they did in Luther Burbank's day. Choosing the businesses to include and those to ex-

clude has been one of the most difficult requirements of this book, and defining the criteria by which I make that decision has been no small task. First of all, I have let my own tastes, my own compulsions, guide me and have included those products that I love most. I am a cook fueled by my senses, by taste, and texture, and aroma, not by theory, or duty, or order. I am sure not everyone will agree with me and I am sure that there are wonderful things that I have missed. There came a time when I simply had to stop the field work, had to stop the research, and get this all down on paper. I have included products that are easily accessible and those that can stand up to an onslaught of demand should that be one of the results of increased attention. I avoided mentioning very small businesses, those that offer a limited quantity of produce or just one item, or for a very limited season. Smaller businesses are more delicate, more easily overwhelmed by too much attention. I have avoided too much discussion of specific farms, with a few notable exceptions, in favor of more detailed discussion of the Farm Markets, since they are the best way for the retail buyer to find the offerings of our many family farms. Enjoy my view of Sonoma's bountiful pantry, and be sure to discover it on your own, as well.

As a starting point for your voyages, the Farm Trails organization is useful. Since the Farm Trails organization was started in 1973 by the agricultural commissioner, John Smith, small growers and processors have joined together to encourage people to buy direct from the farms. The organization promotes its member farms primarily through its detailed guide map, and most members display the familiar green Farm Trails membership sign and number. Farm Trails includes more than 150 members, who offer more than 120 types of locally produced goods and a variety of other products, such as organic beef and lamb, game birds, smoked meats and poultry, cheese, oysters, berries, vinegar, garlic, organic produce, homespun angora wool, fresh and dried flowers, live and cut Christmas trees, carriage rides through the wine country, earthworms, feathers, firewood, even live fish and birds. The members span the spectrum from those with shiny production and retail facilities, such as Korbel Champagne Cellars or Sonoma Cheese Factory, to the tiny family farm, such as Buzzard's Roost Ranch, which specializes in eggs, angora wool, and farm animal tours for children. The most exotic is probably Pet-a-Llama Ranch in Sebastopol, where they raise llamas and sell garments and blankets made from handspun llama wool. The Farm Trails organization shows an interesting cross section of the creativity and variety of Sonoma County's agriculture.

Farm Trails also sponsors the annual Gravenstein Apple Fair held in Sebastopol's Ragle Park each summer, an extremely successful, definitely homespun, fair that has earned itself great affection, as well as the nickname "the sweetest little fair in Sonoma." Farm Trails gives financial support to local 4-H clubs and offers several scholarships through the Future Farmers of America organization each year. Extremely suc-

cessful in its efforts, Farm Trails has become a prototype for associations of small farms throughout the country. If you are planning to visit Sonoma, or if you are just interested, you can send for a free copy of the current Farm Trails map (see Addresses, beginning on page 269). The map in this book, on pages 36 and 37 does not duplicate that map, but I do occasionally refer to it.

DAIRY ALCHEMY
Camembert ▼ Jalapeño *Jack* ▼
St. George ▼ *Chèvre* ▼ *Sonoma Jack* ▼
"California Gold" Dry Jack

The process of transforming milk into cheese is simple. Much like winemaking, it involves just a few steps that are basically unchanged since man discovered just what can happen to the juice of the vine, or the milk of the cow, goat, or sheep. Cheese is simply fermented milk, a process engendered by either acid or rennet. And, as in winemaking, the subtle differences in raw ingredients combined with the simple process of fermentation produce endless variations on this basic theme. All aspects of its environment influence cheesemaking, from the air the animals breathe, to the food they eat, to the mood and temperament of the cheesemaker. We are able to produce great cheese here in Sonoma because we have the conditions for producing great milk, and those conditions have inspired the talented cheesemakers among us. Sonoma County is blessed with land that cows love. The low, rolling hills please them, and the mild temperatures allow a tranquil life that results in outstanding milk products. There is good food available at a good price, and the air here is, for the most part, kept clean and fresh by the nearby Pacific Ocean. The dairy industry is the second largest segment, after wine, of Sonoma County's 586,447-acre agricultural sector, and many farmers, dairymen, and cheesemakers work their dairy alchemy, transforming millions of gallons of milk a year into a delicious array of products.

Most visible is perhaps the California Cooperative Dairy, whose white, green, and red signs decorate, not only many of our winding country roads, but also many of our highways, such as the Gravenstein Highway and the Lakeville Highway. A statewide venture, it is by far our largest dairy operation, with 540 dairy farms in the cooperative. The milk is delivered to the California Cooperative Creamery, which supplies the nearly sixteen-million gallons of milk that Clover-Stornetta Farms, Inc., processes each year as the principal milk supplier for Sonoma, Marin, Lake, Mendocino, and Solano Counties. Milk from the California Cooperative Dairy also goes to Sonoma Cheese Factory, Vella Cheese Company, Marin French Cheese Company, and many more producers, in and out of Sonoma County. In addition, the Creamery sells many of their own products, wholesale and retail. Their butter and mozzarella cheese are distributed under the California Gold label (and should not be confused with Vella's California Gold, an aged dry Jack), and they produce six types of Cheddar and three types of Jack cheese that are sold throughout all the western states, and distribution in the Midwest is just beginning.

VELLA CHEESE COMPANY

Some of the smaller cheesemakers receive milk from just one particular dairy in the cooperative. It is, according to Ignazio Vella, the rigorous care taken in all steps of cheese production, including those concerning the cows and their feed and the quality of their milk, that allows the cheesemaker to go on to practice his art, that of transforming a consistently high-quality milk into a consistently high-quality, delicious cheese. Ignazio Vella is one of our local cheesemakers who has accomplished this with great success.

I have enjoyed frequent visits to the Vella Cheese Company since I first came to Sonoma and, while researching this book, I went again. I happily sampled many of their cheeses, including ones I had not tried since the Vellas expanded their product line. As I complimented him profusely on his *Jalapeño* Jack, Ignazio Vella snapped good-naturedly, "Don't call it pepper Jack!" He had just finished telling me the story of this delicious cheese, that it is full of fresh red and green *jalapeño* peppers shipped in from a special source in New Mexico, unlike the various "pepper Jacks" that use the cheaper pimiento, other peppers, and black pepper that spoil the taste of the fresh *jalapeños*. "Oops, just a slip of the tongue," I assured him, out of the habit of years of referring to pepper Jack cheese. It will not happen again. Besides, it is impossible to confuse this delightful cheese with any other. The burst of flavor of the fresh *jalapeños* is unmistakable and compellingly good, and I love the texture of the block cheese, slightly firm and perfect for grating.

The history of Vella Cheese has been well documented in a variety of sources, including Laura Chenel's book, *American Country Cheese*, in which the story of Sonoma's first cheese factory is described in detail. The creamery was started by Joe Vella, who arrived in this country from his native Sicily in 1906. World War I made it nearly impossible to get Italian grating cheeses, and it was this lack that led to the development of Vella's Dry Jack cheese, still the company's most popular product. In 1923, Tom Vella, Ignazio's father, joined his older brother Joe at the creamery. Since then, Vella Cheese has gone through a variety of partnerships, including a long-term, advantageous relationship with Kraft and an association with Celso Viviani, a member of another Sonoma family well known for its success in cheesemaking.

Vella Cheese Company markets its products under the Bear Flag brand, which is well distributed in many areas outside Sonoma County and available by mail to anyone who calls the toll-free number. If you find yourself in Sonoma County, try to fit in a visit to the charming little stone building that has withstood many an earthquake and has housed the Vella Cheese Company since 1931.

LAURA CHENEL'S CHÈVRE

Though made in one of the youngest of Sonoma County's cheese factories, Laura's delicious goat cheeses have probably received more national press and attention than any other of our products and have helped to spawn a new American industry. In 1979, just two or three cheesemakers were experimenting with this French style of goat cheese; now there are dozens, including several here in northern California. Laura Chenel's Chèvre has become a part of the basic grammar of my cooking here in Sonoma; I love her cheeses and would be at a loss without them. I am particularly pleased with the wide variety she offers, a variety that makes it possible to infuse numerous dishes with the subtle, earthy flavor of goat cheese. Their simplicity makes the fresh cheeses, such as the chabis, plain or coated with herbs or spices, useful for cheese courses and in soups and vegetable *pâtés*. The complexity that develops as the cheese ages makes it an interesting and delicious substitute for more traditional hard grating cheeses in such recipes as Sonoma Risotto (page 137). Retail distribution is increasing and Laura Chenel's Chèvre is easily available through mail order. When visiting Sonoma, call the tasting room, and stop by for a sampling of these delightful cheeses.

RACHEL'S GOAT CHEESE OF SONOMA COUNTY

This small family farm produces just two types of chèvre, chabis and *fromage blanc*, which are available in several different flavors, including plain, dill, and, the most popular, herb and garlic. The chabis is also available with a black pepper coating, and occasionally a *fromage blanc* with smoked salmon and chives is available, though only at the facility, Me Gusta Organic Farms, in Sebastopol. Most of the three to four hundred cheeses that Rachel produces each week are sold at the Marin County Farmer's Market; they are also sold at Real Foods at the corner of Sutter and Polk Streets in San Francisco. A member of the Farm Trails organization, Me Gusta Farms encourages visitors to the farm and I would encourage you to go if you are in the area. Rachel raises happy goats and lets them dry up in the fall. Production begins again in March, so plan your visit or your order accordingly.

REDWOOD HILL FARM GOAT DAIRY

Jennifer Lynn Bice and her husband, Steven Schack, share a compelling passion for raising goats. Jennifer's parents started the dairy, which is nestled in the hills between Sebastopol and Occidental, in 1968, when their only product was goat's milk. She and Steven took over the dairy in 1978, when her parents moved to Hawaii. In 1985, they added a rich, delicious yogurt to their product line. Today, they offer several goat cheeses, made in the Italian style. Feeling that the market was becoming crowded with producers of French-style goat cheese, Jennifer and Steven decided to develop another type and have done so quite successfully with their goat ricotta, mozzarella, and feta cheeses. They have plans to expand their offerings in the near future, continuing in the Italian tradition with both a fresh and an aged goat cheese.

Both got their start in their beloved world of goats in the show ring, where they showed as hobbyists and saw the dairy as a way to make the goats pay for themselves. Today, most of their income comes from their milk products, though they continue to show their prize-winning goats, which include Saanens, Nubians, Alpines, LaManchas, and Toggenburgs. They also offer breeding stock, breeding services, and attend the births of all the kids (between one hundred and one hundred fifty a year) born at Redwood Hill Farm.

Their products are sold in specialty food stores throughout the Bay Area, Los Angeles, and in six other states, Hawaii, Oregon, Washington, Nevada, Arizona, and Texas. In Sonoma County, you can find them at Pasta Etc., Food for Less, Traverso's, and most natural food stores.

SONOMA CHEESE FACTORY

"We take our work very seriously—we feel that good cheese is as much a part of gracious living as good wine," commented David Viviane, the president of Sonoma Cheese Factory, while we talked one day on the square in the town of Sonoma. David is serious about his appreciation of cheese, so much so that, as a member of the Milk Advisory Board, he developed "Cheese Tasting California Style," a simple set of instructions designed to highlight the subtleties of cheeses in much the same way as wine tastings can reveal the nuances of wine. This is just an example of the good marketing ideas that have come from this deceptively small factory. Their marketing program is so effective, and the distribution of their cheeses so good, that one has the impression that they are much bigger, more remote, and less accessible than in fact they are. The entire operation is housed at 2 Spain Street, where customers can not only sample and buy all of the company's products, but also choose from a huge array of imported cheeses, fine wines, breads, beers, and delicatessen items, and watch nearly the entire cheese-making process, from the milk and enzyme being pumped into the large vats to the fermented curds being cut, drained of whey, and finally gathered up to be pressed into the rounds of famous Sonoma Jack cheese. In addition to the traditional Jack sold under the Sonoma Jack label, Sonoma Cheese Factory produces Onion Jack, Garlic Jack, Caraway Jack, Hot Pepper Jack, Sonoma Lite, Sonoma Teleme, No Salt Added, and Sonoma Cheddar cheese. All of their products are available by mail order.

JOE MATOS CHEESE FACTORY

To the same degree that Sonoma Cheese Factory is highly visible both in its location and its distribution, St. George cheese and the tiny, hidden little cheese factory in which it is produced are invisible. On a lightly traveled country road, tucked away down a long driveway without even a sign to direct you when the driveway forks, is a family farm that produces a country-style, semisoft cheese named for the island in the Azores where the Matos family lived before coming to Sonoma County. St. George cheese is a slightly sharp, full-flavored cheese made entirely from milk from the family's herd of cows that graze alongside the driveway. Most of the cheese is sold by mail order

to the Portuguese community in northern California, and the rest is sold through their Farm Trails advertising and by word of mouth. I love this cheese as much as I love the trip to the factory, a singular, quiet place, with no advertising, no hustle and bustle, no hard sell. In fact, it is sometimes hard to find anyone around to sell you the cheese at all. But there is a bell on the little counter, and it is definitely worth the wait.

MARIN FRENCH CHEESE COMPANY

This sweet little cheese factory has a bit of an identity problem. Is it a Sonoma business or a Marin business? Its name, Marin French Cheese Company, accurately places it geographically; its address places it in Petaluma. It has a Petaluma phone number and the easiest way to get there is to start on D Street in Petaluma and drive west for nine miles. You will see it spring up among the low, rolling hills like an oasis. This French-style cheese factory is, in fact, six miles over the Marin County line, but has identified itself primarily with Petaluma since its beginnings in the northern Marin uplands in 1865. The company produces its cheeses under the brand name of Rouge et Noir. Although the cheeses are produced in a traditional French style, they are very different from their French counterparts. For many, the difference is delicious. Rouge et Noir brand cheese is distributed in a variety of markets throughout the country, as well as in most large supermarkets and many specialty shops in California. The Camembert, schloss, Brie, and breakfast cheese that this charming little plant has been producing for over 120 years are also available by mail. Marin French Cheese Company is one of my favorite spots for a picnic, too, especially just after the spring rains when the surrounding hills are green, the pond at the factory is high and full of ducks, and the redwinged blackbirds are plentiful. Pick up a loaf of Sonoma French Bakery's sourdough from The Petaluma Market and head west.

PLEASURES OF THE FLESH

Rocky the Range Chicken ▼ *Smoked Duck* ▼ *Pekin Duck* ▼ *Andouille Sausage* ▼ *Pacific Oysters*

It is probably more difficult to find out where your main course has come from than it is to find out about any other part of your meal. The world of corn-fed beef and spring lamb is not as accessible as those of other aspects of agriculture in Sonoma. The county produces a variety of outstanding meat from carefully tended, well-fed animals, that makes its way regularly to restaurant chefs throughout the country, but only infrequently graces the tables of local residents at home. In Healdsburg Bruce Campbell raises outstanding Sonoma lamb, of which many local residents have never heard, much less tasted. The Sonoma Baby Lamb raised by Pat and Bart Ehman is distributed only to professional chefs. On a few local ranches, organically fed beef, lamb, and pork are produced without the hor-

mones and various medications that permeate most retail meat these days, but these products are generally only available in large quantities. Some local meat does make its way to the retail market at places such as Willowside Meats, which offers Sonoma ranch beef, lamb, and pork when it is available. In general, though, the most efficient way to buy naturally raised meat is in large quantities—half or whole animals—directly from the ranch. Obviously, you must have a freezer to do this, and a large family helps, too, so that the meat does not linger in the freezer too long.

The world of poultry is much more accessible than the world of meat. From the highly visible Rocky the Range Chicken and Willie Bird turkey, to the pheasant, quail, duck, and bronze turkeys sold by members of the Farm Trails organization, Sonoma County poultry is easily available and of outstanding quality.

The federal regulations governing the labeling of meat, poultry, and seafood are narrow and restrictive, and becoming more so. Just what the animals are fed does not have to be disclosed, but claims about how they are raised and what they are fed are rigidly limited. You cannot use the word "organic" in relation to any meat products, nor can you claim that an animal's diet has been vegetarian. Add to that the fact that most meat is displayed in the butcher's case with nothing other than the name of the cut and its price, and you realize that you have a market that conveys very little information to the consumer. With few exceptions, we do not know if the seafood we buy is from our coastal waters or from, say, Monterey or

Mexico. We do not know if the beef is full of hormones and the residues of antibiotics and we do not know how the veal was raised. It is fairly difficult to get accurate information about this very important aspect of our diets, but that can change, especially if consumers make it known that they want the information.

PINE RIDGE FARMS

Pat and Bart Ehman had been providing Sonoma Baby Lamb to professional chefs for some time when, after numerous requests, their Pine Ridge farms added chicken to the repertoire. Thus was born Rocky the Range Chicken and his younger brother, Rocky Junior, the only birds allowed to go to market designated as "range chickens."

Chickens wilt easily in the heat, and the Ehmans found the Petaluma fog belt the perfect climate for Rocky. The chickens are raised in the traditional barnyard fashion of forty years ago: tranquil environment, where they peck at their natural, vegetarian diet at will, and can wander inside or outside as they choose. Most chickens are cramped into one-foot-square cubicles that are kept lit around the clock to encourage the birds to eat their hormone-laden, high-fat diets. Rocky's freedom of choice and healthy diet result in chicken that tastes like chicken used to taste, richer and with a better texture than that of other commercial birds.

The Ehmans originally distributed Rocky to those same professional chefs that used Sonoma Baby Lamb, but word quickly spread and demand grew. The taste of Rocky is so superior to that of the standard chicken we have become accustomed to that many consumers find it worth not only the extra cost but also the extra effort it sometimes takes to find him. One by one, local, independent markets added Rocky to their meat and poultry cases, and found him quite popular. Today, the chickens are distributed throughout California and carried by such supermarket chains as Safeway and Raley's. Rocky is easy to recognize: he is the one with the dark glasses, cowboy hat, spurs, and a smoking gun.

PIOTRKOWSKI SMOKED POULTRY

Smoked foods have become increasingly popular recently, and smoked trout, smoked turkey, and smoked duck appear on menus with increasing frequency. Piotrkowski Poultry offers superior smoked poultry, the only product of the Petaluma family farm headed by Joe Piotrkowski. The poultry—a broad selection including chicken, game hen, duckling, mature duck, turkey, and turkey breast—is immersed in a chemical-free brine bath of water, salt, and brown sugar. No additives of any kind are introduced at any point in the curing or smoking process. After being cured in the brine, the poultry is slowly smoked over hardwoods. The result is delicious: tender, delicate and subtle, with a light but not dominant smoky flavor. All the smoking is done to order to insure absolute freshness, and only a small amount of their product makes it to retail markets. As members of the Farm Trails organization, however, they do encourage purchases direct from the farm and ask for a minimum of one week's notice.

REICHARDT DUCK FARM

The Reichardt family has been raising Imperial Pekin ducks since 1901, when they started the business in South San Francisco. In 1959 they moved to western Petaluma where they have been flourishing ever since. Most of their products are distributed in the Bay Area, particularly San Francisco's Chinatown, but their wonderful, farm-raised ducks find their way to restaurants throughout Sonoma County and beyond, including Sacramento, Fresno, and San Diego, as well as New Orleans. The Petaluma Market carries Reichardt duck for retail sale.

SONOMA SAUSAGE FACTORY

We have many sausage makers in Sonoma County, and some of them, Angelo's Meats in Petaluma and Sonoma, for example, and Willowside Meats in Santa Rosa, offer their sausages for sale only at their retail locations; they have no distribution. Sonoma Sausage Factory, our largest specialty sausage company, not only produces the widest variety but also has a broad distribution of its traditional and innovative products. The sausage maker, Herb Hoeser, has worked in the meat industry for several decades and spent some time working and studying in Germany, learning traditional, old-world techniques. His Sonoma company now offers more than eighty-five varieties of sausages, lunch meats, and smoked meats. The most popular sausage is the North Country, a flavorful but mild sausage that is perfect for grilling. Particularly good is the line of Louisiana-style sausages, which includes

both a fresh and a smoked *andouille*, full of garlic. All the sausages are made entirely of meat, with no fillers and no harmful additives.

The retail facility on the square in downtown Sonoma is particularly pleasant. All of the products are available for sale, and there are always several samples set out for shoppers to try.

BAY BOTTOM BEDS

The waters of Tomales Bay, immediately south of Sonoma County, are the home of millions of delicious Pacific oysters. Adventurous farmers who tend their watery acres far from the gardens, pastures, and vineyards of their inland counterparts work to revive an oyster business that had fallen victim to overharvesting many decades ago. Improved techniques of cultivation and excellent growing conditions have led to a booming shellfish industry in northern California, where businesses such as Marin County's Hog Island Farm Shellfish Company and Sonoma County's Bay Bottom Beds are continually expanding to meet a growing demand.

Two types of Pacific oysters, the *miyagi* and the kumamoto, are farmed on the west coast of the Pacific Ocean, where *miyagis* are by far the most plentiful. Bay Bottom Beds, a company based in Santa Rosa, raises its *miyagis* just off Preston Point Rock at the northern end of Tomales Bay, where the bivalves are bathed in a mix of salt and fresh water, an environment that provides a nutrient-rich diet. The owners, Lisa Jang and Jorge Rebagliati, work to make their family farm as efficient as possible without sacrificing the wonderful quality of the oysters. Both Lisa and Jorge hold masters degrees in Aquaculture Management from Oregon State University and this knowledge, along with years of hands-on experience, has resulted in a new and highly successful method of cultivation. A Preston Point *miyagi* has a harder shell and is much easier to open than other Pacific oysters. As Lisa and Jorge sought to improve the shells of their oysters, they did not realize that the process would also result in an oyster with a better, more delicate taste, but that has been the result. The oysters from Bay Bottom Beds are outstanding.

Lisa and Jorge harvest and distribute their oysters throughout Sonoma County, where you will find them at an increasing number of markets and restaurants. You might also see them shucking and serving their oysters at events such as the Symphony of Food and Wine, where the delicious Preston Point *miyagis* are always popular.

STRAW INTO GOLD

Specialty Breads and Pastries

Sonoma County is blessed with several gifted bakers who work their magic with wheat and rye and corn and a multitude of other grains, transforming them into the delicious loaves that keep us well fed and happy. We have no need to travel to San Francisco for that city's famous sourdough bread, as delicious as it is. We have bakeries in Sonoma that keep us well supplied with traditional baguettes, flutes, rounds, and pull-apart loaves.

SONOMA FRENCH BAKERY

Not to stop at Sonoma French Bakery when visiting in Sonoma is unthinkable, though if you are there much past noon, the bread will be sold out for the day. Happily, it is distributed to a number of markets throughout the county and, as the supply arrives in the late morning, it is often available during the afternoon. I generally use their full-sized sourdough loaves for the Greek Lamb Loaf on page 167. Their baguettes are delicious, too, though best suited for eating. They are not suitable for croutons. The crust is too, well, crusty, and the bread crumbles a great deal when sliced thinly. Besides, anything this delicious in its natural state should be eaten simply, with as few changes to its essential nature as possible. Make croutons with a more ordinary baguette, one that has a chewier, moister crust.

COSTEAUX FRENCH BAKERY

All of the bread made in the Costeaux French Bakery is superb and so are the exquisite desserts, a variety of homey cookies and sweet rolls, elegant pies, cakes, and chocolate confections of all types. The bakery, in Healdsburg, also has a concession in Petrini's, the high-quality supermarket on Fourth Street in Santa Rosa. It tends to sell out early, too, especially on the weekends. Of all the traditional breads made locally, Costeaux's pull-apart sourdough is my own favorite and is an essential part of any *Bagna Cauda* (see page 221). It is just the right size for dipping into the hot, garlicky sauce, and its outer crust and inner moistness make it perfect for soaking up that sauce.

DOWNTOWN BAKERY AND CREAMERY

Lindsey Shere, who is the pastry chef at Chez Panisse, has her northern outpost in downtown Healdsburg. At the Downtown Bakery and Creamery she and her daughter Thérèse offer a wonderful selection of house-made ice creams and sorbets, breads, cakes, pastries, puff pastry for home baking, and a *focaccia* that is a favorite of Gaye LeBaron, the newspaper columnist. Not much of an ice cream fan myself, I still find the Wild Plum Sherbert worth a trip to Healdsburg—even if you live in, say, Fayetteville, Arkansas.

ALVARADO STREET BAKERY

The specialty bakery with perhaps the largest distribution currently is Alvarado Street Bakery, a local Rohnert Park business that began twelve years ago as part of a cooperative effort to establish an alternative food system. The company has been extremely successful and its bread is currently one of the two nationally distributed natural breads made in Sonoma. The organic sprouted breads and bagels are available in all fifty states and the sprouted whole-wheat tortillas almost everywhere except the southeast. In most of the country the bagels and breads are sold frozen; in all nine counties in the Bay Area and in Mendocino, Santa Cruz,

and Los Angeles, they are available fresh. The bakery maintains a fleet of bread trucks that carries its wares from Fort Bragg in the north to Santa Cruz in the south, a practice that has been immensely helpful to its success. There are no oils in the sprouted grain breads and all the grains used are organic, which makes the bread very popular in natural food stores across the country. If you are unfamiliar with the bread, check with a natural foods store in your area. If the store does not carry it and is unable to find the distributor who does, call the Rohnert Park offices (see Addresses, page 252), you will be directed to the distributor in your area.

Of all of Alvarado Street Bakery's products, I believe the best are the sprouted whole-wheat sourdough loaves, the whole-wheat tortillas, and the sprouted wheat dinner rolls and hot dog rolls. In fact, when the inspirational sandwich that later became The Farm Market Sandwich (page 108) was first offered to me, it was on a hot dog bun from the Alvarado Street Bakery. Do not let the name fool you: the only relationship it has to what we generally know as a hot dog bun is the name.

BROTHER JUNIPER'S BAKERY

I have saved the best part of Sonoma's bakery story for last. If you have no other reason to visit Sonoma, Brother Juniper's Bakery provides one. This is bread to make you swoon, and swoon I do every time I walk down the hall of the unlikely building that houses the small but expanding facility. This is baking, this is bread, at its lovingly produced best. Brother Peter Reinhart, the baker and inspiration behind this highly successful operation, loves his craft and has gone to great lengths to retain the intimate, hands-on relationship so essential to the production of good bread, while expanding to meet an ever-growing demand. Brother Juniper's began in 1985 as a small café and bakery, and it did not take long for the autumnal aroma of their heavenly Struan bread to make its imprint on our culinary imaginations, not to mention our palates (and our hips). Struan bread has a long tradition beginning in western Scotland, where it was a harvest bread for the Michaelmas celebration made with whatever grains were harvested that year. It is a rich, slightly sweet bread that is at its best when toasted, a process that brings out the nutty quality of the grains. The polenta used in Brother Juniper's recipe gives the bread a beautiful sparkle, and the brown rice holds in the moisture, giving it a much longer life than most breads. The café was known for its baked goods, but it also served exquisitely fresh, original green salads long before *mesclun* was a word on every foodie's lips. Delicious salad dressings, soups, chilis, gumbo, barbecued chicken, and more, all prepared with the same care and dedication that went into the baked goods made Brother Juniper's café extremely popular with the locals, even though it held barely twenty people and frequently a long line for both café and take-out service. We were sad to see it close, as it did early in 1989, but happy because we all knew that its closure meant expansion for the bakery. It meant that the wonderful bread previously available in only a few restaurants and at the café would now see wider distribution. It also meant that many of Brother Peter's "experimental breads," a Monday tradition at the café, might be added to the standard list of products. Some of those experiments are now among the best-selling items of the expanding bakery.

WILD ABOUT PASTA AND RICE

Fresh Pasta ▼ *Fresh Dried Pasta* ▼ *Wild Rice*

Grain is a wonderful gift from nature. Without grain, it would be hard to make bread, or pie crust, or cakes, or any number of wonderful things we take for granted. Without it, we would have no pasta, and, with the range and diversity of pasta, I can't imagine a greater culinary void than a world of food without it. Now that fresh pasta is increasingly common, that range has been greatly expanded. When fresh pasta first burst onto the food scene, it came with a number of annoying pretensions that immediately put some people off. Others fell for the show completely, showing their ignorance by declaring, "Oh, I never use anything but fresh pasta. . . ." It seems that reason has triumphed, and fresh pasta has taken its rightful place as one of many great styles of pasta, perfect for certain occasions and recipes, but not the only choice of the discerning. Few things satisfy the soul like a platter of mom's spaghetti made with good imported dried semolina pasta. I prefer to use dried spaghettini for Spaghetti alla Carbonara Sonoma (page 129). But for fresh ravioli or cannelloni, for fettuccini with wonderful cream sauce, fresh pasta is outstanding.

PASTA ETC.

In 1984, Bernard and Maria Soltes opened a little pasta shop and delicatessen in Santa Rosa, next to Petrini's Market. It was an immediate success, and they have expanded the shop to include a small bakery. It is still their fresh pasta that is the focus of Pasta Etc., and well it should be. This is the best fresh pasta I have ever tasted. It is frequently said that fresh pasta should be made with flour and semolina should be reserved for the dried versions. I have never agreed. I like the texture, the firm bite, of a fresh pasta made with semolina, which is what Bernard and Maria use for theirs. Over the years, they have developed a number of unusual flavors for pasta, all of which are delicious, and frequently quite beautiful, too. The pumpkin-rosemary pasta, a favorite in fall, is every bit as beautiful as it is delicious. I have had few flavored pastas that have managed to be so evocative of the real thing as this version. The wild mushroom pasta is another outstanding flavor, with a richly marbled appearance. Each day, they offer several different flavors, with some favorites, such as garlic-basil, available all the time. A few local restaurants use Pasta Etc., but there are no retail sales except at the shop on Fourth Street.

MENDOCINO PASTA CO.

Fresh dried pasta is an interesting concept and, at first glance, a contradiction in terms. But Don Luber, the owner and chief pasta maker of Mendocino Pasta Co. knew a great concept when he saw it and has created a thriving business air-drying the fresh pasta that had become so popular in Mendocino County restaurants. Don moved the business to Cotati, in the heart of Sonoma County, and set up a drying process identical to that used by Timber Crest Farms to dry fruits and tomatoes. The result is a pasta with a long shelf life, that can be widely distributed without refrigeration, yet has the flavor and texture of a freshly made pasta. The intensity of flavor of most fresh pasta is diminished in drying, but Don has managed to produce a number of dried pastas with outstanding flavors. Country garden vegetable is subtly evocative of a summer garden; tomato-jalapeño has a good strong hint of fire. Mendocino Pasta Co. makes nearly ten different flavors for retail distribution, by a network that is increasing all the time. Carried throughout northern California, Los Angeles, and Hawaii in Safeway stores and specialty shops and available by mail order in the Rykoff catalogue (see page 258), Mendocino Pasta Co. products are easily available.

An interesting aspect of the company's marketing program is the Master Chef Series, a program for which well-known chefs throughout northern California design recipes for specific flavors of pasta. These recipes accompany each eight-ounce package of pasta and are included to encourage novice cooks to try the new pasta. Several chefs in Sonoma County have contributed recipes.

BUONA PASTA

Larry Urmini, of Urmini and Sons' Herb Farm, is father to another thriving business,

Buona Pasta, located inside the Fiesta Market in Sebastopol. His excellent pasta, made in the traditional style, which is to say, with flour, not with semolina, comes in a variety of flavors. His black pepper pasta is vibrant with peppery flavor, and the saffron pasta he occasionally makes is delicious. In addition to the standard cuts of pasta, from angel hair to fettuccini, Buona Pasta also makes its own ravioli and cannelloni with a variety of delicious fillings. As with Pasta Etc., there is no other retail distribution, so you must visit the store in Sebastopol if you want to try it. But if you happen to live nearby, or be passing through, it is certainly worth the stop.

WILD DISTRIBUTING

Wayne and Susan Toress of Santa Rosa concentrate on a single item in their family business: wild rice, grown at Upper Lake in Lake County, immediately to the north of Sonoma County, and sold under the brand name Naturally Wild at specialty stores throughout northern California and by mail order. In the last ten years or so, wild rice has been one of the few things to have come down in price. When I was a child wild rice cost nearly $7.00 a pound, $27.00 a pound in today's money.

CUTTING EDGE PRODUCE

Mesclun ▼ *Currant Tomatoes* ▼ *Blood Peaches* ▼ *Purple Potatoes* ▼ *Nasturtium Flowers*

When I was visiting The Farallones Institute Garden, Doug Gosling, the tour guide and garden manager, reached his arm in among the lush strawberry greens and drew it out to reveal a handful of tiny white alpine strawberries. I put one in my mouth, and it was an experience I will not forget. The little jewel melted nearly instantly, releasing a burst of the essence of strawberry, followed by a lingering taste very much like that of white chocolate. On another day, I stopped by Laguna Farms to pick up some golden tomatoes and Scott Mathieson, who grows them, appeared, wine glass in hand, to offer me a taste of a rare 1976 Zinfandel. Ah, Sonoma. It is moments such as these that make researching our farms a sheer delight.

The produce farms of Sonoma are among the most beautiful, most interesting, and most innovative aspects of agriculture in the county. From the specialized farms such as Lucky Duck that are concentrating on a single item, in this case, *mesclun* salad mix, to the diverse, bountiful gardens such as that of The Farallones Institute, which specializes in reviving heirloom species, our produce farms show the dedication, innovation, and creativity of our growers. With the disappearance of the family farm, there has been a steady decrease in the types of foods produced, and it is farms such as these in

Sonoma that will be instrumental in reversing that trend.

Other farmers concentrate on more traditional crops that have been long established in our county. The apple is the best known of the fruits we grow, but we are not limited to apples. Two kiwi farms, both members of the Farm Trails organization, offer that once-exotic fruit, and the luscious figs grown here are perhaps our best-kept secret, our most valuable untapped resource. Crane melons were developed here by the Crane family more than fifty years ago, and are still grown at the original site and sold at the Crane Melon Barn on Petaluma Hill Road in Santa Rosa. Sonoma Valley offers us luscious strawberries and, throughout the county, we are blessed with wonderful raspberries, blackberries, loganberries, olallieberries, and blueberries. Two farms, Urmini and Sons' Herb Farm and Ocean Song Gardens, concentrate on common and unusual herbs, with each offering dozens of varieties.

It was the bounty of our farms that first drew attention to Sonoma as a prime growing region. At the same time, it is our farms that are the most invisible, the most mysterious to many of the people living in their midst. The average shopper chooses produce from the local market without much thought about its source, and even though that attitude has been changing over the last few years, most residents never think about where their food has been grown, much less ever see the beautiful farms that feed them and their families. It is understandable; we all, including the farmers who grow the produce, live busy lives. Showing the public the farm is no more of a priority to the grower than seeing it is to the consumer. The best ways to take advantage of Sonoma's wonderful produce farms are by shopping at the various Farm Markets, using the Farm Trails map to guide you to specialty farms that interest you, and by frequenting markets that sell produce from Sonoma. Sonoma County Agricultural Marketing Program (SCAMP) (see page 249) offers seasonal tours of local farms and some farms and gardens offer occasional public tours for a small fee.

THE FARALLONES INSTITUTE GARDEN

Certain gardens operate out on the creative edge of gardening, and warrant a closer look. The magical Farallones Institute Garden is one and it commands closer attention. Operating in the belief that companion planting, healthy plants, rich soil, and a bit of intuition is the most productive equation for success, the Farallones gardeners leave the weeds and creatures that infest any garden to seek their own healthy balance; the garden is organic in the truest sense of the word. The soil at the Farallones is the most beautiful I have seen anywhere, rich and dark and crumbly, the kind you love to rub between your hands because it feels so good. A few weeds grow amid the huge stalks of corn, the strawberries, the green beans, the specialty lettuces, but not many. Plenty of bees feed from flowering vines, but I noticed no harmful insects at all. The Farallones is a lush, bountiful, living garden, as full of whimsey and good spirits as it is of wonderful produce. You can imagine mythical garden fairies making their home here.

A particularly interesting aspect of the garden is its revival of heirloom varieties of produce. During a summer visit, I was impressed with the uncommon fruits and vegetables that thrive under the loving hands of the dedicated staff. Small green tomatoes were sweet and slightly spicy; rose-speckled Butter lettuce was delicious, as well as beautiful; and the purple fingerling potatoes were the best I have ever eaten. One potato, the name of which even the Institute does not know, had a warm pink skin with a subtle iridescent glow and a wonderful flavor and texture once cooked. It was in the lush gardens of The Farallones that I had my first bite of a sweet and spicy blood peach. The *mesclun* salad mix that The Farallones produces is truly glorious, a combination of up to forty varieties of wild and cultivated greens, herbs, and flowers.

To help insure the success of their revival program, The Farallones, by encouraging restaurants to feature this produce, hopes to educate the public about the panorama of antique fruits and vegetables that could be easily available once again. Locally, Truffles restaurant regularly offers a variety of items from The Farallones, as do Chez Panisse and Oliveto in the East Bay, and other locations do so occasionally. If consumer demand increases, more farmers will be en-

couraged to follow the lead of The Farallones, and perhaps produce of this quality will be available to the retail shopper, too.

MAXI FLOWERS A LA CARTE

I do not believe I have ever seen an article about Sonoma County, certainly not one in the national press, that did not mention edible flowers. From recipes to photographs, flower petals have become inseparably linked with Sonoma. For that reason, it is surprising that one of the county's major growers of edible flowers, Maxi Flowers à la Carte, sends ninety percent of the harvest elsewhere, to San Francisco and Napa, to Florida, Massachusetts, Arizona, and Rhode Island. Four years ago, all of Maxine Sisson's business was with local chefs and caterers. Now, most of the demand comes from beyond our borders, as chefs throughout the country have been influenced by the style that emerged from Sonoma. On two acres in Sebastopol, Maxi Flowers produces about eighteen types of edible flowers, which chefs use as garnish, in salads, or as appetizers, spread with a bit of cheese or *pâté*. Pansies with their wide range of colors and sizes are the most popular variety. Next in popularity are the delicious nasturtiums, whose sweet flowers have a peppery bite to them.

Edible flowers are not likely to find their way into the retail marketplace with much regularity. They are too delicate, for one thing, and few home cooks grace their dinner plates with roses or snapdragons, but they do add a subtle, delicious aspect to a

DISCOVERING SONOMA'S DIVERSITY

dish. And as long as gardens such as Maxi Flowers continue to thrive, we will find their delicate flowers gracing the plates in fine restaurants throughout the country.

LAGUNA FARMS

Scott Mathieson and Jennifer Joell operate a thriving organic farm, controlling pests by crop rotation and companion planting. Best known for their *mesclun* salad mix, a bright colorful mix full of flower petals and crisp young greens, they also grow an excellent selection of other vegetables. Several different types of beets, harvested when young and tender, make their way from Laguna Farms to the markets and tables of Sonoma each season. They offer several varieties of basil in beautiful, bushy, healthy stalks full of the intensity of flavor found when the herb is properly grown.

It is the tomatoes that Laguna Farms grows that most dazzle both my eye and my palate. From the tiny jewel-like currant tomatoes, red and yellow, to larger slicing tomatoes in a palette of shades, Laguna Farms tomatoes are outstanding. When tomatoes like this are offered from an organic farm, it gives you great hope for the future of organic farming. It is hard to imagine eating a supermarket tomato after a taste of these.

CANNARD FARMS

Speaking with Bob Cannard about his farm and about his vision for the future of our communities is nearly as delightful as eating his food. One winter night as the full moon rose over his garden, I had the opportunity to do both. With a passionate intensity usually associated with childhood excitement, he showed me the solar-powered scythe he is developing to be used for natural, energy-efficient weed control between rows of crops. As he handed me tastes of the vegetables we had just picked, he talked about sweetness in foods as the expression of their completeness. That completeness can be achieved only when all aspects of a plant's life, from the soil and air that it lives in to the minerals that nourish it and the gardener who protects it, work together in natural harmony. A taste of radicchio from his garden illustrated this concept with immediate clarity. It was not unpleasantly bitter like radicchio can be, but sweet and flavorful with a bitter finish that was both subtle and pleasant. The world needs more farmers like Bob Cannard who see through the surface complexity of modern life to a simplicity that can not only provide us with wholesome, delicious foods, but may also be the key to our survival.

Bob's contributions to the survival of agriculture in Sonoma County are varied and extremely important. He helped create the Sonoma County farm market and is a founding member of SCAMP. Since 1974, his class in commercial organic agriculture at Santa Rosa Junior College has been inspiring a new generation of farmers who perfect their skills at the six acre garden he manages for the college. Propelled by a vision of self-sufficient, agriculturally-based communities, most of Bob's energy is focused in the Sonoma Valley where he farms his many acres and is starting a community garden in the town of Sonoma. Bob is a strong advocate of diversity in farming and grows a variety of fruits and vegetables—potatoes, onions, broccoli, beans, tomatoes, berries, peaches, apricots, salad greens, and fennel, to name a few—all mixed together in happy, controlled chaos. Weeds are intermingled with edible crops and are trimmed back only when they interfere with the growth of the planted crops. The soil of Cannard Farms is so healthy that there is no problem with pests of any kind.

In 1985, Bob was chosen from among eighteen farmers to be the grower for Chez Panisse Restaurant in Berkeley, which uses about sixty-five percent of what he grows. A few other restaurants, such as Postrio in San Francisco, also use his marvelous produce. Those who relied on his weekly participation in the Santa Rosa farm market can find his fruits and vegetables at the farm market in the town of Sonoma on Fridays, though he no longer attends the market himself. Many of us miss him and his warmth and enthusiasm, but know that his work to take Sonoma's bounty beyond our borders is one of the things that will help to insure its survival.

DISTILLING THE ESSENCE

Vinegars ▼ *Preserves* ▼ *Dried Fruits* ▼ *Roasted Peppers* ▼ *Dried Tomatoes*

Fix in your mind's eye a vision of tomatoes as far as you can see, shiny seductive plum tomatoes, tons of them, piled high on top of one another all the way to the hori-

zon. Think of box cars full of golden peppers winding their way to their destination. Imagine steaming cauldrons of berries, their aroma rising above the huge kettles that hold them and drifting out over the fields, above the vines they clung to just a few hours before. Picture a tree heavy with its fruit, fruit full to bursting with sugar, fruit drawing nutrients from the branches, from the trunk, from the roots that sink down deep into the soil to drink in the essential water, the water that gives the fruit its life.

After you have this image firmly fixed in your mind's eye, imagine the enormous whirr of activity that must go on hour after hour, day after day, all season long, to extract from those tomatoes, peppers, berries, apples, pears, apricots, at just the right moment, their essence, their lush sweetness, to transform them, at the peak of their flavor, into dried tomatoes and roasted peppers, into berry jams and berry vinegars, apple butters and apple juices, and all the other marvelous products that we so casually take off the shelf in the market or at home when the whim strikes us. This transformation occurs all over Sonoma County, nearly all year long and is no simple task, but rather a challenge that has been met with enormous skill and talent throughout the county, by the small individual farmer who produces a few cases of perfect apple butter to the grower with huge facilities, such as those of Timber Crest Farms, that process tons of fruit and vegetables each year and distribute them throughout the country. Businesses such as Matthew's Mustards of Petaluma, Kozlowski Farms of Forestville, G. L. Mezzetta, Inc. and Happy Haven Ranch of

Sonoma, to name a few, all work at extracting, preserving, transforming fruits and vegetables from their natural state into some form of delicious essence.

It seems that every week there is a new brand of some delicious condiment made in Sonoma on the market. They are entirely too numerous to mention them all. I have highlighted the best of what Sonoma offers in the way of condiments and preserved foods, but that is not to say that there are not others worth discovering.

TIMBER CREST FARMS

Heading west out of Healdsburg along Dry Creek Road, one finds among the vineyards and the wineries, Timber Crest Farms, producers of Sonoma brand dried fruits, dried tomatoes, nuts, and several delicious specialty condiments. Another of Sonoma County's successful family-run farms, Timber Crest has been in production since 1957. Interestingly, not only are nearly all of the products made from organically grown, naturally fertilized produce, but all aspects of processing and production are organic. Fruit is allowed to mature naturally, with no poison sprays, dusts, or weed killers used. Fruits and vegetables are washed with water rather than being treated with chemical detergents or mold inhibitors. Timber Crest never uses sulfur dioxide, common in most dried fruits, nor is anything fumigated. The shorter time required to dry tomatoes in hot air rather than in the sun eliminates the need for salt.

Ruth Waltenspiel, who is the wife of the owner, Ronald Waltenspiel, not only handles public relations for the business, but also has developed a number of delicious recipes. I frequently use her Dried Tomato Tapenade in my cooking, and find the line of three fruit butters absolutely wonderful. You might try using the Pear Butter in place of the chutney in the recipe for Lavosh Sandwich on page 86. The Dried Tomato Bits are perfect for providing that intense dried tomato flavor important to such dishes as Polenta Loaf, page 138, and Sonoma Meatloaf, page 162. The Marinated Dried Tomatoes, which are packed in olive oil, are outstanding, too, perfect to eat simply as a snack, and delicious in any recipe that calls for sun-dried tomatoes.

Do not be put off by the dark, rich complexion of the dried fruit. This is the true color of naturally dried, unsulphured apricots, pears, and peaches that have been allowed to sweeten on the tree. A single taste should convince you that this is dried fruit at its best.

Sonoma brand products are sold in markets throughout Sonoma County and beyond and distributed to chefs throughout the country. They are also easily available to the home cook by mail order. Merely call or write the company (see Addresses, page 252) and request the current catalog, which comes complete with suggestions for use and recipes.

G. L. MEZZETTA, INC.

"I like peppers; I know how they should taste," Ron Mezzetta remarked one morning from behind his desk, a desk cluttered with an enormous jumble of products and produce: peppers in all shapes and colors, cocktail onions, olives, olive oil, grape leaves, and more. This was clearly the desk of a man intimately involved in his business, just as his comment revealed an obsession with the peppers his company produces.

G. L. Mezzetta, Inc., has been operating since the mid-1950s, producing their wares under private labels, primarily for the food service industry. In the early 1980s, Mezzetta moved from San Francisco to Sonoma, launched the Mezzetta label, and began distribution for retail sales. It has been a successful decade for the family-owned company, and Mezzetta products are distributed in major as well as specialty markets throughout northern California. Distribution in southern California began in 1989, and the products can be found in other regions throughout the country. The company is currently expanding the line to include horseradish and will be developing a mail-order service at the same time.

Roasted sweet peppers are one of the great joys the palate can experience, and they are never better than just after they have been roasted and peeled, preferably by your Italian grandmother. But not all of us are blessed with such happy ancestry, nor do we all have access to good peppers as often as we need them, at a price we can afford. It was a $5.99 per pound price tag on sweet red peppers that sent me to the shelves seeking a reliable substitute, and I went through several brands before I came upon Mezzetta.

Peppers, to be acceptable, must be pre-

pared in a certain way. First of all, they must be high-quality peppers, most of which are grown in California, primarily in Gilroy, Fresno, and Vacaville, where the hot summers yield a pepper with the desirable high sugar content. Secondly, the peppers must be fire-roasted, left to rest in their own steam, and then peeled of the charred skin. This is the best time to eat peppers, but it is possible to preserve them without too much loss of flavor. It is at this point of preserving that many manufacturers go wrong, loading their peppers with huge quantities of vinegar. At times, you may want a good strong dose of fine red wine vinegar added to your peppers, but not as a constant diet; it eclipses their sweetness, one of their finest qualities. Mezzetta uses just enough citric acid for proper preserving, and this restraint explains why this is the only brand I find an acceptable substitute for peppers hot from the fire.

Mezzetta has scores of other products, including imported Greek and California olives, capers, minced ginger and garlic, crushed garlic, and pickled California vegetables. I prefer the grape leaves (which never crumble) to the imported brands. A newly introduced product is an excellent as well as authentically *sun*-dried tomato, which is packed in olive oil. Most commercial dried tomatoes are air-dried now, a shorter and more practical process for large-scale production. Mezzetta has, however, found a way to use the older, more natural technique of drying the plump Roma tomatoes in the sun, and the result is outstanding.

If you cannot find Mezzetta brand products, you might talk to your favorite local market about trying to get them. You can also reach the company directly to see when mail order will begin. As their ads say, "Don't forgetta Mezzetta."

KOZLOWSKI FARMS

Several years ago I was invited to judge a berry cooking contest, a prospect that proved more pleasant in the anticipation than in the execution. There were not a lot of entries and, considering the quality, that was certainly a blessing. Most were at best mediocre, many cloyingly sweet, with the sugar overshadowing the character of the berries. Happily, one of the recipes did offer the voluptuous pleasure that a proper, and properly treated, berry will always yield. It was a simple item, a soft chocolate truffle topped with a perfect red raspberry. But the truffle was precisely made, creamy, not overly sweet, with a subtle hint of raspberry liqueur wedding it perfectly to its crowning berry. This was not just a truffle with a berry stuck on top. Whoever made it had a subtle and sensitive palate; I gave it the highest rating possible, and it was awarded a blue ribbon. I was quite surprised when I discovered that the source of the yummy little morsel was none other than Carmen Kozlowski's eleven-year-old granddaughter, Kimberly Every. Berry magic must be in the genetic code; the Kozlowskis have been dazzling the palates of Sonomans since the early 1950s, and they continue to do so with their ever-expanding array of fine products and family recipes.

When Julia Child stopped by Kozlowski Farms to film a segment of "Good Morning America," the products of this family-owned farm were catapulted into the national culinary scene. The photograph of Julia and Carmen that appeared in *The Press Democrat* graces the wall of the retail store, enticing visitors and marking the visit that has brought hundreds to the small Forestville facility. It is a wonderful place to visit. While you are there, you can sample before you make your purchases and there are lots of recipes available. They also sell exquisite berry and apple pies and turnovers, baked on the premises by the family. In addition to red raspberries, black raspberries, golden raspberries, blackberries, boysenberries, loganberries, and blueberries, and several varieties of apples, Kozlowski Farms is well known for its fruit vinegars and fruit butters to which no sugar is added. No fruit vinegar I have tasted is as full of true berry flavor as Kozlowski's. It is rich and full flavored, with a taste that does not diminish with cooking or when added to other ingredients, as will happen with many other fruit vinegars on the market. The No Sugar Added Apple Butter has long been the standard by which all other similar products are judged. They have added plum and pear butters to the line, and now offer ten fruit conserves, all prepared without the addition of processed sugar. My favorite Kozlowski products, other than the vinegars, are the Tomato Chutney and the Apricot Jam, which I always use in my Pork with Apricot Sauce (page 171). Their original, old-fashioned-style jams continue to be popular, and they offer several California Wine Jellies, too. Ol' Uncle Cal's Sweet-N-Hot Mustard is a favorite among locals, and the newly added Red Raspberry Mustard gives a wonderful dimension to recipes that include raspberry vinegar. Try it in a vinaigrette. California Style Barbecue Sauce, with its addition of Cabernet Sauvignon, is perfect for barbecued meats and poultry, especially when you just do not feel like making your own. Kozlowski Farms products are distributed to fourteen states for retail sale and are widely available in the Bay Area and throughout California. In addition to their individual products, they offer a number of boxed gift packs, all of which are available by mail order (see Addresses, page 252). Write for a current catalog.

D A R K   H A R V E S T

Chanterelle ▼ *Shiitake* ▼ *Crimini* ▼ *Pom Pom Blanc* ▼ *Oyster*

By now, my songs of praise for the marvelous growing conditions in Sonoma County must be wearing a bit thin, or sounding slightly clichéd. But they are all true, and even the exotic fungus loves the climate, loves the atmosphere. Mushroom growers, that dedicated, strange bunch who do their farming far from the sun's warming rays, who toil in the dark, coaxing from murky mediums their fragile dark crops, have long known how favorable the climate is to their charges. The mushroom exporting business is thriving throughout the country, with thirteen hundred commercial cultivators of

shiitakes alone, where once there was only one. That one was the enormously successful Gourmet Mushrooms, Inc., right here in Sonoma, and the leader in production and diversity among the four commercial growers of common and exotic fungi.

GOURMET MUSHROOMS, INC.

When Malcolm Clark, a medical research biologist, decided to abandon a lucrative administrative career for the more compelling task of attempting to cultivate the elusive shiitake, he began searching for a location for his fledgling business. Having evolved and perfected a special growing technique that produces excellent shiitakes in much less time than do traditional methods, he discovered that the mushrooms flourish in the same conditions that it takes to produce good Gravenstein apples. In Sebastopol the Gravenstein has thrived since it was first planted by Russian settlers early in the nineteenth century. Not only does Sonoma County have the required conditions for the cultivation of the temperamental mushroom, but also it is close to the Pacific Northwest, a rich reserve of a variety of mushrooms, and it is from these resources that Gourmet Mushrooms, Inc., supplies the local and European demand.

The success of Gourmet Mushrooms, Inc., is well documented by now, and the company continues to be a pioneer in the exotic mushroom market. In addition to being one of the world's largest producers of the dark, richly delicious shiitake, Clark's operation has developed its own variety of mushroom, the Pom Pom Blanc. The company raises a vast selection of mushrooms and gathers and distributes tons of those types that defy attempts at cultivation, such as the highly valued morel, chanterelle, and cèpe.

Much of the production is distributed to chefs locally and throughout the country, in part because of demand and in part because such delicacies as morels, black chanterelles, and even shiitakes are uncommon in our home kitchens. But that is changing, and it is easy to see an increase in the retail distribution of wild mushrooms. It is a trend we can only hope will continue, and can encourage by asking our local grocers to provide them for us.

In Sonoma County, Sebastopol's Fiesta Market features a selection of seasonal mushrooms from Gourmet Mushrooms, Inc., year round, making the frequently hard to find varieties easily accessible to local shoppers as well as to visitors who discover this great market.

DONALD B. MILLS, INC.

Donald B. Mills has been providing commercial and button mushrooms to markets and restaurants in northern California since the late 1960s. The company recently began the organic production of the brown mushroom, sold as the Golden Crimini, a mushroom similar in shape and size to the standard white, but with a greater depth of flavor, both raw and cooked. Although better tasting, having a longer shelf life, and being more disease resistant, the brown mushroom has been largely shunned in favor of the white, which yields more per foot of growing space. Commercial growers made this choice in the late sixties when mushrooms were becoming popular and seem reluctant to switch now, in part because of the time and money required for the commercial production of a new strain. Mills is giving it a shot, though, and hopes that the demand for an organic brown mushroom will stay high enough to make production profitable.

PETALUMA MUSHROOM FARM

The Petaluma Mushroom Farm is primarily a wholesale facility producing several thousand pounds of commercial white mushrooms each week and supplying much of the demand in the Bay Area. They have also experimented with small-scale production of the brown crimini and the shiitake. The company is a member of the Farm Trails organization, with retail sales available at the farm, though no tours are currently offered.

SONOMA COUNTY WINE

Sonoma County, with its scores of microclimates—specific climatic and soil conditions in well-defined geographical areas—is the most diverse wine growing region in the country. The story of Sonoma County wine is as rich, varied, complex, and colorful as the wines produced by our nearly 150 winemakers.

Do not be confused by those who mistakenly join Sonoma County and the nearby Napa County into a single entity. Those of us who live either in Sonoma or in Napa never think of ourselves as part of that larger, misconceived whole. Sonoma and Napa are separated by the Mayacamas Mountains, which not only provide a distinct geographical boundary, but also contribute to vastly different weather and growing conditions, and the resulting variation in crops as well as temperaments. Napa lies in an inland valley where the summers are hot and dry; Sonoma stretches from the mountains all the way to the Pacific Ocean, with great variation in terrain, soil, climate, and elevation throughout the county. The agricultural industries of each county reflect these geographical and climactic differences. Napa is well known, and deservedly so, for its beautiful vineyards, delicious wines, and elegant wineries. It is specifically focused; Sonoma is diverse. This diversity is reflected not only in our geography and agriculture, but in our character as well. I believe that it is this diversity, this combination of land and sea, this variation in terrain, climate, crop, and temperament that makes Sonoma County such a remarkable region of the country.

In the fertile Sonoma Valley, named the Valley of the Moon by Jack London, General Mariano de Guadalupe Vallejo began making wine in the 1830's and was quickly challenged by a flamboyant political exile from Hungary, "Count" Agoston Haraszthy, whose many passions included winemaking. During a visit to the county, Haraszthy was impressed with the possibilities of the region and purchased sufficient land to plant his vineyards and build the palatial estate that he christened Buena Vista. A friendly rivalry grew between Haraszthy and Vallejo, as they frequently competed against each other in state and international competitions. Each year, the birth of Sonoma County winemaking is celebrated in the Vintage Festival, which includes a blessing of the grapes and a re-creation of two of our most notable marriages, that of two of Count Haraszthy's sons to two of General Vallejo's daughters.

Haraszthy's Buena Vista vineyards flourished in the early 1860s. Although General Vallejo with his French winemaker, Victor Fauré, generally received more medals than did the Count, it was Haraszthy who became known as the father of California viticulture. In 1866, his flamboyance and propensity for excess caught up with him, and he left Sonoma Valley for new ventures in Nicaragua, where folklore speculates that he met his maker in an alligator-filled river in 1869. By the time the phylloxera vine louse, which caused an epidemic of damage

throughout the country, had ravaged the Sonoma vineyards, Haraszthy's son had left the failing wine estate of Buena Vista to become a wine merchant in San Francisco. The effect of the earthquake in 1906 was considerable throughout Sonoma County; the tunnels of Buena Vista collapsed, and Count Haraszthy's glorious estate was all but forgotten by the time the fanaticism of Prohibition struck the final blow to much of the local wine industry.

Although some wineries managed to cling to life by making sacramental wines, it took several decades for the wine industry to recover fully from Prohibition. In the 1940s, new owners brought Buena Vista back to life as a producing winery, but revival in general was slow. In 1973, Sonoma County had only twenty wineries. That the industry would eventually flourish seems, in retrospect, inevitable. The growing conditions are simply too outstanding to go unnoticed and unused.

A CLIMATE BLESSED BY BACCHUS

Sonoma County is blessed with wonderful and diverse weather, and unlike specific regions in Europe that support a single varietal grape, with enough variation in climate that we harvest more than fifteen types of wine grapes. Bacchus, the god of wine, has smiled on Sonoma. Originally, before the viticultural areas known as appellations of origin were established, four major valleys were recognized as important, distinct growing areas. Sonoma Valley, running from the southernmost tip of the county nearly to Santa Rosa and nestled between the Mayacamas and Sonoma Mountains, is the home of our oldest wineries. The other three valleys, Alexander, Dry Creek, and Russian River, etched by the Russian River and its tributary creeks as it winds its way to the Pacific Ocean, make up the largest grape growing region in the county. Along with the development of government-approved wine growing appellations came the recognition and exploitation of several specific microclimates within the four areas. Currently nine appellations of origin are recognized and several others are emerging, as our winemakers continue to discover the rich diversity of our soil and climate.

Those areas of the county cooled by the Pacific Ocean on the west and by San Pablo Bay on the south excel in the production of varietals that thrive in the cool summers and warm winters that the sea air guarantees. Carneros-Sonoma, at the southern end of Sonoma Valley, the Russian River Valley, and Green Valley at its southwest corner, are especially well suited to Riesling, Gewürztraminer, Pinot Noir, and Chardonnay grapes, which flourish in the cooler conditions. As you move inland from the sea, north from the bay, you encounter the warm parts of the county, where Cabernet Sauvignon, Merlot, and Sauvignon Blanc thrive in the appellations of Knights Valley, Chalk Hill, Dry Creek Valley, and Alexander Valley. In the hottest regions, portions of Dry Creek Valley and Alexander Valley,

the hearty, sun-loving Zinfandel and Petite Sirah grapes ripen to glorious perfection. The slope of a hillside, a soil type, an elevation, proximity to the banks of the Russian River, influence growing conditions so that a single vineyard may exist within its own microclimate. In the generally hot climate of Alexander Valley, there are cooler areas where Chardonnay thrives. This is true of all regions, all appellations. This is one element that can make the study of Sonoma County wines seem so overwhelming, almost intimidating; it is also the element that is so exciting, and has drawn master winemakers from all over the world.

WINE AND FOOD

Winemaking in Sonoma should, perhaps, be the focus of its own book, its own specialized study. With so many wineries in operation today, it is simply impossible to address the art of winemaking as part of a book on another subject. Therefore, I am offering only the barest overview of a rich and wonderful aspect of the county. There are many ways to gain access into the world of Sonoma wines, many ways to explore it and study it on your own. Our Wine Library, in the Healdsburg branch of the Sonoma County Library is an outstanding resource. Several excellent books contain information that will help guide you, especially *The Wines of America* by Leon Adams (McGraw-Hill, New York, 1985), and *American Wine* by Anthony Dias Blue (Harper & Row, New York, 1988). Adams provides historical and personal descriptions of dozens of our wineries; Blue provides an excellent guide to specific wines and I consult his book frequently.

The best advice anyone can offer you about wine is to enjoy it and, as in all things gastronomic, let your palate be your guide. The overwriting of some critics, the pretentiousness of some so-called connoisseurs, and the intimidating variety of wines and wineries can make the whole question of wine overwhelming, when it is really a very simple matter. Wine can be a delicious element of any meal, however casual, however elegant, and you are the ultimate judge. Winemakers today are making a special attempt to link wine with food, with meals, in an attempt to demystify it, to make it more accessible to the average consumer. For the most part, this has been a good and effective trend, though it has also spawned the unfortunate concept of "food wine," a notion that further enshrouds wine with the element of mystery that the advertisers were hoping to dispel. Do not be confused by this new concept.

You can, of course, get very detailed in your wine explorations, an activity comparable to any other hobby we enjoy, tennis, for example, or bird watching, or making beer at home. Subtlety and nuance are interesting and pleasing aspects of wine and can be explored endlessly for your own pleasure and entertainment. It is not, however, necessary to master the world of wine, to understand its specialized vocabulary, or even to know very much about it, to enjoy wine with your meals. It is only necessary to taste some wines and find those you like.

For the novice wine drinker who wishes to explore the subtleties of pairing wine and food, *Red Wine with Fish* by David Rosengarten and Joshua Wesson (Simon and Schuster, New York, 1989), is entertaining and informative. Garnished liberally with the authors' irreverent sense of humor, the book walks you through the world of wine and food pairing, destroying conventional wisdom, offering interesting perspectives, and making sound suggestions. They even "turn out some mean chow" in the process, and offer numerous recipes to illustrate the process of pairing.

I have not given wine recommendations with specific recipes, because, first of all, that is not how I cook, nor how I eat. With my own fondness for highly-spiced, peasant-style foods, I frequently prefer beer, particularly a good ale from one of my favorite small breweries. I do enjoy wine, especially a buttery Chardonnay or a velvety Cabernet Sauvignon, but my recommendations would have been personal and arbitrary, based on the chance meetings I have had with certain wines, not based on the broad, comprehensive research I would feel compelled to do to make such recommendations. Secondly, these recipes stand on their own. Certainly, any meal is enhanced with a fine wine or beer, but I did not want that consideration to eclipse your enjoyment of these recipes. Rather than making specific suggestions, I have chosen to discuss briefly most of the varietals grown in Sonoma and make general, categorical recommendations when I have such a preference. You will find listings of Sonoma

County wineries beginning on page 260. Occasionally, when my own taste suggests it, I have recommended wines to go with the recipes in my book.

SONOMA VARIETALS

WHITE WINES ▼ These wines should be served chilled, and, if a variety of wines is being poured, should precede any reds, whose richer, more robust flavor will eclipse that of the delicate whites. The exception is dessert wines, whose sweetness allows them to stand on their own at any time.

Chardonnay A rich, full-bodied white wine, made from grapes that flourish in cooler areas of the county. Frequently it has a buttery quality and nicely complements light poultry, shellfish, veal, and pastas with cream-based sauces.

Chenin Blanc A light and fruity white that works well with luncheon salads, and is equally suitable for light poultry and egg dishes and seafood that is not too heavily sauced; Chenin Blanc is also a pleasant refreshment on a hot day.

Fumé Blanc (also known as *Sauvignon Blanc*) This is the typical "dry white wine," and the aroma can vary widely. A fine companion to shellfish and other seafood, light poultry, and pasta.

Gewürztraminer With its floral scent and fruity flavor, frequently reminiscent of grapefruit, this white wine is excellent with spicy foods, such as cream-based curries, that are not too hot. You will also enjoy this wine with fruit salads.

Johannisberg Riesling A white wine full of fruity flavor, generally with a bit of tartness. Those on the sweet side are excellent companions to spicy fare and will generally hold their own with a hot curry or a spicy *chile verde*.

Muscat A rich, sweet wine with the aroma of apricots. This is an excellent dessert wine and works well with appetizers, too, especially in hot weather.

BLUSH WINES ▼ These wines generally have a slightly pink to a rosy pink glow from the red grapes from which they are made. They, like the whites, should be served chilled.

White Zinfandel This blush wine has, in the last few years, become enormously popular, creating wine converts throughout the country. It is fresh and fruity, a highly drinkable wine.

RED WINES ▼ What, exactly, does it mean to say that red wine should be served "at room temperature," a recommendation most of us have heard time and again. Whose room? What season? It means that the bottle of wine should feel cool, but not refrigerator-cold, to the touch. If it does not, place it in the refrigerator for thirty minutes before serving.

Cabernet Sauvignon A big, rich, full-bodied wine that is an excellent accompaniment to the heartiest of meals, including those of duck, beef, lamb, and turkey.

Gamay Beaujolais The lighter, fruity quality of this red makes it easily accessible to anyone who finds the more robust reds overwhelming. A perfect choice for poultry and any but the most delicate seafood.

Merlot One of the softer red wines, with a highly appealing velvet smoothness that is making this varietal increasingly popular. Heavy beef, lamb, and game dishes would overwhelm its more delicate qualities, but Merlot is delicious served with veal, poultry, and grilled seafood.

Petite Sirah Robust, deeply colored, and very high in tannin, this wine is an excellent accompaniment to grilled meats, roast turkey, and other such hearty fare.

Pinot Noir A light and elegant red that is perfect with roast pork, veal, and other light meat dishes, though its classic pairing is with prime rib.

Zinfandel A dry, robust wine that can be very complex, frequently with hints of raspberries, pepper, and, occasionally, chocolate. This is the perfect California red wine to serve with spaghetti, pizza, grilled steaks, and other beef dishes.

SPARKLING WINE ▼ Sonoma winemakers produce numerous excellent sparkling wines, any of which is appropriate at any time. The irrepressibly festive air of champagne makes it a welcome addition to any occasion. Not only must it be served chilled, it must be *opened* chilled. Opening warm bottles of champagne can be at best inconvenient, at worst, dangerous, since they frequently explode, shooting their contents everywhere.

THE FUTURE

If there is a single exciting trend in Sonoma County wine, I believe it is the matching of food and wine in a more deliberate manner than has been done in the past. Wineries are developing food programs, in part, I believe, to insulate themselves and their product from a growing hysteria not unlike that of Prohibition. To move wine out of the bar, out of the realm of the drinker, and into the dining room and the kitchen, seems to offer some protection from those who want to condemn it as an evil intoxicant. This is not the only motivation, however. Winemakers and chefs are finding the pairing of food and wine an exciting, creative arena for their talents, and many wineries are adding professional kitchens and hiring chefs.

Currently, Simi Winery in Healdsburg offers, under the direction of Mary Evely, a chef who frequently works with other well-known chefs in the county, luncheons that highlight specific wines. Chalk Hill Winery offers a full-day, master chef series at which Sonoma County's finest chefs share their skills and their knowledge of our produce and our wines with the county's sous chefs working to refine their craft. In addition to these classes for professional chefs, the winery offers a general series, called "A Way of Life," that focuses on Sonoma style in general and includes, in addition to classes on food and wine, discussions of architecture, interior decorating, entertaining, and design, all of which reflect our regional heritage. Ferrari-Carano Vineyards has plans for a major food facility, and Lyeth Vineyard and Winery has recently placed a full-time chef on the staff.

TOURING
SONOMA

Area map ▼ *Theme Tours* ▼ *Itineraries* ▼
Shopping Lists ▼ *Restaurant*
Recommendations

You certainly do not have to visit Sonoma County to take advantage of our abundance or of the style of cooking that is evolving here. Many of the products discussed in this book are available elsewhere in the country and through mail order (see Addresses, page 252). But should you have an opportunity to explore the county at first hand, do so. I do not recommend trying to cover the entire county in one day; it is virtually impossible, and you will end up exhausted and dissatisfied if you try. If you have only one day to spend here, study the maps and itineraries that follow and choose the area that most appeals to you. This is such a lush, diverse region that there is enough to see, enough to eat, and enough to do that all

manner of tastes and inclinations should be happily sated.

Ideally, the best way to visit Sonoma County is during the week to avoid the weekend madness that can reach a fever pitch at the height of tourist season, now May through October. It is also helpful to plan some of the specific details of your trip and make the necessary phone calls in advance (see Addresses, beginning on page 252). Be sure to work in enough time just to relax and wander, to enjoy the beautiful, sweeping views, country roads, and quiet parks.

If a picnic is your idea of a good time, be sure to bring supplies: a good knife and corkscrew are essential, and whatever other niceties you prefer, a blanket, a tablecloth, plates and silverware, a good English mystery. (I had a friend who kept her car equipped at all times with a well-stocked picnic basket, including her favorite Dorothy Sayers novel. All it took was a stop at a local delicatessen or fruit stand, and she was ready for a wonderful road-side picnic.)

I have, in devising these various tours of Sonoma, made several assumptions about your intentions. First, I am assuming that you are interested in cooking and that you are following my suggested itineraries in part as shopping trips, with the intention of purchasing the raw materials for cooking from this book or from your own favorite recipes. When I make specific suggestions for purchases, I do not intend that those should be the only things you buy at a particular place. Some things you should not overlook, but give yourself time to browse and pick up anything else that interests you.

Almost every itinerary includes suggestions for wine tasting, opportunities for you to acquaint yourself with Sonoma County wines. The purpose of wine tasting is just that, to sample and to acquaint yourself with specific wines and to consider which ones to purchase. If you wish to indulge in more than just a light sampling of our wines, I encourage you to do so with a nondrinking driver so that your tour of the area will be safe as well as enjoyable.

I recommend that you use a Farm Trails map (see page 5) as well as the map in this book (pages 36 and 37), and that you acquaint yourself with both the geography of Sonoma and with the businesses listed. Doing so will bring the narrative adventures into clearer focus. In addition, this will not only make it easier to navigate once you're

here, but will allow you plenty of time to rearrange my suggested itineraries to suit your specific interests and tastes.

I have not led you to all of my favorite places in Sonoma, though I have tried to include as many as were practical. I had to take certain things into consideration: logistics and timing; the ability of a facility to accommodate large numbers of guests; the likelihood that a place would still be there by the time you read the book. I have kept a few secrets, revealed several others, and tried to present the county I love in all its grand diversity while still respecting and protecting the privacy we all value. I hope you find it to be the treasure that I have, that you enjoy it as thoroughly, no matter how brief your visit. Welcome to Sonoma!

SPRINGTIME IN PETALUMA

10:00 ▼ Volpi's Italian Market, Deli, and Speakeasy
11:00 ▼ Marin French Cheese Company
12:00 ▼ Pre-arranged ranch visits (see text)
3:30 ▼ Garden Valley Ranch
5:00 ▼ Johnson Oyster and Seafood Co.
7:00 ▼ The Petaluma Market

My itinerary for Petaluma is organized differently from the ones that follow, to allow you to take advantage of some distinctive aspects of the area. On several ranches in

Petaluma natural beef, lamb, and specialty poultry are raised without hormones or antibiotics, and most businesses require advance notice if you wish to purchase their products. **Piotrkowski Smoked Poultry** is known for its outstanding smoked duck, which must be ordered at least a week in advance. **Matt Sikora,** open all year, raises red and bronze turkeys, several breeds of geese, and a variety of other poultry. Lamb, beef, and chicken are available from the **Pimentel Family Farm,** and **Rocking Heart Ranch** specializes in corn-fed beef and custom lamb. These products are available in different quantities at different places, and you should ask the specific ranches about their policies.

Spring is a perfect time to visit the Petaluma area. The hills are still lush and green, and red-winged blackbirds are plentiful. Start your Petaluma adventure early in the day, beginning with a stop at **Volpi's Fine Italian Market, Deli, and Speakeasy,** which has been in business since 1925 and is still housed in the original building, where you may also want to return for your final stop of the day. Volpi's is an absolute delight, a mixture of Italian and American, of old and new. They offer everything from *focaccia* to *cannellini* beans, fresh pasta made on the premises and Vella's Dry Jack cheese. Spend some time browsing; this is a food lover's haven. Select a few items for a picnic lunch; you might try one of their Italian sandwich specialties, Paminos, accompanied by some fire-roasted peppers and a salad from the delicatessen. This is also a great opportunity to do some shopping for your pantry at home.

One of the particularly interesting aspects of Volpi's is the Speakeasy in the back of the store. Regulars gather here daily for an afternoon beer or glass of wine and are entertained by the storekeeper's husband, John, on accordion and piano. If you arrive after the store closes at 6:00 P.M., there is a bell near the front door. Mary Lee Volpi operates a wonderful slice of old Italian-Americana here; I hope you enjoy it as much as I do.

When you leave Volpi's, head west to the **Marin French Cheese Company,** where Rouge et Noir cheeses are made. If you are so inclined, you can tour the facility or simply purchase some of their French-style cheeses, both for your lunch and to take home. Outside, there are picnic tables bordering the duck-filled pond, a perfect place to relax and have some lunch. Be sure to watch for the red-winged blackbirds; they seem to love this area.

After you leave the cheese factory, the itinerary allows you the afternoon to make pre-arranged visits to ranches nearby. You should try to finish in time to visit **Garden Valley Ranch,** the facility that provided all the roses for Caroline Kennedy's wedding. The garden is stunningly beautiful, with beautiful seasonal flowers in addition to two acres of exhibition-quality roses.

Before heading home with your purchases, you might want to buy some Pacific oysters, which are at their most flavorful in the spring. The retail outlet and restaurant of the **Johnson Oyster and Seafood Co.** is open all year and offers their Drake's Bay oysters on the half shell, barbecued, or deep-fried. A selection of local seafood is also available. On your way out of town,

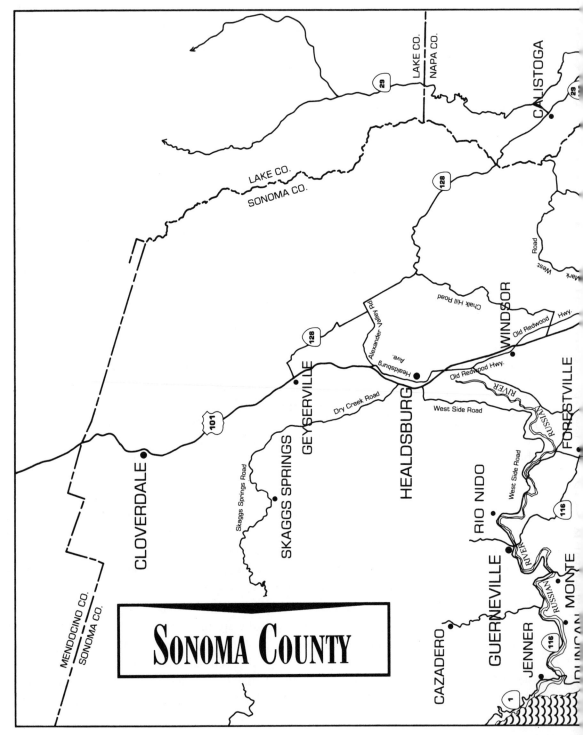

SONOMA COUNTY

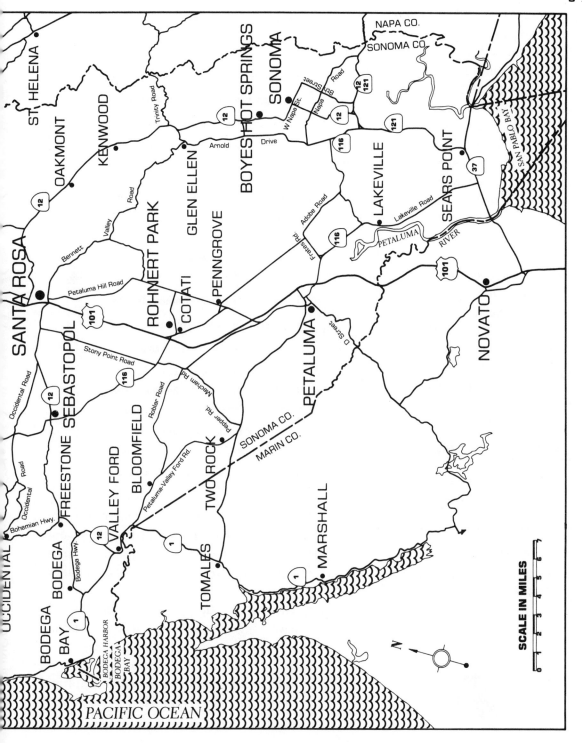

consider a visit to **The Petaluma Market,** an outstanding supermarket. From Harris Ranch corn-fed beef to Kozlowski, Vella, and Green Valley Farm products, The Petaluma Market is a shopper's delight. It has an excellent imported foods section, fine organic produce, and outstanding cheeses and pasta. If you have been unable to find a good selection of Sonoma County products, this is your opportunity.

There are many wonderful places to visit in Petaluma that are not on this itinerary, most of whose hours conflict with my suggestions here. If you would prefer seeing some of the other points of interest, the **Petaluma Mushroom Farm,** for example, or **Angelo's Meats,** instead of the ranch visits I have suggested, just consult your Farm Trails guide and devise your own tour. Regardless of the specifics of your Petaluma adventure, I'm sure you will enjoy its country charm.

SHOPPING LIST

- ▼ **Meats and poultry from ranch visits**
- ▼ **Lunch items from Volpi's**
- ▼ **A selection of Rouge et Noir cheeses**
- ▼ **Oysters and seafood**
- ▼ **Local products from the Petaluma Market**

SONOMA WINE AND CHEESE TOUR

9:30 ▼	**Sonoma French Bakery**
10:00 ▼	**Vella Cheese Company**
11:00 ▼	**Sonoma Cheese Factory**
11:30 ▼	**Sonoma Sausage Factory**
12:00 ▼	**Sebastiani Winery, for tasting**
12:45 ▼	**Buena Vista Winery, tasting and picnic**
2:30 ▼	**Happy Haven Ranch (call ahead)**
3:00 ▼	**Smothers Brothers Winery**
3:30 ▼	**Kenwood Vineyards**
4:15 ▼	**Grand Cru Vineyards**
5:00- 7:00 ▼	**Relax in the park; have a drink at the Sonoma Mission Inn; shop**
7:30 ▼	**Dinner at Kenwood Restaurant and Bar**

A wine and cheese tour of the town of Sonoma can be accomplished without your ever leaving the downtown area, or it can be expanded to cover the entire Sonoma Valley while racking up lots of miles on your car. The style of your explorations is up to you. I have designed a day that combines a bit of both worlds, with the morning spent on a walking tour, and the afternoon covering a wider area by car. Before you start your trip, you should call **Happy Haven Ranch** and let them know the time you would like to come and you should make dinner reservations at **Kenwood Restaurant.**

With your Farm Trails map in hand and an ice chest in your car, plan to arrive at Sonoma's town square in the morning so that you will have plenty of time for exploring, and so that you will be sure to get a couple of loaves of sourdough bread from **Sonoma French Bakery,** your first stop, before they sell out, as they always do. Walk the couple of blocks from the bakery to **Vella Cheese Company,** where you will begin the first of the day's many tastings. Vella's Bear Flag brand cheeses are delicious; sample several to find your favorites. You might purchase three or four small portions (less than a pound) for a picnic lunch later and buy larger portions of your favorite varieties, being sure to include a wheel or a half wheel of the Dry Jack. It keeps well when stored properly and, once you are used to cooking with it, you will not want to be without it.

When you leave Vella, return to the town square, where you will find the **Sonoma Cheese Factory** on the north side of the square, on Spain Street. A main attraction is the viewing window in the back of the store that allows you to watch nearly the entire process of cheesemaking, which is augmented by a video explaining the procedures. In addition to their own cheeses, all of which are available for tasting, Sonoma Cheese Factory has a full delicatessen selling domestic and imported meats and cheeses, prepared foods, breads, beer, wine, and other beverages. After tasting the various flavored Sonoma Jack and Cheddar cheeses, make your purchases, keeping in

mind that the small rounds make excellent gifts.

Your next stop is just around the corner, on the west side of the square, where **Sonoma Sausage Factory** offers its fare for retail sale. Be sure to take home several packages of *andouille* sausage, both fresh and smoked; it freezes well and is perfect in a variety of recipes, including Frank's Crêpes (page 175), Potato Soups (page 103), or your favorite red beans and rice. I suggest you try Hawaiian *linguiça*, North Country, hot beer, and hot Creole sausages, too, and any others among the numerous housemade products they offer. There are always several samples available, which you should certainly try, and choose your favorites for your picnic lunch. If you have much of an appetite after all your tasting, select some other items, their german potato salad, for example, to complete your picnic. If you feel so inclined, you should take a look at **Sign of the Bear,** the wonderful cookware store almost next door to the Sausage Factory.

Your final stop before leaving the Square is **Sebastiani Vineyards,** at Spain and Fourth Streets, where the Sebastiani family has made its wines since 1904, and where you will do your first wine tasting of the day. If you are an inexperienced taster, it is best to just follow the lead of the person conducting the pouring. In addition to purchasing wines you particularly enjoyed, you might consider a copy of Sylvia Sebastiani's cookbook, *Mangiamo (Let's Eat)*, which has sold five thousand copies a year since its publication in 1970. Return to your car and store your purchases carefully, out of the sun. Any dairy or meat products should be kept in your cooler, with adequate ice packs. With your Farm Trails map as your guide, head east on East Napa Street to Buena Vista Winery on Old Winery Road, the state's oldest winery, and one of its most beautiful. Tasting is done in the new, modern tasting room, so be sure not to miss the old stone building, with its tunnels, its huge oak casks, and pictorial history of the early years of California's wine industry. Picnic tables line the courtyard; enjoy a leisurely lunch in this idyllic setting before setting off on a busy afternoon of wine tasting.

Happy Haven Ranch is your next stop. Here you should consider picking up a case

---

PICNIC LUNCH

*Sourdough Bread
with a selection of
Sonoma Cheeses & Meats*

▼

*Salads from Sonoma Cheese Factory &
Sonoma Sausage Factory*

▼

Buena Vista Wine

SHOPPING LIST

- ▾ **2 loaves of French bread**
- ▾ **Bear Flag brand products:**
  wheel of Dry Jack
  Butter, 1 or 2 pounds
  Jalapeño Jack
  Garlic Basil Jack
  others according to taste
- ▾ **Sonoma Cheese Factory products:**
  Traditional Cheddar
  Onion Jack
  others according to taste
- ▾ **Sonoma Sausage Factory products:**
  ***Andouille,* fresh and smoked**
  North Country sausage
  Hot Beer sausage
  other meats according to taste
  items for picnic lunch
- ▾ **Hot Pepper Jams, green and red**
- ▾ **Wine**

---

of Hot Red Pepper or Hot Green Pepper Jam. Both are exquisite, the best versions of this particular style I have ever come across. They offer several other varieties of jams and chutneys, which you should taste, taking your favorites with you to use at home or for gifts.

You are now ready to spend the rest of your afternoon wine tasting, either at the wineries I recommend or at others of your own choosing. I have chosen fairly well-known wineries that are used to accommodating large numbers of visitors to their facilities on a regular, drop-in basis. Some of the smaller, specialty wineries offer tours and tastings by appointment only, and it did not seem fair to single out any one of them for inclusion here. If wine is of special interest, I suggest that you research this region and substitute those wineries that most appeal to your particular tastes for my more general recommendations.

Most of the wineries and many of the other points of interest close by 5:00 P.M., which leaves you with two free hours before dinner, unless you feel like eating early. In warm weather, it is always pleasant to relax in Sonoma's town square. There are also plenty of stores, galleries, and antique shops throughout the valley to keep you busy. Dinner at Kenwood Restaurant should be quite a treat: neither too noisy, nor too quiet, it is the perfect place to linger over a leisurely dinner after a day of wine tasting. It is one of the best restaurants in all of Sonoma County and frequently offers an utterly delicious, velvety shrimp bisque.

A FARM MARKET MORNING

9:00 ▾ **Farm Market**
10:30 ▾ **Costeaux French Bakery, Pasta Etc., McCoy's Cookware**
11:30 ▾ **Traverso's**
1:30 ▾ **Korbel Champagne Cellars**
2:00 ▾ **Armstrong Woods**
6:00 ▾ **Dinner at Sizzling Tandoor**

This excursion is designed with the thought that you will return home by evening, to store your many purchases and to begin to use them by the next day. Let's begin our Farm Market journey by imagining a trip on a warm July morning, when sweet berries, peaches, nectarines, and corn will be plentiful and when there might, depending on the weather, be some of the first locally ripened tomatoes. A Wednesday morning is the perfect time for your adventure; you

will not encounter weekend traffic and will be able to enjoy Sonoma at a more leisurely pace.

The centrally situated **Farm Market** will get your morning off to a perfect start, leaving you an afternoon of leisure, which I suggest you spend exploring Armstrong Woods, a regional park in the heart of the Russian River redwoods. Study your favorite recipes, in this book and elsewhere, and make a shopping list. Consider whether there are any seasonal specialties you should take advantage of; I suggest Gravenstein apples and strawberries for chutney (page 224), fresh corn for salsa and chowder (pages 219 and 99), raspberries for any number of delights. Take a couple of shopping baskets with you. A collapsible one on wheels and made of fine wire mesh will be very helpful at the Farm Market, and it never hurts to have a couple of others available for carrying supplies into a park or along a trail for a picnic, or for just holding purchases at your different stops (it is the ecological way to do it). It is also a good idea to put an ample cooler in your trunk. It will allow you to purchase items that need to be kept cool, including some of the glorious flowers from the Farm Market, which I can never resist. Cars get hot, even on mild days, and you do not want your produce wilting, your cheese melting, or your caviar growing all sorts of interesting little bacteria.

Try to arrive by 9:00 A.M. when the Farm Market opens. Frequently, the best and most delicious seasonal items are snapped up quickly, especially during berry season. When I go to the Farm Market, I get those items I have planned in advance, say, a twenty-pound box of garlic from **Rocky Creek Gardens** or a dozen ears of corn for a corn salsa and some perfect golden tomatoes. After placing these items in the cooler, I return to wander leisurely, observing, maybe tasting, and buying whatever catches my eye or tickles my culinary imagination. You might say that this is when my Muse and I go shopping; it is a trip she quite enjoys. If you have any questions about the market, you will find the manager, Hilda Swartz, always friendly and helpful.

When you leave the Farm Market, head east on Highway 12 (which requires a right turn out of the parking lot followed by the next two left turns possible), and continue on Farmer's Lane to Fourth Street, where you should turn left and then right into the shopping center on the corner. **Costeaux French Bakery** has a concession in **Petrini's Market** and by 10 A.M. each morning their wonderful breads, still hot from the bakery in Healdsburg, should have arrived. Pick up a loaf of their pull-apart French bread and a couple of sourdough flutes. If sweets are your passion, Costeaux has a great array that will please any palate. Next to Petrini's you will find the delightful **McCoy's Cookware**, where any food lover will be happy browsing. The best fresh pasta in town is available next door at **Pasta Etc.**; don't leave without a good supply. While all the flavors are first class, I particularly recommend the wild mushroom and the black pepper. The black squid ink pasta is also a special treat, though it is only available in the fall or if someone has placed a special order and they have made a little extra for retail sale. Maybe you will be lucky. Bernard and Maria Soltes, the

owners, will be more than happy to help you figure out how much pasta will suit your needs and will also help you select items from among their many prepared foods, including their award-winning Pesto Mascarpone Torta, essential for a picnic. The Soltes also operate the little bake shop across from Pasta Etc., in which they sell a variety of desserts and breads from Brother Juniper's Bakery and Sonoma French Bakery.

Your next stop should be at **Traverso's Gourmet Foods and Wine,** one of my favorite shops in all of Sonoma County. It is on the corner of Third and B Streets (drive west until Fourth Street deadends into Santa Rosa Plaza; turn left; go two blocks, and you are there). This is the market and delicatessen where I stop frequently just to soak up the Italian warmth and hospitality of owners, Louis and Enrico Traverso, the two brothers from Genoa who started this business in Santa Rosa in 1929, and the rest of the staff, all of whom are every bit as friendly as Louis and Rico. Traverso's has an outstanding selection of cheeses, including many from our local cheese factories. If you will not be stopping at **Laura Chenel's, Vella,** or the **Sonoma Cheese Factory,** you can pick up some of their products here, in addition to the excellent products made by **Redwood Hill Farm.** The shop also sells a vast array of imported cheeses and meats, including creamy Italian Gorgonzola, pancetta, exquisite prosciutto from Parma, and *soprassatta*, which looks like salami, but has much more flavor. There's a huge selection of imported dried pastas, and Traverso's also has a number of fresh dried pastas from **Mendocino Pasta Co.** This is a place to browse, a place to pick up a bar of Swiss chocolate, a new kind of mustard, a jar of sun-dried tomatoes. If wineries are not on your itinerary for the day, this is also the place to get your wine, including a bottle for your picnic. Bill Traverso, Louis' son, who has been on the board of directors of the Harvest Fair for many years, knows Sonoma County wines as well as anyone and he is always happy to help you with your selections. If you were able to get some black squid ink pasta, pick up a small jar of golden caviar from Traverso's freezer section for the Black Angel Pasta on page 128. As long as you have brought a cooler to hold your purchases, the caviar will keep for a few hours. Add any items from the extensive delicatessen selection to your picnic, and you are ready to head north to Armstrong Woods for a Sonoma County picnic in the redwoods. On your way to the woods, you will drive right past **Korbel Champagne Cellars,** with its beautiful summer garden. It would be a shame to miss it.

If you decide to stay for dinner in Santa Rosa, the **Sizzling Tandoor** will provide you with some truly outstanding Indian fare. Sonoma County is lucky to have an Indian restaurant of this caliber, and your day at Armstrong Woods would end perfectly with a rich and spicy curry for dinner.

SHOPPING LIST

- ▾ **Farm Market:**
    Fresh flowers
    Garlic and garlic braids
    Fruits and vegetables
    Herbs
    Eggs

- ▾ **Costeaux:**
    Pull-apart and flute sourdough bread; pastries as needed

- ▾ **Pasta Etc:**
    Fresh pasta sheets for cannelloni (wild mushroom, if available)
    Black squid ink pasta, if available, cut in "angel hair" strands (¼ pound per serving)
    Black pepper pasta
    ¼ pound Pesto-Mascarpone Torta
    Biscotti
    Brother Juniper's Cajun Three-Pepper Bread

- ▾ **Traverso's:**
    Golden caviar
    Selection of cheeses
    ¼ pound soprassatta
    Mezzetta Fire Roasted Peppers
    Mustard: Dessaux Dijon, Sonoma Coast, or Matthew's
    Mendocino Pasta Company's tomato-jalapeño pasta
    Wine
    Chocolate

PICNIC MENU

French Bread with Pesto Mascarpone Torta
& Roasted Peppers

▼

Cajun Three-Pepper Bread with Mustard,
Bear Flag brand High-Moisture Jack,
Ripe Tomatoes, and Soprassatta

▼

Biscotti, Chocolate, & Fresh Fruit

▼

Sonoma County Wine

THURSDAY NIGHT DOWNTOWN MARKET

12:00 ▾ **Lunch at Ristorante Siena**
2:00 ▾ **Laura Chenel's Chèvre (call ahead)**
3:00 ▾ **Imwalle Gardens**
4:00 ▾ **Sonoma Museum**
6:00 ▾ **Thursday Night Market**
      Treehorn Books
      Last Record Store
      Sawyer's News
9:00 ▾ **Ma Stokeld's Old Vic**

The **Thursday Night Downtown Market,** held weekly in downtown Santa Rosa from May through September, surprised every-

one with its immediate, overwhelming success. The event tapped into the spirit of local residents as if they had been eagerly awaiting its arrival, and for young and old alike Fourth Street became the place to be every Thursday evening. The closing of several blocks of Fourth Street, from B to E Streets, lends a festive air to the event, and most retail shops remain open. The Thursday Night Market is really a street fair, with a dazzling array of musicians, jugglers, and booths of delicious prepared foods, in addition to farm vendors selling their locally grown fruits, vegetables, and other products. **Kozlowski Farms** comes out for the event, offering not just their berries, jams, butters, and vinegars, but their baked goods as well. Raspberry, blackberry, and apple pies and tarts tempt passersby with their golden crusts and fragrant aromas. **Vella Cheese Co.** frequently attends the market, offering their Dry Jack, High-Moisture Jack, and Butter cheese. The sellers vary from week to week, and from year to year, making the market a continual panorama of the best foods and food products Sonoma County offers.

If you live anywhere in the County, this is an easy excursion. If you are coming from out of the area specifically for the market, you should arrive earlier in the day and visit some other points of interest. I recommend your arriving in time for lunch at **Ristorante Siena,** the casual Italian restaurant in west Santa Rosa at which Michael Hirschberg is the chef. You will not be far from **Laura Chenel's Chèvre,** where you can sample her fine goat cheeses in the tiny tasting room.

Just be sure to call ahead. You will also be close to **Imwalle Gardens,** which is always worth a visit. The local produce available there depends, of course, on the time of your visit, but you will never fail to find beautiful, tempting fruits and vegetables, many of them grown on the premises. When making your purchases, do keep in mind that you will be at the Farm Market in a few hours. Store your cheeses and your produce properly and head downtown, where you can leave your car in one of the garages and spend the rest of the afternoon and evening walking. **The Sonoma Museum** is an interesting place to visit, and the perfect way to spend some time before the market opens. There is also a small museum retail store, featuring gifts of local interest.

The Farm Market begins at 5:30 P.M., and there are plenty of things to explore before then. **Traverso's** is within walking distance, as is the **Studio Kafe,** a combination bar, café, and radio station, where you can stop for a drink. Several restaurants line Courthouse Square, including **Orlando's,** with its companion, **Deli Rose, Caffe Portofino's, Prospect Park,** and **La Vera Pizza.** Stroll past these and survey their menus for future reference, if you like, but save your appetite for the street fare that will be available after 5:30 P.M. It is not often that we have the chance, in this country anyway, to eat delicious street food. This is one of those occasions. Unlike the fast, generic food often seen at county fairs, the selection at the Thursday Night Market, offered by some of our best local restaurants, is excellent. You will not go hungry.

SHOPPING LIST

- ▾ Selection of Laura Chenel's Chèvre: Taupinière, Tome, Chabis, Calistogan
- ▾ Fruits and Vegetables
- ▾ Vella cheese

Several downtown stores are worthy of a visit during your market visit, too. **Treehorn Books** sells used and rare books and an outstanding collection of new cookbooks. I have found several first editions of the works of M. F. K. Fisher, who makes her home here in Sonoma County. Treehorn Books also offers beautiful, limited editions from small specialty presses certain to interest the collector. **The Last Record Store** is an essential stop for the lover of popular music. The store features an informed selection of new, used, and frequently hard to find, albums (yes, on black vinyl), in a variety of categories, including blues, classic rock and roll, modern rock, punk, and jazz. The broad collection of compact discs includes, in addition to current, popular titles, opera and classical selections. Next door to the record store is **Sawyer's News,** with the best selection of magazines, periodicals, and newspapers in the county.

Complete your Farm Market evening with a pint of ale from **Ma Stokeld's Old Vic,** the English pub next to Sawyer's News. It is an entertaining place, and you never know what special event might be taking place the night you walk in. It could be Beatles Trivia Night, Open Mike Night, which features the band, "Stupid White People," or, well . . . at the Old Vic, you just never know. The place is perfect for a great beer and a bit more local color to end your evening.

SEBASTOPOL'S FARMS

▼▼▼▼▼▼▼▼▼▼▼▼▼▼▼▼▼▼▼▼▼▼▼▼▼▼▼▼▼▼▼

9:00 ▼	**Joe Matos Cheese Factory**
9:30 ▼	**Formica's Berry Farm**
10:30 ▼	**Mary Mary's**
11:00 ▼	**Urmini & Sons' Herb Garden (call ahead)**
11:30 ▼	**Fiesta Market**
12:00 ▼	**Me Gusta Farms (Rachel's Goat Cheese)**
12:30 ▼	**Picnic Lunch in Ragle Park**
1:30 ▼	**Kozlowski Farms**
2:00 ▼	**Walker Apples**
2:45 ▼	**Caswell Vineyards (call ahead)**
3:30 ▼	**Redwood Hill Farm (call ahead)**
4:15 ▼	**Iron Horse Vineyards (call ahead)**
DUSK ▼	**Dinner at Russian River Vineyards**

▲▲▲▲▲▲▲▲▲▲▲▲▲▲▲▲▲▲▲▲▲▲▲▲▲▲▲▲▲▲▲

One of the best ways to explore western Sonoma County, especially Sebastopol, is to drive around, off the main roads. Hand-painted signs offering "Berries," "Ranch Eggs," "Fresh Produce—Honk Twice" will beckon you to try some of the county's best-kept secrets, the bounty of the family farm.

Most offer just a few items in season, and it would be overwhelming were I to name them here; they are best discovered by chance, as you drive through the beautiful countryside. More visible, but just as charming, are those places I recommend for your tour of Sebastopol, if you decide to take my suggestions rather than do your own exploring.

This trip is designed for sometime in the summer, late enough—July or August—so that there are plenty of ripe tomatoes, several types of apples, and fresh garlic, too. Be sure to make the necessary phone calls before you start out; you want to be sure all the stops on your itinerary will be open. From Highway 101, head west on Highway 116 to Llano Road and follow it to the **Joe Matos Cheese Factory** for their St. George cheese. Return to Highway 116 and, using your Farm Trails map (see pages 4 through 6), proceed to the nearby **Formica's Berry Farm,** which offers raspberries and boysenberries from June through October. You might consider making some berry vinegar or berry jam, in which case you should call ahead and request a few flats. Next on your itinerary is **Mary Mary's,** an organic garden that receives so much business that it does not advertise. "Closed Rainy Days & Mondays" the sign outside says, but I am assuming that you will encounter good weather and arrive on another day.

Let your Farm Trails map guide you to the north side of Sebastopol and your next stop, **Urmini and Sons' Herb Farm,** where you will find more than a hundred varieties of culinary and medicinal herbs. The Urminis offer plants as well as cut herbs, so you can begin an herb garden at home, or expand yours with some exotic varieties, such as the saffron crocus. Not far from the herb farm, you will find one of the best supermarkets in Sebastopol, **Fiesta Market.** Stop by to pick up a few things for your lunch at Ragle Park. I recommend a loaf of Brother Juniper's bread and some chilled sparkling cider. At **Me Gusta Organic Farms (Rachel's Goat Cheese),** your last stop before lunch, be sure to add to your purchases. If you are lucky, Rachel will have some *fromage blanc* with salmon and chives, a variety she makes occasionally and sells only at the farm. If it is not available, any of the other delicious varieties will go perfectly with the bread and berries you have just purchased.

After a light lunch in the park, you might enjoy a walk. Ragle Park is a relaxing, beautiful area, perfect for walking or for a quick nap in the sun. Once you have rested, it will be time to head to **Kozlowski Farms,** where, with luck, they will have some of their delicious golden raspberries. Be sure to read about Kozlowski products on page 24, so you'll have an idea of what you would like to buy. Go on to **Walker Apples,** at the end of Upp Road, a scenic dirt lane in northern Sebastopol, where Shirley and Lee Walker offer samples of their twenty-three types of apples. Not far from Walker Apples is **Caswell Winter Creek Farm and Vineyard.** If you want to see this facility on a week day, you will need to call ahead; on weekends, it is open from 10:00 A.M. through 5:00 P.M. In addition to varietal, hand-bottled wines,

they offer a selection of vinegars, jellies, jams, olive oil, apples and pears in season, and hard apple cider. They are considering pressing their own olive oil. If they do, they will be the first in Sonoma County.

If you are interested in seeing a goat dairy in operation, the next stop on your itinerary should prove delightful. **Redwood Hill Farm,** which has more than a hundred milk goats, is an interesting place and well worth a visit. The goat's milk products are delicious, and you should definitely take some home with you. Far from the world of goat farming, **Iron Horse Vineyards** produces outstanding sparkling wines. Tours and tasting are available by appointment every day except Sunday. Iron Horse also offers excellent varietals and, if wine is of particular interest to you, you might want to taste with the intention of buying by the case.

Depending on the time of year of your visit, you will probably have a few hours before your twilight dinner at **Russian River Vineyards,** time for a ride to the coast and a walk along the beach, or time to spend browsing through downtown Sebastopol, where you will find two bookstores and an

---

PICNIC IN THE PARK

Brother Juniper's Struan Bread with Rachel's Goat Cheese and Ripe Tomatoes & Peppers

▼

Raspberries

▼

Sparkling Cider

SHOPPING LIST

- ▾ **St. George cheese**
- ▾ **Raspberries**
- ▾ **Tomatoes**
- ▾ **Corn**
- ▾ **Melons**
- ▾ **Peppers**
- ▾ **Garlic**
- ▾ **Specialty lettuces**
- ▾ **Green beans**
- ▾ **Fresh herbs**
- ▾ **Brother Juniper's bread**
- ▾ **Rachel's Goat Cheese**
- ▾ **Golden raspberries**
- ▾ **Apples**
- ▾ **Redwood Hill Farm goat's milk yogurt and cheeses**
- ▾ **Wine and champagne**

excellent herb shop. When you arrive at Russian River Vineyards, ask to be seated outside if the weather is comfortably warm. A special attraction here, apart from the restaurant, the winery, **Topolos at Russian River Vineyards,** and a small bed-and-breakfast facility, is the nightly emergence of hundreds of little brown bats who make their home in the towers opposite the restaurant courtyard. At dusk, the bats crawl from their daytime sleeping quarters to sweep out over the vineyards for their nightly meal, which may take them dozens of miles from home and which will rid the farmers'

fields of pounds of harmful insects. I love the food that Robert Engel and Christine Topolos, the chefs, offer and I find Jerry Topolos a wonderfully charming host, but it is the sight of the bats' nightly journey that sends me back to Russian River Vineyards time after time. While you may not share my particular passion for these flying nocturnal mammals, I am sure you will share my pleasure in the wine and food. The Greek and American specialties are all delicious, and you may want to complement your meal with the winemaker's special wine suggestions, an option that offers you a different Topolos wine with each course. It is a delicious way to familiarize yourself with their outstanding wines, particularly if you arrived after the downstairs tasting room closed. Though I did not suggest it in my itinerary, you could, when planning your trip, arrange for an overnight stay at the vineyards, perhaps to coincide with a local event that interests you, say, the Gravenstein Apple Fair held in August. Just think, you might wake up in time to see the bats, their tummies full from a night of munching, return home for their day's sleep.

ALEXANDER AND DRY CREEK VALLEYS

9:00 ▼	Westside Farms
9:45 ▼	Sonoma Antique Apple Nursery
10:30 ▼	Middleton Gardens
11:30 ▼	Timber Crest Farms
12:30 ▼	Picnic lunch at Trentadue Winery
1:30 ▼	Nervo Winery
2:15·	Alexander Valley Wineries:
4:45 ▼	Alexander Valley Fruit and Trading Company
	Johnson's Alexander Valley Wines
	Alexander Valley Vineyards
	Field Stone Winery
	Chalk Hill Winery
5:30 ▼	Sonoma County Wine Library
7:00 ▼	

This particular adventure sends you exploring the farms of the Dry Creek Valley and the wineries of the Alexander Valley, two of the warmest areas in all of Sonoma County. It is a busy day, with lots of stops, and I recommend that you bring a picnic lunch with you from home, rather than stop for lunch or picnic supplies once you are here. You will be able to pick out some wonderful fresh fruit to augment your picnic, and then relax over a leisurely dinner after your exploring. If you would rather stop somewhere here to pick up things for a picnic, I recommend **Volpi's Fine Italian Market** in Peta-luma (see page 35) or **Traverso's Gourmet Food** (see page 42) in Santa Rosa. Be sure to bring a cooler with you for your picnic and your perishable purchases, and to secure dinner reservations at **Tre Scalini** before beginning your excursion.

Summer, when the farms of Dry Creek will be at peak production, is an excellent time to visit Healdsburg. Your first stop is at **Westside Farms** (you need to call ahead), for their free-range eggs, gourmet popcorn, grapes, and produce. If you have any interest in growing your own fruit, you will love the **Sonoma Antique Apple Nursery**, which has more than seventy varieties of apples and other types of fruit and nut trees, as well. They also hold tastings of their different apples each year; if this is of interest to you, you should send away for their catalogue, which includes a tasting schedule. Just down the road is **Middleton Gardens,** where you will find many delicious varieties of peaches and melons. Apples, vegetables, and strawberries are among the other offerings of this wonderful family farm. After leaving Middleton Gardens, wind your way over Dry Creek Road to **Timber Crest Farms,** where you can browse through the little retail store selling their delicious products. If it interests you, arrange in advance for a tour of the processing center. I once visited during the height of tomato season, and found the process in which plump, ripe Roma tomatoes were transformed into the various dried tomato products fascinating.

After Timber Crest Farms use your Farm Trails map (see pages 4 through 6) to guide you from the shortcut over Lytton Springs Road to Geyserville Road, to **Trentadue**

Winery. A lovely picnic area is available at this family-run winery, so if you are ready for lunch, this is the spot. Your next stop, **Nervo Winery,** is a beautiful example of turn-of-the-century architecture in Sonoma County. Nervo wines are available only at the winery and are sold young, with the thought that you will age them, though the whites are ready to drink when sold. This family-owned and -operated winery is charming and has none of the slick modernization to be found in many local facilities.

I have allowed you the rest of the afternoon to explore the wineries of the Alexander Valley, suggesting six different stops. **Alexander Valley Fruit and Trading Company** is well known for its highly drinkable wines ("user friendly," the brochure describes them), as well as for its gift packs of Sonoma County products. In addition to outstanding varietal wines, **Johnson's Alexander Valley Wines** has a 1920s pipe organ in the tasting room, and offers occasional concerts. At the original homestead of Cyrus Alexander, built in the 1840's, **Alexander Valley Vineyards** produces eight estate-bottled wines, Chardonnay, Dry Chenin Blanc, Johannisberg Riesling, Gewürztraminer, Pinot Noir, Merlot, Zinfandel, and Cabernet Sauvignon. **Field Stone Winery** offers, in addition to tasting and retail sales, a picnic area and summer evening concerts. If you would like your visit to coincide with one of these concerts, call the winery for specific dates. **Chalk Hill Winery,** last on your itinerary, must be called in advance to arrange for a tour and tasting, but its beautiful stone veranda and fine wines are certainly worth the extra phone call.

Wine tasting generally comes to an end around 5:00 P.M., by which time most tasting rooms have closed. If you want to continue your wine adventure, **The Sonoma County Wine Library,** in Healdsburg, contains a wealth of fascinating information. You can also spend the hours before dinner browsing in downtown Healdsburg. You will find **Toyon Books,** a wonderful, locally owned bookstore, and **Robinson and Company,** an outstanding cookware store, both excellent places to pass the time. **Jacob Horner,** a fine restaurant in its own right, is an excellent place for a glass of wine before dinner. At their beautiful bar, they offer a wide, informed selection of Sonoma County wines. Dinner at **Tre Scalini** is the perfect completion to your day of wine tasting. It is elegant without being pretentious, and the food is absolutely first rate. A saffron risotto I enjoyed there was clearly the work of a highly talented chef, and I have no doubt that you will enjoy the fruits of his labor as much as I have.

The Dry Creek and Alexander Valleys are wonderful and it takes more than a day to

SHOPPING LIST

- ▾ **Peaches**
- ▾ **Popcorn**
- ▾ **Eggs**
- ▾ **Melons**
- ▾ **Dried tomato products**
- ▾ **Dried apricots and cherries**
- ▾ **Plum butter**
- ▾ **Wine**

enjoy them in all their diversity. This tour includes only a few of the wineries in the region and but one of the many worthy restaurants. Asti, the home of **Pat Paulsen's** winery, and Geyserville, a charming town that celebrates May 1 with a genuine Maypole dance, both deserve your attention, as do so many points of interest. The many bed-and-breakfast inns make it easy for you to extend your stay, or to return for a longer visit. I hope you will have time to return many times, and to explore northern Sonoma County at length.

HARVEST FAIR
AWARDS NIGHT

9:00 ▾	**Farm Market**
12:00 ▾	**Bodega Head**
2:00 ▾	**Scott's Bay Grill**
3:00 ▾	**Inn at Valley Ford**
6:45 ▾	**Harvest Fair Awards Night**
9:30 ▾	**Dinner at John Ash & Co. or Restaurant Matisse**

Tickets for the annual Harvest Fair Awards Night in Sebastopol, which is always held on the last Saturday night in September, sell out well in advance of the event, and rooms at our small inns are booked up early in the season. If this tour appeals to you, make your plans and secure the necessary tickets and reservations early. The Annual Harvest Fair Competition is one of the most prestigious medal competitions for wine in the state and is a perfect way to acquaint yourself with some of the best wines Sonoma County has to offer.

Think of Awards Night as a concentrated wine tasting, with delicious appetizers, because that is exactly what it is. You should plan your day accordingly. An early morning visit to the **Farm Market** is always a great way to start the day, whether you actually do any shopping or not. If you will be returning home the next day, plan to take advantage of the abundance of fall produce that will be available, which means making arrangements to store your purchases properly until you get them home. After leaving the Farm Market, head west on Highway 12 to **Bodega Bay** and follow the signs to **Bodega Head,** where you will have a breathtaking view of both the bay and the ocean. Bodega Head is one of my favorite places for just relaxing and listening to the waves; and nothing stimulates the appetite like a few hours at the seashore. Bring some fresh fruit from the Farm Market for your lunch, or stop by **Scott's Bay Grill,** just north of town, for a snack of their delicious fish and chips, the best this side of London. I recommend a light, but late lunch, so that you have an appetite when you arrive at Awards Night, but are not ravenously hungry. If you check in to your room at the **Inn at Valley Ford** at 3:00 P.M. or 3:30 P.M. you will have time for a short nap before getting ready for the gala of Awards Night. The Inn is one of the most charming bed-and-breakfast facilities in Sonoma County. Each room is named for a different heroine of English literature; I am particularly fond of the one named for Molly Bloom. If you haven't already done so, make your reservations for dinner before you head to the fairgrounds. I recommend **John Ash & Co.** or **Restaurant Matisse.** These are two of the best restaurants in the county and both serve food complementary to the wine you will have been sampling. John Ash & Co. is our best-known restaurant, and visitors come from throughout the country to taste the fare of our most famous chef. The restaurant also offers an award-winning selection of wines. Matisse was voted Best Restaurant in the 1989 Celebrate Sonoma Art Awards. Both serve excellent food and both make use of a wide variety of local products, so the choice is up to you.

Arrive at Awards Night early. The Hall of Flowers is sometimes chilly, so take that into consideration when dressing for the event, for which black tie is optional. If you arrive overly hungry, which is not a good idea, be sure to eat something before tasting too many wines. Many of Sonoma's best local bakeries will be offering the breads they have entered in the competition, and restaurants and caterers will be serving their entries, too, so it will not be difficult to dull your hunger. Long lines at many of the food stations make it difficult to move quickly in your sampling, and I suggest you spend as little time as possible in these lines. Eat a little French bread, find your favorite wines, and do not stand in a line until you have surveyed what is offered to find out if it is worth the wait. Remember, this is not dinner. Be sure to make notes of your favorite wines and don't leave without one of the booklets listing the winners. These are passed out as soon as the awards are announced, around 9:00 P.M. A leisurely dinner is the

perfect way to complete your evening of wine tasting.

A HALLOWEEN ADVENTURE

9:30 ▾	Joe Matos Cheese Factory
10:00 ▾	Bengs-Best Ranch
11:00 ▾	Twin Hills Ranch
11:45 ▾	Sebastopol Cemetery
12:30 ▾	Pastorale
1:00 ▾	Lunch at Rocco's
2:00 ▾	Wishing Well Nursery
3:00 ▾	The P&G Art Ranch (call ahead)
4:00 ▾	Western Hills Nursery
5:30 ▾	Tea at Occidental Bakery and Café

As Halloween approaches, busloads of school children arrive to choose their annual jack-o'-lanterns from among acres of golden pumpkins. This annual tradition draws youngsters, their teachers, and their families from throughout the Bay Area to join in the fall festivities, and local pumpkin farmers decorate their fields and stands with scarecrows, talking witches, ghosts, and assorted seasonal goblins. On cold days, hot cider is frequently available. Brightly colored Indian corn, gourds, corn stalks, and winter squash can be purchased at the various fruit stands.

October is a wonderful time to visit Sonoma; it is frequently quite warm and the fall foliage is in full glory. The sunsets are often spectacular, the air is fresh and clear, and the countryside is bathed in the beautiful, haunting light that only October brings. If you can time your visit to coincide with the October full moon, do so and watch those pumpkin fields for the appearance of Charlie Brown's Great Pumpkin. If he is going to appear anywhere, it should certainly be in Sonoma, where the cartoonist, Charles Schulz, lives. For a Halloween Adventure, I have chosen a day spent exploring some of the more out of the way points of interest. This is not a trip that will put you into the heart of the Sonoma County food world, but it will take you to some very special places, and provide you with one of the best hamburgers you will ever have. Be sure to take a Farm Trails map with you, and make any side trips that interest you.

Begin your Halloween Adventure at **Joe Matos Cheese Factory.** While there is obviously nothing particularly seasonal about cheese, you should take advantage of your close proximity to this family facility. The stop will take only a few minutes, as you pick up a large chunk of their delicious St. George cheese, and you will be less than a mile from **Bengs-Best Ranch,** where Stanley and Helen Bengtson create a festive Halloween atmosphere. Choose your pumpkins, corn, gourds, and corn stalks, and then continue north on Highway 116 to Pleasant Hill Road, where you will find **Twin Hill Ranch.** Stock up on local apples and apple products, including seasoned apple wood for your fireplace. On the corner of Bodega Highway and Pleasant Hill Road, you will find Sebastopol's cemetery. Cemeteries are sources of information about a community's history, and I always find an autumn stroll through the gravestones a fitting Halloween tribute. Continue west on Bodega Highway to the small town of **Freestone,** which will appear on your right where Bohemian Highway begins. Freestone is the home of varied delights, from **Pastorale,** a retail shop that sells custom- and ready-made sheepskin products, including seat covers, jackets, hats, vests, rugs, and stuffed animals, to funky and charming **Rocco's,** the converted gas station that serves the county's best hamburgers. Just down the road from Rocco's is the **Wishing Well Nursery,** which you should not miss. It is a good nursery, with an excellent collection of statuary, but all that is eclipsed by the man-made pond on the far side of the parking lot. Three black swans, two females who scorn the solitary male, share the sheltered pond with a floating replica of the Statue of Liberty, made during the Bicentennial Celebration, which you must see to appreciate. A deck overlooks the pond and it is a great place to sit in the sun and relax, either before or after your lunch. At Rocco's do not even consider ordering anything other than a hamburger, especially on your first visit. They are big, juicy, messy, and absolutely delicious. I prefer mine with pepper

---

SHOPPING LIST

- ▾ **St. George cheese**
- ▾ **Pumpkins, for carving and soup**
- ▾ **Indian corn and gourds**
- ▾ **Apples and apple cider**
- ▾ **Herbal wreaths**

Jack cheese, but there is a good selection of cheeses and an outstanding array of very cold beers, the perfect accompaniment. After lunch, spend a leisurely afternoon visiting just two places, the **P&G Art Ranch,** which sells floral and herbal wreaths and handmade paper and has a small gift shop (be sure to call in advance), and **Western Hills Nursery,** on the beautiful Coleman Valley Road, which specializes in native Californian and rare plants. After a quiet afternoon, head west to watch the sun set over the Pacific, or linger over a cup of tea at the **Occidental Bakery and Café.**

A FARM TRAILS CHRISTMAS

DAY ONE

9:30 ▾ **Downtown Healdsburg**

11:00 ▾ **Timber Crest Farms**

12:00 ▾ **Ferrari-Carano Vineyards**

12:45 ▾ **Dry Creek Vineyards**

1:45 ▾ **Hop Kiln Winery**

2:30 ▾ **Lytton Springs Winery**

3:15 ▾ **Madrona Manor**

7:00 ▾ **Dinner**

DAY TWO

10:30 ▾ **Brunch at Chateau Souverain** (optional; see text)

12:00 ▾ **Kozlowski Farms**

1:00 ▾ **Larson's Keneko Farm**

1:30 ▾ **Pelikan Spring Farms**

2:30 ▾ **Choose a Christmas tree (see text)**

4:00 ▾ **Pet-a-Llama Ranch**

Everyone agrees that Christmas shopping is not the most pleasant of tasks, and it is frequently carried out in less than pleasant conditions: crowded malls and department stores with tired clerks and grumpy shoppers. I have suggested an alternative here, one that combines personal pampering and efficient gift shopping that will result not only in a more pleasant experience for you, but also in interesting gifts for your family and friends. Why not spend the weekend gathering original and delicious products in beautiful Sonoma rather than buying massproduced trinkets in a crowded shopping center? People will appreciate the effort, they will enjoy the foods you give them, and you will have a great time in the process. You will also be helping to preserve one of the most beautiful agricultural regions in the country. A Farm Trails map is essential for this tour. Make sure you get one, either by writing to the address on page 269, or by picking one up at one of the many locations in Sonoma County where they are available. Study the map, make changes to suit your particular preferences, and make whatever advance arrangements are recommended by Farm Trails. A well-organized plan will make your shopping trip not only more efficient but more enjoyable as well.

Once you have made the necessary phone calls and secured the required reservations for this trip, you should organize your gift list and make an estimate of the quantities you will need to buy to make the baskets I am suggesting. You may also want to make up baskets of specific products, such as wine, that include, not just a selection of Sonoma County wines, but also some wine-based products, such as jellies, mustards, and vinegars, and a map of our wine regions. For the serious cook, build a basket around a copy of a local cookbook and include local products such as raspberry and blueberry vinegars, flavored pastas, goat cheeses, sun-dried tomatoes, and apricot jam. You can even make baskets for some of the children on your list, introducing them to whole-some snacks such as dried apricots, and including a wooden toy from **Grandpa's Workshop.**

Arrive in downtown Healdsburg in the morning. Do not miss the **Downtown Bakery and Creamery** and make the short walk to **Costeaux French Bakery,** where you can pick up a loaf of bread for lunch at one of the wineries you will be visiting. The **Salame Tree Deli,** on the square near the Downtown Bakery is a good place to pick up some other items for lunch, or you can wait until you have headed out on Dry Creek Road and stop at the **Dry Creek Store,** a colorful, local market established in 1881. Close to downtown you will also find the Healdsburg branch of the Sonoma County Library, which houses the **Sonoma County Wine Library,** an impressive collection, sure to delight the wine scholar. After your explorations, head northwest, with your Farm Trails map as your guide, to **Timber Crest Farms,** where you can purchase Sonoma brand dried tomato products, dried fruits, fruit butters, and nuts. If you will be making a large number of gift baskets, consider buying the larger quantities and re-packaging them yourself in decorative containers. Be sure to pick up some of their recipe pamphlets to include with your gifts; they offer many helpful, delicious suggestions. If you call ahead, you can arrange for a tour of the area where they dry and package their products.

For the rest of the afternoon, explore the wineries of the Dry Creek region, either the ones I have suggested or others you prefer. **Ferrari-Carano Vineyards and Winery,** whose classic varietals are made from their Alexander and Dry Creek Valley harvests, will soon be the site of a full culinary arts center. **Lytton Springs,** set in a beautiful, old vineyard, is known for its outstanding Zinfandels. A pictorial history of the county's early hop industry may be seen at **Hop Kiln Winery,** which is in a landmark hops barn. **Dry Creek Vineyard** produces outstanding wine that you can taste in their large, elegant tasting room. Baskets of Costeaux bread sit beside jars of Dry Creek's own mustard, and will keep the hunger pangs at bay. Both Hop Kiln Winery and Dry Creek Vineyard have picnic facilities.

By the time you are ready to head to nearby **Madrona Manor,** your trunk should be full of Christmas gifts, acquired almost effortlessly. Check into your room at the manor, where you can relax before dinner, or go out for more exploring on your own. Dinner at Madrona Manor, where Todd

Muir is the executive chef, will be a wonderful experience. If you are not inclined to turn in early, consider a movie at the **Raven Theater** in Healdsburg, without a doubt the best, most comfortable movie house in the county. With a snack bar that sells special, Midwest popcorn with *real* butter and shakers full of freshly grated Parmesan cheese, Cajun sausages, Italian sodas, good mineral waters, Twinings brand teas with real half-and-half instead of powdered milk substitute, and good chocolate, this is the only theater north of San Francisco that offers edible food.

The second day of your holiday excursion is flexible. You can have a light breakfast and begin your shopping early, arriving at **Kozlowski Farms** well before noon. You might want to alter the suggested itinerary and treat yourself to brunch at **Chateau Souverain,** where Gary Danko, a nationally lauded chef, makes a point of using Sonoma County products in classical French country cooking. This diversion will not allow you as much time to browse at each stop as I have allowed, but you will certainly start the day deliciously. Once you do begin your shopping, use your Farm Trails map (see pages 4 through 6) to guide you to **Kozlowski Farms,** your first stop. After making your gift selections, you might want to try one of the berry or apple tarts they offer fresh each day, especially if you have had only a light breakfast. Your next stop, **Larson's Keneko Farms,** won't take long. Pick up some of their fresh ranch eggs and a flat of persimmons for chutney (see the recipe on page 224), which you can put in decorative half-pint jars and include in your gift baskets.

After leaving Larson's, stop at **Pelikan Spring Farm,** a working flower farm, where you will find herbs, vinegars, flowers, wreaths, garlands, and a special Christmas boutique.

By this time, you should have selected most of the Sonoma delicacies you need to fill your gift baskets, and it will be time to choose your Christmas tree. There are dozens of Christmas tree farms in Sonoma County and thirty-nine of them are mem-

SHOPPING LIST

- ▾ **Dried fruit:**
  Cherries, apricots, pears
- ▾ **Dried tomato products:**
  Bits, Chutney, Tapenade,
  Marinated
- ▾ **Plum butter**
- ▾ **Wine**
- ▾ **Vinegars: Herb and fruit**
- ▾ **No-Sugar-Added Apple Butter**
- ▾ **Apricot jam**
- ▾ **Raspberry mustard**
- ▾ **Raspberry fudge sauce**
- ▾ **Assorted jams and jellies**
- ▾ **Tiny jars of Ol' Uncle Cal's Sweet-n-Hot Mustard, and assorted jams and jellies**
- ▾ **Persimmons**
- ▾ **Christmas wreath**
- ▾ **Dried flowers**
- ▾ **Christmas tree**
- ▾ **Baskets**

bers of the Farm Trails organization. I suggest five possibilities, chosen because they differ from the traditional choose-and-cut tree farms. **Canfield Tree Farm** offers landscape trees and live Christmas trees in containers, in addition to trees that you choose and cut. **Forever Yours** offers live trees in containers and miniature table-top conifers. **The Apple Tree-Christmas Tree** offers, in addition to trees you choose and cut, apples, apple products, dried fruit and nuts, honey, ornaments, and gifts. **Good's Holiday Tree Ranch** is conveniently situated on Gravenstein Highway just north of Sebastopol and offers, as well as the traditional trees to choose and cut, wreaths and garlands. **Fisher Farm** has an excellent selection of varieties on their three-and-a-half-acre farm. Remember, you do not have to choose your tree at the first place you stop; you can visit

several. I once spent the entire day going from farm to farm, looking for the perfect Christmas tree. Well after night had fallen and a good rain storm had set in, I found a beautiful tree, one that I have never forgotten.

After you have selected your tree, you can visit **Pet-a-Llama Ranch,** where you will find beautiful handspun llama wool garments and blankets, perfect gifts for someone special. You might want to take a quick trip into Santa Rosa, where you can find numerous baskets at **Cost-Plus,** or you might want to have an early dinner before heading home, in which case I suggest something hearty, such as ribs at Sebastopol's **Pack Jack Barbecue,** or one of the house specialty pizzas or pastas at **Pizza Gourmet** in Cotati.

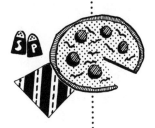

THE YEAR
IN FEASTS

Each season in Sonoma is filled with reasons to celebrate, and celebrate we do. The blossoming of the apple trees, the apple harvest, the wine crush, the beginning of fall, the beginning of spring, the end of spring, all of these natural events are opportunities for the community to get together and revel once again in the county's abundance. We have Harvest Festivals, Fisherman's Festivals, Heritage Celebrations and Living History Days, Garlic Cook-Offs, Fall Color Parades, Rose Parades, a Citrus Fair, even a Slug Festival. Cinco de Mayo, Adobe Harvest Festival, Valentine's Day Wine Tasting, Halloween, and Día de Los Muertos all have their audiences, enthusiastic followings that keep the celebration alive. Sonoma County celebrates its heritage, its abundance, its uniqueness in a year-round kaleidoscope of feeds, festivals, celebrations, tastings, and fairs that range from the homespun town park crab feed to the grand, black tie gala.

It is impossible to keep up with all of the celebrations in Sonoma; new ones appear with increasing frequency. Some disappear after a year or two, others become traditions, growing year after year. Some are unfortunately nothing but marketing tools to promote a particular business, but the ones that really reach out to the community and contribute something to it have a chance of sparking interest and continuing.

An entire book could be written on the celebrations in Sonoma, of its food, wine, and heritage. What I have done here is to list those of particular longevity, quality, or interest. Some of Sonoma's fairs feature food and crafts primarily from out of the area; those I have excluded all together. Others may offer food that is simply standard carnival fare, not of interest to the real food lover, and those I have excluded, too. I have tried to cover all of those that strive for authenticity, that attempt to evoke a particular aspect of Sonoma County, that celebrate our native abundance.

Several of the fairs and celebrations include professional competitions, such as Celebrate Sonoma and its Art Awards, and the Harvest Fair medal competition, one of the most esteemed wine competitions in California.

The annual **Celebrate Sonoma Festival,** a three-day extravaganza of Sonoma County art, food, music, and crafts, began in 1989 with a Gala Buffet Dinner (the menu appears on page 60), followed by the first annual Sonoma County Art Awards. Several well-known local chefs donated their time to plan and execute a menu that would celebrate Sonoma's bounty in a buffet for five hundred guests. The event, sponsored by Bandiera Winery, began with a reception for the artists whose work was being shown and who had been nominated for awards. Special Recognition Awards were presented at the reception, including an award for Outstanding Cooking Teacher which went to John Ash, a well-known chef in Sonoma. Lisa Jang and Jorge Rebagliati from Bay Bottom Beds were on hand with their Preston Point *miyagi* oysters on the half shell, and a luscious selection of Sonoma County

cheeses were accompanied by breads from our best local bakers, including Brother Juniper's, Costeaux French Bakery, Alvarado Street Bakery, and Sonoma French Bakery.

Elaine Bell prepared cheeses and pâtés to be eaten with the delicately delicious flower petals grown by Maxi Flowers à la Carte. Jim Gibbons, the chef of Jacob Horner restaurant in Healdsburg, provided an outdoor barbecue of local free-range chickens and wild boar sausages. Josef Heller, Lisa Hemenway, and I worked in the kitchen of the Luther Burbank Center for the Performing Arts to present the feast. Local wineries were on hand pouring their best selection of Sonoma County wines, and a staff of about one hundred volunteers worked together to make the event progress smoothly.

Following the dinner, the Sonoma County Art Awards were presented by local community leaders and celebrities, as a variety of musicians and dancers entertained the crowd. The event began a new tradition in Sonoma County, an organized forum of recognition for the vast array of talent in our community.

The Harvest Fair Awards Night in September (see page 51) is always a particularly exciting affair, as restaurants, caterers, bakers, and winemakers gather to serve samples of those delights that they entered in the official competition earlier in the month. The awards are presented after an hour or two of tasting, and the air is charged with expectation as everyone awaits the announcement of the year's Sweepstakes awards, indicating the best of the show. Other events, such as the Harvest Fair itself the following weekend, acknowledge the amateur winemaker, beer maker, and home cook with special ribbon competitions.

I tend to see our local festivities from an interesting vantage point, often from the inside. Occasionally, one of the organizations putting on an event enlists my services, particularly where the food is concerned, and I end up down in the machinery of the event, watching the wheels turn. Sometimes I am preparing the food, because our local fundraisers are among the best forms of exposure for a chef without a restaurant. I participate each year in the Symphony of Food and Wine, The Harvest Fair Awards Night, Celebrate Sonoma, and several Farmlands Group wine and food tastings. I hope to be instrumental in reviving the extremely popular Great Garlic Cook-Off. Frequently I attend an event in my capacity as a local writer; sometimes I am invited to be a judge. The opportunity to view our local celebrations from a variety of vantage points is one of the joys of my work. In whatever capacity you may find yourself in Sonoma, even as a visitor, attend one of our many celebrations if at all possible. For some of them, such as Harvest Fair Awards Night, you will need to plan in advance, because tickets are limited and sell out early. For other events, those with a relatively unlimited capacity such as the Harvest Fair, can be attended on the spur of the moment if you suddenly find yourself with a free afternoon that coincides with one of our local community parties. Use the list I have provided on page 270, and call the Chamber of Commerce of that specific town for more information. Increasingly many of our local wineries are hosting their own celebrations and festivals, and it is

always helpful to be on the mailing lists of as many of the wineries as possible if these sorts of events are of special interest to you.

What follows are brief descriptions of some of our best food and wine events, with sample menus, some from specific events, some honoring specific seasons. If the recipe for a dish is included in this book, I have given the page reference. I love to read menus, even if I am not going to recreate the entire meal; imagining an event through its many dishes is one way a food lover can find pleasure and a cook can find inspiration. I hope you enjoy the menus, too. Following the menus are specific monthly listings of food and wine events in Sonoma.

CELEBRATE SONOMA
GALA BUFFET DINNER

CHEFS
▼
Elaine Bell, Jim Gibbons, Josef Heller, Lisa Hemenway, and Michele Jordan

APPETIZERS
*Preston Point Oysters
on the Half Shell
Sonoma County Breads & Cheeses
Edible Flowers filled with
Cheeses & Pâtés*
▼

DINNER

Farm Market Salad (page 205)

▼

Laguna Farms Mesclun
with Dried Tomato Vinaigrette

▼

Smoked Chicken Linguini

▼

*Roast Pork Loin with
Chicken-Apple Sausage Stuffing &
Apricot Sauce (page 171)*

▼

*Wild Boar Sausage
with Peach Chutney*

▼

*Grilled Free-Range Chicken
with Santa Rosa Plum Sauce*

▼

Shiitake Strudel (page 181)

▼

Pasilla *Peppers stuffed with Goat Cheese,
topped with Yellow Tomato Salsa
(pages 182 & 220)*

THE JADED PALATE'S TRIBUTE TO
THE LOVERS OF THE STINKING ROSE

**The Farmlands Group Tasting
of Cabernet Sauvignon Wines
Summer 1988
Chateau St. Jean Winery**

This menu caused quite a sensation when I offered it at one of The Farmlands Group wine and food tastings. Word quickly got out that someone was serving *garlic and chocolate*. People were astonished. Some were reluctant to try it, but most found the combination delicious.

*Roasted Garlic Braid (page 78)
served with
Edible Rose Petals, Sun-Dried Tomato
Cheese Torta, & Croutons*

▼

*Bagna Cauda with Steamed Artichokes &
Costeaux Bread (page 221)*

▼

*Transylvanian Chocolate Cake:
Chocolate Cake with Chocolate
Buttercream Frosting smothered in
Caramelized Garlic Slivers (page 243)*

LATE SUMMER BRUNCH AT
IRON HORSE VINEYARDS

CHEF

▼

Lisa Hemenway

Audrey Sterling, of Iron Horse Vineyards, asked Lisa Hemenway, a local restaurateur, for a simple menu for a small gathering (which turned out to comprise seventy people, including seven members of the U.S. Senate). The produce for the event came from Audrey's garden and was a great success in spite of the unseasonal rain and proliferation of bees. Sonoma County is a wonderful place in which to cook in part because there are people, like Audrey and Lisa, who are interested enough in fresh, wholesome foods to make an event like this possible.

*Fresh Corn Blini with Smoked Salmon
Iron Horse Champagne*

▼

*Cold Poached Breast of Free-Range Chicken
with Lemon, Thyme, & Yellow
Tomato Salsa (pages 142 & 220)*

Three Vegetable Tarts
(Carrot, Spinach, & Summer Squash)
Iron Horse Chardonnay

▼

Local Goat Cheese marinated in Herbs
served with Bruschetta
Iron Horse Cabernet Sauvignon

▼

Poached Comice Pears with Chocolate
Sauce & Pistachios,
Garnished with a Rosette of
White Chocolate Mousse &
Confetti of Charentais
Melon

A SPRING LUNCHEON

CHEF
▼
John Ash

John Ash has been influential in the culinary world of Sonoma County since he opened his first restaurant here a decade ago. Currently, he travels throughout the world introducing chefs to the foods and cooking techniques we use in California, and Sonoma. He designed this menu especially for this book.

Fresh Halibut wrapped in Chard
with Lobster & Ginger Beurre Blanc
(pages 152 & 213)
Matanzas Creek Sauvignon Blanc

▼

Warm Red Cabbage Salad with
California Goat Cheese & Bacon
(page 208)
Rafanelli Zinfandel

▼

California Four-Nut Torte (page 236)
Piper Sonoma Brut

A TASTE OF SONOMA

CHEF
▼
Josef Heller

This menu is featured at chef Josef Heller's restaurant, La Province, in Santa Rosa.

Smoked Bodega Salmon
with Onion & Capers
Korbel Brut Champagne

▼

Spinach Salad La Province
(page 195)
topped with Laura Chenel's Goat Cheese

▼

Petaluma Duck in Raspberry Sauce
(page 144)
Geyser Peak Reserve Alexander 1983
Cabernet Sauvignon

▼

Pears Poached in Red Wine served over
Vanilla Ice Cream (page 230)
deLoach Late Harvest Gewürztraminer

SONOMA COUNTY SPRING DINNER

CHEF
▼
Michael Hirschberg

The Restaurant Matisse in Santa Rosa is known for its special dinners pairing the best of the county's wines and food.

A Sonoma Coast Mixed Grill
with Oysters, Salmon, & Rockfish
Matanzas Creek 1987 Sauvignon Blanc
▼
Shiitake, Morel, & Pom Pom Mushrooms
in Puff Pastry
Sonoma Cutrer 1987 Russian River Valley
Chardonnay
▼
Springtime Salad of Artichokes,
Fennel, & Haricots Verts
▼
Roast Quail with Fresh Sage Pasta
Joseph Swan 1985 Zinfandel
Gary Farrell 1985 Zinfandel
▼
Warm Santa Rosa Goat Cheese Timbale
with Healdsburg Dried Tomatoes
▼
Cloverdale Orange Tart
Chateau St. Jean 1986 Alexander Valley
Riesling Select Late Harvest

1990 TRIBUTE TO M.F.K. FISHER

CHEFS
▼
Lisa Hemenway and Michele Jordan

The highlight of the 1990 Celebrate Sonoma's *Sonoma County Art Awards* was the presentation of the Lifetime Achievement Award to Mary Frances Kennedy Fisher in recognition of her career as America's premier food writer. It was an honor and a joy to participate in a tribute to this remarkable talent without whom careers such as mine may not have even existed. Now in her 80's, Mrs. Fisher has made her home since the 1960's in the small town of Glen Ellen here in Sonoma County, where she continues to shape her fine prose and to delight and charm her friends and admirers with her unending enthusiasm, curiosity, and zest for life.

Marinated Grapes and Onions
(page 225)
Farallones Institute Gardens Mesclun *with*
Fresh Mozzarella grilled in Grape Leaves
Grilled Range Chicken Breasts with
Lemon-Currant Compote
Wild Rice with Currants & Walnuts
Haricots Verts
Sonoma County Berries with
Lemon Genoise
▼
Breads by Mezzaluna Bakery
▼
Sonoma County Wines
Korbel Blanc de Noir Champagne
1987 Chalk Hill Chardonnay
1988 Melim Vineyards Maacama Creek
Cabernet

LATE SUMMER LUNCHEON
AT QUIVIRA WINERY

CHEF
▼
Bea Beasley

Bea Beasley, a graduate of the California Culinary Academy in San Francisco, had the enviable position of chef aboard Chateau St. Jean's private rail car, a job that took her throughout the United States, cooking for food and wine writers, restauranteurs, and chefs. In 1986, she launched Bea Beasley & Co., a specialized catering service that showcases local wines.

Prosciutto with Hearts of Palm
& Crane Melon
Quivira 1988 Dry Creek Valley
Sauvignon Blanc
▼
Salad of Petaluma Smoked Duck Breasts
with Dried Cherries, Oranges, &
Hazelnuts (page 202)
Quivira 1987 Dry Creek Valley Zinfandel
▼
Laura Chenel's Calistogan Goat Cheese
served with Raspberry-Basil Butter
(page 212) & Baguette Slices
Quivira 1987 Dry Creek Valley Zinfandel

HOG ISLAND'S DAY
OF HORSES, HOGS, AND TRUFFLES

CHEF
▼
Mark Malicki

Hog Island Oyster Co. celebrated its oysters by throwing a huge party on the bay, with chef Mark Malicki preparing the menu, and Iron Horse Vineyards pouring the wine. In spite of the early fall rain and cool temperatures, it was a wonderful event, one that will be remembered by everyone who indulged in the glorious abundance and variety of oysters.

Oyster Bisque
with Croutons, Crème Fraîche & Caviar
▼
Oysters on the Half Shell
with Assorted Sauces:
Spicy Mignonette (page 216)
Balsamic Vinegar Mignonette
Red & Green Pepper Vinegar
Homemade Cocktail Sauce
▼
Barbecued Oysters with Assorted Sauces:
Yellow Curry & Coriander
Smoked Red Pepper & Arugula
Chinese Black Bean, Ginger &
Garlic Sauce
▼
Cold Poached Oysters
with Ginger Zabaglione & Julienned
Cucumbers & Beets
▼
Panfried Oysters
with Rock Shrimp, Corn &
Pancetta Ragout
▼

*Moonshadow Farms Spit-Roasted Pig
with Glazed Onions &
Caramelized Asian Pears*

▼

Lemon Bars

▼

Almond Biscotti

▼

Chocolate Walnut Cookies

▼

*Iron Horse Vineyards Wines &
Sparkling Wines*

ORGANICALLY GROWN WEEK DINNER

CHEF

▼

Mark Malicki

The movement towards organically grown foods of all kinds is seeing increasing momentum in Sonoma County, and 1989 marked the first Organically Grown Week, seven days of cooking demonstrations, lectures, and the promotion of this wonderful, natural alternative to overprocessed and chemical-ridden foods. A special dinner at Truffles restaurant in Sebastopol, at which several illustrious members of the food industry were guests, was the highlight of the week.

*Roasted Herb & Vegetable Breads with
Stueve's Certified Raw Butter*

▼

*Vegetable Broth with Leek Envelopes filled
with Roasted Vegetables
Matanzas Creek 1987 Sauvignon Blanc*

▼

*Potato & Fennel Terrine (page 184)
with Herbed Summer Vegetables
Vinaigrette
Lemon Verbena Sorbet (page 233)
Frei Vineyards 1988 Carignane Blanc*

▼

*Roasted Pepper, Tomato, & Basil Lasagne
with Goat Milk Ricotta*

or

*Spit-Roasted Chicken
with Roasted Rocambole Garlic &
Golden Chanterelle Ravioli
Frei Vineyards 1988 Pinot Noir*

▼

Gardener's Salad

▼

Floating Island with Strawberry Sauce

A FALL DINNER
FROM RUSSIAN RIVER VINEYARDS

CHEFS

▼

Robert Engel and Christine Topolos

Russian River Vineyards, on Highway 116 in Forestville, just up the road from Kozlowski Farms, is a particularly charming place to visit. It is situated on a hill overlooking acres of vineyards and its carefully tended gardens follow the natural cycles of native plants.

*Steamed Mussels with Chardonnay &
Fresh Herbs (page 152)
Korbel Natural Champagne*

▼

Butternut Squash Soup with Mace
(page 102)
Topolos 1987 Chardonnay

▼

Red-Leaf Lettuces with Smoked Chicken,
Sesame Oil, & Raspberry Vinegar
Dressing (page 201)
Topolos 1987 Sauvignon Blanc

▼

Roast Duckling with Madeira &
Black Currants (page 145)
Topolos 1986 Pinot Noir

▼

Christine's Cheesecake (page 236)
Topolos Late Harvest Riesling

FALL DINNER

CHEF

▼

Todd Muir

Todd Muir, the executive chef at Madrona Manor, designed this menu for a special event at Clos du Bois Winery. Madrona Manor, a beautiful bed-and-breakfast inn, is well known for its visiting chef series, a program at which chefs from all over Europe come to present special versions of the cuisine from their particular regions.

Seafood Sausages with Tomato Coulis
Calcaire 1987 Chardonnay

▼

Pumpkin Soup with Turkey Quenelles,
Chives, & Cranberry Cream

▼

Sonoma Rack of Lamb
with Red Wine Sauce,
Baby Vegetables, & Polenta
1985 Marlstone

▼

Wild Huckleberry Pie with Crème Anglaise
1986 Fleur d'Alexandra

WINTER LUNCHEON

CHEF

▼

Mary Evely

Mary Evely, a self-taught chef, is the director of the Food and Wine Program at the Simi Winery in Healdsburg. She specializes in food and wine pairings and provides a number of special luncheons at the winery each year, frequently working with other fine local chefs. A brochure about the series is available from the winery.

Smoked Chicken & Fennel Salad
(page 200)
Simi Rosé of Cabernet Sauvignon

▼

Wild Mushroom Risotto (page 137)
Simi Cabernet Sauvignon

▼

Apple Tart with Polenta Crust (page 240)
Simi Muscat Canelli

SONOMA'S CELEBRATIONS

ANNUAL EVENTS

JANUARY ▾

Petaluma Crab Feed, Petaluma. This annual fundraiser organized by the Lion's Club attracts about six-hundred seafood lovers for the all-you-can-eat event.

FEBRUARY ▾

Sonoma Museum's Valentine's Day Romancing the Vine Wine and Dessert Tasting, Santa Rosa. Established in 1985, this is an elegant evening tasting of some of the county's finest wines.

Winter Wine Fest, Rohnert Park. About twenty wineries and nearly as many restaurants and caterers gather to brighten up winter with one of the year's earliest wine tastings.

Citrus Fair, Cloverdale. Wine and beer tasting; cooking demonstrations.

MARCH ▾

Russian River Slug Fest, Monte Rio. Slug recipe contest with prizes for the best appetizer, best entrée, and best dessert; always held the Sunday after the Ides of March.

Russian River Wine Barrel Tasting, Cloverdale to Sebastopol. Wineries that are members of the Russian River Wine Road organization offer tastings directly from the cask.

APRIL ▾

Blessing of the Fleet and Fisherman's Festival, Bodega Bay. Attracts up to twenty-five thousand revelers. A parade on the bay of decorated fishing boats is the centerpiece of this community's celebration of its historic fishing industry. In addition to the ceremony at sea, there are plenty of opportunities to sample Sonoma County wine and food.

Butter and Eggs Day, Petaluma. Celebrates Petaluma's history as "the egg capital of the world" with a march through Petaluma's quaint downtown area in tribute to their agricultural heritage; attracts over twenty-thousand people.

Symphony of Food and Wine, Santa Rosa. Since 1975, dozens of wineries and scores of caterers and restaurants have gathered to offer samples of their wares, accompanied by the Santa Rosa Junior Symphony, all to benefit the Volunteer Center.

Apple Blossom Festival, Sebastopol. Celebrating the blossoming of the apple trees that line the hills and valleys in great splashes of white lace. The festival includes a parade, cooking contests, and tastings of local foods and wines.

MAY ▼

Luther Burbank Rose Parade and Festival, Santa Rosa. The annual tribute to Luther Burbank is always held on the third Saturday in May. Dozens of rose-covered floats gather near Burbank's downtown residence and wind their way to the Veteran's Memorial Building. In 1990, the event was expanded to include the week before and the week following the parade, with a variety of special exhibitions, receptions, and garden shows. The Luther Burbank Gardens holds an Ice Cream Social each year the day after the parade.

Valley of the Moon Chili Cook-Off, Sonoma. Sponsored in part by the International Chili Society; attracts up to two-thousand chili lovers. In 1986, the winner of the Valley of the Moon Chili Cook-Off went on to become the World Champion Chili Cook.

Living History Days, Petaluma. An ongoing series held at General Vallejo's adobe fort, the event gives a view of 19th century life through food and crafts demonstrations and tours of the fort.

Russian River Wine Fest, Healdsburg. As many as fifty wineries gather in the downtown Healdsburg Plaza to pour their wines while musicians perform in the gazebo. Food booths offer an array of local and international foods, and wine-oriented arts and crafts are for sale.

FFA County Fair, Geyserville. A four-day celebration under the auspices of the Future Farmers of America organization that begins on the Thursday night of Memorial Day weekend with a parade, followed by three days of festivities that include animal judging and sales, a cake sale, and a chili contest.

JUNE ▼

Bear Flag Celebration, Sonoma. On June 14, 1846, twenty-three Americans seized Sonoma, in what is now called The Bear Flag Revolt, from General Vallejo and declared California an independent republic. The new nation lasted only twenty-three days but is celebrated annually at this event.

Cotati Jazz Festival, Cotati. A tradition begun in the 1970s; two days in which prominent jazz musicians play in various bars and restaurants in Cotati.

Something's Brewing, Santa Rosa. Boutique breweries from throughout California and beyond gather to pour samples of specialty ales, lagers, and stouts; a benefit for the Sonoma County Museum.

JULY ▼

Celebrate Sonoma, Santa Rosa. The Luther Burbank Center for the Performing Arts is the home of this three-day celebration honoring the arts and artists of Sonoma County; the event begins with a Gala Dinner and presentation of the Sonoma County Art Awards and includes cooking demonstrations, wine tastings, and food tastings.

Fort Ross Living History Day, Fort Ross. A celebration of Russian Heritage with authentic food, costumes, music, games, and dancing.

Sonoma County Fair, Santa Rosa. This quintessential county fair draws thousands from throughout the Bay Area. The fair includes a spectacular flower show, professional rodeo, outstanding live music, and The Pasta King's famous pesto spaghetti, in addition to all the standard county fair attractions from midway rides and games to livestock judging.

AUGUST ▾

Petaluma River Festival, Petaluma. A mid-August festival with food and beverage booths, live music, and a parade of decorated floats to support public park development along the Petaluma River.

Gravenstein Apple Fair, Sebastopol. A two-day tribute to the native Gravenstein, featuring apples in all forms, from dolls and trivia contests to pies and fritters.

Wine Showcase and Auction, location varies. The gala centers around a grand auction of Sonoma County Wines and is preceded by receptions and barbecues held at different wineries throughout the county.

SEPTEMBER ▾

Russian River Jazz Festival, Guerneville. Since 1977 seven- to eight-thousand music lovers have gathered on the second weekend in September for outstanding music on the river.

Harvest Fair Awards Night, Santa Rosa. Held on the Saturday preceding the Harvest Fair (see below), usually the last Saturday in September. A tasting of all the entries in medal competitions for wine, French bread, professional appetizers, and miniature desserts; presentation of awards.

Cloverdale Grape Festival, Cloverdale. Cooking demonstrations, wine tastings, displays, and music.

Scottish Games, Santa Rosa. Labor Day

weekend is the time of the Scottish Games and Gathering, the second oldest and largest in America. In addition to athletic competitions, there is Scottish food, Highland dancing, and bagpipe bands.

Valley of the Moon Vintage Festival, Sonoma. The oldest vintage festival in California features the blessing of the grapes, recreation of historical events, and a grand parade.

OCTOBER ▾

Harvest Fair, Santa Rosa. Always the first full weekend in October; includes art show, grape stomp, barbecue, wine tasting of all medal winners, cooking demonstrations, and Sonoma County retail market.

Living History Days, Petaluma. See May listing.

Champagne and Spirits Ball, Sonoma. Gloria Ferrer Champagne Caves is the site of an annual Halloween costume gala.

Geyserville's Fall Color Festivals, Geyserville. The last weekend in October; features a stationary parade (you walk past it), a chili contest, two pumpkin contests, growing and carving, and a pie-baking contest.

Oktoberfest, Little Bavaria Restaurant, Guerneville. Celebrates fall in the German tradition.

ARTrails of Sonoma County, throughout the county. The last two weekends of October offer an opportunity to see local artists in their studios, with works on display and for sale. A map of participating artists and their studio locations is published each year and is available at most museums and galleries.

NOVEMBER ▼

Fall Open House. Many wineries have their annual fall open house on Thanksgiving weekend, Friday through Sunday. Call your favorite winery for more information.

DECEMBER ▼

Sonoma County Museum, Santa Rosa. Exhibitions illustrating the national heritage of different countries. In 1988 the subject was Italy; in 1989 it was Russia. Local restaurants plan special menus in conjunction with the event.

Holiday Candlelight Tours, throughout the county. The Sonoma County Museum sponsors six tours of historic bed and breakfast inns; refreshments and entertainment are part of the event.

SEASONAL EVENTS

Stage a Picnic, Geyserville. From the first weekend in May to the last weekend in October, weather permitting, half-day tours in a stage coach, pulled by beautiful strawberry roan Belgian draft horses, of Alexander Valley vineyards and wineries are offered, complete with gourmet picnic lunch.

Farmlands Group Wine Tastings, throughout the county. A continuing series of tastings focusing on specific varietals, with Best of the Reds and Best of the Whites presented each spring; restaurants and caterers in Sonoma County supply the food for these popular and fun events.

SCAMP Farm Tours, throughout the county. Once each season, the Sonoma County Agricultural Marketing Program (SCAMP) offers a tour of specialty farms.

Romantik Culinary Festival, Healdsburg. Each winter Todd Muir, the executive chef of Madrona Manor, invites master chefs from various regions of Europe to recreate their native cuisines. Regional European wines complement the festive dinners.

A
Sonoma
Cookbook

To crave and to have are as like as a thing and its shadow. For when
does a berry break upon the tongue as sweetly as when one longs to taste it,
and when is the taste refracted into so many hues and savors of
ripeness and earth,
and when do our senses know any thing so utterly
as when we lack it?
And here again is a foreshadowing—the world will be made whole. For
to wish for a hand on one's hair is all but to feel it. So whatever we may
lose, very craving gives it back to us again. Though we dream and hardly
know it, longing, like an angel, fosters us, smooths our hair, and brings
us wild strawberries.

MARILYNNE ROBINSON

Housekeeping

(New York: Farrar, Straus, Giroux, 1980)

About the Recipes

The following recipes come from several sources. Most were developed for my catering business and my newspaper column, "The Jaded Palate"; some have their roots in my earliest days in a kitchen. All of them have in some way been influenced by my exploration of Sonoma County, though they reflect my particular style rather than anything that could be described as a Sonoma style, a vague concept that is still evolving. Some of the recipes have been developed specifically for this book by many of our county's finest chefs.

This collection of recipes is different from most in that, generally, authors specifically avoid the mention of commercial products by name, whereas you will notice that I mention brand names frequently. I do so for two reasons: a particular Sonoma product might have been my reason for developing a particular recipe, or I simply prefer the taste of the particular product used. These references should not be construed as advertising; I am paid neither in cash nor in kind for my enthusiastic praise of specific products. And for those who have no access to Sonoma's bounty, I provide generic descriptions of the ingredients so that substitutions can be made.

Substitutions may, at times, present problems. In some recipes, any substitution would produce a parody of the original dish. Some ingredients are interchangeable; some have counterparts in name only. I have offered suggestions for substitutions when I am aware that a product exists that will approximate the original quite closely. Many of Sonoma's local products are obtainable by mail order, but that does not entirely solve the problem. Often it is a matter of judgement—yours as well as mine—and I encourage you to experiment with your own substitutions and variations of my recipes as much as you like. I also recommend that you pay close attention to the seasons and choose foods when they are at their best, or do so as often as possible in this busy world. To my mind, all tomatoes should be home-grown, vine-ripened, and picked within the last ten minutes. All tomatoes are not, and so we compromise.

I hope that these recipes prove enticing enough that you will actually cook from them, and not just enjoy them on the printed page. They have been developed with the home cook in mind, and with few exceptions, you should find them easy to execute. I have tried, too, to fit the recipes into a larger context, the context of my life and the world in which I live. Too often I find cookbooks and their recipes exist in a vacuum, with nothing to locate them in time and space, except, perhaps, the choices of ingredients and styles of cooking. Keep that in mind as you read the introductions to the recipes; at times they are informative; at times they are irreverent or silly; occasionally, they are sentimental. They reveal my life as a person for whom cooking and living are intimately and inseparably joined. I hope they convey what a joyful union it has always been.

APPETIZERS

SONOMA CRUDITÉS

The ubiquitous vegetable platter makes its appearance, with little variation that would evoke any specifics of place, or region, or time, or personality, on buffet tables of all types. A four-star hotel may offer more elaborate garnishes but, in general, these platters are made up of carrot rounds or sticks, celery sticks, green onions, radishes, cherry tomatoes, olives, and cabbage, and accompanied by a cheese or sour-cream-based dip. These platters may be a welcome sight to dieters and refreshing when the rest of the food is not very good, but there is nothing particularly interesting, or delicious, or compelling about them. I have often wondered why, in an area with such an abundance and variety of fresh vegetables, more chefs and caterers have not come up with more inspired versions.

Because I am frequently asked to provide vegetable trays in my catering services, I have experimented over the years with com-binations of seasonal vegetables to find the most visually appealing, delicious, and popular. I try to make the offerings not only delicious, but also interesting. The possibilities vary seasonally, of course, and I offer several different suggestions here. I have found that it is best to concentrate on just two or three different types of vegetables and choose a dipping sauce that goes perfectly with your choices. For example, I find that if am serving Bagna Cauda (page 221), the most popular accompaniments are grilled or baked eggplant rolls, artichokes, and chunks of pull-apart bread from the Costeaux French Bakery. At Christmas, pieces of steamed and marinated new potatoes and briefly steamed broccoli and cauliflower florets are well received and are particularly delicious dipped in Cranberry Mayonnaise (page 210). Also, do not neglect leafy greens when preparing your platters of crudités. With the specialty greens now available, there are many delicious possibilities that will add interest to your platter.

SEASONAL CRUDITÉS

Choose several of the following seasonal vegetables for your appetizers, along with the appropriate sauces listed below. Don't be afraid to experiment with unusual combinations. Let your palate be your guide.

SPRING

asparagus, briefly steamed

mushrooms, enoki, oyster, and crimini

Belgian endive

young spinach leaves

sugar snap peas

baby artichokes, steamed until just tender

young lettuce leaves

very young and tender carrots, trimmed and served whole

SUMMER

golden tomatoes—use only the best, home-grown tomatoes

currant tomatoes, red and gold

purple radishes

wax beans

Blue Lake green beans

peppers, sweet red and gold bell

jícama, peeled and sliced

lemon cucumbers, cut in wedges

Armenian (English) cucumbers, cut in ¼-inch rounds

FALL

artichokes

golden beets and white beets, cooked until just tender, peeled, and sliced

ground cherries

late tomatoes

arugula

purple fingerling potatoes, cut in half, length-wise, cooked until tender, and marinated in olive oil and lemon juice

Grilled Eggplant Rolls, page 84

baby avocados, unpeeled and cut in half lengthwise

Belgian endive

pomegranate seeds, for garnishing

WINTER

new potatoes, cut in quarters, cooked until just tender, and marinated in olive oil and lemon juice

broccoli florets, blanched for two minutes

cauliflower florets, blanched for two minutes

artichokes, steamed, leaves pulled from the heart, and arranged decoratively

white beets and golden beets, cooked until just tender, peeled, and sliced

Belgian endive

SAUCES

Aïoli, page 211

Bagna Cauda, page 221

Cranberry Mayonnaise, page 210

Hummus, page 222

Raspberry Mayonnaise, page 210

Yogurt-Mint Sauce, page 218

SONOMA ANTIPASTO SPEARS

MAKES 12 TO 14 SKEWERS

Timbercrest Farms feature their Sonoma brand Marinated Dried Tomatoes in an

amusing appetizer, the recipe for which is part of their collection.

8 ounces dried tomatoes marinated in olive oil

1 pound (3 medium) new potatoes, cooked until just tender and cut into 1-inch cubes

½ pound medium shrimp, cooked and shelled

1 scallion with top, thinly sliced

1 tablespoon chopped fresh thyme

2 cups bite-sized raw vegetable pieces: pepper, celery, cucumber, zucchini

Drain the oil from the tomatoes into a large bowl and set aside the tomatoes. Add the potatoes, shrimp, onion, and thyme to the oil and mix to coat well. Cover and refrigerate for 1 hour.

To assemble, alternately thread tomatoes, potatoes, shrimp, and raw vegetables onto 6-inch bamboo skewers. Season with salt and pepper as desired. Serve on a decorative platter, garnished with a sprig of currant tomatoes, if available, or some fresh herbs.

SONOMA ANTIPASTO PLATTER

SERVES 4

Fresh cheese (I would use Laura Chenel's Chèvre and Vella's Dry Jack) and fresh vegetables, garnished with beautiful grape leaves: nothing could be more Sonoma. Be

sure to offer plenty of hot sourdough bread along with this country-style appetizer.

3 Japanese eggplant
  Extra-virgin olive oil

1 sweet red pepper

1 tablespoon red wine vinegar

½ baguette, thinly sliced

3 ounces chèvre (goat cheese)

2 tablespoons fresh Pesto (page 221)

8 fresh grape leaves

4 sprigs fresh basil
  Marinated Onions (page 225) or
    Marinated Onions and Grapes
    (page 225)

3 or 4 medium golden tomatoes

1 clove garlic

¼ cup grated Dry Jack cheese or Parmesan

¾ cup Corn Salsa (page 219)

Cut off the stem end and slice each eggplant lengthwise in ¼-inch-wide strips. Place on a cookie sheet, drizzle with olive oil, and bake at 325 degrees until soft and tender, about 20 minutes. Roast the pepper over a flame or under a broiler until the skin is charred. Steam in a paper bag for 20 minutes. Remove the blackened skin, stem, and seeds, and slice the pepper into thin strips. Toss with vinegar. Place slices of baguette on a cookie sheet, drizzle with olive oil, and bake at 300 degrees for 15 to 20 minutes, until crisp. With a fork, blend the chèvre and Pesto together and refrigerate until ready to use.

To serve, place 2 grape leaves, off-center, on each of 4 serving plates. Divide the goat cheese among the 4 plates, placing it on the grape leaves. Garnish with a small sprig of fresh basil and surround with several croutons.

Arrange a small mound of Marinated Onions or Marinated Onions and Grapes on each serving plate. Slice the tomatoes into rounds and divide them among the serving plates. Cut the garlic clove into slivers, sprinkle them on the tomatoes, and drizzle with a little olive oil. Top with the dry Jack cheese. Arrange the eggplant and peppers attractively on the plates. Top the eggplant with a small quantity of Corn Salsa and place a tablespoon or two in center of the plates. Serve with hot crusty bread.

VARIATION ▾ Arrange all the items on a large serving platter and have guests help themselves.

ROASTED GARLIC

SERVES 4 TO 6

Once an unfamiliar, exotic treat, roasted garlic has become nearly a staple in many kitchens, frequently replaces the butter once served with French bread, and is found on many local restaurant menus. Sonoma County loves its garlic and celebrated its deliciousness at The Great Garlic Cook-Off in Cotati in 1987 and 1988, an event that there is interest in reviving.

   3 large, firm heads of garlic
   ½ cup extra-virgin olive oil
   ¼ cup water
   2 sprigs fresh thyme
      Freshly ground pepper
      Salt

Remove the loose outer skin of the garlic and place the heads in a small baking dish. Pour olive oil over the garlic and add the water, thyme, salt, and pepper. Cover and bake at 325 degrees for 45 to 60 minutes, until the garlic is the consistency of soft butter. Remove the garlic from the dish, cool, and serve with a mild, creamy cheese and croutons.

Reserve the cooking liquid to make a delicious vinaigrette.

VARIATION ▾ To serve a large number of people, and provide a spectacular centerpiece that is fairly easy to accomplish, roast a whole garlic braid, rather than a large number of separate bulbs. Begin with a braid of fresh garlic. Rub the braided stem end with olive oil and wrap it in aluminum foil to keep it from burning during the cooking process. Place the braid, bulbs down, in a 3-inch-deep baking dish large enough to allow the braid to lie flat. Add about ¼ inch of water to the bottom of the pan. Add 1½ cups of olive oil, drizzling it over the braid. Cover tightly with aluminum foil and place in a 325 degree oven. After 30 minutes, remove the foil and brush the braid with the olive oil. Cover with foil again and continue to cook until the garlic is the proper consistency, about 1 more hour. Remove the braid from the oven, let it cool slightly, and transfer it to a decorative serving platter. Surround with croutons and serve. To eat the roasted garlic, carefully remove a single clove from the root and squeeze its contents onto a crouton that has been spread with cheese.

GRAPE LEAVES

It is hard to conjure up a mental picture of Sonoma County without a grape leaf coming into focus. The wine industry plays a major role in our economy, and the enjoyment of wine is an integral part of life here, with wine tastings providing the focal point for social events as diverse as political fundraisers, nonprofit benefits, wakes, and memorial services. Transforming the simple, sweet juice of the grape into the complex mystery of wine is part of life in Sonoma County. The grapevine is a concrete part of our day-to-day life, too, a highly visible feature on our diverse landscape. Driving to work in Santa Rosa, or Sonoma, Healdsburg, or Sebastopol, one finds it nearly impossible not to pass fields of newly planted vineyards or of old, heavy vines, gnarled in age, from whose sturdy trunks emerge delicate vines, leaves, and grapes. Our rolling hills are covered with them, and we find their manmade representations everywhere, too, from serious fine art to the comic caricature.

The grape vine appears on posters and wine labels, earrings, corkscrews, T-shirts, and bolo ties. Buffet tables at celebrations of our county's abundance are adorned with grape vines, and the leaves frequently serve as coasters or little plates to hold small portions of food. I love to drink in the grapevine's visual beauty, but in my opinion, the best way to enjoy the grape leaf is in the tra-

ditional Greek style, wrapped around a bite-sized morsel of delicious food. Whether cloaking a simple piece of local cheese or holding an elaborately prepared mixture of meat and spices, it is a real treat and one that never fails to delight those whom we feed. If you are lucky enough to have access to a vineyard, use fresh grape leaves. If not, you can enjoy them preserved.

Gather grape leaves direct from the vine, in the early summer, when they are young and tender. To begin your harvest, grab a handful of rubber bands and a basket. Choose leaves that are not too big, nor too small. I find they are most suitable when they are between three and a half and four inches across. Pick a dozen or so, stacking them in your hand, all in the same direction, carefully roll them up, and secure them with a rubber band. Drop that batch into your basket and continue picking until you have enough to suit your purposes or until you have taken as many as your grapevines can offer without suffering. They keep well when frozen or preserved in brine, so gather as many as you think you will need until next year, being careful not to strip any one vine, because the leaves serve as sunshades for the delicate grapes.

When you arrive back in your kitchen, make up a large pot of brine using two teaspoons of pickling salt to each quart of water. Bring the brine to a boil. Remove the rubber bands from your grape leaves and submerge them, a stack at a time, into the brine for thirty seconds, holding the stack with kitchen tongs. Remove them from the brine and drain in a colander. At this point, your grape leaves are ready for use or storage. Follow your recipe of choice, one of the suggestions below, or preserve them for another occasion. To freeze them, simply wrap the bundles in aluminum foil and indicate on a label the number of leaves per package. To preserve them in brine, roll them in tight bundles and place in wide-mouthed pint jars. Bring to a boil enough of the cooking liquid to cover, and add one cup of fresh lemon juice for each quart of liquid used. Cover the grape leaves, place lids on the jars, and process for fifteen minutes in a boiling water bath. To use the preserved leaves, remove them from the jar and soak in cool water for five minutes.

In addition to the following recipes, here are several simple ways to enjoy grape leaves:

▼ Wrap marinated rounds of goat cheese (the one-ounce cabecou works perfectly) in a single blanched leaf and grill or bake until cheese is melted. Serve with hot French bread.

▼ Stuff the cavity of a rainbow trout with a mixture of herbs, lemon zest, and bread crumbs, brush with olive oil and lemon juice, wrap in two or three grape leaves (as many as it takes to fully wrap the whole fish), brush the leaves with olive oil, and grill or bake until done, about seven or eight minutes on each side.

▼ Use strips of grape leaves to tie strips of baked eggplant around squares of feta cheese.

▼▼

BERKELEY DOLMAS

SERVES 6 TO 8 AS AN APPETIZER; 4 AS A MAIN COURSE

I first tasted grape leaves prepared this way, not in Sonoma, but in the hills of Berkeley, following the annual Stanford-Berkeley football game (what was I doing there?). I have been recreating them here in Sonoma ever since that first bite.

30 to 40	grape leaves, fresh or preserved
1	pound ground lamb
6 to 8	cloves garlic, minced
1	tablespoon fresh oregano, chopped
1	small can (7½ ounces) tomato sauce
½	cup beef stock
¼	cup extra-virgin olive oil
	Juice of 2 lemons
1	tablespoon fresh, cracked black pepper

Rinse preserved grape leaves under cool water and set aside. Sauté the ground lamb, breaking it into small pieces with a fork. When nearly done but still slightly pink, add the garlic. Sauté for 2 minutes, add the oregano, stir, and remove from heat. After the mixture has cooled, stuff the grape leaves. To fill, place a leaf on a flat surface with the dull side up. Place 1 teaspoon of filling in the center. Fold the bottom of the leaf up over the filling and fold the two sides, one after the other, over the top of the filling. Roll the bundle up to the tip of the leaf and set aside, seam-side down.

Line a shallow baking dish with any leftover leaves. Blend together the tomato sauce, stock, olive oil, lemon juice, and pepper. Place the dolmas in baking dish. Pour the sauce over. Bake at 325 degrees for 40 minutes.

Serve warm as an appetizer, or over rice as a main course.

CEVICHE DOLMAS

MAKES ABOUT THREE DOZEN DOLMAS

I created these spicy seafood dolmas especially for the 1986 Harvest Fair, at which they received a Silver Medal.

1	pound red snapper fillets
¾	cup fresh lime juice
1	teaspoon salt
Half	a red onion, minced
1	tomato, peeled, seeded, and diced
10	radishes, finely chopped
1	bunch cilantro, chopped with large stems removed
3	jalapeño peppers, seeded and diced
1	very ripe avocado, peeled and mashed
	Juice of 2 limes
	Salt to taste
35 to 40	grape leaves preserved in brine

The night before serving, place the snapper in a shallow glass or ceramic container and cover with the ¾ cup lime juice. Sprinkle with 1 teaspoon salt. Refrigerate. Turn the fillets every few hours to insure even marinating.

When ready to assemble the dolmas, drain the snapper well and cut into small, ¼- to ½-inch cubes, being sure to find and discard the bones. Set aside.

Place the minced onion, tomato, radishes, cilantro, and peppers in a mixing bowl. If you have a food processor, process the avocado with the juice of the 2 limes until very smooth. If not, beat the avocado and juice together, making as smooth a mixture as possible. Add to the other ingredients and toss the salsa well. Add salt to taste.

Soak the grape leaves in warm water for about 10 minutes to remove the brine. Drain on paper towels. Add the snapper to the salsa and mix lightly. To assemble, place a single grape leaf on a cutting board, dull-side up, and smooth it out. Place 1 teaspoonful of snapper mixture in the center of the leaf and wrap into a tight little package, tucking in ends so the seviche will not slip out of the sides. Continue until you have no more leaves, or no more filling. Chill for at least 1 hour, but no more than a few hours, before serving.

THAI DOLMAS

with Yogurt Sauce

MAKES THREE DOZEN APPETIZERS

This spicy twist on the traditional herbed dolma *makes for delightful little surprise packages. Coconut milk adds a mysterious, sweet, rich element that provides a perfect counterpoint to the fresh mint.*

2/3 cup fruity, extra-virgin olive oil
8 stalks green garlic or scallions, finely chopped
1/4 cup finely minced fresh dill
1/4 cup chopped Italian parsley
1/2 cup finely chopped cilantro
1/2 cup finely chopped fresh mint
4 jalapeño peppers, with seeds, finely chopped
1/2 cup dried currants
1 cup Arborio rice (Italian short-grained rice)
  Juice of 1 lime
1/3 cup coconut milk (page 274)
2/3 cup boiling water
30 to 40 grape leaves, preserved or fresh
  Yogurt-Mint Sauce (page 218)

Heat the olive oil gently and slowly. Add the green garlic, herbs, and peppers. Sauté over low heat until they wilt and become fragrant. Stir in the currants. Add the rice and sauté for 5 minutes, stirring constantly. Add lime juice, coconut milk, and boiling water, stir, and cook until all the liquid is absorbed. The rice will not be quite done.

After the mixture has cooled, fill the grape leaves with 1 teaspoon filling per leaf. To fill, place a leaf on a flat surface with the dull side up. Place the filling in the center. Fold the bottom of the leaf up over the filling and fold the 2 sides, 1 after the other, over the top of the filling. Roll the bundle up toward the tip of the leaf and set aside, seam-side down.

Line a large pot with any extra leaves and place the dolmas on top. Make a second and third layer as needed. Pour in about 2 cups of water, or as much as is needed barely to cover the dolmas. Set a heavy plate on top of the dolmas, bring the liquid to a simmer, and cook for 45 minutes. When cooled, carefully remove the dolmas from the cooking liquid. You may serve them immediately or you may chill them. Serve with Yogurt-Mint Sauce on the side.

THREE-PEPPER CHÈVRE AND CROUTONS

SERVES 8 TO 10

This dish can be made successfully with other bread if Brother Juniper's is not available, but it will suffer considerably from a lack of the spicy chipotle peppers, which are worth whatever effort it takes to find them. Luckily, they are widely available in Sonoma County and in California in general, because of the large Mexican population throughout the state. If they are hard to get, make sure you stock up when you do find them.

1 loaf Cajun Three-Pepper Bread (Brother Juniper's Bakery) or sourdough bread, sliced
  Olive oil
1 pepper chèvre (5 ounces)

1 pyramid chèvre (8 ounces) or, if available, 1 Taupinière (9½ ounces)

¼ cup puréed chipotle peppers in adobo sauce (see page 274)

2 large cloves garlic, finely chopped

1 jalapeño pepper, finely chopped, with seeds

2 eggs, beaten

⅓ cup flour

Fresh cilantro

Brush the bread with olive oil and toast it in the oven until crisp. Cut each slice diagonally in quarters. Set aside.

Mix together both cheeses, 1 teaspoon of the chipotle peppers, the garlic and the *jalapeño*. Add the eggs and blend well. Beat in about half the flour. Shape into a log, 2½ to 3 inches in diameter and roll it in the remaining flour. Chill until firm.

Place on an oiled cookie sheet and brush liberally with the remaining chipotle purée. Place in a 400-degree oven for 25 to 30 minutes. Place the cilantro on a serving platter and carefully place the log of cheese on top. Surround it with croutons and serve immediately.

STRIPED TOMATO BRIE

SERVES 4 TO 6

This recipe is from the file of Timber Crest Farms and was designed to be used with their dried tomatoes. You may also use dried tomatoes marinated in oil; simply disregard

the instructions on how to reconstitute dried tomatoes.

1 ripe, round, 8 ounce, Brie cheese

⅓ cup (½ ounce) sliced, dried tomato halves

¼ cup butter, softened

2 tablespoons chopped fresh basil

1 tablespoon minced shallots

¾ cup chopped, toasted walnuts (¼ cup chopped coarsely, ½ cup chopped finely, for the garnish)

Place the wrapped cheese in the freezer until firm, but not frozen (about 1 hour). Reconstitute the dried tomatoes by placing them in boiling water for 2 minutes. Remove the tomatoes from the water, drain and chop them, and set them aside. With a sharp knife, halve the cheese horizontally; set aside. Beat the butter until smooth and creamy. Beat in the tomatoes, basil, and shallots. Mix in the walnuts. Spread the tomato mixture evenly on the cut side of one cheese half. Cover with the remaining cheese, cut side down; press gently. Roll the cheese on its side in additional toasted walnuts, finely chopped, to coat the tomato layer. Cover and chill until firm. Serve cut into thin wedges. Accompany with crackers and sliced baguette.

VARIATION ▾ Use the Raspberry-Basil Butter on page 212 as a filling. After filling the cheese, spread a small amount of the butter mixture on the sides. Roll in the walnuts until the sides are completely coated. Serve chilled and cut into thin wedges, accompanied by sweet French bread.

EGGPLANT MOZZARELLA ROLLS

with Roasted Sweet Peppers

MAKES 25 TO 30 ROLLS

This dish has consistently been one of Jaded Palate's most popular appetizers. Vegetarians love it, and it has even been known to turn confirmed eggplant haters into true believers. It is, of course, best made with fresh roasted peppers, but if they are not available, remember the slogan: "Don't forgetta Mezzetta."

5 or 6 Japanese eggplants, each 5 to 8 inches long, or 2 small or 1 large regular eggplant
         Olive oil
3 ounces fresh mozzarella cheese, well chilled
1 cup roasted sweet peppers cut in julienne (see glossary page 279)
4 cloves garlic, sliced
3 tablespoons red wine vinegar, raspberry vinegar, or Balsamic vinegar
   Toothpicks

Slice the Japanese eggplant vertically into ¼-inch-wide strips. If you are using regular eggplant, cut them, widthwise, into ¼-inch-wide slices and cut the slices lengthwise into strips approximately 1¼ inches wide.

Pour a thin layer of olive oil on a sheet pan. Arrange the eggplant slices on top. Drizzle each slice with a little more olive oil and bake at 325 degrees until soft, creamy, and slightly golden. Drain on paper towels and allow to cool. Slice the mozzarella into thin pieces. Cover the surface of a slice of eggplant with a few pieces of the mozzarella. Roll up lengthwise and secure with a toothpick. The rolls may be refrigerated for several hours before serving, but it is not necessary. Toss together the peppers, garlic, and vinegar.

To serve, reserve 2 tablespoons or so of the roasted peppers and spread the rest over the surface of a serving platter. Arrange the eggplant rolls on top and use the reserved peppers as a garnish. Guests use the toothpicks to spear a couple of pieces of pepper as they pick up an eggplant roll.

BAGELS AND CREAM CHEESE

What a delight bagels and cream cheese can be. With the Grateful Bagel selling its wares in both Santa Rosa and Sebastopol, Sonomans are never far away from a good, fresh bagel. I find their cocktail bagels (known commercially as Junior Bagels) a welcome addition to a buffet table, and also good to take along on picnics. Spicing up the cream cheese with some of these variations makes for an added treet.

EACH VARIATION MAKES ENOUGH FOR 18 COCKTAIL BAGELS OR 6 TO 8 REGULAR-SIZED BAGELS

CREAM CHEESE WITH FRESH HERBS

    6 ounces old-fashioned cream cheese
    2 ounces unsalted butter
    2 ounces imported Gorgonzola cheese
       (optional)
    ¼ cup fresh chopped herbs: thyme, chives,
       savory, cilantro, marjoram, basil,
       Italian parsley, oregano
    2 cloves garlic, pressed
    1 teaspoon lemon zest
       Salt and pepper (optional)

By hand, blend together the cream cheese and butter until smooth. If you like Gorgonzola cheese, it is a wonderful addition to this blend. Add it with the butter, and use a fork to mash the firmer chunks. Add the herbs, garlic, and lemon zest, and mix well. Taste, and add salt and pepper if desired. I like to add a generous quantity of fresh ground black pepper.

CURRIED CREAM CHEESE WITH CHUTNEY

In the section on lavosh sandwiches is a recipe for curried cream cheese (page 87).

DRIED TOMATO CREAM CHEESE

    8 ounces old-fashioned cream cheese
    3 ounces chèvre
    3 tablespoons puréed dried tomatoes
       packed in oil
    2 teaspoons fresh thyme, chopped
    2 large cloves garlic, pressed

Blend the cream cheese and chèvre together by hand until smooth. Add the remaining ingredients and blend well.

PESTO CREAM CHEESE

    8 ounces old-fashioned cream cheese
    ⅓ cup Pesto, or more to taste (page 221)

Mix together, by hand, until smooth.

ROASTED PEPPER CREAM CHEESE

    2 roasted sweet red peppers, peeled and
       seeded
    8 ounces old-fashioned cream cheese
    2 tablespoons capers (optional)

Purée the roasted peppers in a blender or food processor. By hand, combine with the cream cheese until smooth. Mix in the capers, or top the cream cheese with capers after spreading it on bagel.

To serve, you can simply place the cheese mixture in a small crock and surround it with the bagels, or you can be more decorative. I line a small, decorative mold with plastic wrap, press the cheese mixture into the mold, and chill it. When it is well chilled, I unwrap the cheese, invert it onto a decorative serving plate and garnish with one of the central ingredients that flavor the cheese, a sprig of fresh basil with the Pesto

Cream Cheese, for example, or roasted pepper cut into a decorative shape for the Red Pepper Cream Cheese.

GRAND BAGEL PLATTER

This is an excellent centerpiece for an appetizer buffet, and one I serve frequently at various events in Sonoma County. Make three types of flavored cream cheese, choosing tastes that go well together. My favorite combination is Dried Tomato, Herb, and Pesto. Line a decorative mold, one that is large enough to hold all the cheese, with plastic wrap. Layer the cheese blends. I press in the dried tomato version first, followed by the herb blend, and finish with the pesto, being sure to press firmly and evenly after each addition. Chill the mold well, invert on a large, decorative platter, and surround with plenty of sprigs of fresh herbs. Garnish the top of the mold with decorative pieces of the ingredients you used, making, perhaps, a dried tomato flower, with a basil flower center, and chive stalks.

This is definitely an opportunity to be creative. Surround your cheese mold with plenty of sliced cocktail bagels. Try some of the seasoned bagels available; my favorite is the garlic.

You can also add some accompaniment to your Grand Bagel Platter, basing your choices on items that will go well with the cheese blends you have chosen. I recommend the following possibilities:

thinly sliced smoked salmon
golden caviar
slices of red onion
capers
whole cloves of roasted garlic (wonderful with Pesto)
thinly sliced roast beef (excellent with the herb blend)
slices of avocado
slices of roast turkey (make an herb blend with plenty of sage)
cranberry relish
fresh tomatoes, in season
roasted sweet peppers, julienned
tapénade (olive spread)

▼▼

LAVOSH SANDWICHES

The first time I ever saw lavosh Middle Eastern cracker bread sandwiches (also known as aram sandwiches), I thought they were a great idea. I also assumed, mistakenly, that they must be delicious. I was expecting some marvellously flavored filling to complement their appearance. I was disappointed. They were dry and bland, filled uninterestingly with roast beef or turkey, lettuce, and tomato. It seemed such a wasted opportunity, and I set out to come up with some versions that would take advantage of this perfect little vehicle for appetizer sandwiches.

Two of the fillings call for chutney. If you make your own, use your favorite version, or you may want to try one of the chutneys in this book. There are also good commercial chutneys available, including a tomato chutney made by Kozlowski Farms and Sonoma brand Dried Tomato Chutney. Sample a variety until you find your favorites.

The following recipes are all for 2 squares of Armenian cracker bread, each measuring about 6 by 8 inches, an amount that can be easily doubled or tripled if you require more. Begin the same way whenever you make these sandwiches. Wet the cracker bread on each side, wrap in a damp tea towel, and set aside for 1 hour. The bread should be flexible, but not saturated with water; it should not tear when you lift it. If it seems too damp, leave it exposed to the air for a few minutes before rolling. After building the sandwich, roll the bread up like a jelly roll, wrap it tightly, and refrigerate long enough to chill all the ingredients. When ready to serve, remove the roll from refrigerator, unwrap, and slice it ¼- to ⅜-inch thick. Arrange on a serving platter, garnish, and serve.

CURRIED CREAM CHEESE AND CHUTNEY

    8 ounces old-fashioned cream cheese
    4 ounces unsalted butter
    ¼ cup diced yellow onion
      Olive oil
    4 cloves garlic, minced
    2 teaspoons hot curry powder
    1 teaspoon ground cumin
    1 teaspoon grated fresh ginger
    ¼ teaspoon ground turmeric
    ¼ teaspoon cayenne pepper
    2 squares cracker bread, softened
    ¾ cup chutney
    2 cups fresh greens: arugula, mizuna, or
      mesclun mix

By hand, or in a mixer fitted with a dough hook, blend together the cream cheese and butter. Sauté the onion in a small quantity of olive oil until soft and transparent. Add the garlic and sauté for 2 minutes. Add the spices, stir well about a minute, and remove from the heat.

When the mixture has cooled slightly, add it to the cream cheese and butter and blend well.

Spread both pieces of cracker bread with the cheese mixture. Top the cheese with a thin coating of chutney. Spread the greens over the surface. Roll, chill, slice, and serve as directed above.

HUMMUS, EGGPLANT, AND ROASTED PEPPERS

    1 medium eggplant
      Olive oil
    1 cup hummus (page 222)
    2 squares cracker bread, softened
    1 cup (2 or 3 red bell peppers) roasted
      peppers, cut in julienne (see glossary
      page 279)
    ½ cup chopped Italian parsley

Cut the stem end from the eggplant. Slice the eggplant lengthwise into strips ¼-inch wide. Sprinkle with salt, place in a colander, and let stand for 30 to 60 minutes. Pour about ¼ cup olive oil onto a cookie sheet. Heat the oven to 350 degrees. Wipe any excess moisture from the eggplant slices and arrange them on the cookie sheet. Drizzle with more olive oil, about ¼ cup. Place in the oven until soft and tender, about 25 minutes. Eggplant should be very creamy but not darkened beyond a medium golden. Remove from the oven and drain on paper towels.

Spread ½ cup hummus over the surface of both pieces of cracker bread. Cover with eggplant. Spread roasted peppers evenly on top of the eggplant. Sprinkle with Italian parsley, and roll up according to the general directions given above.

TURKEY, CREAM CHEESE, AND CRANBERRY CHUTNEY

This is a great appetizer around the holidays, either when you have leftover turkey, or when you want to add some traditional flavors to a nontraditional meal. It can, and should, be made several hours before serving.

> 2 tablespoons + 2 ounces softened butter
> ¼ cup yellow onion, finely diced
> 1 tablespoon celery, finely diced
> 2 tablespoons fresh sage leaves, finely chopped
> 8 ounces old-fashioned cream cheese
> 2 squares cracker bread, softened
> 4 to 6 ounces cooked, sliced turkey
> ½ to ¾ cup Cranberry Chutney (below)
> Fresh sage, for garnish

Melt 2 tablespoons of the butter in a small sauté pan. Add the onion and celery and sauté until soft and transparent. Add the sage leaves and sauté for another 2 minutes. Set aside to cool. By hand blend the remaining 2 ounces butter with the cream cheese. Add the cooled onion mixture and blend well. Spread the surface of both pieces of cracker bread with the cream cheese mixture. Cover the surface with turkey meat and top with cranberry chutney, spreading it evenly. Roll up, wrap, and refrigerate the sandwiches according to the general directions above. Slice, garnish with sprigs of fresh sage, and serve.

CRANBERRY CHUTNEY

> 4 cups cranberries
> 8 cloves garlic, minced
> 1 onion, diced
> 2 *jalapeño* peppers, seeded, stemmed, and cut in very thin strips
> 1 cup golden raisins
> ¾ cup + ¼ cup brown sugar
> ½ cup cider vinegar
> 1-inch piece of ginger, peeled and chopped
> ½ teaspoon each: dry mustard, ginger, allspice, cardamom, cloves, and cayenne pepper
> 2 pears, peeled, cored, and diced

In a large pot, bring to a boil all the ingredients except the pears and ¼ cup of the brown sugar. Stirring frequently, simmer until the mixture is very thick. Add the pears and remaining brown sugar, and, stirring constantly, simmer for another 10 minutes. Remove from the heat. Cranberry Chutney may be stored for up to 4 weeks without processing.

▼▼▼▼▼▼▼▼▼▼▼▼▼▼▼▼▼▼▼▼▼▼▼▼▼▼▼▼▼▼▼▼▼▼▼▼

POLENTA ROUNDS
with Pesto and Dried Tomatoes
MAKES ABOUT 60 ROUNDS

These charming little appetizers are a perfect way to use dried tomato bits.

3½ cups water
1 teaspoon salt
¼ cup dried tomato bits or chopped dried
  tomatoes
1 cup polenta
3 tablespoons butter
3 cloves garlic, pressed
3 ounces imported Gorgonzola cheese
1 cup grated dry Jack cheese or Parmesan
½ cup grated imported Romano Pecorino
  cheese
  Pastry bag fitted with a star tip
75 petit four cups
¾ cup Pesto (page 221)

Bring the water, with salt added, to a boil. Stir in the dried tomato bits. Slowly pour in the polenta, whisking as you pour to discourage the formation of lumps. Lower the heat and cook the polenta for 10 minutes, stirring constantly. When mixture has begun to thicken, stir in the butter and garlic and keep stirring until the butter is melted. Break up the Gorgonzola cheese and add it to the polenta. Stir until well incorporated. Add the Jack and Romano cheeses and stir well. Cook over low heat for another 5 minutes, stirring constantly. Remove from the heat and let sit until it just begins to set and has cooled somewhat. Stir every couple of minutes.

Place the polenta in the pastry bag and wrap the bag in towel to shield your hands from the hot polenta. Arrange the *petit four* cups on a sheet pan. Squeeze about a teaspoon of polenta into each cup. It should form a perfect bite-sized star. Top each serving with about ¼ teaspoon of pesto, arrange on serving platter, and serve hot or at room temperature.

CARPACCIO OF SALMON

SERVES 1

Michael Hirschberg, the owner of Restaurant Matisse in Santa Rosa highlights Pacific salmon in this delightful appetizer. It is one of my favorite ways to eat salmon and works equally well using fresh tuna.

2 ounces salmon or tuna
1 teaspoon lemon juice
1 teaspoon capers
½ teaspoon minced red onion
½ teaspoon minced radish
½ teaspoon chopped fresh herbs: parsley,
  thyme, basil
  Dash of salt
1 tablespoon extra-virgin olive oil

Slice the fish across the grain into thin portions. Place each portion between squares of plastic wrap (measuring about 12 inches by 12 inches) and carefully but firmly pound the fish with a broadsided cleaver until it spreads out to about 6 inches in diameter and less than ⅛-inch thick. Store the slices, separated by pieces of plastic wrap in the refrigerator until ready to serve.

Remove the fish from the refrigerator and peel off 1 layer of plastic wrap. Position the fish on a plate and then remove the top sheet of wrap. Paint a small quantity of lemon juice onto the fish and then sprinkle with capers, onion, radish, and herbs. Add just a dash of salt, then drizzle with olive oil. Serve immediately.

SALMON AND RASPBERRY JEWELS

with Raspberry Hollandaise

MAKES 2 TO 2½ DOZEN

Every now and then, I just have to show off with something very complex and dazzling. Usually I end up with a major, labor-intensive dish on my hands, like this one that received a silver medal at the 1989 Harvest Fair. If making the little rounds that I describe is simply too much for you, poach the fillets, chill them, and serve them whole, topped with the sauce and garnished with the raspberries. This is a wonderful luncheon dish or main course for a summer dinner.

1	pound salmon fillets (small fillets will give the best results)
	Round toothpicks
2	tablespoons black raspberry vinegar
1	small onion, quartered
	Several black peppercorns
	Juice of 1 lemon
	Raspberry Hollandaise Sauce (page 212)
25 to 30	nasturtium leaves measuring 2 to 3 inches across
½	pint red raspberries
3 or 4	nasturtium blossoms

Using a very sharp knife, cut thin, lengthwise strips of salmon from the fillet. Using your left index finger as a spacer, wrap the salmon—not too tightly—around itself and carefully secure with a toothpick. Each salmon round should be between 1¼ and 1½ inches across, with a space in the center. Fill a flat-bottomed, heavy skillet about half full of water. Add the raspberry vinegar, onion, peppercorns, and lemon juice. Carefully place the salmon rounds into the skillet. Place over very low heat and slowly heat the water until it is almost simmering. Turn the burner off; let salmon cool in the skillet for 10 minutes, or until water is cool enough for you to reach in and remove salmon by picking up the toothpicks. Chill.

To assemble, have the Raspberry Hollandaise Sauce hot. Arrange the salmon rounds on top of nasturtium leaves on a decorative serving platter. Top each with a small spoonful of Hollandaise. Place a raspberry on top of each salmon round, garnish with a few nasturtium flowers, and serve immediately.

SONOMA MEXICANA

Mexico and Mexican culture have always been a part of life in California. Many of the names throughout Sonoma reveal our Mexican roots; there are annual celebrations of Mexico's traditional holidays, and nowhere are these roots more evident today than in the availability of a wide variety of imported Mexican products, products that make the Mexican recipes throughout this book possible. Much of the food of any culture has to do with cooking style and technique, but certain ingredients are crucial to an authentic execution. The availability of such items as *chipotle* peppers and *achiote* have allowed me to evoke certain flavors of Mexico and present them in a style that has evolved here in Sonoma.

▼▼▼▼▼▼▼▼▼▼▼▼▼▼▼▼▼▼▼▼▼▼▼▼▼▼▼▼▼▼

MEXICAN CHICKEN WINGS

SERVES 4 TO 6

    2 tablespoons achiote (page 272)
    1 jalapeño pepper, seeded and coarsely
        chopped
    4 cloves garlic
    ¼ cup warm water
       Juice of 1 lemon
    ½ teaspoon cayenne pepper
    2 pounds (about 20 to 24) chicken wings,
        often sold as "drumettes"
       Sour Cream Dipping Sauce
    ½ cup sour cream
    ¼ cup half-and-half
    ½ cup cilantro leaves
    1 jalapeño pepper, seeded and minced
       Salt to taste

In a blender or food processor, place the achiote, chopped *jalapeños*, garlic, water, lemon juice, and cayenne and blend well. Rub each of the chicken wings with the mixture and place them in shallow dish. Pour any remaining sauce over and refrigerate for 2 or 3 hours, or overnight. Place the wings on a baking sheet and brush them well with sauce. Bake at 325 degrees for about 40 minutes, turning once and brush-

ing with more sauce. Blend together the sour cream and half-and-half. Chop the cilantro and stir it into the sour cream mixture, along with the minced *jalapeño*. If desired, add salt to taste. Remove the wings from the oven and arrange them on serving platter, on top of cilantro sprigs if you wish, and place the sour cream sauce in the center in a dish. Use the sauce as a dip for the "drumettes."

▼▼▼▼▼▼▼▼▼▼▼▼▼▼▼▼▼▼▼▼▼▼▼▼▼▼▼▼▼▼

CHIPOTLE CHICKEN WINGS

SERVES 4 TO 6

A can of peppers and some lime juice, a few cloves of garlic and some chicken wings? What is the big deal, you might ask; why is this in a Sonoma cookbook? Trust me. Few things I have ever served have resulted in such cries of pleasure as these simple appetizers. Chipotle peppers have a distinctive flavor that is extremely hot, but so delicious that even those who admit to "wimpy palates" have begged for more.

    1 can (8 ounces) chipotle peppers in
        adobo sauce (page 274)
       Several (8 to 10) cloves of garlic
    ¾ cup water
       Juice of 2 limes
    2 pounds chicken wings, often sold as
        "drumettes"
    ½ cup sour cream

Purée *chipotle* peppers with the garlic, water, and lime juice. Place the chicken wings in a baking dish that will just hold them all in a single layer. Pour the *chipotle* sauce over them and bake at 350 degrees for 45 to 60 minutes. Remove from the oven. Arrange the wings on a serving platter and place the sour cream in a bowl in the center of the platter. Serve at once.

▼▼▼▼▼▼▼▼▼▼▼▼▼▼▼▼▼▼▼▼▼▼▼▼▼▼▼▼▼▼▼

MEXICAN POLENTA ROUNDS

MAKES 60 ROUNDS

Because of the wide ethnic diversity in Sonoma, there is a great deal of cross-cultural experimenting among chefs in Sonoma. Done carefully, with respect for the traditional qualities of specific ingredients, such experimentation can produce wonderful results. Here I have combined elements of country food from two sources, Mexico and Italy, into a dish that is evocative of both cultures and delicious in its own right.

3½ cups water
1 teaspoon salt
3 tablespoons puréed chipotle peppers in adobo sauce (page 274)
1 cup polenta
3 tablespoons butter
3 cloves garlic, pressed
1½ cups grated Cheddar cheese

Pastry bag with star tip
75 petit four cups
1 cup Corn Salsa (page 219)
1 large bunch cilantro

Bring the water and salt to a boil. Add the *chipotle* peppers. Slowly pour in the polenta, whisking as you pour to discourage the formation of lumps. Lower the heat and cook for 10 minutes, stirring constantly. When the mixture has begun to thicken, stir in the butter and garlic and continue to stir until the butter is melted. Add the cheese and stir until well incorporated. Taste and add salt if desired. Cook for another 5 minutes over low heat, stirring constantly. Remove from heat and set aside to cool, stirring every couple of minutes.

After about 10 or 15 minutes, but before the polenta has set up, place it in the pastry bag. Fill each *petit four* cup with about 1 teaspoon polenta, which should form a perfect, bite-sized star. Top each serving with about ½ teaspoon Corn Salsa. Cover a serving platter with the cilantro, arrange the *petit four* cups on platter, and serve.

▼▼▼▼▼▼▼▼▼▼▼▼▼▼▼▼▼▼▼▼▼▼▼▼▼▼▼▼▼▼▼

STEAK DE LOS MUERTOS

MAKES APPROXIMATELY 4 DOZEN APPETIZERS

This spicy variation of traditional steak tartar is named in honor of Día de los Muertos, a Mexican holiday that is observed on November 1 and 2, and is being celebrated with increasing interest here in northern California.

- 2 pounds freshly ground, high-quality steak
- ½ cup fresh chopped cilantro
- 1 jalapeño pepper, seeded and very finely chopped
- 4 raw egg yolks
  Salt and freshly ground black pepper
- 1 baguette, thinly sliced
  Olive oil
  Garlic
- 1 cup salsa (your favorite homemade or commercial)

Mix together the steak, cilantro, *jalapeño*, egg yolks, salt, and pepper. Chill. Brush the slices of baguette with olive oil and garlic. Place in an oven at 250 degrees until crisp and golden. Form the steak mixture into little balls and place them on the baguettes. Make an indentation in the top of each and add a little salsa.

The steak may also be served with tortilla chips. Try using one of the brands of blue corn chips now available. They are delicious and look dramatic.

THAI BEEF ROLLS

MAKES 3 DOZEN ROLLS

This appetizer, which won a gold medal at the 1989 Harvest Fair Awards Night, arose out of the desire to find an easy appetizer variation of the Thai Lime Beef Salad on page 197, a dish devised for black chanterelles from Gourmet Mushroom Inc. The original dish, I might add, stands up so well on its own that the chanterelles are an optional ingredient.

- 5 cloves garlic
- 5 serrano chilies
- 2 tablespoons Thai fish sauce
- 4 tablespoons lime juice
- 1 tablespoon sugar
- 2 market steaks (about 1 to 1¼ pounds)
- ¼ pound fall salad mix, with mint leaves (page 276)
  Yogurt-Mint Sauce (page 218)

Several hours before serving, grind together the garlic and chilies in a mortar and pestle or a small food processor until finely ground. Remove to a small bowl and add the fish sauce, lime juice, and sugar. Pour over the steaks and refrigerate. One hour before serving, remove the beef from the refrigerator and let it come up to room temperature.

Just before serving, grill it quickly until just rare, about 4 minutes on each side. Cut the beef into thin, cross-grained strips. Wrap each piece of beef around several leaves of salad mix and secure with a toothpick. Put the remaining salad mix on a serving platter, arrange the beef rolls on top, and place a small bowl of Yogurt-Mint Sauce (page 218) in the center for dipping. Serve immediately.

▼▼▼▼▼▼▼▼▼▼▼▼▼▼▼▼▼▼▼▼▼▼▼▼▼▼▼▼▼▼▼▼▼▼▼

MEATBALLS STUFFED WITH ROASTED GARLIC

MAKES ABOUT 3 DOZEN MEATBALLS

These labor-intensive little morsels were one of the first signature dishes developed at the Jaded Palate, and the making of 750 of them for our first large party is permanently imprinted on all our minds. It is not something any of us would do willingly again. It is infinitely easier to make thirty or forty of them, and will not take you until 3 or 4 in the morning to accomplish, I promise. If it still seems too formidable a task, use the variation given at the end of the recipe.

30	whole, medium-sized cloves garlic
6 or 7	cloves garlic, minced
3	shallots, minced
	Olive oil
3	sprigs fresh thyme
1	cup fresh bread crumbs
¾	pound ground pork
¾	pound ground beef
½	pound freshly grated dry Jack cheese or fresh Parmesan
	Salt and pepper

Roast the whole garlic cloves according to the directions on page 78, but separate the cloves before covering them with oil. When done, remove from the cooking liquid and allow to cool. Carefully peel each clove and set aside.

Sauté the minced garlic and shallots in a little olive oil for 2 to 3 minutes, being careful not to brown them. Chop the thyme. Combine the garlic, shallots, thyme, bread crumbs, pork, beef, and cheese. Season with salt and pepper.

To form meatballs, put about 1 tablespoon of meat mixture in the palm of your left hand and form into a ball. Make an indentation with your thumb and insert a peeled clove of roasted garlic. Pinch the meat mixture back together. Sauté the meatballs over medium heat, turning when browned. When all are well browned, cover the pan and cook for 10 to 15 minutes.

The meatballs may be served as an appetizer, with a little bowl of crème fraîche on the side for dipping. They are also excellent served over pasta. I use angel hair pasta, which I toss first with a little of the liquid from the roasted garlic, top with meatballs, and garnish with a spoonful of crème fraîche and a small sprig of fresh thyme.

VARIATION ▾ Instead of stuffing each individual meatball, work ½ a cup of puréed roasted garlic quickly into the meatball mixture. Form into balls and cook as directed above.

WILD MUSHROOM TRIANGLES

MAKES ABOUT 60 TRIANGLES

Always a crowd-pleaser, these crunchy little packages took a gold medal in the 1988 Harvest Fair competition. The creamy Chèvre Sauce adds a rich element to the crackle of the filo that made the crowds scramble for "just one more of those triangles from heaven," as one of their fans put it. If the wrapping process seems prohibitively long and difficult to you, try one of the variations at the end of the recipe.

    1 **cup butter**
    3 **shallots, minced**
  1½ **pounds mushrooms: a blend of shiitake, chanterelle, field, and/or button**
    3 **tablespoons Madeira**
    1 **teaspoon fresh thyme**
   ¼ **cup chopped Italian parsley, plus one large bunch for garnish**
    6 **ounces Taupinière, grated**
    1 **pound package filo pastry**
       Chèvre Sauce (page 214)

Melt ⅔ cup butter in heavy saucepan, add the shallots and simmer until they are transparent (about 10 minutes). Clean the mushrooms, remove any woody stems, and chop coarsely. Add to the shallots and butter and sauté until soft. Add the Madeira, thyme, and chopped parsley. Taste and season with salt and pepper if desired. Stir in the Taupinière and remove from heat (It is this mixture that is referred to as "mushroom *pâté*" below.)

In a small, heavy saucepan, melt the remaining butter. Prepare the filo pastry by cutting a two-inch piece off of the rolled filo. Cover the large, uncut portion of the filo pastry with a towel and set aside. It is essential that you keep any filo that you are not working with at the moment covered or it will dry out. Roll out the smaller piece of filo and place two strips on your cutting board. Brush a small amount of the melted butter in a corner of one of the strips and place the other piece of filo on top of it. Brush the entire surface of the top piece with butter. Place one heaping teaspoon of the mushroom mixture at the bottom right corner of the strip of pastry and fold the corner up to form a triangle. Continue folding in a triangle shape, end over end, until the entire strip is folded. This process is very similar to the traditional manner of folding a flag. Place the finished triangle on a greased cookie sheet and repeat the process until done. If you have a work space that is large enough, work on six triangles at a time. When all the triangles are folded, brush their surfaces with melted butter. Bake at 400 degrees for 20 minutes, until the triangles are lightly browned. Remove and serve hot on a bed of Italian parsley with Chèvre Sauce for dipping.

VARIATIONS ▾ Omit the filo pastry. Serve as a mushroom *pâté*, either warm or chilled. Garnish with plenty of finely chopped Italian parsley and surround with rye toast triangles. ▾ Select about 3 dozen mushrooms, standard commercial, crimini, or shiitake, and remove the stems. Simmer for 4 to 5 minutes in 1½ cups olive oil and enough added water to cover. Add a bay leaf, sprigs of fresh herbs, and peppercorns to the liquid. Remove with a slotted spoon, drain in a colander, and place on a cookie sheet. Fill each mushroom with the mushroom *pâté*, and garnish each with a leaf of Italian parsley. Serve immediately or chill and serve. Strain and reserve the cooking liquid for future use, to make, say, a vinaigrette, or as the oil in ratatouille.

SOUPS

CRANBERRY-ZINFANDEL SOUP

SERVES 4 TO 6

One of Sonoma's fine Zinfandels is the ideal companion for cranberries in this festive soup, perfect for a Christmas Eve or New Year's Eve dinner party. Its bright, clear flavor stimulates the palate, making it the perfect opening for rich, holiday fare.

- 12 ounces fresh cranberries
- 1½ cups water
- ½ cup sugar
- 1½ cups Zinfandel or other fruity, full-bodied red wine
- 5 whole cloves
- 1 cup fresh orange juice
  Sour cream or crème fraîche
  Orange peel, rind removed and sliced in very thin 1-inch strips

Simmer the cranberries in the water until their skins pop, about 10 minutes, turn the mixture into a blender or food processor, and process until smooth. Return to the pan, add the sugar, ¾ cup of the wine, and the cloves. Simmer for 10 minutes. Add the remainder of the wine and the orange juice. Simmer for another 5 minutes and pour through a fine strainer or sieve. Serve hot or chilled.

To serve, top each portion with a spoonful of sour cream or crème fraîche and several strips of orange peel.

PLUM SOUP FOR A. J.

SERVES 4

With a name like this, yes, of course, there is a story. As I was browsing through my newly arrived copy of Season by Season, The Sonoma County Farmer's Market Cookbook, *I came upon a recipe, "Plums for A. J." After reading the accompanying anecdote, I realized it must have been named for an old friend whom I had not seen in quite a long time. Instead of just making the simple phone call that would have solved the question, I wrote a column about the process of deduction that led to my assumption. The day after publication, my suspicions were confirmed by a phone call from A. J. himself, who was more than a little surprised to find an analysis of his character spread across Sonoma's food pages. It seemed fitting that I not only name this recipe for my dear friend, but that I offer him the first bowl of this delicious soup, which I did. I think he approved.*

2 pounds Santa Rosa Plums
3 cups medium dry white wine
¾ cup homemade chicken stock
⅓ to ⅔ cup sugar
2 tablespoons butter
¼ cup crème fraîche or 2 tablespoons sour cream, thinned with half-and-half to make up ¼ cup

Cut the plums into chunks, removing and discarding the pits. Place them in a heavy, nonreactive saucepan and cover with 2 cups of the white wine and the chicken stock. Cover the pot and simmer until the plums are tender. Remove from the heat and transfer the plums with a slotted spoon to a food processor or blender. Process until very smooth and set aside.

Return the saucepan with the cooking liquid to the heat, add sugar to taste, depending on the sweetness of the fruit, and simmer on high heat until the mixture is re-duced by one third. Reduce the heat to low, add the plum purée, and stir well. Stir in the butter a tablespoon at a time, waiting until the first has melted before adding the second. If necessary, thin the soup with a little more white wine until you have the desired consistency. Heat thoroughly.

Place in individual serving dishes and slowly drizzle each with 1 tablespoon crème fraîche. Serve immediately. (This soup will keep for several days in the refrigerator, but with some loss of flavor.)

▼▼▼▼▼▼▼▼▼▼▼▼▼▼▼▼▼▼▼▼▼▼▼▼▼▼▼▼▼▼▼▼▼▼▼▼

GAZPACHO

SERVES 4

Few things evoke the essence of summer or soothe against its heat like a bowl of gazpacho made from thoughtfully, carefully grown produce. You cannot mask the quality of the ingredients in a dish such as this one, and the success of a gazpacho is completely dependent on that quality. If you do have access to superior produce, this is a perfect way to display its wonderful flavors.

VERSION 1
1 small red onion, peeled and diced
2 small cucumbers, peeled, seeded, and diced
1 red bell pepper, cored, seeded, and diced
2 small zucchini, diced

¼ cup minced garlic
8 medium golden tomatoes
¾ cup chicken stock
½ cup extra-virgin olive oil
1 lemon
　Tabasco sauce
　Salt and pepper

In a large bowl, toss together the onion, cucumber, pepper, zucchini, and garlic. Plunge 3 of the tomatoes into boiling water for 10 seconds. Remove and set aside. Seed and chop the remaining 5 tomatoes and add to the vegetables. Peel the other 3 tomatoes and seed them. Place in a blender or food processor with the chicken stock and purée until smooth. Add this mixture to the chopped vegetables, along with the olive oil. Stir well. Add the juice of the lemon, Tabasco, and salt and pepper to taste. Chill before serving.

VARIATIONS ▾ Omit the Tabasco sauce and add ¼ cup chopped fresh herbs: chives, oregano, thyme, marjoram, basil, dill, summer savory. ▾ Omit the Tabasco sauce. Add 2 diced *jalapeño* peppers. Substitute the juice of 1 lime for the juice of 1 lemon. Add ½ cup chopped cilantro leaves and top with a spoonful of Jalapeño Aïoli (page 212).

VERSION 2
4 or 5 large ripe tomatoes, peeled, seeded, and chopped
2 or 3 cloves garlic, minced
1 or 2 golden bell peppers, seeded and diced
2 lemon cucumbers, peeled, seeded, and diced

1 red onion, peeled and thinly sliced
1 ripe but not too soft avocado, diced
3 cups light beef stock or chicken broth
½ cup extra-virgin olive oil
3 to 4 tablespoons lemon juice
　Fresh herbs: basil, thyme, parsley, cilantro
　Salt and pepper to taste
　Tabasco sauce

Toss the vegetables together. Add them to the stock. Stir in the olive oil and lemon juice to taste. Add the chopped fresh herbs. Season with salt, pepper, and Tabasco. Chill thoroughly before serving.

▼▼▼▼▼▼▼▼▼▼▼▼▼▼▼▼▼▼▼▼▼▼▼▼▼▼▼▼

CORN CHOWDER

SERVES 4

Betsy Timm, who is the publicist for the Farm Trails organization, loves this soup, and makes it regularly. It is a simple recipe that highlights the flavor of the corn, so be sure to use the best, freshest corn you can find.

6 ears corn
¼ pound bacon
1 small red onion, thinly sliced
5 small new red potatoes, cut into quarters
1 green and 1 red pepper, seeded and cut into small dice
3 cups chicken stock
1 cup heavy cream

Salt and pepper

Cayenne pepper

3 tablespoons cilantro leaves

Cut the kernels from the ears of corn with a sharp knife. In a large pot, cook the bacon until crisp. Remove the bacon and drain. Sauté the onion in the bacon grease until soft and transparent, about 10 minutes. Add the potatoes and peppers and sauté for another 5 minutes. Add the chicken stock, bring to a boil, reduce the heat, and simmer until the potatoes are tender, about 10 minutes. Add the corn, simmer for 2 minutes, and add the cream and seasonings. Crumble the crisp bacon and stir it into chowder. Garnish each serving with a sprinkling of cilantro leaves.

TOMATO-CILANTRO SOUP

S E R V E S   4

Since I first ran this recipe in my weekly column in the summer of 1986, it has become by far my most requested recipe. People who have misplaced their copy or have heard about it from a friend call for copies frequently. For a beautiful variation, use golden tomatoes instead of red. The result is dazzling!

1 medium yellow onion, chopped

¼ cup virgin olive oil

5 cloves garlic, minced

2 cups chicken broth

3 to 4 pounds fresh ripe tomatoes, peeled, seeded, and chopped

1 large or 2 small bunches fresh cilantro

1 tablespoon Madeira (optional)

Salt and pepper

¼ cup sour cream

¼ cup heavy cream

Sauté the chopped onion gently in the oil until very soft, about 20 to 25 minutes. For the last 2 minutes, add the minced garlic. Stir in the chicken broth. Add the tomatoes and stir well. Simmer for about 15 minutes. Remove the soup from the heat. If you have a portable immersion blender, use it to blend the soup. If not, put the soup in a blender or food processor and blend briefly. Return to the saucepan. Add the Madeira. Cook over low heat for 5 minutes. Remove the cilantro leaves from the large stems and chop finely. Stir into the soup and remove from the heat. Add salt and pepper to taste. Mix the sour cream and heavy cream together and top each bowl of soup with a spoonful. The soup is also delicious served with Jalapeño Aïoli (page 212) as the topping.

BODEGA BAY CHOWDER

SERVES 6

Charles Saunders, chef at the Sonoma Mission Inn, combines salmon and saffron in this wonderfully fragrant chowder. Although Charles serves his version ungarnished, I find topping each portion with a spoonful of Saffron Aïoli (page 211) a very pleasing addition.

- ⅛ cup olive oil
- 1 cup mixed root vegetables (onions, carrots, celery, parsnips), diced
- ¼ cup fennel, diced
- ½ cup Sauvignon Blanc
- 1 quart fish stock, hot
- ¼ cup sweet white corn
- ½ cup potatoes, diced
- ½ cup fresh tomatoes, seeded and diced
- 1 tablespoon fresh thyme, chopped
- 2 tablespoons Kalamata olives, pitted and chopped
- ¾ pound salmon fillet, diced
  Pinch of saffron threads
  Salt and pepper

Place the olive oil in a large soup pot and add the diced vegetables and fennel. Saute for about 15 minutes or until the vegetables are soft. Add the white wine and the hot fish stock and simmer for 15 minutes. Add the corn and the potatoes and simmer an additional 10 minutes. Stir in the thyme, olives, salmon, and saffron. Remove the chowder from the heat and add salt and pepper to taste. Serve immediately.

SHIITAKE-CHÈVRE SOUP

SERVES 6 TO 8

This soup is rich and heavenly, a perfect showcase for both of the featured ingredients. Remember that, although rich, goat cheese has a much lower fat content than cheese made from cow's milk.

- ½ cup butter
- 3 large shallots
- 12 ounces shiitake mushrooms
- ¼ cup Madeira or sherry
- 2 cups chicken stock
- 2 cups heavy cream
- 4 ounces chabis
- 4½ ounces Taupinière (if not available, use an extra 4 ounces chabis)
- 1 cup half-and-half
- 2 tablespoons minced chives
- 1 teaspoon freshly ground black pepper
  Salt to taste

Melt butter in a large saucepan. Saute shallots for 5 minutes. Remove the stems from the mushrooms and set aside a quarter of them. Finely chop the remaining mushrooms, using a food processor if possible, and add them to the shallots. Sauté until soft. Slice the reserved mushrooms into thin strips, add them to the chopped mushroom mixture, and stir. Cook until the mushrooms wilt. Add the Madeira and simmer for 2 to 3 minutes. Add the chicken stock and simmer, over low heat, for 5 minutes. Add the cream. Crumble the goat cheese, add it to soup, and stir until the cheese has melted and is well incorporated into the soup. Thin with half-and-half. Stir in the chives and pepper. Taste and add salt and more pepper as desired. Serve with plenty of hot French bread.

BUTTERNUT SQUASH SOUP

SERVES 4

This sweet and creamy soup developed by Russian River Vineyards starts their Fall Dinner (page 65).

> 1 small butternut squash (about 2½ or 3 pounds)
> 3 tablespoons flour
> 3 tablespoons butter
> 1½ cups milk
> 1½ cups chicken stock
> Salt, white pepper, and ground mace to taste
> 1 teaspoon Worcestershire sauce
> ½ cup heavy cream or half-and-half
> 2 tablespoons dry sherry (optional)

Cut the squash in half, remove the seeds, place cut-side-down on a roasting pan with half an inch of water in the bottom. Bake in the oven at 350 degrees until very soft, approximately 1 hour. Or, if desired, cut into pieces and steam. Let cool, remove the skin, and purée in a food processor, blender, or food mill.

Make a roux of the flour and butter; let it cool. Warm the milk and stock together, whisk in the roux, bring to a simmer, and cook for 10 minutes, until slightly thickened.

Add the puréed squash to the thickened base, salt and pepper sparingly (use no salt if your stock is already salted). Add ⅛ teaspoon mace or more as desired. Each serving is topped with a shake of mace; take this into account.

The final consistency of the soup depends on how much water the squash absorbs in cooking. Adjust with cream or half-and-half at the end. Garnish each serving with a spoonful of unsweetened whipped cream and a shake of mace.

PUMPKIN SOUP

with Roasted Garlic and Croutons

SERVES 4 TO 6

Vast fields of orange, especially along Gravenstein Highway in Sebastopol, herald the onset of fall each year, and busloads of children from throughout the Bay Area make their way to Sonoma in the annual tradition of selecting their Halloween pumpkins. There is more than one way to carve a jack-o'-lantern, though. I recommend your carving some up to be steamed or baked and used to make this delicious soup. They may not be smiling, but you will be.

> 1 medium onion, minced
> 3 tablespoons butter
> 2 cups chicken broth

2 cups steamed and mashed pumpkin
        4 tablespoons Roasted Garlic Purée
            (page 222)
        1 tablespoon brown sugar
  1-inch piece fresh ginger, peeled, chopped,
            and pressed through a garlic press
  1 to 2 cups half-and-half
          Salt and pepper
          Ground cinnamon and cloves
            (optional)
        1 small baguette

Sauté the onion in butter over low heat until golden, about 15 minutes. Add the chicken broth. Whisk in the pumpkin and roasted garlic. Blend well. Add the sugar and ginger. Simmer for about 5 minutes. Add the half-and-half until you have the desired consistency. For a smoother soup, strain the mixture through a fine-meshed sieve before adding the half-and-half. Season with salt and pepper and with ground cinnamon and clove to taste, if desired.

Slice the baguette very thinly. Brush with oil reserved from roasting the garlic. Place in slow oven (250 degrees) until dry.

To serve, you can scoop out a medium-sized pumpkin and use that as a tureen. Serve the croutons on the side. For individual servings, top each with one or two croutons.

POTATO SOUPS

I love soup and I especially love soup made with a hearty base of potatoes, onions, and garlic. I offer only some of the variations I have made over the years, lest you think I am a fanatic on the subject. Occasionally I have the opportunity to go sailing on San Francisco Bay, an activity I dearly love, and the Potato Soup with Chipotle Peppers and Sausage is the perfect antidote to the bone-chilling cold such a trip sometimes includes. Any of these variations will warm, soothe, comfort the chilled body or flagging spirit, not to mention delight the eager taste buds.

BASIC POTATO SOUP

with Three Variations
SERVES 4 TO 6

        ¼ cup butter or olive oil
        1 medium onion, diced
   3 or 4 cloves garlic, minced
        2 pounds red potatoes
        2 cups chicken stock
          Water
          Salt and pepper

Melt the butter in a large pot. Add the onion and sauté over low heat for about 20 minutes, until just golden. Add the garlic and sauté for another 2 minutes. Meanwhile, wash and trim the potatoes and cut into large dice. Add the chicken stock to the sautéed onions and garlic. Add the potatoes and enough water to cover the potatoes completely. Simmer until the potatoes are just done, about 20 minutes. Remove from the heat and purée in a food processor, or partially purée the soup with an immersion blender, if available. At this point, follow the instructions for whichever variation you have chosen.

SPINACH AND POTATO SOUP

      1 large bunch spinach
3 or 4 cloves garlic, minced
         Olive oil
         Nutmeg
         Sour cream or crème fraîche,
           for garnish

Rinse the spinach well, dry, and chop it finely. In a sauté pan, sauté the minced garlic in a little olive oil for about 2 minutes. Add the spinach and toss over heat until wilted. Stir into the potato soup. Season with nutmeg, salt, and pepper. Top with a little sour cream or crème fraîche.

BROCCOLI AND POTATO SOUP

1 head broccoli
   Sour cream or crème fraîche, for garnish

Trim the broccoli and cut into very small dice. Steam very quickly, about 2 minutes. Add to the potato soup and mix together well. Season with a little salt and plenty of black pepper. Top with a little sour cream or crème fraîche.

PEPPERS AND POTATO SOUP

8 or 9 fresh pasilla or poblano peppers,
         roasted, seeded, and diced (see
         glossary page 279)
         Dash cayenne pepper
         Jalapeño Aïoli (page 212)

Add the peppers to the potato soup and blend well. Season with salt and pepper and a dash of cayenne. Top each serving with Jalapeño Aïoli.

POTATO CHEDDAR SOUP

SERVES 6 TO 8

 5 tablespoons olive oil
 2 cups yellow onion, minced
 1 cup carrots, peeled and finely chopped
 3 pounds potatoes, diced
 6 cups chicken stock
 3 cups grated Cheddar cheese
½ cup fresh chopped dill or ½ cup minced
     Italian parsley
    Salt and pepper to taste

Heat the olive oil in a large soup pot. Add the onion and sauté over low heat for about 15 minutes. Add the carrots and sauté for another 10 minutes. Add the potatoes and chicken stock. Stir the mixture and add water as needed to cover the potatoes completely. Cover the soup pot and simmer over low heat until the potatoes are tender, about 20 minutes. Remove from heat. Blend the soup with an immersion blender, if available, or in a food processor. Return the soup to low heat. Slowly stir in the cheese. Add the dill or parsley and season to taste. Serve immediately.

minutes. Add the potatoes, chicken stock, and enough water to cover. Stir, cover the pot, and simmer over low heat until the potatoes are tender, about 20 minutes. Remove from the heat, add the *chipotles*, and blend the soup with an immersion blender if available, or with a food processor. In a sauté pan, sauté the sausage until nearly done. Add garlic, sauté for another minute, and stir into the soup. Reserving a tablespoon or 2 for garnishing, add the cheese and stir. Taste and add salt if desired. Top each serving with a small sprinkling of grated Cheddar.

POTATO SOUP WITH CHIPOTLES AND SAUSAGE

SERVES 6 TO 8

- 5 tablespoons olive oil
- 2 cups yellow onion, minced
- 3 pounds potatoes, diced
- 6 cups chicken stock
- ½ cup puréed chipotles in adobo sauce (page 274)
- 2 pounds spicy sausage, hot Creole or andouille, cut in half lengthwise, then sliced ¼-inch thick
- 1 head garlic, cloves peeled and minced
- 2 cups grated Cheddar cheese
  Salt to taste

Heat the olive oil in large soup pot. Add the onion and sauté over low heat for 15 to 20

DEBUREAU'S MASQUERADE SOUP

SERVES 6

This soup is named for the pierrot in the classic French film, Children of Paradise, *by Marcel Carné, not only because of the striking black and white contrast in its presentation, but because the soup itself is a bit of a masquerade. When the culinary ex-*

plosion was outdoing itself in presentation, and food as art was at its most pretentious, I designed this elegant presentation of two peasant soups to poke fun at the way in which chefs and food stylists were taking themselves so seriously. Although Debureau's soup is guilty of the excessive presentation I was criticizing, it was offered in lighthearted fun and really is an unpretentious, delicious soup. Appearance is an important element in our enjoyment of food, but let us not get carried away. Serve this soup in attractive bowls, preferably of black china.

BLACK BEAN SOUP

1½ cups black beans (soaked overnight in water and drained)
1 small onion, diced
5 cloves garlic, minced
1 teaspoon cumin seed
1 teaspoon salt
Pinch pepper

WHITE BEAN SOUP

1½ cups small white beans (soaked overnight in water and drained)
1 small onion, diced
1 small carrot, peeled and diced
1½ teaspoons ground cumin
¼ to ½ teaspoon cayenne pepper
Salt to taste

GARNISH

¼ cup crème fraîche
¼ cup Garlic and Cilantro Sauce (page 214)

For the black bean soup, cover the beans with water and simmer until tender, about 40 minutes, adding more water as needed. Meanwhile, sauté the onion in a little olive oil until tender, adding the garlic for the last 2 minutes. Stir into the cooked beans. Add the seasonings. Purée about half of the soup in a blender or food processor and return to the soup pot. Blend well and correct the seasoning.

For the white bean soup, cook the white beans as you did the black beans. Sauté the onion and carrot in a little olive oil until tender. Stir into the cooked beans. Add the seasonings. Puree the soup in a food processor or with immersion blender. Add water to reach the desired consistency. Correct the seasoning.

To serve pour equal quantities of each soup into serving bowls *at the same time*, pouring carefully so the soups do not mix together. Pouring from small pitchers will make this easier. Next, top the soup with a pattern of crème fraîche that has been thinned with a little cream or half-and-half. Finally, top the soup with another pattern using the Garlic and Cilantro Sauce. Serve immediately.

SANDWICHES

AVOCADO AND ZUCCHINI SANDWICHES

SERVES 4

Originally designed to perk up bored vege-tarians who frequented my restaurant in Cotati, this sandwich quickly became a fa-vorite of meat eaters, too. It is a great way to use up some of that extra zucchini most of us have at the peak of summer. I would use the whole wheat bread from Alvarado Street Bakery and Sonoma brand Jack cheese.

3	cups grated zucchini
3 or 4	cloves garlic, minced
	Juice of 1 lemon
8	slices whole-wheat sourdough bread or 4 sourdough French rolls
2	avocados, peeled and sliced
1½	cup grated Jack cheese
	Aïoli (page 211) or a good mayonnaise
	Watercress or arugula

Toss the grated zucchini with the garlic and lemon juice. On each of four slices of bread, place half a sliced avocado. Top the avocado with the zucchini and garlic mixture. Divide the cheese among the four sandwiches. Place in a 400 degree oven or under the broiler (not too close) and cook until the cheese is melted, but not browned. While the sandwiches are cooking, toast the re-maining four slices of bread and spread with *aïoli* or mayonnaise. Remove the sand-wiches from the oven, top with a handful of watercress or arugula, and place the slices of toast on top. Cut in half diagonally and serve immediately.

CHICKEN AND RASPBERRY SANDWICH

MAKES 1 SANDWICH

Chicken and raspberries are among the most marvelous combinations of flavors. This is a particularly simple, informal way to enjoy them.

1 French roll or 2 slices French bread
  Raspberry Mayonnaise (page 210)
1 small red onion, cut into rounds
  Half a chicken breast or 4 to 5 ounces
    roasted or sautéed chicken meat
  Shredded red cabbage
  Fresh raspberries

Split the rolls. Spread them liberally with Raspberry Mayonnaise. Place some rounds of onion on the bread and top with chicken. Top the chicken with cabbage. Add some fresh raspberries. Place on serving plates with plenty of raspberry mayonnaise on top piece of bread. Garnish the plate with more raspberries.

FARM MARKET SANDWICHES

MAKES 4

One Saturday morning, I was giving a cooking demonstration at The Farm Mar-

ket, making and giving out samples of Bagna Cauda Sauce, using the wonderful garlic from Rocky Creek Gardens. Bob Cannard, a local grower, came to my table, scooped a bunch of the sauce onto a sandwich, and handed it to me. I think you'll enjoy it as much as I did.

4 whole-wheat hot dog buns
4 sprigs very fresh basil
1 medium cucumber, peeled and cut
    lengthwise into strips
2 medium golden tomatoes, sliced
1 medium red onion, thinly sliced
¼ cup Bagna Cauda Sauce (page 221) or
    extra-virgin olive oil and several slices
    of garlic

Open the buns and place a sprig of basil in the center of each. Top with strips of cucumber and slices of tomato and onion. Drizzle sauce over each sandwich. If you are using olive oil, drizzle each sandwich with about 1 tablespoon oil and top with several slices of garlic.

ROASTED PEPPER SANDWICHES

SERVES 4

Although nothing beats fresh roasted peppers, this is a great way to enjoy Mezzetta's when fresh are unavailable. The Cajun bread comes from Brother Juniper's Bakery; St. George cheese is made only by Joe Matos; as a substitute, I would choose Vella's Jack.

        Extra-virgin olive oil
    8 slices Cajun Three-Pepper Bread or 4
         sourdough rolls
    ¼ pound soprassetta (an Italian salami-
         style meat)
  1½ cups (4 to 5 peppers) roasted sweet
         peppers, cut in julienne (see glossary
         page 279)
    3 cloves garlic, thinly sliced
    4 slices cheese or about 1 cup grated
         St. George or Jack cheese
       Fresh greens: fall salad mix or arugula

Brush a generous quantity of olive oil on one side of each of the slices of bread and toast them in the oven until the bread is just beginning to brown lightly. Remove bread from oven. On four slices of the bread, place several slices of *soprassetta*. Toss the roasted peppers with the garlic and divide among the four sandwiches, placing the peppers on top of the meat. Top the peppers with cheese and place in an oven or under the broiler until the cheese is just melted. Top the cheese with a handful of greens, place the

other slice of bread on top, cut the sandwich in half and serve immediately.

VARIATION ▼ Bake ¼-inch thick slices of eggplant drizzled with plenty of olive oil in a 350-degree oven until soft, creamy, and slightly golden, and add them to the sandwich, between the soprassetta and the peppers.

For a delicious vegetarian version, omit the meat.

SPRING SANDWICHES

MAKES 4 SANDWICHES

What food heralds the arrival of spring more clearly than the first tender stalks of asparagus? Try this unusual way to enjoy them. A version of this sandwich made with Armenian cracker bread would be delicious; read about lavosh sandwiches on page 86.

    1 pound fresh asparagus
    2 tablespoons Dijon-style mustard
       Mayonnaise (homemade or a good
         commercial brand)
       Black peppercorns
    1 teaspoon chopped fresh dill
    8 slices dark rye bread
    8 thin slices prosciutto or smoked pepper
         ham
       Thin slices torpedo onion (optional)

Cut the tough ends from the stalks of asparagus. Boil the spears for 2 to 3 minutes until just tender. Rinse under cool water, chop coarsely, and place in a food processor. Add 2 tablespoons mustard and process for about 30 seconds, until well blended but not puréed. Remove the asparagus mixture to a mixing bowl. Add the mayonnaise, a tablespoon at a time, until mixture acquires a good spreading consistency. Add some cracked black pepper and the dill. Blend well, taste, and correct seasoning.

Toast the bread. Spread 4 slices generously with the asparagus mixture. Spread the other 4 slices thinly with mustard. Fold 2 slices of prosciutto or ham on top of the asparagus spread and top with some crushed black pepper and rings of onion. Top with the other slice of bread, cut diagonally, and serve.

SONOMA MISSION BURRITOS

**SERVES 4 AS A MAIN COURSE
SERVES 8 TO 10 AS AN APPETIZER**

Charles Saunders, executive chef at the Sonoma Mission Inn, developed this California-style burrito using locally raised turkey and cheese from the Sonoma Cheese Factory. You can make a delicious variation using Bear Flag brand Jalapeño Jack and the Jalapeño Aïoli on page 212. These delicious burritos are easily portable, making them a perfect picnic item; just remember to keep them properly chilled.

½ **cup mayonnaise, homemade or commercial**

1 **teaspoon serrano chile, seeded and chopped**
¼ **teaspoon cumin**
¼ **teaspoon chili powder**
½ **teaspoon oregano, chopped**
1 **tablespoon lime juice**
4 **8- to 9-inch flour tortillas**
¾ **pound smoked turkey breast, sliced thin**
¼ **pound Jack cheese, sliced thin**
1 **ripe avocado, sliced**
⅛ **pound sprouts (radish, sunflower, or alfalfa)**

In a small bowl combine the mayonnaise with the serrano chile, cumin, chile powder, oregano, and lime juice. Set the mixture aside.

Warm the tortillas and place them on your cutting board. Top each tortilla with slices of the turkey followed by slices of the cheese, filling the center of each tortilla but leaving a portion on either side free of the ingredients. Spread one tablespoon of mayonnaise over the surface of the cheese and top with the sprouts, tomato, and avocado. Fold over the uncovered portion of the tortilla that is nearest you and roll the tortilla like a jelly roll. Repeat the process with each tortilla. Cut each burrito in half and place it on a serving plate. Serve immediately with additional mayonnaise on the side. To serve as an appetizer, cut in smaller portions and arrange on a serving platter.

CHICKEN AND ASPARAGUS *EN CROUTE*

SERVES 4

This dish is perfect for a spring lunch. Serve it with a Chardonnay, not too oaky, or with chilled champagne. Early spring strawberries, tossed with a little Balsamic vinegar and black pepper, or with a little lemon juice and sugar, make the perfect accompaniment.

1	pound boneless chicken breasts or meat from roaster
	Butter
20 to 25	thin stalks fresh asparagus
2	shallots, minced
1	tablespoon minced garlic
1	cup heavy cream
¼	cup Dijon-style mustard
2	teaspoons fresh thyme leaves
4	croissants, split in half lengthwise

If beginning with uncooked chicken, sauté it in a little butter until just done but still moist. Remove from the pan and set aside. If using roasted chicken, cut it into thin strips and allow to come up to room temperature. Cook the trimmed asparagus in rapidly boiling water for 2 to 3 minutes, rinse quickly in cool water, set aside, and keep warm.

In the pan drippings from the chicken (or in a little butter), sauté the shallots for 4 to 5 minutes, making sure they do not brown. Add the garlic and sauté for another 2 minutes. Add the cream, stir to blend, and reduce slightly. Stir in the mustard and thyme.

Cut the sautéed chicken into thin strips, stir into the mustard cream sauce, and heat thoroughly. Split the croissants in half and heat. Place them on individual serving plates. Divide the asparagus among the servings, placing it on the bottom half of each croissant. Divide the chicken among the servings, placing it on top of the asparagus. Place the top half of the croissant next to the filled half, garnish with sprig of thyme, and serve immediately, open-faced.

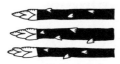

JADED PALATE'S BLT

MAKES 4

I have always loved having pancetta, *the Italian unsmoked bacon, left over from a catering job, especially in summer when there are lots of fresh tomatoes around to make my favorite version of a classic American sandwich.*

¼	pound thinly sliced pancetta or very thin slices of smoked duck
1	very fresh loaf of French bread
	About ½ cup Aïoli (page 211)
	Fresh basil leaves
4	ripe, homegrown tomatoes, sliced

If you are using it, cook the pancetta until just crispy. Cut 8 slices of bread diagonally and about ½-inch thick. For each sandwich, spread both sides of the bread with plenty of *aïoli*. Cover one slice of bread with fresh basil leaves and top with thick slices of tomato. Top the tomato with slices of duck or the crumbled pancetta and place the second slice of bread on top.

CROQUE SEÑOR

MAKES 1 SANDWICH

This is the spicy Mexican cousin of the traditional French Croque Monsieur, *a grilled or fried sandwich of ham and cheese. I would use Brother Juniper's Cajun Three-Pepper bread or Alvarado Street Bakery's Whole-Wheat Sourdough. My Cheddar would come from the Sonoma Cheese Factory and the Jack would be Vella's Jalapeño Jack.*

2 slices of bread
  Butter
2 teaspoons puréed chipotle in adobo
    sauce, thinned with a tablespoon of
    olive oil
  Cheddar cheese
  Jalapeño Jack cheese
1 pasilla or poblano pepper, roasted,
    peeled, and seeded
  Fresh cilantro

Butter one side of each slice of bread. Brush the other side with the puréed *chipotle*. Place

one slice of bread butter-side down and top the *chipotle*-covered side with plenty of cheese and top that with the pepper and a handful of cilantro. Place the other slice of bread, butter-side up, on top. If you have a stove-top toasting iron for making *croques*, place your sandwich inside and toast it over the flame of a gas burner, as you would any other sandwich. If you do not, melt a little butter in a heavy skillet and fry the sandwich for 2 to 3 minutes on each side, until it is nicely browned and the cheese is melted. Serve immediately.

JALAPEÑO BURGERS

SERVES 3

This recipe began as an act of desperation. It was one of those days in the little Cotati restaurant I was operating, and I did not have time to work on my daily special, one of the most popular features of the restaurant. We came up with this at the last minute, offered it with our best Mexican beer, and, much to my surprise, watched it become one of our most popular specials.

8 cloves garlic
3 jalapeño peppers, chopped, with seeds
1 pound ground chuck (not extra lean)
  Salt to taste
3 slices jalapeño Jack cheese
  Slices of fresh avocado
  Jalapeño Aïoli (page 212)
  Cilantro

Mince the garlic and combine with the *jalapeños*. Blend into the ground chuck, along with salt to taste. Form into three thick patties. Grill the burgers over medium-high heat, or broil, for 4 minutes. Turn, top with a slice of cheese, and cook for another 3 to 4 minutes for rare hamburgers. Top each burger with several slices of avocado. Have rolls heating or toasting while the hamburgers cook. Spread the rolls with *aïoli*, top with the meat, and garnish with sprigs of cilantro.

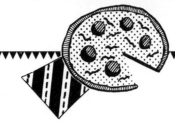

BREADS, PIZZA, AND CALZONE

BROTHER JUNIPER'S FRENCH BREAD

MAKES 2 LOAVES

This recipe comes to us from Brother Peter Reinhardt, the immensely talented master baker, at Brother Juniper's Bakery in Forestville. Try the Strombolini variation that follows the main recipe to create some exciting filled rolls.

4½ cups unbleached all-purpose flour or
    bread flour
 1 tablespoon salt
 1 tablespoon yeast
    About 1½ cups cool, not cold water

Mix all the ingredients except ¼ cup of the water in a clean bowl. Stir with a large spoon and then work with your hands until a ball is formed. Add more water if needed.

Turn out the ball onto a clean, solid tabletop and begin to knead with the heel of your hand, turning the dough over on itself every time it spreads out. Knead for about 10 minutes. The dough should be tacky but not sticky. If it is too wet, gradually add small quantities of flour. If it is too dry, add a few drops of water and work them in.

Place the ball of dough in a clean, oiled bowl. Cover with plastic wrap and allow it to rise at room temperature for approximately 1½ hours, until double in size. Punch it down and fold it back into a ball. Let it rise again for about 1 hour.

Punch it down and divide into 2 balls. Roll 1 ball into a rectangle, fold it in thirds, pinch the seam closed, and turn it over, seam-side down. Roll it out again and fold it again. Repeat once more, and pinch seam together carefully. You should have a baguette shape. Repeat the process with other ball of dough.

Sprinkle some polenta on a baking sheet large enough to hold both loaves with at least 2 inches between them. Cover and allow to rise for 1 hour.

Preheat the oven to 425 degrees (375 degrees for a convection oven). Uncover the dough and make three diagonal slashes across the top of each loaf with a serrated knife. Spray with cold water in a mist bottle. Place in the oven and spray every two minutes three times. Leave to bake, checking about 10 minutes after the last spray. The bread should begin to turn a deep, golden brown. When it reaches a rich color, turn off the oven and allow it to sit for 10 minutes. Remove from the oven. Let stand at least 15 minutes before slicing.

STROMBOLINI

MAKES 1 ROLL

Strombolini are delicious little rolls that resulted when I asked Brother Peter Reinhardt of Brother Juniper's Bakery to enter something in the Second Annual Great Garlic Cook-Off. This was what he came up with. For two years in a row, Brother Juniper's won first place with a Garlic Strombolini, thus beginning what is now a well-loved tradition in Forestville. Peter hopes to perfect a way of distributing Strombolini in the retail marketplace, perhaps frozen, to be baked at home.

Strombolini is a concept rather than a recipe and it is not necessary to provide specific quantities or instructions. You should have fun coming up with your own variations.

1 recipe Brother Juniper's French Bread
   (page 114)

FILLING
3 cups, chosen from among the following;
   always include some blend of cheeses:
      onion, diced
      garlic, minced
      roasted red pepper, diced
      roasted garlic, peeled and chopped
      green or black olives
      mung bean sprouts
      shredded cheese: Cheddar, Jack, dry
         Jack, Swiss, mozzarella, Parmesan,
         Romano
      dried or fresh herbs: parsley, oregano,
         basil, thyme
      spices: cayenne pepper, paprika,
         ground cumin, cumin seed

   Polenta

Roll out the dough into a rectangle. Spread the ingredients over the dough as you would in making a pizza. Roll up like a jelly roll. Slice into pieces about 1-inch thick. Lay the slices out on a sheet pan sprinkled lightly with polenta. Let them rise for 30 minutes. Bake at 350 degrees for approximately 30 minutes, or until the cheese is golden. Serve hot.

CHEESE BREAD

MAKES 4 SERVINGS

Cheese Bread is another delicious tradition that began in the old days of my restaurant,

The Brass Ass. On Thursday nights, when scores upon scores of students would pour in to pour down beer in celebration of the start of the weekend, we would prepare a hundred or more of these and frequently sold out. This version has been updated and freshened, to make a great idea taste as good as possible.

4 sourdough French rolls (unsliced)
¼ cup butter
4 cloves garlic, minced
1 tablespoon Italian parsley, minced
1⅓ cups grated garlic Jack cheese
⅔ cup grated mozzarella cheese
2 teaspoons chopped fresh herbs: thyme, oregano, marjoram, chives

Make 4 crosswise cuts in each French roll, being careful not to cut all the way through. Set aside. Melt the butter in a saucepan, add the garlic, and sauté for 2 minutes. Add the parsley, stir, and remove from the heat. Brush each cut of bread with the garlic butter. Blend cheeses together and stuff them into the cuts in the bread. Sprinkle with the chopped herbs. Place in 400-degree oven until the cheese is melted and bubbly, about 15 minutes. Serve immediately.

These can also be made on a grill. Just wrap each roll in foil and place on the grill, away from hottest part. Grill until cheese is melted.

▼▼

SAVORY ITALIAN BREAD PUDDING

SERVES 6 TO 8 AS AN ACCOMPANIMENT
MAKES ABOUT 50 APPETIZER SERVINGS

I decided that savory bread pudding might be interesting after I accidentally left the sugar out of a bread pudding for 75 guests. I corrected that little problem by drenching the pudding in a sweet and wonderful Lemon Whiskey Sauce, and began experimenting with the idea I had accidentally stumbled upon. Because both are flavored with oregano, I choose to make this recipe with Brother Juniper's Oreganato Bread and usually make it with Sonoma brand Dried Tomato Tapenade.

Olive oil
1 loaf San Francisco-style sourdough bread
¾ cup pine nuts
1 cup fresh, grated St. George cheese or Fontina
2 teaspoons chopped fresh oregano
4 eggs
3½ cups milk
2 tablespoons puréed sun-dried tomatoes
3 cloves garlic

Rub a 9- by 13-inch baking dish with olive oil. Cut the bread into ¾-inch squares and place in the baking dish with the pine nuts, cheese, and oregano and toss. In a mixing bowl, beat the eggs until creamy and light. Beat in the milk. Add the sun-dried tomatoes and press in the garlic. Mix well. Pour the custard over the bread mixture. Place in a 350-degree oven, immediately lower the heat to 300 degrees, and bake for 40 minutes. Increase the heat to 425 degrees and bake until lightly and evenly browned, about 15 minutes.

This bread pudding can be served just as it is, with sauce or gravy from an accompanying roast, or it can be cut into small squares and served, at room temperature, as an appetizer.

Latin-Style Cheese Bread

S E R V E S   4

This version of Cheese Bread resulted in more groans from the kitchen staff than did any other of my recipes. They hated stuffing the peppers into the cuts in the bread and complained about slicing the avocados. But the result was so delicious that even my overworked, grumpy cooks had to admit it was worth the effort.

4 sourdough French rolls, unsliced
¼ cup extra-virgin olive oil
2 tablespoons freshly minced garlic
1 cup (2 to 3 peppers) roasted, seeded, and sliced sweet peppers (see glossary page 279)
1½ cups grated jalapeño Jack or other Jack cheese
1 ripe but slightly firm avocado, cut lengthwise into slices

Make 4 crosswise cuts in each French roll, being careful not to cut all the way through. Brush the inside of the cuts with plenty of olive oil. Place some minced garlic in each cut and then top with slices of roasted peppers. Stuff each cut full with the cheese and place the rolls in a 400-degree oven until the cheese is melted and bubbly, about 15 minutes. Remove from the oven and place a slice of avocado in each cut, on top of the melted cheese. Serve immediately.

Pizza and Calzone Dough

MAKES 2 LARGE, 10- TO 12-INCH PIZZAS OR FOUR SMALL TO MEDIUM CALZONES

To say that we in Sonoma County like pizza is like saying we drink water; so what else is new? Everyone everywhere likes pizza and Sonoma County is no exception. One local restaurant has, however, distinguished itself among all the others and is producing more than just your average cheese and sausage pizza. Pizza Gourmet in Cotati makes a mean Marguerita-style pizza with olive oil, garlic, and cheeses, topped with sliced Roma tomatoes and basil. They have taken specialty pizzas a step further with such delights as the Mexicana, the Gilroy, with roasted garlic, and a variety of other unusual and delicious combinations.

To make a good pizza or calzone, you must first begin with a good dough recipe. After much experimenting, I have finally found one with which I am satisfied.

1 package or 1 tablespoon yeast
1¼ cups warm water
4½ cups all-purpose flour
1 teaspoon salt
2 generous tablespoons extra-virgin
olive oil

Place the yeast and ¼ cup of the warm water in a mixing bowl and set aside for 10 minutes. Stir in the remaining cup water and 1 cup flour. Add the salt and olive oil and stir. Add the remaining flour, cup by cup, mixing each completely before adding the next until you have just ½ cup left. Turn the dough out onto a floured surface and knead until smooth and velvety, about 7 minutes, working in as much of the remaining flour as the dough will take. Place the dough in a clean bowl well coated with olive oil. Cover with a damp towel, set in a warm place, and let it rise for 2 hours. Punch it down, let it

rest for 5 minutes, and form it into the desired shape.

SONOMA COAST PIZZA

SERVES 4

Pizza Gourmet has offered the recipe for one of their most popular specialty pizzas. What a great way to evoke the flavors of our coast.

1 Half recipe Pizza Dough (page 117)
   rolled out into a 12-inch circle
   Olive oil
2 to 4 tablespoons garlic, minced
3 ounces fresh crab, cooked
3 ounces bay shrimp, cooked
3 ounces St. George cheese, or
   Gruyère cheese, grated
5 ounces mozzarella cheese, sliced
2 or 3 tablespoons chopped Italian parsley
2 thin slices lemon, cut into quarters
8 sections crab-leg meat (optional)

Cover the pizza dough with a generous layer of olive oil and sprinkle plenty of minced garlic over the surface. Add the crab and then the shrimp to the pizza, spreading them evenly over the surface. Repeat the process with both cheeses. Bake in a 500-degree oven, preferably on a pizza stone, until the cheese is melted and just beginning to turn golden, about 20 minutes. Remove from the oven and glaze the surface with olive oil. Sprinkle with Italian parsley and cut into 8 wedges. Garnish each wedge with a piece of lemon and, if using, a single section of crab leg meat. Serve immediately, with a simple green salad.

ZUCCHINI AND AVOCADO PIZZA

MAKES 1 PIZZA, 10- TO 12-INCHES IN DIAMETER

This pizza is deceptively simple and light. It is also so exquisitely delicious that it seems surely more complicated to make than it is. During the three years that I ran the now-closed Brass Ass Restaurant in Cotati, it was our most popular of the newer style pizzas.

	Half recipe Pizza Dough (page 117) rolled out to a 10- to 12-inch circle
4 to 5	tablespoons extra-virgin olive oil
2	cups grated zucchini
1	tablespoon lemon juice
1 or 2	jalapeño peppers, seeded and diced
5	cloves garlic, minced
2	cups grated cheese, a combination of jalapeño Jack, dry Jack, Garlic Jack, St. George (or Fontina), and mozzarella

2	tablespoons fresh herbs, chopped
1	ripe but firm avocado

Drizzle olive oil over the rolled-out pizza dough until it is well covered. Toss together the zucchini, lemon juice, *jalapeños*, and garlic and spread evenly over the pizza. Top with an even layer of the cheese blend. Bake at 500 degrees until the crust is golden and cheese bubbly, about 15 to 20 minutes. Remove the pizza from the oven, cut into 8 slices, and top each piece with a slice of avocado. Serve extra olive oil and crushed hot peppers on the side.

RATATOUILLE PIZZA

MAKES 1 LARGE, 10- TO 12-INCH PIZZA

This recipe is the result of one of those wonderful moments of serendipity. There I was with extra pizza dough and a great deal more ratatouille than guests. It seemed to be a good idea, so I gave it a try. Voila! I have a new, favorite pizza. The Pizza Dough recipe is enough for two large pizzas. In this recipe the quantities of topping are given for one pizza. Make another type with the rest of the dough, or double the amount of topping.

> Half recipe Pizza Dough (page 117)
> 2 cups Ratatouille (page 181)
> 2 ounces grated Jack cheese
> 2 chaurice or fresh andouille sausages, casings removed
> ¼ cup grated dry Jack cheese

Spread the surface of the rolled pizza dough with the ratatouille and distribute the Sonoma Jack cheese over the top. Briefly sauté the sausages, breaking them up with a fork. Spread half-cooked sausage over the surface and top with dry Jack cheese.

Bake on a pizza stone, if available, at 500 degrees for 15 to 20 minutes, until the crust has started to turn golden. Let the pizza rest for 2 or 3 minutes, slice, and serve.

▼▼▼▼▼▼▼▼▼▼▼▼▼▼▼▼▼▼▼▼▼▼▼▼▼▼▼▼▼▼

ROASTED PEPPER AND SALAMI PIZZA

MAKES 1 PIZZA, 10- TO 12-INCHES IN DIAMETER

Pizza is delicious with a drizzle of extra-virgin olive oil. I keep a shaker bottle filled with oil and a teaspoon of crushed red peppers on hand all the time.

> Half recipe Pizza Dough (page 117) rolled out to a 10- to 12-inch circle
> 4 to 5 tablespoons extra-virgin olive oil

> ¼ pound Italian salami or soprassetta
> 2 cups (4 to 6 peppers) roasted peppers, cut in julienne (see glossary page 279)
> 1 tablespoon red wine vinegar
> ¼ cup freshly minced garlic
> ¼ pound fresh mozzarella cheese, sliced
> 2 cups grated garlic Jack or jalapeño Jack cheese
> 1 large or 2 small ripe tomatoes, cut in rounds
> Fresh basil leaves

Cover pizza dough with a generous layer of olive oil and top with a single layer of salami or *soprassetta*. Toss the peppers, vinegar, and garlic together and spread over the surface of the pizza. Cover with slices of mozzarella and top with grated cheese.

Bake at 500 degrees for 15 to 20 minutes, until the crust is golden and the cheese bubbly. Cut in 8 pieces, top each piece with a slice of tomato and 2 or 3 fresh basil leaves. Serve immediately and pass extra olive oil.

▼▼▼▼▼▼▼▼▼▼▼▼▼▼▼▼▼▼▼▼▼▼▼▼▼▼▼▼▼▼

CREAMY GARLIC CALZONE

SERVES 1 OR 2

Garlic squeezed through a press has more of the characteristic hot garlic taste. This creamy calzone is full of that fire and will delight any garlic lover.

Polenta or cornmeal

One-fourth recipe Pizza Dough
(page 117), rolled out to an 8-inch
round

4 ounces chabis cheese

2 ounces Jack cheese, grated

2 ounces mozzarella cheese, grated

1 ounce dry Jack, or Parmesan grated

6 cloves garlic

2 tablespoons chopped fresh herbs: chives,
basil, thyme, cilantro, oregano, etc.

1 tablespoon chopped Italian parsley

1 teaspoon freshly ground black pepper

Olive oil

Spread a little polenta or cornmeal on your baking surface and place the circle of pizza dough on top. Mix together the cheeses. Press 4 cloves of garlic into the cheese mixture, add the herbs, parsley, and pepper. Blend well. Place the cheese mixture on one half of the pizza dough. Fold the dough over and seal the edges tightly, either by folding and pinching, or by joining with a fork. Drizzle the surface with olive oil. Chop the remaining 2 cloves of garlic and sprinkle them over the surface of the calzone. Bake, preferably on a pizza stone, at 500 degrees, until the crust turns golden, about 20 minutes. Remove and serve immediately.

BARRY'S BIANCA CALZONE

MAKES 1 CALZONE

Pizza Gourmet of Cotati originally offered this popular creamy and spicy calzone only as a special; now it is on their standard menu. An accompanying salad or vegetable that includes citrus or tomatoes will complement the creamy, rich quality of the calzone.

2 or 3 slices bacon

2 slices yellow onion, chopped

1 jalapeño pepper, seeded and diced
Several leaves Swiss chard, cut in
strips, large stems removed
One-fourth recipe Pizza Dough
(page 117)
Olive oil

3 to 4 ounces ricotta cheese

2 tablespoons chopped fresh herbs:
Italian parsley, chives, oregano,
thyme, etc.

½ cup grated mozzarella cheese
Freshly chopped garlic
Coarse sea salt

Fry the bacon until crisp, remove it from the pan, and drain. Sauté the onion and *jalapeño* in the bacon drippings until soft. Add the Swiss chard, stir, and sauté until just limp. Crumble the bacon and toss with the other ingredients. Set aside to cool.

Roll out the dough to an 8- to 10-inch circle and drizzle olive oil over the surface.

Spread the Swiss chard mixture over half of the dough and top with ricotta cheese. Sprinkle fresh herbs over the ricotta and top with mozzarella cheese. Fold the dough over and seal the crust by pinching the edges.

Brush the exposed surface with olive oil and sprinkle with garlic and coarse sea salt. Bake at 500 degrees until golden, about 20 minutes. Serve immediately.

Eggs

Eggs Kozlowski

SERVES 4

A spring brunch is the perfect time to serve this delicious Sonoma version of Eggs Benedict.

- 32 thin stalks of asparagus
- 8 very thin slices prosciutto (optional)
- 1 recipe Raspberry Hollandaise Sauce (page 212)
- 4 English muffins
- 8 fresh ranch eggs
  Fresh raspberries, for garnish, if available

Assemble all your ingredients so that, once you begin, you can proceed quickly. Cook the asparagus until just tender. If using prosciutto, wrap a piece of prosciutto around a group of 4 stalks of asparagus. Hold in a warm oven. Make the Raspberry Hollandaise and hold over hot water. Toast the English muffins and place 2 halves on each of 4 plates. Top each half with four stalks of asparagus. Hold in warm oven. Quickly poach the eggs, no more than 2 at a time, and place 1 egg on top of each muffin half. Top with hollandaise and garnish with a few raspberries. Serve immediately.

Batcakes

FOR 4 CAKES

Bats have long been a pet interest, probably because I loved Halloween so much as a child. Now we are finding out, primarily through the work of the organization, Bat Conservation International, based in Austin, Texas, how important bats are to our environment. Not only do they play a major role in insect control, but they are also responsible for the fertilization of a number of species of plants, including many tropical fruits. They are delightful, intelligent crea-

tures who bond with humans, play like cats, are easy to train, and frequently mate for life. Contrary to popular myth, they are not a health or safety threat to humans; they make the world a safer place by ridding it of insects. Forestville's Russian River Vineyards draws many outside diners in the spring and summer who come to watch the nightly emergence of the little brown bats who make their home in the tower of the guest room. It is beautiful to watch them swoop out over the vineyard on their search for the thousands of mosquitos they will eat that night. Over the years, I have developed recipes that would somehow enable me to focus on bats, so that I could write about them in my column. Many species of the gentle creatures are endangered, and it is only the education of the world that will save them.

 1 bat-shaped cookie cutter
 4 slices pumpernickel or dark rye bread
    Butter
 2 eggs
 4 cloves garlic, minced
    Salt and pepper to taste
 ¼ cup grated dry Jack cheese
 ¼ cup hot salsa

At an angle, cut a bat from the center of each slice of bread. Set the bat shapes aside to make croutons for soup or salad. In a heavy skillet or on a griddle, melt a little butter until foamy. Fry the bread in butter until crisp. While the bread is cooking, quickly beat together the eggs, garlic, salt, and pepper; add the cheese. Turn the bread over, making sure there is enough butter in the pan. Carefully spoon just enough of the egg mixture into the bread to fill the bat-

shaped space. Do not overfill. Carefully stir the egg mixture with a fork to scramble it a bit. Repeat with each slice of bread. Cover the batcakes until the egg has set. Remove from the skillet and invert onto serving plates. Serve a small cup of salsa on the side. For an eerie accompaniment, try some fried purple potatoes.

▼▼

GARLIC OMELETTE

SERVES 1

There are times when nothing provides the proper combination of nourishment and comfort quite like an omelette. If you have never used real ranch eggs, eggs from well-fed, happy chickens, who get to see the sun and run around and act like the barnyard birds they were meant to be, make the effort to find a source. They are so far superior to the pale, flavorless eggs that their less fortunate caged cousins produce that you will never want to shop in a supermarket again.

 2 tablespoons extra-virgin olive oil
 6 large cloves garlic, chopped
 3 fresh eggs
 1 tablespoon fresh herbs, chopped
 ½ cup grated St. George cheese, or
    Taupinière, or dry Jack cheese

In a heavy skillet or omelette pan heat the olive oil and sauté the garlic for 2 minutes. Quickly beat the eggs and herbs together and pour into the pan. Stir quickly with a fork to incorporate the garlic into the eggs. When the eggs are almost set, add the cheese. Fold the omelette over and cook until the cheese is melted. Serve immediately.

▼▼▼▼▼▼▼▼▼▼▼▼▼▼▼▼▼▼▼▼▼▼▼▼▼▼▼▼▼▼▼▼▼▼▼▼

TORTILLA ESPAÑOL

S E R V E S   4

Jim Gibbons, who is the owner and chef at the restaurant, Jacob Horner, in Healdsburg developed this recipe and its original use of aïoli.

1   green bell pepper
1   red bell pepper
1   red onion
3   tablespoons olive oil
3   cloves garlic, minced
3   ounces prosciutto, sliced thin and cut into thin strips
9   eggs
    Salt and freshly ground pepper
    Aïoli (page 211)
2   tablespoons each Italian parsley, and chives

Cut the peppers and onion into a fine julienne and cook slowly in olive oil until they are barely resistant. Add the minced garlic, cook for 1 minute, and add the prosciutto. Mix well and remove from the heat. Spread the mixture out on a sheet pan and divide into three equal parts.

Place three of the eggs in a bowl and whip well. Season with salt and pepper. Add one portion of the pepper mixture, mix well, and pour into a hot, oiled omelette pan.

Cook until set, turn, and cook another minute or 2. Slide out onto a sheet pan and let cool.

Repeat this process twice. Allow all three omelettes to cool.

Spread the *Aïoli* on top of two of the omelettes, and stack all three, with the uncoated omelette on top. Spread the top layer with *Aïoli* and sprinkle with the parsley and chives.

Refrigerate until well chilled and cut into wedges to serve.

▼▼▼▼▼▼▼▼▼▼▼▼▼▼▼▼▼▼▼▼▼▼▼▼▼▼▼▼▼▼▼▼▼▼▼▼▼

SONOMA JACK SOUFFLÉ

S E R V E S   6

This soufflé, which comes from the Sonoma Cheese Factory, is excellent served with Caesar Salad, Sonoma Style (page 195), Baked Cherry Tomatoes (page 186), and a good white wine, such as a Fumé Blanc.

    Butter for the soufflé dish
2   tablespoons imported, freshly grated Parmesan cheese (optional—use for a slightly sharper flavor) + extra for lining the soufflé dish
2   tablespoons butter
2   tablespoons flour
½   cup hot milk
5   eggs, separated
8   ounces Jack cheese, grated
    Salt and white pepper
    Cayenne pepper

Preheat the oven to 350 degrees. Butter a 2-quart soufflé dish or casserole and sprinkle all the buttered surfaces with the extra Parmesan cheese. Melt the 2 tablespoons butter in the top of a double boiler; add the flour gradually, stirring to make a smooth paste. Slowly add the hot milk and cook gently for 4 minutes, or until the mixture thickens slightly. Remove from the heat, cool slightly, and add the egg yolks, one at a time, alternating with small additions of the cheeses. When all the egg yolks and cheese have been added, return to heat, and stir until the cheese is entirely melted and incorporated into the sauce. Remove from the heat, season with salt, white pepper, and cayenne to taste, and cover tightly to prevent the formation of a skin. Let cool.

Beat the egg whites until stiff but moist, and *very gently* fold them into the cheese sauce. Pour into the buttered soufflé dish and bake until the top is golden and the soufflé puffy, about 35 to 40 minutes. Serve immediately.

▼▼▼▼▼▼▼▼▼▼▼▼▼▼▼▼▼▼▼▼▼▼▼▼▼▼▼▼▼▼▼

GOAT CHEESE AND ARTICHOKE TART

SERVES 4 AS A FIRST COURSE

This is a delicious way to enjoy the flavor of chèvre. The recipe was developed by Laura Chenel, a well-known cheesemaker.

CRUST
   2 ounces fresh goat cheese, such as
      log or chabis

   2 tablespoons butter
   ¾ cup flour
   ½ teaspoon salt

CUSTARD
   4 ounces goat cheese
   1 egg
   ¼ cup heavy cream
   ½ tablespoon fresh thyme
      Salt and pepper to taste

TOPPING
   4 baby artichokes
   1 red pepper
  10 cloves garlic

Mix together the ingredients for the crust. Chill the dough for 1 hour and then roll it out to fit a 7½-inch tart pan with a removable bottom. Prebake the shell in a 400-degree oven for 10 to 15 minutes, or until the pastry begins to firm and turn golden.

Mix together the custard ingredients until velvety in texture. Pour into the prebaked, cooled tart shell and spread evenly.

Cut the artichokes in half. To make the topping, trim the tender leaves of the baby artichokes and boil in salted water until soft, about 15 minutes. Roast, skin, and seed the red pepper, and slice it into strips. Skin and roast the garlic, and cut each clove in half. Top the custard decoratively with an interesting pattern of artichokes, peppers, and roasted garlic halves and bake in a 350-degree oven for 40 minutes.

MEXICAN QUICHE

S E R V E S   6   T O   8

There is only one thing you need to remember about quiche: Real men everywhere, including here in Sonoma, eat anything they want.

 1 small yellow onion, finely diced
   Olive oil
 6 cloves garlic, minced
 ½ pound chorizo sausage, bulk or casings
   removed
 2 fresh jalapeño peppers, seeded and
   diced
   10-inch springform pan, lined with
   shell of pâté brisée
 1 cup jalapeño Jack or mild raw-milk
   Cheddar cheese, grated
 2 eggs
 1½ cups heavy cream
 1 teaspoon achiote, if available
 ¼ teaspoon nutmeg
 ¼ teaspoon cayenne pepper
 ¼ teaspoon salt
   Fresh cilantro

Saute the onion in a little olive oil until soft and golden. Add the minced garlic and sauté for 2 minutes. Crumble the *chorizo* into the sauté pan and cook, stirring constantly, for about 15 minutes. Add the fresh *jalapeños*. Cool the mixture slightly and place in the pastry shell. Top with the cheese. Beat the eggs with the cream. If using *achiote*, moisten it with a little warm water and stir into the cream mixture. Add the seasonings

and pour over the cheese. Sprinkle a little cayenne pepper over the top if you wish. Bake for 35 to 40 minutes at 375 degrees. Garnish with fresh cilantro.

ROASTED PEPPER AND GARLIC QUICHE

S E R V E S   6

The combination of the sweet roasted peppers and nutty flavored roasted garlic makes this vegetarian quiche unusually delicious; a great alternative to standard versions.

   10-inch springform pan, lined with a
   shell of pâté brisée
 1½ cups roasted red and yellow peppers,
   cut in julienne
 ¾ cup grated St. George cheese
 ½ cup Roasted Garlic Purée (page 222)
 3 eggs, beaten
 2 cups heavy cream
 1 teaspoon fresh thyme
 ½ teaspoon salt
 ¼ teaspoon white pepper

Place roasted peppers in the pastry shell, spreading them evenly on the surface. Top with cheese. Beat together the garlic purée, eggs, cream, thyme and salt and pepper. Pour into the pastry shell and bake at 375 degrees for 35 to 40 minutes. When done, a knife inserted at the edge should come out clean. Cool before serving.

PASTA

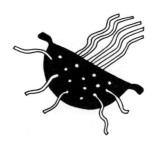

▼▼▼▼▼▼▼▼▼▼▼▼▼▼▼▼▼▼▼▼▼▼▼▼▼▼▼▼

BLACK ANGEL PASTA

SERVES 2

This is one of my favorite dishes and not merely because it is so visually stunning. When Pasta Etc. began making their black pasta, I was entranced both by its appearance and by its delicious flavor, so subtly evocative of the sea. It seemed the perfect background for the delicate flavor of golden caviar. Served with a crisp, dry champagne, it is sublime, and ideal for a hauntingly delicious Halloween dinner, a tradition I heartily recommend.

  ½ pound fresh black (squid ink) or
        black pepper angel hair pasta
  3 tablespoons unsalted butter
      Juice of 1 lemon
3 to 4 ounces golden caviar
  2 sprigs Italian parsley, for garnish
  2 lemon wedges

Cook the pasta in boiling, salted water for 30 to 45 seconds. Toss with butter until the butter has melted and the pasta well coated. Squeeze lemon juice over the pasta and toss again.

Place on warmed serving plates. Divide the caviar between the 2 portions of pasta, placing it on top. Garnish each portion with a sprig of parsley and a wedge of lemon. Serve immediately.

SPAGHETTI ALLA CARBONARA SONOMA

SERVES 4

In Third Helpings *(Penguin Books, New York, 1984), Calvin Trillin suggests that our national Thanksgiving dish be changed from turkey to spaghetti carbonara. Certainly, the luscious strands of egg and cheese-coated pasta have made me swoon more often than even the best roasted turkey. Try this dish with Hearts of Butter Lettuce with Lemon Vinaigrette (page 216), some hot French bread, and a full-bodied white wine; you may be on your way to a new family tradition. For a particularly festive touch, begin the meal with Cranberry-Zinfandel Soup (page 97), accompanied by a blanc de noir champagne.*

    1   tablespoon olive oil
    4   cloves garlic, minced
    ¼   pound pancetta, diced
    3   eggs
    3   tablespoons chopped Italian parsley
    2   teaspoons fresh, cracked black pepper
    1   teaspoon salt
    1   cup freshly grated dry Jack or Parmesan
        cheese
    ½   pound dried imported spaghettini or
        spaghetti

Heat the olive oil in a heavy skillet. Have a large pot of rapidly boiling water ready. Add the garlic to the skillet and sauté for 2 minutes. Add the *pancetta* and cook until it is just crispy. Remove from the heat. While the *pancetta* is cooking, beat the eggs together in a large bowl until they are very well mixed. Add the parsley, pepper, salt, and cheese. Cook the pasta in boiling water until just done. While it is cooking, add the *pancetta* and any pan drippings to the egg and cheese mixture, stirring quickly to break up the *pancetta*. Drain the cooked pasta and place it in a bowl with the egg mixture. Toss quickly and continuously until all the pasta is well coated. The heat of the pasta will cook the egg. Serve immediately.

FETTUCCINI ARMANDO

SERVES 4

Half the fun of making this whimsical version of Fettuccini Alfredo was naming it; the other half was eating it.

    2   shallots, minced
    5   cloves garlic, 3 minced and 2 thinly
        sliced
    2   jalapeño peppers, seeded and minced
    2   tablespoons olive oil
    2   cups heavy cream
    1   cup half-and-half
    2   tablespoons achiote
    2   ripe tomatoes
    1   tablespoon lemon juice
    1   tablespoon extra-virgin olive oil
    ½   teaspoon salt
    12 ounces fresh fettuccini

In a saucepan, sauté the shallots, minced garlic, and *jalapeños* in the olive oil until soft. Add the cream and ½ a cup of the half-and-half and simmer to reduce by one-third. Mix together the remaining ½ cup half-and-half with the *achiote*, using a fork to break apart the *achiote*. Stir this mixture into the sauce.

Chop the tomatoes and toss them with the sliced garlic, lemon juice, olive oil, and salt. Set aside.

Have a pot of rapidly boiling salted water ready. Cook the fettuccini in the boiling water, drain, and place in large bowl. Pour about half of the sauce over and toss until all the strands of pasta are well coated. Place on individual serving plates, spoon more sauce over, and top each serving with a generous spoonful of the tomato mixture. Serve immediately.

RANCHER'S PASTA

SERVES 4 TO 6

Timber Crest Farms wants to be sure that everyone who buys their dried tomatoes knows what to do with them, so they include several recipes with each package, and have special recipe pamphlets available, too. The following recipes, using their Sonoma brand Dried Tomato Halves, are two of the many delicious recipes they offer.

- 12 halved dried tomatoes
- 16 ounces fettuccini

- 1 cup olive oil
- 8 cloves garlic, coarsely chopped
- 1 cup Kalamata olives, halved
- 1 teaspoon oregano
  Salt and pepper to taste
- 8 ounces grated dry Jack cheese

Soften the dried tomato halves in boiling water for 2 minutes and slice into strips. Cook the pasta according to the directions on the package.

Heat the oil over medium heat in a large skillet. Add the garlic and sauté for 2 minutes. Add the olives, tomatoes, oregano, salt, and pepper.

Drain the pasta and toss it with the garlic and olive mixture and the grated cheese. Make sure all pasta is well coated and serve immediately.

SONOMA PASTA

SERVES 4 TO 6

- 3 ounces halved dried tomato
- 8 slices thick-cut, smoked bacon
- 16 ounces fettuccini
- 2 tablespoons fresh garlic, minced
- 12 medium basil leaves, slivered
- 1 cup whole black or Kalamata olives, pitted

8 ounces goat cheese
Salt and pepper to taste

Drop the dried tomato slices into boiling water for 2 minutes. Drain and cut them into long slivers. Set aside.

Cut the bacon into ¼-inch pieces and brown well in heavy skillet. Remove the bacon with a slotted spoon to a paper towel to drain; reserve the bacon drippings in the skillet.

Cook the pasta, according to the directions on the package, in rapidly boiling water. While the pasta is cooking, sauté the garlic in the bacon drippings for 2 minutes. Add the basil leaves and dried tomatoes and toss well. Add the olives and sauté until well heated. Immediately before draining the pasta, break the cheese into pieces and toss it with the garlic mixture. Drain the pasta, add it to the sauce and toss well. Add salt and pepper to taste, place on a serving platter, and serve immediately.

Sun-Dried Tomato Pasta

SERVES 2

This recipe is the essence of simplicity. It is perfect for a fast meal during the holidays when we're all pressed for time, or perfect when unexpected guests drop by. Dried tomatoes are such an easy staple to keep on hand, you might as well have a few simple

uses for them up your culinary sleeve. This recipe is most easily prepared when you have both commercially puréed dried tomatoes and dried tomato halves packed in oil on hand. If you do not, you will need to purée them yourself.

6 ounces fresh sun-dried tomato pasta, cut
    in double fettuccini strands or 4
    ounces imported dried fettuccini
1 cup heavy cream
1 tablespoon puréed dried tomatoes packed
    in oil
    Freshly cracked black pepper
2 oil-packed dried tomato halves, julienned

Cook the pasta in plenty of boiling, salted water. Reduce the cream over high heat by one-third. Stir in the dried tomato purée. Add the pasta to the sauce and toss well. Arrange on two plates, and top with plenty of freshly cracked black pepper, and garnish with the julienned strips of dried tomato.

Pasta alla Campagna

SERVES 4 TO 6
AS A MAIN COURSE

This delicious, country-style pasta comes from the Vella Cheese Company's own recipe file. Serve this as a hearty main course or use it to accompany grilled or roasted meats.

1 pound Swiss chard
1 cup pecans, chopped

1 pound bacon, chopped
2½ cups penne (quill-shaped dry pasta)
3 cloves garlic, pressed
½ teaspoon crushed dried hot pepper or
more to taste
3 teaspoons Dijon-style mustard
3 tablespoons red wine vinegar
2 cups grated dry Jack cheese

Have a large pot of boiling, salted water ready.

Wash the chard and drain it. Trim off the tips of the chard stems and discard. Finely slice the stems and leaves, keeping them separate. Set aside.

Place the pecans in a large frying pan over medium heat and stir until they darken slightly, about 5 minutes. Remove from the pan and set aside.

Place the chopped bacon in a pan over high heat. Stir frequently until the bacon is browned and crisp. Drain on paper towels.

Cook the pasta until just tender and drain. While the pasta is cooking, discard all but 6 tablespoons of the bacon fat. Add the chard stems, garlic, and dried hot pepper to the pan and sauté over medium heat until the stems are limp, about 10 minutes. Add the leaves and stir until limp and tender. Remove from the heat.

In a large bowl, stir together the mustard and vinegar. Add the pasta and toss. Add the cheese, greens, and bacon; toss well. Top with the pecans and serve.

CANNELLONI

One of the best uses for fresh pasta, home-made or store-bought, is in cannelloni or any of the little pasta packages, such as ravioli, tortellini, and so on, that obviously cannot be made from dried pasta. Cannelloni made with fresh pasta are easy and lend themselves to a wider variety of fillings than do the smaller ravioli and tortellini.

General Directions:

▼ Begin with fresh pasta sheets about 1/16-inch thick and 5-inches square.

▼ Allow 3 or 4 tablespoons of filling per cannelloni.

▼ Spread a little sauce or a little olive oil on the bottom of the baking dish before putting the cannelloni in.

▼ Bake for no more than 15 to 20 minutes. If the filling ingredients need more cooking than this, they should be partially cooked in advance.

▼ Reserve a little extra sauce to top the cannelloni when it comes out of the oven.

▼ Allow 2 cannelloni per serving.

SPINACH CANNELLONI

S E R V E S 1 0

1 bunch spinach, rinsed and stems
removed
Olive oil
4 or 5 cloves garlic, minced
¾ pound fromage blanc or ricotta
cheese

¼ pound prosciutto, cut into match
   sticks
6 ounces dry Jack cheese, grated
2 eggs
   Freshly ground black pepper
   Nutmeg
20 sheets (5- by 5-inch) spinach pasta

SAUCE
   Olive oil
1 medium onion, chopped
8 cloves garlic, minced
4 cups tomato sauce
1 cup red wine
1 teaspoon nutmeg
½ teaspoon ground cloves
½ teaspoon cinnamon
   Salt and pepper

To make the filling, chop the cleaned spin-ach and sauté it in olive oil until just limp. Add the garlic and stir well for 2 minutes. Place in mixing bowl. Blend in the cheese and prosciutto. Beat the eggs and add them to the mixture. Season with plenty of fresh black pepper and nutmeg and blend well. Set the mixture aside.

To make the sauce, heat the olive oil in a heavy saucepan, add the onion, and sauté until golden. Add the garlic and sauté for 2 minutes. Add the tomato sauce and wine and simmer for 30 minutes. Thin with wa-ter if necessary. Season with nutmeg, clove, and cinnamon. Add salt and pepper to taste.

To assemble, place the spinach pasta squares on a flat surface. Spread the spinach mixture over entire surface, leaving a ¼-inch margin all around. Roll up loosely. Spoon a little sauce into the baking dish.

Add the cannelloni and top with sauce. Bake for 15 minutes. Remove from the oven and top with a little more sauce. Serve immediately.

CANNELLONI PRIMAVERA
SERVES 10

½ pound fresh asparagus, tough ends
   removed
½ pound fresh Blue Lake green beans
   Butter
2 small zucchini, cut in julienne
1 red pepper, cut in julienne
¼ pound shiitake mushrooms
3 cloves garlic, minced
   1-inch piece fresh ginger, peeled and cut
   into very small julienne

SAUCE
2 cups heavy cream
1 cup half-and-half
2 egg yolks
1 tablespoon butter
1 teaspoon ground ginger
20 sheets (5- by 5-inch) fresh pasta

To make the filling, parboil the asparagus and cut into 1½-inch pieces. Do the same with the green beans. Melt some butter in a heavy skillet, add the zucchini and the pep-per and sauté for about 5 minutes. Add the mushrooms and sauté for another 5 min-utes. Add the asparagus and green beans. Add the garlic and toss well. Add about half of the fresh ginger. Toss the mixture well and set aside.

To make the sauce, place the cream and the rest of the ginger over medium-high heat and reduce by one third. Combine the egg yolks and ground ginger and add a couple of tablespoons of the cream mixture. Add the egg mixture to the cream and stir well. Swirl in the butter in small pieces. Set the sauce aside.

To assemble, place the pasta sheets on a flat surface. Place 3 tablespoons vegetable mixture on each sheet and roll it up loosely. Put a little sauce in the bottom of the baking dish, place the cannelloni in the dish and top with sauce. Bake for 15 minutes, remove from the oven, and top with more sauce.

LEMON, DILL, AND SCALLOP CANNELLONI

SERVES 4

> 1 pound fresh calico scallops or bay
>   scallops
> Flour
> Butter
> 2 cloves garlic, minced
> Juice of 1 lemon
> 2½ cups heavy cream
> 1 teaspoon lemon zest
> 1 tablespoon fresh dill, finely chopped
> Dill sprigs for garnish
> Thin round lemon slices for garnish
> 8 sheets (5- by 5-inch) pasta, lemon-dill
>   if available

To make the filling, rinse the scallops and pat them dry. Toss with some flour, place in strainer, and shake off any excess flour. Melt butter in a saucepan with the garlic and sauté for 2 minutes. Add the scallops and toss to coat with butter. Add the lemon juice and toss again. Stir in ½ cup of the cream and remove from heat. Set aside.

To make the sauce, combine the remaining cream with the lemon zest and chopped dill in a heavy saucepan. Reduce the cream by one-third. Set aside.

To assemble, place the pasta sheets on a flat surface and divide the scallops among the 8 squares. Roll them up loosely and place in baking dish that you have coated with sauce. Top with more sauce. Bake for 15 minutes. Remove from the oven, spoon a little more sauce over, and garnish with a sprig of dill and a slice of lemon. Serve immediately.

▼▼▼▼▼▼▼▼▼▼▼▼▼▼▼▼▼▼▼▼▼▼▼▼▼▼▼▼▼▼▼▼▼▼▼▼▼

SONOMA CANNELLONI

SERVES 5 OR 6

Pasta Etc. has made some pastas that I find truly inspirational. Their wild mushroom pasta is one of those, and this recipe was developed specifically for that pasta, though it can be made with a simple dried cannelloni shell.

> ½ ounce dried porcini mushrooms,
>   soaked in ½ cup hot water for
>   30 minutes
> 2 to 3 tablespoons butter
> 2 shallots, minced
> 1 tablespoon garlic, minced
> ¾ pound fresh mushrooms, tough
>   stems removed and thinly sliced
>   (use a mixture of seasonally
>   available mushrooms, but be
>   sure to include plenty of
>   shiitakes)

¼ cup pine nuts
3 tablespoons Madeira
10 or 12 squares (5- by 5-inch) wild
mushroom pasta
¾ cup grated Taupinière cheese
Chèvre Sauce (page 214)

Drain the porcini, reserving the liquid to use in a soup stock, and set aside. Melt the butter in a heavy sauté pan and sauté the shallots until transparent. Add the garlic and sauté for 2 more minutes. Add the fresh mushrooms and sauté for several minutes, until they begin to give up their water. Add the pine nuts and Madeira and sauté for 3 minutes. Remove from the heat. Slice the porcini into small strips and toss with the mushroom mixture.

To assemble, place squares of pasta on a working surface. Spread the mushroom mixture over each piece. Carefully roll up the squares of pasta and mushroom and place them in a baking dish into which you have spooned several tablespoons of Chèvre Sauce. Spoon more sauce over each cannelloni. Bake in a 325-degree oven for 15 to 20 minutes. Remove from the oven, place on serving plates, and garnish with fresh chopped herbs. Serve immediately.

Halloween Pasta Rolls

S E R V E S   8

The black and orange pastas that provide a dramatic visual effect as well as a delicious flavor are not essential to the success of this dish. If such exotic pasta is not available to you, try this recipe with a simple fresh pasta dough.

4 sheets black (squid ink) pasta, rolled out
to measure 11 by 16 inches
4 sheets pumpkin-rosemary pasta, rolled
out to measure about 11 by 16 inches
Pumpkin stuffing (recipe follows)
Goat cheese filling (recipe follows)
Olive oil
Chèvre Sauce (page 214)

Fill 2 sheets of black pasta and 2 sheets of pumpkin-rosemary pasta with pumpkin stuffing by spreading the filling across the entire surface of the pasta sheet. Carefully—and fairly tightly—roll the pasta lengthwise and place on a cookie sheet lined with aluminum foil. Brush the surface of the pasta with olive oil.

Fill the remaining 4 sheets of pasta with the goat cheese filling and roll them in the same fashion. Place on a cookie sheet and brush with olive oil. If you are not going to cook the pasta rolls immediately, cover and refrigerate them.

To cook, place the rolls in a 325-degree oven for 20 minutes. While they are cooking, make the Chèvre Sauce.

To serve, place about 2 or 3 tablespoons Chèvre Sauce in the center of each of 8 serving plates. Place half a roll of black pasta and half a roll of orange pasta, each with a different filling, in the center of each plate. Spoon plenty of sauce over the pasta rolls, grind black pepper over the top, and garnish the plates with sprigs of rosemary. Serve immediately.

The pasta rolls may also be sliced about ½-inch thick and served on a platter as an appetizer.

PUMPKIN STUFFING

1 small pumpkin or 3 acorn squash
2 heads garlic
   Several sprigs fresh rosemary
   Olive oil
   Fresh cracked black pepper
1 teaspoon nutmeg

Remove the stem end of the pumpkin, scrape out all the seeds and fibers and cut into large chunks. Place on baking sheet. Remove the loose outer skin from the garlic heads and place in a small baking dish. Place a sprig of rosemary on each piece of pumpkin and one in the baking dish with the garlic. Drizzle both the pumpkin and the garlic with olive oil, adding enough oil to the garlic to cover the bottom of the dish to a depth of about ¼ inch. Add about ½ cup water to garlic and cover tightly. Place both pumpkin and garlic in a 350-degree oven for about 1¼ hours, until the pumpkin is tender when pricked with a fork and the garlic is the texture of soft butter. Remove from the oven and let cool.

When cool enough to handle, scoop the flesh of the pumpkin from the skin, place in a large mixing bowl, and mash well with a

fork. Using your thumb, pull the root from each head of garlic. Place the garlic on a cutting surface and, with the heel of your hand, remove the soft pulp. Add the garlic pulp to the pumpkin and blend together well. Chop enough fresh rosemary leaves to make about 1 tablespoon and add this to mixture. Add about 1 teaspoon fresh cracked black pepper along with the nutmeg. Blend together and taste. Adjust the seasoning. Set aside until ready to use. This mixture may be kept in the refrigerator for 2 to 3 days.

GOAT CHEESE FILLING

2 cups drained fromage blanc
5 ounces pepper or herb goat cheese
8 ounces Taupinière
2 eggs, beaten
½ cup mixed fresh herbs, chopped: Italian
   parsley, thyme, basil, oregano
4 cloves garlic, minced
¼ teaspoon nutmeg
½ teaspoon salt
2 teaspoons puréed chipotle peppers in
   adobo sauce

Blend together the cheeses and stir in the eggs. Add the remaining ingredients and mix until smooth. Taste and adjust seasonings if necessary. Set aside or refrigerate until ready to use.

SONOMA RISOTTO

SERVES 4

The best saffron in the world is produced in Spain and Italy, but with our fertile soil and our wonderful growing conditions, well, you just never know what might happen.

1 tablespoon butter

2 tablespoons extra-virgin olive oil

1 small onion, finely chopped

3 cloves garlic, minced

3 tablespoons calvados or brandy

1 cup Arborio rice

1½ cups homemade chicken stock

2½ cups dry champagne

¾ cup grated dry Jack cheese

¼ cup grated Tome cheese

Salt and freshly ground black pepper

Pinch of saffron (optional)

It will take about 30 minutes of constant attention to make your risotto. Melt the butter with the olive oil in heavy frying pan. Add the onion and sauté for 10 minutes. Add the garlic and sauté for another 2 minutes. Add the calvados or brandy and, very carefully, set it aflame. It will burn itself out quickly, adding a slightly caramelized flavor. Stir in the rice, and cook for 5 minutes, stirring constantly. Have the chicken stock simmering. Over medium heat, begin to add hot stock, ½ cup at a time, to the rice, stirring constantly. Continue to add stock after each addition has been fully absorbed. After the last addition of stock, during the last 10 minutes of the cooking, begin to add the champagne, ¼ cup at a time. Stir constantly so that the rice neither sticks to the pan nor burns. When done, the rice will still be firm to the bite, but the center will not be hard or dry. When it reaches this stage, stir in the cheeses and salt and pepper to taste. The risotto will be creamy. If it seems too dry after the addition of the cheeses, add a little more champagne, being sure to stir well. Remove from the heat and, if using, stir in the saffron. Serve immediately.

WILD MUSHROOM RISOTTO

SERVES 6

Mary Evely, the director of the Food and Wine Program at Simi Winery in Healdsburg, makes use of the abundance of local mushrooms in this recipe from her Winter Luncheon (page 66).

½ pound wild mushrooms, cleaned and cut into ¼-inch pieces

6 tablespoons unsalted butter

1 small clove garlic, minced

Salt and fresh cracked black pepper

4½ cups low-salt chicken stock

3 tablespoons olive oil

¼ cup minced onion

1½ cups Arborio rice

½ cup minced Italian parsley

6 tablespoons grated Asiago cheese

Sauté the mushrooms in 3 tablespoons of the butter over high heat for about 2 minutes. Lower the heat to medium, add the garlic, and sauté briefly. Season with salt and pepper and set aside.

Add water to the chicken stock to increase the amount of liquid to 5½ cups. Bring to a boil and hold over medium-low heat.

Melt the remaining 3 tablespoons butter with the olive oil in a heavy skillet. Add the onion and cook over medium heat until transparent. Add the rice and stir until it is well coated. Add a ladleful of the simmering stock, turn the heat to high, and stir continuously so that rice does not stick to skillet. When the stock has been completely absorbed, add another ladleful. Repeat the procedure until about half the stock has been used. Stir in the mushrooms and parsley and continue adding stock and stirring between ladlesful until the rice is done. It should be firm to the bite, but not dry in the center of the grain.

Remove from the heat and stir in cheese. Top with freshly cracked black pepper and serve immediately.

▼▼▼▼▼▼▼▼▼▼▼▼▼▼▼▼▼▼▼▼▼▼▼▼▼▼▼▼▼▼

POLENTA LOAF WITH PESTO

SERVES 4 TO 6

Several community organizations in Sonoma County sponsor Polenta Feeds as effective fundraisers. If polenta is not a staple in your kitchen, one taste of this creamy, garlic-infused version should make it so. Be sure to look at the appetizer version on page 88.

3½ cups water, lightly salted
1 cup polenta
¼ cup sun-dried tomato bits
5 cloves garlic, pressed
1 cup dry Jack or Parmesan cheese, grated
4 ounces imported Gorgonzola cheese
Extra-virgin olive oil
¾ cup Pesto (page 221)
Sprigs of fresh basil
2 sun-dried tomatoes, packed in oil, cut in strips

Bring the water to a boil in a large, heavy pot. Slowly whisk in the polenta, making sure each addition is well incorporated into the water to avoid lumps. Over medium heat, stir constantly until the mixture thickens. Add the sun-dried tomato bits. Continue to stir until the mixture becomes very thick, for a total of about 20 minutes. Add the garlic and cheeses and remove from the heat. Stir well and set aside.

Coat a 5-cup decorative mold, bread pan, or quiche pan with a liberal quantity of olive oil. Spread one-third of the polenta in the bottom of the mold. Let it sit for a minute or 2. Spread half of the Pesto over the polenta. Repeat. Finish with the final third of the polenta. Let the mold stand in a warm place until the polenta is well set, about 20 minutes. Unmold onto a serving platter and garnish with basil leaves and strips of sun-dried tomatoes.

POULTRY

BROILED CHICKEN WITH MUSTARD

SERVES 4

If you are fond of a particular type of mustard, Matthew's Honey-Jalapeño, for example, or Dry Creek's Fumé Blanc Mustard, try it in this recipe. I love the unmistakable flavor of a traditional Dijon-style mustard, but this dish lends itself well to experimentation. Also try it sometime with Kozlowski Farms Raspberry Mustard, for which I have given a variation.

- 4 half chicken breasts or 8 chicken thighs, bone-in
- 3 cloves garlic
- ½ cup Dijon-style mustard
- 2 teaspoons soy sauce
- 1 teaspoon fresh thyme leaves
- 3 tablespoons olive oil
- 1 cup fresh bread crumbs

Rinse the chicken and pat it dry. Place, skin-side down, under a broiler about 5 or 6 inches away from the heat. Broil for 8 minutes, turn, and broil for 5 minutes.

While the chicken is broiling, make the mustard sauce. Press the garlic into the mustard, add the soy sauce and thyme, and mix. Slowly mix in the olive oil.

Remove the chicken from the oven. Coat the underside (not the skin-side) with plenty of the mustard sauce and then cover with bread crumbs. Place under the broiler for 5 minutes. Turn it carefully. Coat the skin-side with mustard sauce, top with bread crumbs, and broil for 5 minutes. If you like your chicken very well done, broil for an additional 5 minutes before coating it with mustard and bread crumbs and then broil for an additional 5 minutes once it is coated. Serve immediately.

This is excellent served with rice. After you've removed chicken from broiler pan, add a little water to pan, place it over heat, and scrape up the pan drippings. Add any leftover mustard sauce, heat thoroughly, and use as a sauce over the rice.

VARIATION ▾ Use ½ cup raspberry mustard, and substitute 1 tablespoon raspberry vinegar and 1 tablespoon raspberry syrup for the soy sauce. Proceed as above.

▼▼▼▼▼▼▼▼▼▼▼▼▼▼▼▼▼▼▼▼▼▼▼▼▼▼▼▼▼

GRILLED CHICKEN WITH LEMON BUTTER

S E R V E S   6

The matriarch of the Kozlowski family, Mrs. Carmen Kozlowski, is quite a cook. She continues to develop wonderful recipes to be included in the packaging of the company's products and she has offered a delicious version of an old favorite for this book.

  ¾ cup butter
  1 tablespoon grated lemon peel
  6 cloves garlic, crushed
  1 teaspoon thyme
     Salt and pepper
  3 free-range broiler-fryers, halved
  1¾ cups apple cider

Prepare coals for grilling. Blend together the butter, lemon peel, garlic, thyme, salt, and pepper. Make several slits 1-inch long and ½-inch deep in the meaty areas of the chicken and insert 1 teaspoon of the butter mixture into each slit.

Arrange the chicken, skin-side up, on a lightly oiled grill and cook 5 inches from the coals. Baste frequently with the apple cider. Turn after 15 minutes and cook until done, another 5 to 10 minutes.

▼▼▼▼▼▼▼▼▼▼▼▼▼▼▼▼▼▼▼▼▼▼▼▼▼▼▼▼▼▼

CHICKEN WITH HALVED HEADS OF GARLIC IN WINE SAUCE

S E R V E S   4

My editor, John Harris, deserves credit for the inspiration that resulted in this dish. We appeared together on a morning talk show, John talking about garlic and the various garlic festivals occurring that summer, I promoting Cotati's garlic festival and giving a cooking demonstration. This is the dish that evolved from John's suggestion that I try the recipe for Halved Heads of Garlic in Sauce from his Book of Garlic *(Aris, Berkeley, Calif., 1974).*

For this recipe the heads of garlic must be large and firm. Otherwise, when cut in half horizontally, they may fall apart. If you have only small heads of garlic, just cut about a quarter inch off the root end; this will give you a surface to sauté and will keep the bulbs intact.

  4 heads garlic
  2 tablespoons olive oil
  2 tablespoons butter
  1 free-range chicken, cut up, 4 to 5
     pounds

1 cup homemade chicken stock
1 cup dry white wine
3 or 4 jalapeño peppers, chopped
½ cup cilantro leaves (optional)
Salt and pepper to taste

Cut each of the 4 heads of garlic in half, as you would a grapefruit. The cut cloves will be held in their skins much as grapefruit segments are held together. Heat the oil and butter in a saucepan and sauté the bulbs, cut-side down, over moderate heat until the garlic meat begins to brown. Remove from the pan and set aside. In the same pan, brown the pieces of chicken for 4 or 5 minutes on each side. Return the garlic to the pan. Add the chicken stock, wine, and peppers. Cover the pan with a tight lid and braise over low heat until the liquid is reduced and thickened and the garlic cloves are soft when poked with a knife, about 45 to 50 minutes.

To serve, arrange the half heads of garlic cut-side up on a plate with the pieces of chicken. Spoon the sauce over, garnish with the peppers, and cilantro, if using. Eat the garlic as you would an artichoke, using your teeth to pull the purée out of the skin.

CHICKEN AND VEGETABLE PACKETS

SERVES 4

The dishes that Ruth Waltenspiel develops for the dried tomatoes from Timber Crest

Farm are not only delicious, but also are very simple and quick to prepare. For this she uses Sonoma brand Dried Tomato Bits.

Kitchen parchment or aluminum foil
2 cups julienned vegetables: zucchini, carrots, red bell peppers, red onions
4 boned and skinned chicken breast halves, about 6 ounces each
¼ cup (¾ ounce) ground dried tomato
¼ cup lemon juice
Handful fresh basil leaves, if available
4 teaspoons minced garlic
Salt and pepper to taste

Preheat the oven to 400 degrees. Cut four circles each 12 inches in diameter from kitchen parchment or foil. Fold each circle in half and unfold. Divide the vegetables among the four circles, placing next to the fold. Top with the chicken breast halves and sprinkle with the remaining ingredients. Refold the parchment over the chicken so that the cut edges meet. Fold and roll up the edges all the way around to seal. Place on baking sheet and bake for 20 minutes, until the packets are browned and puffed. Transfer to plates and cut open to serve.

CHILLED POACHED BREAST OF CHICKEN

with Yellow Tomato Salsa

SERVES 4

Lisa Hemenway's choice of an entrée for luncheon at the Iron Horse Vineyard (menu on page 61) is very simple to recreate at home.

   4 chicken breasts, each about 8 ounces
   ½ cup olive oil
   1 clove garlic, minced
   1 bunch lemon thyme (reserve a few sprigs
      for garnish), chopped
   ¼ cup lemon juice
      Salt and pepper
   2 cups chicken stock
      Yellow Tomato Salsa (page 220)

Marinate the chicken breasts overnight in olive oil, garlic, lemon thyme, lemon juice, salt, and pepper.

   Heat the oven to 375 degrees. Remove the chicken from the refrigerator, allow to warm to room temperature, place in a baking dish, and cover with hot chicken stock. Bake in the oven until the breasts are done to medium rare, about 12 minutes. Remove from oven and let them cool in the stock. Remove from the stock and chill.

   To serve, place the breasts on individual serving plates, top with Yellow Tomato Salsa, and garnish with a sprig of lemon thyme.

RASPBERRY PATCH CHICKEN

SERVES 4 TO 6

Simple flavors and simple preparation denote this dish; it is perfect on a hot summer night, served with your favorite blush wine. Because it is the chicken I always use, this recipe was developed with Sonoma's local bird, Rocky the Range Chicken, in mind; for the same reason, I would also use Kozlowski Farms' Raspberry syrup.

   1 roasting chicken, preferably free-range
      Salt and pepper
   1 cup fruity white wine
   ¼ cup raspberry syrup
   1 bunch Italian parsley
   2 tablespoons butter
      Fresh raspberries, for garnish

Rinse and pat the chicken dry. Sprinkle it inside and out with salt and pepper. In a small mixing bowl, combine the wine and raspberry syrup. Rub the mixture into the skin of the chicken. Cut the large stems off the parsley and place it in the breast cavity of the chicken. Place the chicken on a rack in a roasting pan and roast in a 425-degree oven for about one hour, until just done, but still moist and tender. When done, remove the chicken from the roasting pan and let it sit for about 15 minutes before carving.

   Place the roasting pan over low heat and with a whisk, scrape up the pan drippings from bottom of pan. Whisk in ½ cup of the syrup and wine mixture and simmer for 5 minutes. Stir in the butter, 1 tablespoon at a time, until melted and the sauce is slightly thickened.

Carve the chicken, place the pieces on a platter and drizzle them with a little of the sauce. Surround with fresh raspberries and pass extra sauce on the side.

▼▼▼▼▼▼▼▼▼▼▼▼▼▼▼▼▼▼▼▼▼▼▼▼▼▼▼▼▼▼▼▼▼▼▼▼

ROAST CHICKEN
with Wild Rice Stuffing
SERVES 4 TO 6

This is my favorite way to prepare roast chicken. The wild rice and the garlic absorb the juices and the flavors of the chicken during the roasting process, making the whole dish rich and succulent.

1 cup wild rice

2 tablespoons dried porcini mushrooms, soaked in ½ cup hot water (optional)

2½ cups chicken stock or 1 can (14½ ounces) chicken broth, diluted with water to make 2½ cups

Olive oil

1 head garlic, cloves separated and peeled

¾ cup shelled pine nuts

2 tablespoons fresh herbs, chopped (I use summer savory, oregano, thyme, and sage)

1 chicken (4 to 5 pounds), free-range if available

Salt and pepper

Wash the wild rice and place it in a medium saucepan. Strain the mushrooms, add the liquid to the chicken stock, and pour over wild rice. Bring to a boil and cook for about 40 minutes, until the liquid has been absorbed.

In a heavy skillet, pour enough olive oil to coat the bottom well. Over medium heat, sauté the whole cloves of garlic for about 3 minutes, stirring constantly. Add the pine nuts and cook for another minute. Remove from the heat and toss the mixture with the wild rice. Cut the reconstituted mushrooms into small pieces and add them to the rice mixture. Stir in the fresh herbs.

Rinse and dry the chicken. Salt and pepper the inner cavity and fill it with the wild rice stuffing. Bind the legs together and place the chicken on a roasting rack. Rub the skin with olive oil and season with salt and pepper.

Roast in 425-degree oven for 20 to 25 minutes per pound. Any extra wild rice stuffing can be placed in a covered baking dish and put in the oven with the chicken for the last 25 minutes of cooking.

When done, remove the chicken from oven and let it stand for 15 minutes before carving. Remove the stuffing to a serving platter, carve the chicken, arrange the pieces around the stuffing, and serve.

▼▼▼▼▼▼▼▼▼▼▼▼▼▼▼▼▼▼▼▼▼▼▼▼▼▼▼▼▼

CHICKEN LIVERS

with Garlic and Chorizo over Pasta

SERVES 4 TO 6

This dish is excellent served with a baked tomato and a salad of roasted sweet peppers and sliced garlic. Those who like both garlic and liver will appreciate this marvelous marriage of ingredients.

> 1 medium onion, minced
> Olive oil
> ½ pound chorizo sausage, bulk or casings removed
> 1 head garlic, minced
> 1½ pounds chicken livers
> 1 teaspoon fresh thyme
> ½ teaspoon sage
> ½ teaspoon allspice
> Juice of 1 lemon
> Salt and pepper
> 1 pound imported, dried spaghetti
> Sprigs of fresh thyme and slices of lemon, for garnish

Sauté the onion in a little olive oil, until transparent. Add the *chorizo* and sauté until almost done. Add the minced garlic and sauté for 2 minutes. With a slotted spoon, remove the *chorizo*, garlic, and onion mixture from the pan to a warm plate. Rinse, dry, and trim the chicken livers. Slice them and sauté quickly in the pan juices. Return the *chorizo* mixture to the pan and toss well with the livers. Add the herbs, allspice, and lemon juice. Cook the pasta according to package directions. Drain and toss with just

enough olive oil to coat. Place on large serving platter, top with the livers, and garnish with sprigs of thyme and slices of lemon.

▼▼▼▼▼▼▼▼▼▼▼▼▼▼▼▼▼▼▼▼▼▼▼▼▼▼▼▼▼

DUCK WITH RASPBERRY SAUCE

SERVES 2

The chef, Josef Heller, offers this succulent dish as the main course of his Taste of Sonoma Dinner, the menu for which is on page 62.

> 1 duck, 4½ pounds
> 1 carrot
> 1 stalk celery
> ¼ small leek
> 1 medium onion
> 2 cups chicken or beef stock
> 2 tablespoons brandy
> 1 pint fresh raspberries, puréed, with a few berries set aside for garnish
> 1 teaspoon honey
> 2 teaspoons sugar
> 2 teaspoons soy sauce

Separate the duck breasts from the leg and thigh pieces. Season the duck with salt and sauté in a little olive oil until golden brown. Place in a roasting pan and bake at 400 degrees for 45 minutes. Remove the breasts from oven and set aside. Chop the vegetables coarsely, add them to the roasting pan, and cook for another 45 minutes. Remove legs and thighs, add the stock or boullion, brandy, and raspberries to the pan, and simmer for 15 to 20 minutes. Strain the sauce and discard the vegetables. Add the honey, sugar, and soy sauce.

Bring the duck to the proper serving temperature in a hot oven. Place 1 leg and 1 half-breast on each of 2 serving plates. Spoon sauce over, garnish with a few fresh raspberries, and serve.

▼▼▼▼▼▼▼▼▼▼▼▼▼▼▼▼▼▼▼▼▼▼▼▼▼▼▼▼▼▼

ROAST DUCKLING

with Madeira and Black Currants

SERVES 4

Most of the preparation for this recipe is done the day before serving; the results are delicious and certainly worth the extra time for a special dinner. Sautéed red potatoes and green beans make an excellent accompaniment. My thanks are due to Bob Engle of Russian River Vineyards whose recipe it is. It was originally published in his book, A Chef's Notebook.

PREPARATION DAY

¼ teaspoon fennel or anise seed
½ teaspoon caraway seed
3 tablespoons paprika
¼ teaspoon white pepper
¼ teaspoon salt
   Generous pinch of allspice
2 ducklings
1 small onion
1 stalk celery

Roast the seeds in a 350-degree oven on a pie tin for 5 minutes to develop the flavor. Grind in a mortar and pestle and combine with the other spices.

Pull the excess fat out of the cavities of the duckling and rinse them, inside and out, with water. Cut off the neck and the wings at the first joint. Pierce the skin with a small sharp knife a couple of times along the breast bone and somewhat more numerously around the thighs and under the wings where the fatty deposits lie.

Sprinkle the skin generously with the seasonings mixture. Lay the ducks, necks, and wing tips in a roasting pan and bake in a 350-degree oven for 25 minutes per pound. Do not use too shallow a pan as the ducks release a great deal of fat.

When the ducks are done, pour off the fat and juices into a container and chill. Set the ducks aside to cool (but do not chill).

Bone the ducklings (see the instructions at the end of the recipe) and refrigerate until the next day.

In a large pot, place the wing tips, necks, backbones, ribs, and any other leftover parts of the ducklings, along with the onion and celery. Just cover with water. Bring to a boil and keep at a strong simmer for several hours to concentrate the flavors and reduce the stock. You should end up with about a quart of duck stock. Strain and refrigerate.

SERVING DAY

> Pan drippings from roasting the
>   ducklings
> Duck stock
> ⅓ cup Madeira
> 4 tablespoons black currants
> 1½ teaspoons raspberry vinegar
> 3 tablespoons cornstarch
> ½ cup water
> Roasted ducklings

Remove the fat from the top of the pan drippings and stock and discard. Combine the pan drippings and the stock in a heavy pot and reduce to about 3 cups. Add the Madeira, currants, and vinegar to the stock and continue reducing until you have 1½ cups of sauce. Mix the cornstarch and water and pour in a thin stream into the sauce, whisking continually. Cook for 5 minutes to thicken. Keep the sauce warm or reheat when needed.

Lay the duck on a sheet pan and bake in a 375-degree oven for 20 minutes. Divide among 4 serving plates and cover with a generous ladle of the sauce.

TO CARVE A DUCK

First of all, look carefully at the duck to see how it is put together. Familiarity with the structure of what it is you need to bone will make the task much easier. Begin by cutting the duck apart at the back bone, using a knife or poultry shears. Next cut straight down the center of the breast bone. The duck will now be in two halves. Use your fingers to pull the breast bone and ribs out from the inside. With a sharp knife cut the breast portion (breast and wing) and leg portion (leg and thigh) apart. Use the tip of the knife to find the hip joints and shoulder joints, and cut at these points to separate carcass. When serving, interlock leg with wing to make an attractively presented portion.

FIESTA SONOMA GRILLED TURKEY

SERVES 6

This recipe, from Rich and Saralee Kunde of Sonoma Grapevines, Inc., first appeared in Season by Season, The Sonoma County Farmers Market Cookbook.

> Half a bunch cilantro
> ½ cup lime juice
> ½ cup Sauvignon Blanc wine
> ½ cup olive oil
> 4 cloves garlic, crushed
> 6 fillets of turkey breast, 6 to 8 ounces
>   each
> Salt and pepper to taste
> Slices of fresh lime

Clean and chop the cilantro and remove the large stems. You should have about ½ cup of leaves. Combine the cilantro with the lime juice, wine, olive oil, and crushed garlic to make a marinade. Pour the marinade over the turkey, cover tightly, and refrigerate for several hours, preferably overnight.

Season the turkey with salt and pepper, and grill 6 inches above medium-hot coals for 8 minutes on each side. Brush with the marinade several times during grilling to give the meat a beautiful golden color.

Serve with a squeeze of fresh lime juice and garnish with slices of lime.

TURKEY RAVIOLI

with Sage Cream Sauce

MAKES 4 DOZEN RAVIOLI,
2½ INCHES SQUARE

I have been thoroughly spoiled by Pasta Etc. I love to work with their fresh pasta and have developed a number of recipes particularly suited to what they offer. If you have a fresh pasta store near you, cultivate a relationship with the staff. If not, you will need to learn to make your own fresh pasta to use recipes such as this one.

- 3 small shallots, minced
  Olive oil
- 1 clove garlic, minced
- 1 pound freshly ground turkey meat
- 2 teaspoons dried sage
- 1 tablespoon finely minced fresh sage
  Freshly ground black pepper
  Salt
- 4 sheets fresh sage pasta, rolled out to measure approximately 11 by 16 inches

- 1 egg white
- 2 tablespoons butter
- 2 tablespoons flour
- 2 cups half-and-half
  Sprigs fresh sage

Sauté 2 of the shallots in a little olive oil until transparent. Add the garlic and sauté for another minute. Add the turkey and sauté until nearly done, breaking up the meat with a fork as it cooks. Add 1 teaspoon ground sage, 1 tablespoon fresh sage, 1 teaspoon black pepper, blend well, and taste. Add salt and more pepper to taste. Cool the turkey mixture until it is easy to handle. It can also be held overnight with no loss of flavor.

To make ravioli, spread out 1 sheet of pasta on your working surface. Score the pasta and cut it into 24 squares, each just slightly larger than 2½ by 2½ inches. Place a teaspoon of the turkey mixture in the center of each of half the number of squares, that is, 12. Quickly brush the edges with a little egg white. Top each square of filled pasta with another square, and seal quickly by pressing the two pieces of pasta together with the tines of a fork. Set aside on a piece of waxed paper and cover with more waxed paper. Repeat until all the pasta is used.

Melt the butter in heavy saucepan and sauté the remaining shallot until transparent. Stir in the flour and the remaining 1 teaspoon of dried sage, crushed, blend well, and cook for 2 minutes. Slowly pour in the half-and-half, whisking continuously. Add a sprig or two of fresh thyme. Simmer for 15 minutes, until the sauce begins to thicken. Remove the sage sprigs before serving.

Gently simmer the ravioli in 2 or 3 batches, until the pasta is tender, about 4 minutes. Drain quickly and carefully, arrange on serving plates, and top with the sage cream sauce. Garnish with a sprig of fresh sage and a sprinkling of freshly ground black pepper.

VARIATION ▾ To make triangular ravioli, rather than the traditional squares, cut the pieces of pasta slightly larger, place the turkey near one corner, brush the edges with egg white, and fold the pasta over to form the triangle. Seal as you would any ravioli, using the tines of a fork.

▼▼▼

ROAST TURKEY OR FREE-RANGE CHICKEN

with Cajun Dressing

S E R V E S   8   T O   1 0   (4   T O   6)

This recipe is excellent with both turkey and free-range chicken, which is rich enough to stand up to its spiciness. It is wonderful when made with Brother Juniper's Cajun Three-Pepper Bread, but a good sourdough should be substituted when that is not available. The smaller quantities given in parentheses are for use with a smaller bird, a chicken of 4 to 5 pounds. Make the larger quantity and you should have enough to stuff a 10 to 12-pound turkey.

½ + ¼ cup butter (⅓ cup + 2 tablespoons)

1 cup chopped yellow onion (1 small)

3 cups chopped celery (2 cups)

1 bay leaf

¼ cup minced garlic (2 tablespoons)

1 pound fresh andouille sausage, casings removed (½ pound)

½ pound chicken gizzards, finely chopped (4 ounces)

¼ pound chicken livers, finely chopped (2 ounces)

2 teaspoons crushed dried oregano

2 teaspoons dried thyme

1 teaspoon freshly cracked black pepper

1 teaspoon salt

1 teaspoon dried mustard

1 teaspoon ground cumin

10 cups cubed Cajun Three-Pepper Bread or sourdough bread (6 cups)

3 eggs

1 tablespoon + 2 teaspoons Tabasco sauce (3 teaspoons)

1 turkey (10 to 12 pounds) or 1 roasting chicken (4 to 5 pounds)

Melt ½ cup (⅓ cup) of the butter in large sauté pan. Sauté the onion for about 10 minutes. Add the celery and bay leaf and sauté until the celery is soft. Add the garlic and sauté for 2 minutes. Crumble in the sausage and cook for 10 minutes, until the sausage is about half done. Add the chicken gizzards and livers and sauté for 5 minutes. Remove the bay leaf. Add all the dried herbs and spices to the meat mixture and toss well. Place the bread cubes in a large mixing bowl, add the meat mixture, and toss together until well blended. Beat the eggs with the tablespoon (2 teaspoons) of Tabasco sauce, pour over the bread mixture, and toss.

Preheat the oven to 450 degrees.

To stuff the bird, rinse, pat it dry, season the breast cavity with salt and pepper, and make sure not to pack the stuffing in too tightly. Close the cavities and place the bird on a rack in a roasting pan. Melt the remaining butter and Tabasco sauce together and baste the skin of bird with the mixture.

Cover with tent of aluminum foil, place in the oven, and reduce the heat to 325 degrees. Cook smaller birds for 20 minutes per pound; larger birds for 15 minutes per pound. For the last third of the cooking time, remove the aluminum foil and baste bird with the butter and Tabasco mixture frequently, every 15 minutes or so. Remove from oven when stuffing reaches an internal temperature of about 160 degrees. Let the bird rest for 15 minutes before carving. Place extra dressing in a baking dish and cook it with bird for the last 30 minutes.

SEAFOOD

CRAB CAKES WITH BLACK BEANS

SERVES 4

Everyone loves crab cakes, and this version is exceptionally good. Since fresh crab is so plentiful around the holidays, I frequently serve this as a New Year's Day brunch, with a bottle of Van der Kamp's Midnight Cuveé sparkling wine, and poached pears or apples for dessert. What a great way to start a new year.

BLACK BEANS

- ¾ cup black beans
  Water to cover + 2 inches
- 1 small onion, quartered
  Several whole cloves garlic
- 4 stalks celery, cut in 4-inch pieces
- ¾ teaspoon ground cumin
- ½ teaspoon salt
- 1 teaspoon Tabasco sauce

Soak the beans overnight. Drain and rinse them, place in a cooking pot, cover with water, and add the onion, garlic, and celery. Cook for about 1½ hours, until the beans fall apart. With tongs, remove all the vegetables and discard. Purée the beans. Stir in the cumin, salt, and Tabasco. Return to the heat and simmer the purée for about 10 minutes, stirring frequently to prevent it from sticking. Set aside and reheat gently just before serving.

CRAB CAKES

- 3 tablespoons butter
- ¼ cup minced onion
- 1 or 2 jalapeño peppers, seeded and minced
- ⅔ cup celery, finely chopped
- 3 eggs, well beaten
- ¾ cup heavy cream
- 1½ cups fresh bread crumbs
- 3 cups fresh flaked crab meat
- 1 tablespoon good quality Dijon-style mustard
- 2 tablespoons fresh lemon juice

3 tablespoons chopped Italian parsley
    Salt and pepper to taste
    Flour and butter, for frying
8 wedges lime and several sprigs
    cilantro, for garnish

Melt the butter in a sauté pan. Add the onions and sauté until they are translucent. Add the *jalapeños* and cook for another 3 minutes. Add the celery and cook for 2 or 3 minutes. Remove from the heat and set aside to cool briefly. Add the vegetables to the beaten eggs. Stir in the cream and add 1 cup of the bread crumbs, the crab meat, mustard, lemon, juice, and parsley. Add salt and pepper to taste and chill for at least 2 hours.

If the crab mixture is too moist to be formed easily into cakes, add the remaining ½ cup of bread crumbs. Form into cakes about 3-inches across and dust lightly on both sides with flour. Melt butter in a heavy skillet until foamy. Sauté the cakes for about 4 minutes on each side. Serve immediately, with the black beans: Ladle about ½ to ¾ cup black beans in the center of each of 4 serving plates. Agitate the plate so the beans form a pool over the surface of the plate. Place 2 crab cakes on top of each plate of sauce. Garnish each plate with 2 wedges of lime and several sprigs of cilantro. Pass extra limes and extra chopped cilantro on the side.

▼▼▼▼▼▼▼▼▼▼▼▼▼▼▼▼▼▼▼▼▼▼▼▼▼▼▼▼▼▼▼▼▼▼▼▼▼

PASTA WITH CLAMS, GARLIC, AND JALAPEÑOS

SERVES 4

Know your peppers! *I have accidentally made this dish so hot that it felt as if it were searing our skin as we ate it. Peppers vary greatly in heat and, if you run across a particularly hot batch, be sure to discard all of the seeds and the interior ribs, where the heat is most intense. Also, be sure to protect your hands with gloves during the preparation. The oil from the peppers remains on your skin and, if you mistakenly rub your eyes or other delicate tissues, you will suffer considerable pain.*

 2 tablespoons olive oil
 2 tablespoons butter
6 to 10 cloves garlic, minced
 2 jalapeño peppers, seeded and minced
 2 tablespoons chopped Italian parsley
½ cup dry white wine
 1 small can (6 ounces) minced clams
 2 pounds fresh clams, in their shells
    Salt
½ pound dried angel hair pasta
¼ cup chopped cilantro
    Jalapeño Aïoli (page 212) (optional)

Heat the olive oil and butter in a heavy skillet. Add the garlic and peppers and sauté for 2 minutes. Add the parsley, wine, and all the clams, with the liquid from the canned clams. Bring to a simmer, cover, and steam the clams open.

Meanwhile, cook the pasta in plenty of

boiling salted water and drain. Place the pasta in a large serving bowl and pour the sauce over, holding the fresh clams back in the pan. Toss the pasta and sauce, top with the clams, and sprinkle with chopped cilantro. Serve immediately, with a spoonful of *Jalapeño Aïoli* on each serving.

STEAMED MUSSELS

with Chardonnay and Fresh Herbs

S E R V E S   4

Bob Engel and Christine Topolos, who are the chefs at The Russian River Vineyards, have provided this recipe as part of their Fall Dinner Menu on page 65.

- 4 dozen mussels
- 2 tablespoons olive oil
- 2 tablespoons butter
- 1 teaspoon minced garlic, or more or less, to taste
- 1 tablespoon fresh minced herbs: parsley, thyme, oregano, dill, or any combination of these
- ½ cup Chardonnay wine

Scrub the mussels and pull their beards off. Heat the olive oil and butter together in a broad shallow skillet over medium-high heat. Add the mussels and shake to coat them with oil. Add the garlic and reduce the heat if necessary to keep the garlic from browning. Sauté for 2 minutes or so, add

the wine and herbs, cover, and steam until the mussels have opened.

FRESH HALIBUT WRAPPED IN CHARD

with Lobster and Ginger Beurre Blanc

S E R V E S   4

John Ash begins his Spring Luncheon (page 62) with this delicately delicious steamed halibut. The Beurre Blanc, with its sweet, seductive scent of fresh ginger, draws together the various flavors and textures into a medley of sheer delight. It is a good idea to make the Lobster and Ginger Beurre Blanc before you begin preparation of the halibut. You can hold it over warm water until you are ready to use, but not for longer than one hour.

- 4 pieces very fresh halibut, 5 ounces each
  Salt and pepper
- 4 medium leaves Swiss chard, blanched and hard stems removed
- 6 ounces mushrooms, thinly sliced
- 1 bunch scallions, thinly sliced
- 2 tablespoons butter
  White wine
- 2 small leeks, cut in small julienne
- 2 medium carrots, cut in small julienne
- 1 sweet red pepper, cut in small julienne
- 3 ounces shiitake mushrooms, sliced, with tough stems removed

Lobster and Ginger Beurre Blanc
(page 213)

¼ cup salmon caviar

Season the halibut lightly with salt and pepper. Wrap each piece in a leaf of chard. In a sauté pan, quickly cook the regular mushrooms and scallions in 1 tablespoon of butter. Place the wrapped fish on top of the mixture, add a splash of dry white wine, cover, and cook gently until the fish is barely done, about 8 to 10 minutes.

Quickly blanch the julienned vegetables, drain, toss them together, and set aside, warm. Sauté the shiitake mushrooms in the remaining butter and set aside. Remove the fish from the heat.

On a warm plate, spoon some of the *Beurre Blanc* and agitate the plate to distribute the sauce evenly. Arrange a bed of the julienned vegetables in the center. Place the cooked fish on top, spoon more *Beurre Blanc* over the fish, and garnish with the lightly cooked, sliced shiitake mushrooms and fresh salmon caviar.

SMOKY SWEET SALMON

SERVES 4

The sweetness of the salmon blends wonderfully with the smoky flavor of the chipotle peppers in the salsa. The pineapple adds a bright element that makes the dish perfect on a hot summer night. Fettuccini Armando (page 129) would make a wonderful

accompaniment, complemented by a chilled Gewürztraminer.

4 fresh salmon fillets
Smoky Sweet Salsa (page 220)
Slices of fresh pineapple
Sprigs of cilantro

To grill, have the coals hot. Brush the salmon fillets with a little of the liquid from the Salsa and place on the grill. Cook until the salmon is heated through and has just turned pink. Do not overcook. Place the fillets on individual serving plates and spoon Salsa down the center of each. Garnish with a slice of pineapple and sprig of cilantro. Serve immediately.

VARIATIONS

▼ If you cannot grill the salmon, broil it, again being sure not to overcook it.

▼ Poached, chilled salmon would be delicious served with this salsa.

FISH, FANTASTIC AND FAST

SERVES 4

Timber Crest Farms developed this recipe to highlight their Sonoma brand Dried Tomato Bits, which it does beautifully. This makes a perfect dinner when you are really too busy, but still want a home-cooked meal. I would serve it with pasta tossed with butter and Vella Dry Jack cheese and a green salad.

4 fillets fish (snapper, sea bass, or orange roughy), each about 6 ounces
¼ cup ground dried tomato
¼ cup lemon juice
2 tablespoons fresh thyme
4 teaspoons minced fresh garlic
 Salt and pepper

Preheat the oven to 400 degrees. Place the fish on individual pieces of aluminum foil or kitchen parchment. Top the fish with the ground tomato, lemon juice, thyme, garlic, salt, and pepper. Wrap the fish and seal the edges by folding securely. Place on baking sheet and bake for 12 minutes. Remove to individual plates and serve immediately.

▼▼▼▼▼▼▼▼▼▼▼▼▼▼▼▼▼▼▼▼▼▼▼▼▼▼▼▼▼▼▼▼▼▼▼▼▼

SNAPPER WITH CAYENNE, GARLIC, AND LEMON

SERVES 4

I had a friend who always complained about fish being "boring." He had just been told that his blood pressure was extremely high and he would have to cut down on the huge amount of red meat he consumed daily. He acted as if he were completely deprived, whining endlessly about the fish he was condemned to eat for the rest of his life.

To shut him up, I came up with this recipe. He liked it, but did not stop complaining.

¼ cup all-purpose flour
2 tablespoons cayenne pepper
4 medium-sized snapper fillets
 Butter for sautéing
8 cloves garlic, finely minced
½ cup white wine
 Juice of 2 lemons

Mix the flour and cayenne together. Dredge the fillets in the flour mixture, making sure that the fish is well coated. In a heavy skillet, preferably of cast iron, melt 2 or 3 tablespoons butter. Sauté the garlic for 2 minutes. Add as many fillets of fish as will fit comfortably in the pan. Sauté for about 3 minutes, then turn. Add ¼ cup of the wine and the juice of 1 lemon. Cover the pan. Cook for about 5 minutes, until fish is just done, not overdone. Add more butter to the pan and repeat the process until all the fish is cooked. Hold the fish in a warm oven. Add another 2 tablespoons butter to the pan, allow it to melt, and stir in more lemon juice to make a sauce with the butter and pan drippings. Pour the sauce over fish and serve.

RISOTTO

with Snapper and Pesto

SERVES 4 TO 6

Nothing can replace a properly made risotto, and I find the constant attention that it demands a rather soothing, focused way to spend thirty minutes or so. Obviously, it is not something you will always have the time to do, but when the opportunity presents itself, this is a delicious untraditional twist on the standard version of the classic Italian dish.

Be sure to have all your ingredients assembled and well organized because the timing of this dish is important: the Pesto may be made first and set aside at room temperature; time the cooking of the risotto and the fish so that the fish is done slightly before the risotto. The fish may be held briefly in a warm oven and you need to give the risotto your full attention for the last five minutes of its cooking. Then, once it is done, the dish should be assembled quickly and served as soon as possible.

RISOTTO
- 1 can (14.5 ounces) chicken broth mixed with 3 cups water
- 2 tablespoons butter
- 3 tablespoons extra-virgin olive oil
- ½ small yellow onion, finely chopped
- 1 cup raw Arborio rice
- ¾ cup freshly grated dry Jack cheese

SNAPPER
- 3 to 4 tablespoons butter
- Several cloves garlic, minced
- ¼ cup flour, mixed with 1 teaspoon white pepper and ½ teaspoon salt
- 4 fillets snapper
- ¼ cup dry white wine
- ½ cup Pesto (page 221)
- Sprigs of fresh basil, for garnish

To make the risotto, bring the broth to a steady simmer. Place 1 tablespoon butter and the olive oil in a heavy skillet. When the butter is melted, sauté the onion over medium-high heat until translucent. Add the rice and stir well to coat thoroughly. Sauté for 2 minutes. Add ½ a cup of the simmering broth and stir well as it cooks. Scrape the sides of the pan and be sure to loosen any rice that may stick to the bottom of the pan. The cooking should be lively, but not so rapid that the liquid evaporates too quickly. Adjust the heat accordingly. Add more liquid, ½ a cup at a time. The rice is done when it is tender, but still firm to the bite. Near the end of the cooking, after about 20 minutes, it is a good idea to add the liquid ¼ cup at a time so as not to drown the near-done rice.

When you estimate that the rice is about 5 minutes from being done, add the remaining 1 tablespoon of butter and all of the cheese. Mix well. Taste the risotto and salt it if necessary.

To sauté the snapper, melt the butter in a heavy skillet and sauté the garlic for 1 minute. Dredge the snapper in the flour mixture, shake to remove any excess, and sauté the fish on one side for 3 or 4 minutes. Turn the fillets and add the wine. Sauté for another 3 or 4 minutes. If necessary, hold in a warm oven until the risotto is ready.

To serve, place the risotto in a serving

dish, top with the sautéed snapper, and spoon the Pesto over. (Have the Pesto at room temperature and add 2 tablespoons very hot water before spooning it onto the risotto and fish.) Garnish with basil sprigs and serve immediately.

SEAFOOD STEW

SERVES 4 TO 6

Achiote, a spice blend based upon the annatto seed and imported from Mexico is what makes this Seafood Stew so delicious. Achiote can be hard to find, so I suggest your stocking up when you do find it. A good version of this dish can be made without it but, with the achiote, *it is spectacular.*

1 cup sliced leeks, white part only, or 1 cup yellow onion, diced
4 tablespoons olive oil
2 jalapeño peppers, seeded and diced
6 cloves garlic, minced
2 cups peeled, sliced Roma tomatoes
4 cups chicken stock
1 cup new red potatoes, diced
1 cup zucchini, diced
½ pound dried imported pasta, in small shapes

1 pound marinated snapper fillets (recipe follows)
Fresh cilantro
Fresh limes
Flour tortillas
Tabasco sauce, or other hot sauce

In a large, heavy pan sauté the leeks or onions in the olive oil for about 15 minutes. Add the *jalapeños* and garlic and sauté for 3 more minutes. Add the tomatoes, sauté for 5 minutes, and add the chicken stock. Add the potatoes, simmer for 10 minutes and add the zucchini. (If you are not going to serve the stew immediately, remove it from the heat at this time and chill until 30 minutes before serving.)

About 20 minutes before serving, add the dried pasta. Simmer for 10 minutes. Meanwhile, cut the marinated fillets into 1- to 1½-inch chunks. Add them to the stew and simmer for 10 minutes. Serve with fresh cilantro, quartered limes, and hot flour tortillas. Pass the hot sauce.

VARIATION ▼ Serve Garlic and Cilantro Sauce (page 214) with the stew, instead of the cilantro and wedges of lime.

MARINATED SNAPPER FILLETS
3 tablespoons achiote
¼ teaspoon cayenne pepper
3 cloves garlic, pressed
2 tablespoons hot water
1 tablespoon fresh lime juice
1 pound snapper fillets (or other fish)

Blend the *achiote*, pepper, garlic, water, and lime juice together to make the marinade. It should be the consistency of heavy cream. Thin with a little more water if necessary. Rub each fillet thoroughly with the marinade, place in a baking dish and pour any leftover marinade on the fish. Marinate for at least 1 hour or overnight if possible.

TOMATO-JALAPEÑO PASTA WITH CAYENNE SNAPPER AND CORN SALSA

SERVES 4

*I developed this recipe especially for Mendocino Pasta Co.'s Master Chef recipe series, a special feature on the back of each package of their fresh dried pasta. Tomato-*jalapeño *pasta is the perfect companion to the snapper and salsa, but the dish is almost as delicious with a plain, dried pasta.*

    2 fillets of snapper or butterfish, rock cod, sole, or orange roughy
    ¼ cup all-purpose flour
    1 tablespoon cayenne pepper
2 to 3 tablespoons butter
    1 tablespoon garlic, minced
      Juice of 1 lemon
    8 ounces tomato- and jalapeño-flavored pasta or 8 ounces plain, dried pasta

    3 cups Corn Salsa (page 219)
      Sprigs of cilantro

Have a large pot of rapidly boiling water ready when you begin this recipe. Rinse and pat the fish fillets dry. Mix the flour and cayenne pepper together and dredge the fillets in the mixture. Make sure that they are well coated and then pat or shake them to remove excess flour.

In a heavy skillet or on a griddle, melt the butter until it is foamy. Add the garlic and sauté for 1 minute. Add the fillets, sauté for 4 minutes, and turn. Squeeze the juice of the lemon over and cook until the fish is done, another 4 to 5 minutes. When you turn the fillets, put the pasta into boiling water, cook according to the directions on the package, and drain. In a large bowl, place 2 cups of the Corn Salsa. Top with the cooked pasta and toss well. Place the pasta on individual serving plates and top each serving with a fillet of snapper. Top the snapper with several spoonsful of Corn Salsa and garnish with a sprig of cilantro. Serve immediately and pass any extra Corn Salsa on the side.

GRILLED TUNA WITH CORN SALSA AND TORTILLAS

SERVES 4

The whole-wheat tortillas made by the Alvarado Street Bakery are a perfect accompaniment to this dish, but are not essential to its success. If they are unavailable, substitute your favorite type of tortilla.

4 tuna steaks, each about 1-inch thick and
    weighing about 6 ounces
4 whole-wheat tortillas
    Corn Salsa (page 219)
    Wedges of lime
    Sprigs of cilantro

If using an outdoor grill, prepare the coals 45 minutes before you need to cook the fish. Grill the tuna briefly, for 4 or 5 minutes on each side, or broil. The tuna should be cooked only until it is rare. Heat the tortillas while the tuna is cooking. Place the tortillas on four plates, top with the tuna steak, and place about ¼ cup Corn Salsa on top of each serving. Garnish with wedges of lime and sprigs of cilantro. Pass extra Corn Salsa on the side.

TUNA TOSTADAS

SERVES 4

I was well into my adult years before I ever tasted fresh tuna and I could not believe that anything so delicious had been shoved into a can for so many years. Why the taste of fresh tuna was such a well-kept culinary secret for so long, I have no idea. Another point in favor of fresh tuna is that it is not harvested by the inhumane methods that are used for tuna that is to be canned, methods that kill not only the desired tuna, but also the dolphins who swim with them. You can eat delicious, tender fresh tuna with a quiet conscience.

1 pound albacore tuna steaks
⅔ cup lemon juice
⅓ cup olive oil
1 cup black beans
2 stalks celery
5 whole cloves garlic
1 small onion, quartered
2 jalapeño peppers
1 teaspoon cumin seed
1 teaspoon salt
4 corn tortillas
2 tomatoes, if in season, chopped
    Avocado Salsa (page 219)
1 bunch cilantro

The night before serving, marinate the albacore in the lemon juice and olive oil. Soak the black beans in plenty of water.

The next day, drain and rinse beans. Cover with fresh water and add the celery, garlic cloves, and onion, cut in quarters. Add whole peppers, cumin seed, and salt, and simmer over medium heat until the beans are tender, about 40 minutes. Stir occasionally and make sure that the beans do not become too dry, adding water as necessary. When the beans are done, remove them from the heat and discard the celery, garlic, peppers, and onion. When the garlic is cool enough to handle, remove the pulp from the cloves, mash it, and stir it into the beans. Taste and correct seasonings.

Grill or broil the albacore until just done, about 4 minutes on each side for 1-inch steaks. Fry the tortillas until just crisp. Place tortillas on individual serving plates and top each with about ½ cup black beans, drained of excess liquid. Cut the albacore in chunks and divide among the servings, place it on top of the beans. Surround with tomatoes and top with a few sprigs of cilantro. Top cilantro with 2 tablespoons of Avocado Salsa. Garnish with cilantro leaves. Serve immediately and pass remaining salsa on the side.

MEAT

BEEF AND SHIITAKES ON SKEWERS

SERVES 6

Precook the mushrooms briefly in the marinade to make them juicy and succulent when grilled.

- 2 pounds beef tenderloin, cut into 1½-inch cubes
- 1 cup hearty red wine, such as a Zinfandel or Cabernet
- ½ cup fresh lemon juice
- ½ cup olive oil
- 5 cloves garlic, crushed
- 2 teaspoons fresh thyme
  Salt and pepper
  About a dozen 12-inch wooden skewers
  About 24 small to medium-sized shiitake mushrooms, stems removed
  About 24 cherry tomatoes
- 3 medium red onions, quartered or

about 12 very small torpedo onions
- 1 large or 2 small red peppers, cut into 1½-inch squares
- 3 to 4 cups steamed rice

The night before serving, place beef in a nonreactive bowl or crock. Mix together the wine, lemon juice, olive oil, garlic, and thyme. Taste and season with salt and pepper. Pour over beef and refrigerate. Remove from refrigerator about 1 hour before assembling and cooking. At that time, soak the wooden skewers in water until ready to use.

Half an hour before assembling the skewers, heat about 1 cup of the marinade in a small saucepan. Brush the mushrooms clean, remove any hard stems, and place them in the marinade. Simmer for 3 or 4 minutes. Remove the mushrooms with a slotted spoon and drain on paper towels.

To assemble, place 3 or 4 cubes of beef alternately with vegetables, including mushrooms, onto skewers. Grill the kabobs for about 5 minutes on each side. You may also broil the kabobs, turning them after 5 minutes. Heat the marinade. Serve the kabobs over steamed rice and spoon a little marinade over each serving.

VARIATION ▾ If you can find them, you might try substituting crimini mushrooms for the shiitakes. They are similar to the common white mushroom, but have a greater depth of flavor. They are available in Sonoma, organically grown. See the Glossary for more details.

▾▾

SONOMA FAJITAS

S E R V E S   4   T O   6

This recipe won the award in the Best Use of Wine category and a Gold Medal in the 1989 Sonoma County Harvest Fair. It is a very simple dish and one that works well for a summer barbeque. The slight sweetness that the meat takes on from the marinade is a wonderful counterpoint to the spicy acidity of the Corn Salsa. My tortillas came from the Alvarado Street Bakery; others might be substituted.

1½	pounds skirt steak
2	cups poaching liquid from the recipe for Gravenstein Chutney (page 224) or Red Wine Marinade (recipe follows)
4 to 6	whole-wheat tortillas
	Corn Salsa (page 219)
	Sprigs of cilantro
	Wedges of lime

The night before serving, cut the skirt steak into 4-inch strips and place in a shallow dish. Pour the marinade over, cover, and refrigerate. Remove from the refrigerator 1 hour before cooking.

If you are cooking the steak on a charcoal grill, prepare the coals when you remove the steak from the refrigerator. A stove-top grill will also give excellent results.

To cook, remove the steak from the marinade and place on the hot grill. Turn after 3 or 4 minutes for rare steak. Grill on other side for another 3 or 4 minutes. While the steak is grilling, heat the tortillas until they are soft and warm, but not crisp. Remove the steak from the grill, slice in thin strips, and place in the center of the tortillas. Place on individual serving plates or large platter. Top each tortilla with 2 tablespoons of Corn Salsa and garnish with cilantro and lime. Serve immediately and pass more salsa on the side.

RED WINE MARINADE

2	cups red wine
½	cup apple juice
¼	cup sugar
4	cloves garlic, sliced
¼	teaspoon nutmeg
	Juice of 1 lemon

Combine the ingredients and stir over low heat until the sugar has melted. Remove from the heat and allow to cool before using.

SONOMA MEATLOAF

SERVES 6 TO 8

For the ultimate comfort meal, try this with Sonoma Risotto (page 137), a simple green salad, and Apples Poached in Port (page 229); it is perfect for a rainy winter night. This recipe is well named: I would use Sonoma brand Dried Tomato Bits and Dried Tomato Tapenade and Vella's Dry Jack cheese. The Tome is a dried goat cheese made by Laura Chenel.

    1 small onion, minced
    1 shallot, minced
    3 tablespoons olive oil (from roasting
        garlic, if available)
    4 cloves garlic, minced
 1¼ pounds ground chuck
    ½ pound ground pork
    ½ cup ground dried tomatoes
    ⅔ cup grated dry Jack cheese
    ⅓ cup grated Tome (dried goat cheese)
    2 eggs, beaten
    ½ cup Roasted Garlic Purée (page 222)
    ¾ cup fresh bread crumbs
    2 tablespoons chopped Italian parsley
    1 tablespoon chopped fresh herbs: mar-
        joram, thyme, oregano
    1 teaspoon salt
    1 teaspoon fresh ground pepper
    ½ cup oil-packed dried tomatoes

Sauté the onion and shallot in the olive oil until soft and transparent. Do not allow them to brown. Add the minced garlic and sauté for another 2 minutes. In a medium-sized mixing bowl blend together the beef, pork, and sautéed onion mixture. Add the ground dried tomatoes and the cheeses, followed by the eggs, garlic purée, bread-crumbs, herbs, and salt and pepper. Mix well until all the ingredients are evenly distributed throughout the mixture.

Pack the meatloaf mixture firmly into a loaf pan. Spread the oil-packed dried tomatoes over the surface, about ¼-inch thick. Bake in 350-degree oven until done, about 1 hour.

VARIATION ▾ Sauté several medium shiitake mushrooms, either whole or sliced, in a little olive oil for 5 minutes. Place half of the meatloaf mixture in the loaf pan, top with a layer of the mushrooms, add the rest of the meat mixture, and continue as above. ▾ Meatloaf can also be baked in individual loaf pans, which will take only about 20 to 25 minutes to cook, or in decorative molds.

BEEF TENDERLOIN
with Gorgonzola Butter

SERVES 4

Roasted tiny new potatoes and Asparagus in Raspberry Vinaigrette are the perfect accompaniments to this rosemary-infused dish. Serve with your favorite red wine.

    1 cup red wine
    ½ cup fresh lemon juice

½ cup olive oil

5 cloves garlic, crushed

1 tablespoon fresh rosemary, chopped

1 beef tenderloin, fully trimmed, about
2½ pounds

2 tablespoons + 1 teaspoon freshly ground
black pepper

2 teaspoons salt

2 tablespoons minced Italian parsley

3 tablespoons minced fresh rosemary

1 tablespoon lemon zest

3 ounces Gorgonzola cheese

4 ounces unsalted butter

Several small sprigs of fresh rosemary for
garnish

Mix together the red wine, lemon juice, olive oil, garlic, and rosemary. Pour over the beef and let stand, refrigerated, for several hours or overnight. Bring it to room temperature before cooking. Combine 2 tablespoons of the pepper with the salt, parsley, 2 tablespoons of the rosemary, and the lemon zest. Roll the tenderloin in mixture and place on a rack in a roasting pan in a 450 degree oven. Immediately lower the heat to 350 degrees and cook to an internal temperature of 130 degrees for rare, about 15 to 20 minutes per pound.

Combine the cheese, butter, and remaining pepper and rosemary to make a smooth spread. Roll into a tube shape about 1 inch in diameter, wrap in waxed paper, and chill.

When the tenderloin is done, cut into slices about ¼-inch thick. Place 3 or 4 slices on individual plates. Top with a ¼-inch slice of the chilled Gorgonzola Butter, garnish with a sprig of fresh rosemary, and serve.

▼▼▼

NOISETTES OF SONOMA LAMB

with Rosemary Goat Cheese Persillade and Rosemary Cabernet Sauce

S E R V E S   6

This recipe using two of my favorite Sonoma ingredients, lamb and goat cheese, is from Elaine Bell, the owner and chef of Elaine Bell Catering Company and the delicatessen, Lainie's Cuisine, in Sonoma.

2 cups fresh bread crumbs

½ cup Tome, (dry, aged goat cheese)
grated finely

2 tablespoons fresh rosemary, chopped

½ cup Italian parsley, chopped
Salt and pepper to taste

1 loin of lamb, about 3 to 4 pounds,
boned and trimmed of all fat

½ cup flour

3 eggs, beaten

1 cup clarified butter
Rosemary Cabernet Sauce
(recipe follows)

To make the *persillade*, combine the bread crumbs, cheese, rosemary, and parsley. Season with salt and pepper. Cut the lamb into 18 pieces 1-inch square. Dredge the meat in the flour. Dip each piece into the beaten egg and then coat with the *persillade*.

Heat the clarified butter in a skillet until it is smoking hot. Add five or six pieces of meat and brown them on all sides. Repeat until all the meat is browned. Transfer the

1 6 4

pieces to a roasting rack. Just before serving, bake the browned meat in a 350-degree oven for 7 minutes.

To serve, spoon several tablespoons of sauce onto individual serving plates, and agitate to spread the sauce evenly. Divide the meat among the plates, arranging it attractively on top of the sauce. Garnish with a small sprig of fresh rosemary and serve immediately with sautéed fresh spinach.

ROSEMARY CABERNET SAUCE

2 cups demi-glace (see Glossary)
1 cup Cabernet wine, reduced to ¼ cup
1 tablespoon fresh rosemary, chopped

Combine the ingredients in a saucepan and heat through.

LAMB WITH POMEGRANATE SAUCE

SERVES 4

The pomegranate has been one of my favorite fruits since I received my first one while trick-or-treating on Halloween long ago. Much to my mother's dismay, I loved the messy little fruit and looked forward each fall to their arrival in the markets. To me it is still the sight of the first pomegranates that marks the end of summer.

8 small loin lamb chops
½ cup pomegranate concentrate (see Glossary)
½ cup water
2 shallots, minced
3 cloves garlic, minced
A few leaves of fresh mint, crushed
Salt and pepper
Butter
½ to ¾ cup half-and-half
Fresh pomegranate seeds
Sprigs of fresh mint

Remove the bones from the lamb chops. Mix together the pomegranate concentrate, water, shallots, garlic, and mint leaves. Season with a little salt and a few twists of pepper. Place the lamb in a bowl and pour the marinade over. Refrigerate for several hours or overnight.

In a heavy skillet, melt a little butter. When foamy, add the lamb and sauté on 1 side for about 5 minutes. Turn and sauté for another 2 to 3 minutes. Add about ½ cup of the marinade, turn the lamb so that it is well coated, and transfer the meat to a warm plate, covered to keep it hot. Add another ½ cup of the marinade to the skillet, turn the heat to high, and reduce the liquid by half. Add the half-and-half, stir well, and reduce by one-third.

On each of 4 plates, pour a circle of sauce. Slice the lamb and arrange the strips in the center of the sauce. Spoon a little more sauce over the top. Garnish with sprigs of mint and several fresh pomegranate seeds.

LAMB KABOBS

with Rosemary and Lemon Marinade

SERVES 4

This recipe was one of the first I ever developed on my own, for a dinner party where I was trying to impress one of my college teachers. I have been using it ever since, and it is particularly good when made with our fine Sonoma lamb.

> Rosemary and Lemon Marinade
>   (recipe follows)
> 2 pounds lamb, cut into 1½-inch cubes
> 1 pound pearl onions
> ½ pound small mushrooms
>   Skewers
>   Sprigs of rosemary

The night before serving make the marinade and cover the cubes of lamb with about half of it.

To assemble, alternate peeled onions, mushrooms and lamb on skewers. Brush with the marinade. Cook over charcoal or under a broiler for about 8 minutes, turning once. Brush frequently with the marinade. Serve over rice with extra marinade on the side. Garnish with fresh rosemary sprigs.

ROSEMARY AND LEMON MARINADE

MAKES ABOUT 1¼ CUPS

> ½ cup fresh lemon juice
> 6 cloves garlic
> 3 tablespoons chopped fresh rosemary
> ¼ teaspoon fresh thyme leaves
> ¾ cup olive oil

> ¼ teaspoon salt
> ½ teaspoon fresh, cracked black pepper

Place the lemon juice, garlic, and herbs in a blender and blend on high for about 15 seconds. Add the olive oil, salt, and pepper and blend until smooth.

MARINATED LEG OF LAMB

Stuffed with Roasted Garlic Purée

SERVES 4 TO 6

There is something particularly seductive about this combination of flavors. Is it the way the succulent lamb drinks in the flavors of the wine and lemon? Perhaps it is because the creamy roasted garlic when used in this way becomes absolutely irresistible. Perhaps the separate ingredients unite in some unexplained alchemical magic, creating a whole far surpassing the simple sum of the parts. Whatever the explanation, if you want to create enchantment, I recommend this dish with complete confidence.

Half a leg of lamb, boned (about 3 to 4 pounds)

2 cups red wine

1 cup extra-virgin olive oil

½ cup lemon juice

6 cloves garlic, smashed

1 onion, cut in quarters

Sprigs of fresh thyme, oregano, and rosemary

1 teaspoon salt

1 teaspoon fresh, cracked black pepper

¾ cup Roasted Garlic Purée (page 222)

1 tablespoon Italian parsley, chopped

1 tablespoon chopped fresh herbs: thyme, oregano, and rosemary

2 tablespoons butter

Remove the fell (the outer, papery layer) from the lamb. Place the meat in a large glass or ceramic bowl. Mix together the red wine, olive oil, lemon juice, garlic, onion, and sprigs of herbs. Add the salt and black pepper and pour over the lamb. Refrigerate overnight, turning occasionally to insure even marinating.

To cook, remove the lamb from the marinade and pat dry. Preheat the oven to 425 degrees. Place the lamb on your work surface, outside down. Mix the Roasted Garlic Purée with the parsley and chopped herbs and spread the mixture over the surface of the lamb. Roll the meat up and tie it securely. Place on a rack in a roasting pan and pour ½ cup of marinade over. Place in the oven and reduce the heat to 325 degrees. Cook for approximately 20 to 25 minutes per pound for medium-rare, or until the lamb reaches an internal temperature of 135 degrees.

When done, remove from oven and place on cutting board to rest for 15 minutes. Place the roasting pan on a stove-top burner over low heat, add ¼ cup marinade, and scrape up the pan drippings. Add a little water if needed to make about ½ to ¾ cup pan juices. Add the butter, a teaspoon at a time, and stir with a fork or whisk until each addition has been incorporated into the sauce. Place the sauce in a serving dish. Slice the lamb about ½-inch thick and place on a serving platter. Spoon a little of the sauce over and garnish with a few sprigs of fresh herbs. Serve immediately and pass the sauce on the side.

Oven-Roasted Leg of Lamb

with Sausage Stuffing and Mustard Glaze

SERVES 6 TO 8

This recipe was the focus of my first column for The Sebastopol Times and News in March of 1986. I received a phone call the

day after publication complaining that the local market had completely run out of leg of lamb. I was astounded to realize that people had actually read what I had written. It was a completely magical revelation, and writing that column remains one of my favorite things to do.

1 leg of lamb, boned, 6 to 8 pounds
  Olive oil
1 small onion, chopped
8 cloves garlic, minced
1 pound Italian sausage, removed from the
  casings
2 tablespoons Dijon-style mustard
1 teaspoon fresh thyme
1 teaspoon fresh summer savory
1 cup fresh bread crumbs
1 tablespoon butter

MUSTARD GLAZE
¾ cup Dijon-style mustard
½ cup olive oil
1 teaspoon soy sauce
1 teaspoon fresh thyme leaves
1 teaspoon fresh summer savory
3 cloves garlic, pressed

Remove the papery outer covering of the lamb (the fell) and set the meat aside. Heat the olive oil in a heavy skillet. Sauté the onions until soft. Add the garlic and sauté for another 2 minutes. Add the sausage, crumble it with a fork, and cook until about half done. Stir in the mustard and herbs. Toss with the bread crumbs and remove from the heat.

Place the boned leg of lamb, outside down, on a flat working surface. Spread the stuffing over the inside of the lamb, roll it

up, and tie. Place on the rack of a roasting pan. Make the glaze by whisking all the ingredients together until smooth. Spread the glaze over the surface of the lamb and place in a 325-degree oven. Bake for 20 minutes per pound for a medium-rare roast.

When the lamb reaches an internal temperature of between 130 and 135 degrees, remove it from oven and let rest for 15 minutes before slicing. Place the roasting pan over a stove-top burner on low heat. Add ½ cup water and scrape the pan to loosen the drippings. Add any leftover mustard glaze, stir well, and simmer for about 5 minutes. Add the tablespoon chilled butter, a teaspoon at a time, stirring after each addition until the butter is melted. Pour into a sauce bowl. Slice lamb in slices ¼- to ½-inch thick, arrange on a platter, and top with sauce. Pass the remaining sauce on side.

GREEK LAMB LOAF

SERVES 6 TO 8

This dish has a wonderful interplay of flavors, and they are enhanced by the right red wine. Try it with the playfully named Lytton Springs Wineburger or with a Merlot. Kept properly chilled in a cooler and then heated over a campfire, Greek Lamb Loaf is entirely portable. Bring along Greek Salad, Sonoma Style (page 207) and some fresh berries, and you have the perfect afternoon picnic.

> 1 loaf San Francisco-style sourdough bread
> 2 tablespoons garlic, minced
> 1 tablespoon olive oil, with extra for brushing
> 1 bunch spinach, rinsed and chopped
> 1½ to 2 pounds ground lamb
> 1 tablespoon fresh rosemary, finely chopped
> 1 egg beaten
> 6 ounces feta cheese, cut into ½-inch cubes

SAUCE

> ¾ cup tomato sauce
> ½ cup chicken stock
> Juice of 2 lemons
> 1 teaspoon (or more to taste) freshly cracked black pepper
> 1 teaspoon Greek oregano

To make the filling, cut the ends off the loaf of bread and, with your fingers, pull out the soft insides of the bread, making a shell. Use the soft bread to make bread crumbs; you will need ¾ cup; set aside.

Sauté the garlic in a little olive oil for about 2 minutes. Add the spinach and stir until wilted. Set aside. Sauté the lamb until it is about half done. Remove from the heat, cool slightly, then mix with the spinach. Toss with the bread crumbs, add the egg, and blend well. Toss the mixture lightly with the feta cheese.

Fill the inside of the hollowed loaf of bread with the lamb mixture, packing it

fairly well. Wrap the loaf in aluminum foil and brush the top of the bread with a little olive oil before closing. Bake for 25 to 30 minutes.

To make the sauce, blend the ingredients and cook over low heat for about 10 minutes.

When done, remove the loaf from the oven, let it sit for about 5 minutes, and slice into 1-inch slices. Serve with sauce on the side.

▼▼▼▼▼▼▼▼▼▼▼▼▼▼▼▼▼▼▼▼▼▼▼▼▼▼▼▼▼▼▼▼

PERRY'S PORK CHOPS

with Raspberry Vinegar Sauce

SERVES 4

This recipe comes to us from Perry Kozlowski, of Kozlowski Farms and a producer of superior berries—and vinegars.

> 2 tablespoons olive oil
> 3 cloves garlic, minced
> 2 tablespoons flour
> ¼ teaspoon salt
> ¼ teaspoon white pepper
> ½ teaspoon finely chopped fresh rosemary
> 4 large, meaty pork chops
> ½ cup beef stock
> ½ cup dry vermouth
> ¼ cup red or black raspberry vinegar
> ¼ cup half-and-half
> Sprig of fresh rosemary

Heat the oil in a frying pan, add the garlic, and sauté for 2 minutes. Mix together the flour, salt, pepper, and rosemary. Dredge the pork chops in this flour mixture and brown them in the oil and garlic. Drain off any excess fat and add the stock and vermouth. Simmer over *very low heat* for one hour. Remove the chops from the pan and keep warm.

Turn the heat to high and reduce the sauce until it has thickened. Add the raspberry vinegar and stir the sauce, simmering until it has thickened again. Add the half-and-half, simmer, and reduce until the sauce coats a spoon thickly. Taste and adjust seasonings as necessary. Pour the sauce over the chops, garnish with the rosemary sprig, and serve immediately.

▼▼▼▼▼▼▼▼▼▼▼▼▼▼▼▼▼▼▼▼▼▼▼▼▼▼▼▼▼

PORK TENDERLOIN IN RED WINE MARINADE

with Potato and Apple Pancakes

SERVES 6 TO 8

Originally designed as part of my application to Madeleine Kamman's School for American Chefs in St. Helena, this recipe is an unusual but delicious way to combine two of Sonoma County's major products, wine and apples. The pork takes the marinade beautifully, and apple and pork have long been happy companions. The strawberries in the chutney add a new spark.

1 center-cut pork tenderloin, 3 to 4 pounds
2 cups poaching liquid from the recipe for
     Gravenstein Chutney (page 224)
   Salt and pepper
   Potato and Apple Pancakes (page 183)
1 cup Gravenstein Chutney (page 224)
   Strawberries, sprigs of Italian parsley, and
     cilantro for garnish

The night before serving, place the pork tenderloin in a shallow dish and pour the poaching liquid over it. Cover and refrigerate. Remove from the refrigerator 1 hour before cooking. Prepare the pancakes while the pork is roasting.

Remove the pork from the marinade and season it with salt and pepper. Place on a rack in a shallow roasting pan. Cook in slow oven, 300 degrees, for 20 to 25 minutes per pound, until pork reaches an internal temperature of 160 degrees. Remove the pork from oven and let it stand in warm place for 15 minutes before slicing.

To serve, place 2 Potato and Apple Pancakes on each individual serving plate. Slice the pork thinly and place several slices on top of the pancakes. Place a teaspoonful of Gravenstein Chutney in the center of each serving. Place a sprig of parsley and a sprig of cilantro on each plate. Make several slices in each strawberry, from tip to stem, but do not cut all the way through. Press the strawberries against your cutting surface to spread each into a fan-shape and add them to the plates. Serve immediately, passing more Gravenstein Chutney on the side.

CHIPOTLE PORK WITH GARLIC

S E R V E S   6   T O   8

*This dish is every bit as hot as it is deli-
cious, and it is fun to serve for an informal
party. It is easy to prepare, and the taste of
the* chipotle *peppers is distinctive enough to
stimulate lots of conversation. The Root
Salad Tricolor on page 208 is a cooling side
dish. Be sure to have plenty of cold Mexican
beer and other thirst quenchers on hand:
this is hot stuff.*

> 1 pork roast (any type will do), weigh-
       ing about 4 pounds
> 1 or 2 heads garlic, separated and peeled
> 1 can (7 ounces) chipotle peppers in
       adobo sauce
> 1 cup grapefruit juice
> 1 dozen corn or flour tortillas
> 2 limes, cut into wedges
> 2 cups grated Cheddar cheese
> 1 bunch cilantro, large stems removed

Place the pork in a heavy, ovenproof pot
with a lid. Add the garlic. Purée the chipotle peppers and their sauce with the grapefruit juice and pour over the pork and the
garlic. Place in an oven that has been heated
to between 300 and 325 degrees and cook
until the pork begins to fall apart, about 2½
hours. It should be completely fork tender.
Remove from the oven.

Heat the tortillas and wrap them in a
towel to keep hot. Serve the pork surrounded
by hot tortillas, limes, cheese, and cilantro.
Guests fill their own tortillas, topping the
pork and garlic with a squeeze of lime, some
cheese, and cilantro.

PORK ROAST WITH PEPPER JAM

S E R V E S   6

*Happy Haven Ranch, a strawberry farm in
Sonoma's Valley of the Moon, makes the
best hot pepper jam I have ever had. Neither
the red nor the green variety is overly sweet.
In this recipe, the taste of the peppers is
complemented by the use of vinegar.*

> 1 pork shoulder roast, about 4 pounds
       (any type of pork roast will work fine)
> 2 shallots, minced
> 6 to 8 cloves garlic, minced
> 4 to 5 tablespoons olive oil
> 2 jalapeño peppers, chopped, with seeds
> 1 pound chorizo sausage, bulk or casings
       removed
> 1 tablespoon achiote
> ½ cup green pepper jam
> ¼ cup sherry vinegar

Cut a pocket about 2- to 2½-inches wide in
the center of the roast. Sauté the shallots,
garlic, and *jalapeños* in the olive oil. Add
the *chorizo* and sauté, breaking it up with
a fork. Crumble the *achiote*, add it to the

meat mixture, and stir well to incorporate. Drain off any excess fat and set aside to cool. Place the mixture in a pastry bag without a tip, insert the bag into the pocket in the meat, and fill. Coat the pork roast with jam, place on a rack in a roasting pan, and bake at 325 degrees for 25 to 30 minutes per pound, to an internal temperature of between 150 and 160 degrees. While the roast is cooking, baste it occasionally with more pepper jam. When done, remove it from the oven and let it sit for 15 minutes before carving. Place the roasting pan over the flame, add sherry vinegar and a little water, and deglaze. Slice the roast, place on a serving plate, and serve the pan juices on side.

▼▼▼▼▼▼▼▼▼▼▼▼▼▼▼▼▼▼▼▼▼▼▼▼▼▼▼▼▼▼▼▼▼▼▼▼▼

Roast Pork Loin

with Apricot Sauce

SERVES 6 TO 8

The appetizer version of this recipe, called Autumn Pork Cornucopias, received awards in the Best Use of Wine and Best Use of Meat categories and a Gold Medal at the 1988 Sonoma County Harvest Fair. It never fails to bring exclamations of delight at the dinner table.

    Apricot Sauce (recipe follows)
- 1 center-cut pork loin, about 3½ to 4 pounds, bone removed
- 2 tablespoons olive oil
- 1 onion, diced
- 8 cloves garlic, minced
- 1½ pounds chicken-apple sausage, casings removed
- ¾ cup diced, dried apricots
- ½ cup pine nuts
- ¾ cup fresh bread crumbs

Make the Apricot Sauce first and set it aside.

Ask your butcher to cut a pocket down the length of the pork loin or cut it yourself, leaving about 1 inch uncut on each side.

Heat some olive oil in a heavy saucepan and sauté the onion until soft and transparent. Add the garlic and sauté for 1 minute. Add the sausage, break it up with a fork, and sauté until it is just barely done. Add the apricots, pine nuts, and fresh bread crumbs. Stir well and remove from heat. Add a small amount of Apricot Sauce, about 2 tablespoons, to moisten. Set aside to cool.

When the mixture has cooled sufficiently, place it in a pastry bag with wide opening. Insert the tip of the bag into one end of the pocket in the pork as far as it will go and squeeze in about half the mixture. Repeat at other end of pork loin. Place the meat on a roasting rack in a heavy pan and brush with Apricot Sauce. Bake at 325 degrees for 25 to 30 minutes per pound to an internal temperature of between 160 and 180 degrees. Brush frequently and liberally with the Apricot Sauce.

When the pork is done, remove it from the oven and let it rest for 15 minutes. While the roast is resting, scrape the pan drippings from the bottom of the baking dish and add a little water. Place over medium heat to deglaze pan. Add the remainder of the Apricot Sauce to the pan, stir to blend with the pan drippings, and simmer until thoroughly heated.

Slice the pork loin thinly, arrange the slices on a serving platter, and top with several spoonsful of the Apricot Sauce. Pass more sauce on the side.

VARIATION ▾ To serve as an appetizer, do not cut the pocket or stuff the loin. Prepare the stuffing and bake it in the oven, with some of the Apricot Sauce spooned over it, for 30 minutes. Roast the pork according to the directions in the main recipe and, when cool enough to handle, cut it in thin pieces, and roll them into small cone shapes. Secure with picks. Spoon the stuffing into the pork cones and arrange them on a serving platter. Spoon hot Apricot Sauce onto each little cornucopia and serve.

APRICOT SAUCE

MAKES ABOUT 2½ CUPS

```
2 to 3  tablespoons olive oil
     1  medium yellow onion, diced
        Several cloves garlic, minced
     8  ounces apricot jam
    ½   teaspoon ground cinnamon
    ½   teaspoon cumin seeds
    ½   teaspoon ground cumin
     6  whole cloves, coarsely ground
        Pinch nutmeg
   1½   cups orange muscat wine
```

Sauté the onions in olive oil until soft and transparent. Add the garlic and sauté for 2 minutes. Stir in the apricot jam and add the spices. Stir well. Add the wine and stir until smooth and well blended. Simmer for 15 minutes and set aside.

▼▼▼▼▼▼▼▼▼▼▼▼▼▼▼▼▼▼▼▼▼▼▼▼▼▼▼▼▼▼▼▼▼▼▼▼▼▼

POTATO AND APPLE STEW

with Andouille Sausage

SERVES 4

This is a California recipe in the truest sense of the word. It consists almost entirely of Sonoma County products, and I made it for the first time in exchange for an astrology reading. I had met an astrologer who mentioned his love of sausages and asked if I would cook him a dinner in exchange for a reading. It was an offer I could not refuse, and made for a fun evening. Everyone enjoyed the combination of flavors and textures, and the creamy sweet element that the apples contributed was sublime. The evening ended with our astrologer friend pleading for the leftover stew, which I had to package for his long motorcycle ride home. Only in California!

```
   4  tablespoons olive oil
   1  medium onion, chopped
  ½   pound potatoes, preferably yellow fin or
      new red
   2  Gravenstein apples
   2  smoked andouille sausages, about ½ to
      ⅔ pound
   1  tablespoon flour
  ½   cup sweet white wine (Riesling or
      Gewürztraminer)
  ¼   cup water
      Several fresh sage leaves
   1  teaspoon each fresh marjoram and fresh
      thyme, chopped
  ¾   cup grated dry Jack or Parmesan cheese
```

Heat the olive oil in a heavy skillet. Sauté the onion until soft and transparent. Cut the potatoes into medium, 1- by ¼-inch pieces. Add them to the onions. Peel and core the apples, cut them into pieces the same size as the potato pieces and add them to the onions and potatoes. Sauté for 5 minutes. Slice the sausages into ¼-inch-thick rounds, add them to the potato mixture, and sauté for another 5 minutes. Remove the mixture from heat and place in a heavy baking dish. Return the skillet to the heat. Add the flour and scrape up the pan drippings to blend with flour. Slowly add the wine, blend it well with the roux, and simmer for a minute or two. Add the water, simmer for a couple of minutes, and pour the sauce over the potato mixture. Chop the sage leaves and add them, along with the other herbs, to the baking dish. Toss well. Top the stew with the cheese. Cover and place in a 325-degree oven for 30 minutes. Remove and serve immediately with a simple green salad.

▼▼▼▼▼▼▼▼▼▼▼▼▼▼▼▼▼▼▼▼▼▼▼▼▼▼▼▼▼▼▼▼▼▼▼▼▼▼▼

CHICKEN-APPLE SAUSAGES

with Curried Polenta and Chutney Sauce

S E R V E S   4

Gerhard's Napa-made sausages have become immensely popular in Sonoma County and are now available in numerous markets and delicatessens throughout the county. A spicy Gewürztraminer would be particularly compatible with this dish.

POLENTA

1 to 3 teaspoons hot curry powder, to taste
    1 teaspoon salt
    1 cup polenta
    ½ teaspoon turmeric
    1 teaspoon ground ginger or ½-inch piece fresh ginger, peeled and grated
    1 teaspoon ground cumin
    ¼ teaspoon cayenne pepper
    2 tablespoons butter (omit for less fat)
    ¾ cup unflavored yogurt

SAUSAGES

    1 pound (approximately 8) East Indian chicken-apple sausage
    2 cups white wine
    2 tablespoons olive oil
    ½ cup Apricot or Persimmon Chutney (page 223)

To make the polenta, bring 3½ cups water to boil in a heavy pot. Add the curry powder and salt. Slowly stir in the polenta and continue to stir over medium heat until it begins to thicken, about 10 to 15 minutes. Stir in the spices and the butter, if using. Stir until the polenta is very thick and bubbly. Taste and remove from heat when the texture is tender and creamy.

Coat a 10-inch tart pan that has a removable bottom with olive oil and sprinkle it lightly with cayenne pepper. Pour in the polenta, smooth it out evenly, and keep it warm while it sets.

While waiting, place the sausages in a heavy frying pan with 1 cup of the wine. Simmer for about 8 minutes, or until the wine has evaporated. Add the 2 tablespoons olive oil to the pan and brown the sausages. Remove them from the pan and keep hot. Add the remaining cup of wine, turn the heat to high, loosen the pan drippings, and reduce the wine by about half. Stir in the chutney and heat thoroughly. Remove the polenta from the tart pan and place on a serving platter. Cut into 8 wedges. Top each wedge with a sausage and pour sauce over all. Serve immediately, with more chutney and yogurt on the side.

▼▼▼▼▼▼▼▼▼▼▼▼▼▼▼▼▼▼▼▼▼▼▼▼▼▼▼▼▼▼▼▼

SAUSAGE-STUFFED CURRIED ONIONS

SERVES 4

Serve these fragrant and delicious onions as a main course for an afternoon luncheon, or incorporate them into a hearty afternoon tea. A slightly sweet white wine, either a Riesling or a Gewürztraminer, goes perfectly with the spiciness of the curry.

4 medium-sized, round yellow onions, about 4-inches across
3 teaspoons curry powder
1 teaspoon ground cumin
2 tablespoons + a little extra olive oil
1 pound chicken-apple sausages
½ cup golden raisins
⅓ cup fresh bread crumbs
  Salt to taste
1 egg
  Cayenne pepper
1 cup unflavored yogurt
  Chutney

Cut a slice off the root end of the onions so they can stand. Cut a flat slice off the top and carefully peel off the skin. With a very sharp paring knife, cut a cone shape out of the center of each onion. Using a melon ball cutter or a teaspoon, hollow out the inside, leaving a ⅜-inch wall of flesh on the sides and bottom of the onion. Set aside the corings.

Blanch the onion shells in a pot of boiling water, to which you have added 1 teaspoon curry powder, until firm but tender, about 6 minutes. Drain upside down and cool.

Place 2 tablespoons olive oil in a sauté pan. Chop the corings from the onions and sauté them until transparent. Add 2 teaspoons curry powder and the cumin. Remove the sausages from their casings, add them to the onion mixture and sauté for about 5 or 6 minutes. Add the raisins and bread crumbs, toss together well, and remove from the heat. Let cool slightly. Taste and add salt if necessary.

Pour a bit of olive oil into the palm of your hand and rub the outside of each onion. Beat the egg and toss it with the sausage mixture. Fill each onion shell with sausage mixture and place the shells in a baking dish just large enough to hold them. Deglaze the sauté pan with some water and pour those pan juices into the baking dish. Sprinkle with cayenne pepper.

Bake at 375 degrees for 30 to 40 minutes, until tender. Remove the onions from the baking dish to a serving platter. Add a little water to the dish and scrape loose any drippings. Add ½ cup of the yogurt and stir well. Heat but do not boil. Pour the yogurt and pan dripping sauce over the onions and top each onion with a spoonful of chutney. Pass unflavored yogurt and chutney on the side.

FRANK'S CRÊPES

SERVES 4 TO 6

Frank Stanford, the well-known Southern poet and late husband of the artist, Ginny Stanford, loved to cook and enjoyed unusual and uncommon combinations of food. He also loved beer, the beverage of choice with these robustly flavored crêpes. You should enjoy an Anchor Liberty Ale or a Dixie Beer in his honor when you give these a try.

Savory Crêpes (recipe follows)
1 cup Wine Country Applesauce
(page 223)

1 pound new red potatoes
¼ pound butter
1 large red onion, coarsely diced
1 pound fresh andouille sausage
1 pound smoked andouille sausage
2 tablespoons chopped Italian parsley
1 teaspoon fresh thyme
1 teaspoon black pepper
Salt to taste
1 cup crème fraîche or ¾ cup sour cream
mixed with ¼ cup half-and-half
Cayenne pepper
Sprigs of Italian parsley

Mix the crêpe batter and, while it is standing, make the Applesauce and set aside. Cook the crêpes and keep warm.

Cut the potatoes into quarters if they are very small; you want pieces measuring about ¾-inch. Plunge them into boiling water for 5 minutes. Remove, rinse in cool water, and drain. Melt half the butter in a large skillet, add the onion, and sauté for 5 minutes. Add the potatoes and sauté for about 15 minutes, stirring often. Add more butter if the mixture becomes too dry. In a separate skillet, cook the fresh *andouille* sausage in ½ cup water for 5 minutes on each side, turning once. Remove and slice into small pieces. Slice the smoked andouille into small pieces, too. Add the sausage to the potato and onion mixture, toss together well, sauté for another 5 minutes, and remove from the heat. Add the parsley, thyme, and pepper, taste, and add salt as desired.

Fill the crêpes by placing several tablespoons of the filling in the center of each crêpe. Roll carefully and place on plates, 2 per serving for a substantial main course.

Top each crêpe with a tablespoon of crème fraîche or the sour cream mixture and 1 tablespoon of Applesauce. Sprinkle with a little cayenne pepper and garnish with a sprig of Italian parsley. Pass more Applesauce and crème fraîche on the side.

SAVORY CRÊPES

    3 eggs, beaten
    1 tablespoon milk
    1 tablespoon water
    ½ teaspoon Tabasco sauce
    2 tablespoons all-purpose flour
    ¼ teaspoon white pepper
    Pinch of salt

Combine the ingredients and mix well until the batter is very smooth and is the consistency of thin cream. Chill for at least 2 hours or overnight.

To cook the crêpes, melt ½ teaspoon butter in a 5- or 6-inch omelette or sauté pan, preferably nonstick. When the butter is bubbling, pour in enough batter to make a very thin coating on the bottom of the pan. Cook for 1 or 2 minutes, until the crêpe is set. Remove it from the pan with a spatula and stack the crêpes between sheets of waxed paper.

MEAN STREETS SAUSAGE AND POLENTA

SERVES 4 TO 6

I watch Martin Scorcese's classic film, Mean Streets, *at least once a year and enjoy inviting friends over for a big Italian dinner before we start the movie. This spicy sausage dish has been the main course so many times that it is now known by the title of the movie. I prefer to use a hot Italian sausage, without fennel or anise, though you should feel free to use your favorite type of the many that are available. Make the polenta while the tomatoes are simmering and allow it to set in its mold or loaf pan while you finish off the sausage sauce.*

SAUSAGE

       1 pound hot Italian sausage
   2 to 3 tablespoons olive oil
       1 onion, minced
  6 or 7 cloves garlic, minced
       2 cups canned Italian plum tomatoes, with juice
       2 cups canned crushed tomatoes
       1 cup tomato sauce
       1 teaspoon oregano
       1 teaspoon thyme
       ½ cup red wine

Brown the sausage in a little olive oil, remove from pan, and set aside. Add the onion and sauté until golden. Add the garlic and cook for 2 minutes longer. Add the tomatoes and stir well, breaking up the plum tomatoes as you stir. Blend in the tomato sauce and herbs. Simmer over low heat for about 45 minutes. Cut sausages into ½-inch slices. Add the sausages and the wine and simmer for another 30 minutes. Taste and correct seasoning. Serve over polenta and top with a sprinkle of dry Jack cheese.

POLENTA

- 3½ cups water
- 1 teaspoon salt
- 1 cup coarse polenta
- 1 cup grated dry Jack or freshly grated Parmesan cheese
- Olive oil
- Garlic
- Freshly grated Parmesan cheese

Bring the water and salt to a boil. Slowly stir in the polenta. Bring back to the boil and reduce the heat. Stir continuously for 15 minutes. Cook over very low heat for another 10 minutes, stirring frequently. Stir in the 1 cup cheese. Pour the polenta into a decorative mold or loaf pan that has been rubbed with olive oil and garlic and dusted with freshly grated cheese. Let it sit for 20 to 30 minutes, keeping warm. Invert onto serving plate.

RICHARD'S STEAM BEER STEW

SERVES 4 TO 6

There are few things I like better than turning up the radio really loud and cooking while there is a master disc jockey at the controls. No one has ever done a better job than Richard Gossett, a Bay Area radio legend, who has provided the soundtrack for some of my most memorable and enjoyable cooking. He is a full-time brewer of Anchor Steam Beer and that company's other beers and ales, so it seems only fitting that this dish bear his name and be served, of course, with some Anchor Steam Beer or, my favorite, Anchor Liberty Ale.

- 8 to 10 ounces sauerkraut
- 2 teaspoons cumin seed
- ¼ cup olive oil
- 1 yellow onion, chopped
- 3 apples, peeled, cored, and cut into ¾-inch pieces
- 3 tablespoons calvados (optional)
- Thyme and marjoram
- 6 Hot Beer sausages or garlic sausages
- 1 bottle Anchor Steam Beer or dark ale

Drain the sauerkraut of its liquid, toss it with the cumin seed, and spread it over the surface of a heavy, ovenproof dish with lid. In a heavy sauté pan, heat the olive oil and sauté the onion for 5 minutes. Add the apples and continue to sauté for another 10 minutes. If you are using the calvados, add it to the apple and onion mixture and, *carefully,* ignite it. When the flame goes out, all the alcohol will have burned off. Spread apple and onion mixture over the sauerkraut. Sprinkle with thyme and marjoram.

Brown the sausages in a frying pan and arrange them on top of the apple mixture. Pour the beer over all, cover, and place in 350-degree oven for 40 minutes. Remove from the oven and let sit a few minutes before serving.

VEGETABLES

▼▼▼▼▼▼▼▼▼▼▼▼▼▼▼▼▼▼▼▼▼▼▼▼▼▼▼▼▼▼▼▼

APPLE AND ONION TART

SERVES 8

Carol Klesow of Wine Country Cuïsine developed this recipe that includes two well-loved Sonoma County products, apples and Vella's Dry Jack cheese.

  1½ cups flour
   ½ teaspoon salt
   1 cup grated dry Jack or Parmesan cheese
  ⅓ cup + 2 tablespoons butter
   4 tablespoons water
   1 red torpedo onion, sliced
   3 cups Gravenstein apples, sliced

To make the crust, mix together the flour, salt, and ¼ cup of the cheese. Blend in the ⅓ cup butter and the water. Sprinkle your rolling surface with ¼ cup of the cheese, roll out the crust and line a 10-inch tart pan.

Sauté the onion and apple slices lightly in the remaining 2 tablespoons butter. Arrange them in the tart shell and sprinkle on the re-maining ½ cup cheese. Bake at 350 degrees for approximately 35 minutes.

▼▼▼▼▼▼▼▼▼▼▼▼▼▼▼▼▼▼▼▼▼▼▼▼▼▼▼▼▼▼▼▼

ASPARAGUS IN RASPBERRY VINAIGRETTE

SERVES 4

Asparagus and raspberries: it's a marriage made in culinary heaven. This is a light and simple way to combine the two; perfect for an elegant dinner party. It also makes a wonderful lunch, served all by itself, in which case it will not feed four. Enjoy lunch by yourself and indulge.

  1½ pounds thin asparagus, trimmed of tough ends
   2 tablespoons butter
  ¾ cup Black Raspberry Vinaigrette (page 216)
   1 cup fresh raspberries, in season

Cook the asparagus in rapidly boiling water or steam until just tender. Do not overcook.

To serve hot, remove the asparagus to a colander or large strainer and drain quickly. Place on serving plate and top with the butter cut into small pieces. Give the butter a chance to melt and then drizzle with the Raspberry Vinaigrette. Serve immediately.

To serve chilled, transfer the cooked asparagus to a cold water bath to preserve its color. Drain, place in glass or ceramic bowl, and pour the Raspberry Vinaigrette over. Chill. Place on serving plates and garnish with fresh raspberries if available.

▼▼▼▼▼▼▼▼▼▼▼▼▼▼▼▼▼▼▼▼▼▼▼▼▼▼▼▼▼▼▼▼▼

SAUTÉED MUSHROOMS

SERVES 4 TO 6

Everyone loves sautéed mushrooms, whether they are served simply as a side dish, atop a grilled steak, or in a more elaborate dish, such as Sonoma Cannelloni (page 134). However you decide to use them, this recipe, for whatever wild mushrooms happen to be available, is an exciting version of an old standard.

½ cup unsalted butter

6 to 8 cloves garlic, minced

6 cups thickly sliced mushrooms; use a blend of the best wild mushrooms available, shiitakes, cèpes, field, chanterelles, and so on

½ to 1 ounce dried porcini mushrooms, soaked in ½ cup hot water

¼ cup Madeira

1 teaspoon fresh thyme

½ cup pine nuts

Salt and pepper

In a large, heavy skillet, melt the butter until it is just foamy. Sauté the garlic briefly and add the wild mushrooms, tossing them well in butter. Lower the heat and simmer the mushrooms. Drain the porcini and slice into small strips. Add to the other mushrooms and sauté for 15 to 20 minutes, until the mushrooms start to give up their liquid. Add the Madeira and thyme and simmer until the Madeira has evaporated. Add the pine nuts, salt, and pepper and toss well.

▼ Try the Sonoma Cannelloni on page 134.

▼ Serve with pasta and a cream sauce: Toss fettuccini with the Roasted Garlic Cream Sauce on page 214 and top with Sautéed Mushrooms.

▼ Stuff Pasta Shells: Allow 3 or 4 giant shells per person and cook them just barely al dente. Fill with Sautéed Mushrooms and top with Chèvre Sauce, page 214. Bake, covered, in 325-degree oven for 20 minutes. Remove from the oven, top with a little more Chèvre Sauce, and garnish with chopped chives.

SHIITAKE STRUDEL

SERVES 6 TO 8

Lisa Hemenway prepared this delicious strudel for the Celebrate Sonoma Gala Dinner in 1989. It is a perfect way to highlight the rich flavor of shiitake mushrooms.

DOUGH

- 1 cup unsalted butter
- 1 cup cream cheese
- 2½ cups flour
- 1 teaspoon salt
- ¼ cup heavy cream

FILLING

- 1 yellow onion, finely chopped
- 3 cloves garlic, minced
- 2 tablespoons clarified butter
- 8 ounces shiitake mushrooms, tough stems removed
- 1 teaspoon grated fresh ginger
- 3 scallions, finely chopped
  Salt and pepper
- 4 ounces cheese, Doux de Montagne or Fontina
- 1 egg white, with 1 tablespoon water added
- 1 tablespoon toasted sesame seeds

To make the dough, combine the butter and cheese until smooth and creamy. Sift the flour and salt together and gradually add to the cheese mixture. Add the cream and chill for 1 hour.

To make the filling, sauté the yellow onion in clarified butter until lightly browned. Add the garlic and sauté for another 2 min-

utes. Slice the mushrooms and add them to the onions and garlic, along with the ginger. Sauté until the mushrooms are soft. Continue cooking until the moisture released by the mushrooms has evaporated. Remove from the heat, add the scallions, and toss. Add salt and pepper to taste and set aside to cool.

To assemble the strudel, roll out the chilled dough to form a 10- by 12-inch rectangle. Slice the cheese and place it down the center of the dough. Top with the mushroom filling. Fold the pastry over to form a long cylinder and seal the edges with egg white. Brush the top of the pastry with egg white and sprinkle with sesame seeds.

Bake at 400 degrees for 20 to 25 minutes. Remove from the oven, slice, and serve hot.

RED PEPPER AND GARLIC RATATOUILLE

SERVES 8 TO 10

This ratatouille is lighter than traditional versions that call for considerably more tomatoes. Each of the vegetables retains its separate character and flavor, and the whole cloves of garlic become creamy and nutty during the long cooking.

- 8 ounces peeled cloves of garlic
- 8 ounces crimini or commercial mushrooms

2 eggplants, peeled and cut into
1-inch cubes

1¾ cups extra-virgin olive oil
Salt and pepper

1 pound yellow onions, coarsely
chopped

2 or 3 red sweet peppers, cut in medium
julienne

1 or 2 gold sweet peppers cut in medium
julienne

4 zucchini, cut in medium julienne

2 pounds fresh Roma tomatoes, peeled
and sliced or 1 can (28 ounces)
Italian plum tomatoes, drained,
liquid reserved

¼ cup Italian parsley, finely minced

2 tablespoons chopped fresh herbs:
thyme, marjoram, and oregano

Toss the whole garlic cloves, mushrooms, and eggplant together, and place in a roasting pan. Pour 1¼ cups of the olive oil over, sprinkle with 1 teaspoon salt, cover tightly with a lid or aluminum foil, and bake at 350 degrees for 1 hour.

Sauté the chopped onions in the remaining olive oil until soft and transparent. Add the peppers and sauté until both vegetables are soft. Add the zucchini and tomatoes. Blend well and simmer over low heat for 15 minutes. When the eggplant mixture is done, remove from oven and add to the pepper mixture. Toss well. Add the herbs and salt and pepper to taste. If the ratatouille needs any more moisture, add the reserved liquid from the canned tomatoes or 2 tablespoons tomato paste thinned with water to ¼ cup. Simmer over low heat for another 15 minutes. Serve or refrigerate until ready

to serve. This dish improves with age, so it may be made the day before you need it.

VARIATIONS ▾ Grill sausages to accompany the ratatouille. Smoked *andouille* and chaurice are excellent with this dish. Grill 2 sausages per person and serve whole or grill 2 pounds sausage, slice into rounds and stir into ratatouille. ▾ The Ratatouille Pizza on page 119 is a delicious variation. When you make this ratatouille, set aside 2 cups and try the pizza.

▾▾▾▾▾▾▾▾▾▾▾▾▾▾▾▾▾▾▾▾▾▾▾▾▾▾▾▾▾▾▾▾▾▾▾▾▾▾

STUFFED PEPPERS

S E R V E S   4

These stuffed grilled peppers are excellent with roasted meats and are also delicious served with the Tuna Tostadas on page 158.

4 pasilla or poblano peppers

1 cup grated Jalapeño Jack cheese

1 cup grated Jack cheese

1 teaspoon cumin seeds, toasted

2 teaspoons dried Greek oregano

Over hot coals or under the broiler, cook the peppers until the skin is blackened. Place in a paper bag for 20 minutes, or until cooled. Remove the skin, which should peel off easily. Remove the stems and seeds carefully; try not to tear the roasted peppers. Mix together the cheeses, cumin, and oregano. Stuff the peppers with the cheese mixture, packing it fairly tightly. Wrap the peppers individually in foil or place them in a small baking dish, just big enough to hold them. Place in a 350-degree oven until the cheese is melted, about 15 minutes. Serve immediately, with your favorite salsa. Try them with the Corn Salsa, page 219, or the Avocado Salsa, page 219.

VARIATION ▾ Stuff the peppers with the following mixture and serve with Corn Salsa:

- 4 ounces chabis
- 2 ounces grated Taupinière
- 2 ounces grated Jack cheese
- 2 cloves garlic, minced
- 1 tablespoon chopped fresh cilantro
- 1 tablespoon fresh snipped chives

POTATO AND APPLE PANCAKES

MAKES 4 TO 6 PANCAKES, 4-INCHES ACROSS

When I designed a menu for Madeleine Kamman's School for American Chefs, I had no idea that the new recipes I was developing would quickly become some of my favorites, but they have. This variation on a traditional potato pancake makes use of Sonoma's wonderful apples and, served alone or as a light breakfast, is absolutely delicious.

- 2 **medium russet potatoes, about ¾ pound total**
- 2 **medium Gravenstein apples**
- ¼ **cup chopped Italian parsley**
- 2 **teaspoons flour**
- 3 **eggs**
  Salt and pepper
  Oil for frying
  Gravenstein Chutney (page 224)

Cook the potatoes whole in boiling water for 7 to 8 minutes. Remove to cool water. Peel, core, and grate the apples. Wrap the grated apples in cheesecloth and let them stand for about 10 minutes. Wrap the cheesecloth tightly around the apples and squeeze out any excess moisture. Place the apples in mixing bowl, grate in the cooled potatoes, and toss together. Add the parsley and flour to the potato and apple mixture and toss again. Season with a little salt and pepper. Beat the eggs by hand until just foamy, add them to the potato and apple mixture, and blend quickly but well.

In a heavy skillet, heat about ¼ to ⅓ inch of oil until hot. Drop 3 tablespoons of the mixture into the hot oil and flatten it into a cake about 4 inches across. Add more cakes until the pan is comfortably full. Cook until the undersides appear to be well browned. Turn the cakes and cook until golden and crisp. Drain on paper towels and serve immediately, topped with Gravenstein Chutney.

POTATO AND FENNEL TERRINE

S E R V E S   6   T O   8

Mark Malicki, one of Sonoma County's finest chefs, served this delicious potato terrine at a celebration dinner that launched a week of food demonstrations and lectures on the subject of organically raised products. Mark's menu dazzled the crowd of restaurateurs, cookbook authors, and Bay Area celebrities with six delicious courses that included organic wines, butter, and cream. Mark chose some of the more unusual varieties of potatoes available (beautiful pinks, golds, and purples) for the terrine he served that night, but the dish will not be significantly changed if you substitute potatoes that are more readily available, such as new red potatoes or Yellow Fin potatoes.

> 3   russet potatoes, peeled
> 1½   medium-sized fennel bulbs
> 2   dozen assorted small potatoes, pink, purple, or gold, or substitute small, new red potatoes
> ⅓   cup olive oil
> 6   medium new red potatoes
> 1   bunch chives, finely chopped
> ½   cup heavy cream, warmed
>   Salt and pepper

Cook the peeled russet potatoes in salted water until very tender. Follow the same cooking procedure for the fennel. Drain, cover, and keep warm.

Toss the purple, gold, and pink potatoes in a large bowl with the olive oil. Sprinkle with salt and pepper. Place on a sheet pan and roast at 375 degrees until they fall off the end of a knife, about 30 minutes. Cool and peel.

Slice the red potatoes paper-thin and cook in boiling, salted water until tender, about 4 minutes. Drain, cool, and pat dry.

Press the russets through a food mill or potato ricer. Purée the fennel in a food processor until smooth. Mix the puréed potato and fennel together and add the warm cream and salt and pepper to taste.

To assemble, lightly grease a terrine or loaf pan. Place a single layer of the cooked red potatoes in the bottom and along the sides of the pan. Add one third of the russet and fennel mixture and spread it across the surface of the pan. Arrange half of the roasted potatoes in a decorative pattern on top. Add another third of the mixture, smoothing it across the top of the roasted potatoes, and press it down firmly. Repeat with another layer of roasted potatoes and finish with the final third of the russet and fennel mixture. Press firmly. Spread chives across the surface of the terrine, cover, and refrigerate for at least 4 hours.

Remove the terrine from the refrigerator at least 30 minutes before serving. Invert the terrine, remove it from the pan, and slice. Garnish each slice with a strand of chive. Serve at room temperature.

POTATO PANCAKES WITH GOAT CHEESE

MAKES 8 PANCAKES

Laura Chenel developed this delicious recipe using her excellent goat cheese.

- 4 cloves garlic, minced
- 4 tablespoons butter
- 3 ounces shiitake mushrooms, stems removed, and thinly sliced
  Salt and freshly ground pepper
- 3 leaves Swiss chard, ribs removed and sliced en julienne
- 2 eggs, beaten
- 3 tablespoons flour
- 1 pound russet potatoes, peeled, coarsely grated and wrung dry in a towel
  Oil
- 4 ounces goat cheese, sliced into 8 pieces

Warm 2 cloves of the garlic in 2 tablespoons of the butter. Add the mushrooms, salt and pepper to taste, and sauté until browned and the mushroom liquid has been released. Set aside. Warm the remaining garlic in 1 tablespoon of the butter. Add the chard, salt and pepper to taste, and sauté until all the liquid has evaporated.

Mix together the eggs, flour, potatoes, mushrooms, and chard. Add salt and pepper to taste. Heat the oil with the remaining tablespoon butter over medium heat in a large frying pan. Form 8 flat patties with the mixture and cook in the hot butter and oil until golden brown on the underside. Turn and cook until golden brown. While brown-

ing the second side, place a slice of goat cheese on each pancake. Remove from pan and drain on paper towels before serving.

POTATOES VINAIGRETTE

SERVES 4 TO 6

Potatoes and arugula complement each other in both taste and texture, and the acidity of the Mustard Vinaigrette ties the two together perfectly.

- 2 pounds very small new red potatoes
- 2 large bunches arugula
  Mustard Vinaigrette (page 217)

Cut the potatoes in half (or quarters if they are not very small) and boil until just tender. Place in colander and rinse with warm water. Let them drain.

Setting aside a small handful of arugula, arrange the rest on a serving platter and top with the drained potatoes. Pour the Mustard Vinaigrette over. Cut the reserved arugula into thin strips (called a *chiffonnade*) and sprinkle it over the potatoes. This is excellent served with roast leg of lamb.

BAKED PUMPKINS

SERVES 4

When these cute little miniature pumpkins first appeared on the market, they were usually used as a table decoration and frequently were sold lightly varnished, making them entirely unsuitable for eating, even though they were being sold in the produce section of most markets. The word seems to be out that they are actually edible, and they are increasingly available in their natural condition. Their sweetness is more concentrated than that of their big brothers, and they make a perfect single serving.

  4 tiny pumpkins
12 whole cloves garlic, peeled
  4 teaspoons butter or 8 teaspoons extra-
      virgin olive oil
      Fresh, cracked black pepper
      Ground nutmeg or chopped fresh
      rosemary

Cut the tops off the pumpkins, carefully, cutting just low enough to remove the top and stem in one piece. Set the tops aside. Press the center of the cut surface to find the soft spot and, with a sharp knife, cut into the spot. Cut a circle of pumpkin flesh out to reveal the seeds and fibers below. Scoop these out with a small spoon. Rinse out the pumpkins and invert them over paper towels to drain.

Place the pumpkins right-side-up in a baking dish. In each pumpkin, place 3 cloves garlic and either 1 teaspoon butter or 2 teaspoons olive oil. Grind black pepper lightly over the surface of each pumpkin. If you are using nutmeg, sprinkle each pumpkin lightly. If you are using rosemary (especially recommended if you are serving them with lamb), sprinkle about ½ teaspoon in each pumpkin. Place pumpkin tops in baking dish, alongside their mates. Add about ⅛ inch water in the bottom of the dish, just enough to produce a little steam.

Place the baking dish, covered, in a 350-degree oven for about 50 minutes. After 40 minutes, use a fork to test the flesh of the pumpkins. When it is done, it will be very soft and pull away from the walls of the pumpkin easily. After testing, return to the oven for as long as necessary.

To serve the pumpkins, you can use a fork to mash together the garlic and the pumpkin meat and then top the pumpkin with its cap. You can also serve them just as they come out of the oven, leaving the mashing to your guests. Either way, they are delicious as well as beautiful.

BAKED CHERRY TOMATOES

SERVES 4 TO 6

If you have ever grown cherry tomatoes, you know, even if you have just one or two plants, how quickly you can be overwhelmed by them at the peak of their season. I make this recipe dozens of times when tomatoes are in their glory. It is easy, delicious, versatile, and good hot or chilled. You can vary it however you like, adding a few chopped jalapeño peppers for a spicier version, using red wine or raspberry vinegar instead of lemon juice, adding a handful of fresh herb sprigs or several minced shallots. There are generally plenty of cherry tomatoes available for as much experimenting as you might be inclined to do.

1 quart cherry tomatoes (Sweet 100, Toy
    Box, whatever is fresh and available)
  Handful of garlic cloves, peeled and
    sliced
¼ cup extra-virgin olive oil
  Juice of 1 lemon
  Fresh, cracked black pepper
  Salt to taste

Place the tomatoes in a baking dish, add the garlic, and toss. Pour the olive oil over. Squeeze the lemon juice onto the tomatoes and add some black pepper. Place in 350-degree oven for 20 to 30 minutes or until the tomatoes have burst open and the garlic is softened. Remove from oven, taste, and add salt as desired.

▾ Use simply, as a side dish.
▾ Top with a small sprig of basil and serve with pesto, or a pesto lasagne.
▾ Toss with penne or other medium-sized, shaped pasta, top with a little grated dry Jack cheese, and serve with a green salad.

VARIATIONS ▾ Add 2 or 3 anchovy fillets to the tomatoes before baking. Toss with pasta and top with ½ cup grated dry Jack or freshly grated Parmesan cheese. ▾ Immediately after removing from oven, stir in two table-spoons of pesto. ▾ Bake some goat cheese, preferably small rounds such as cabecou or Calistogan, in the oven until just melted. Toss the tomatoes with ½ cup grated Tome cheese, and place on a large serving platter. Top with the rounds of goat cheese and serve with hot French bread.

BLACK PEPPER ZUCCHINI

SERVES 4

Although the quantity of black pepper given in this recipe may seem excessive, try it anyway. Instead of just being a seasoning, the pepper becomes a primary ingredient here and it works very well. Black Pepper Zucchini is the perfect side dish for roasted or grilled meats, especially beef and lamb.

6 zucchini, 4-inches long
2 tablespoons butter
2 tablespoons fresh, cracked black pepper

Cut the zucchini into ¼-inch slices, slightly on the diagonal. Heat the butter in sauté pan until foamy. Add the zucchini and sauté for 4 minutes, tossing to evenly coat in the butter. Add the pepper, toss well again, remove from heat, and serve immediately.

▼▼

ZUCCHINI HUBERT

SERVES 4

This dish is named for the wonderful Algerian chef, Hubert Saulnier, from whom I learned so much about food, and who now cooks on Sunday and Tuesday nights at the Tradewinds bar in Cotati.

  4 to 6 young zucchini, about 4- or 5-inches long

     3 tablespoons extra-virgin olive oil, preferably a green, rather than a golden oil

        Juice of 1 lemon

     4 cloves garlic, peeled and minced

     2 teaspoons ground cumin

        Salt to taste

Remove the stem ends and cut the zucchini into medium julienne. Blanch in rapidly boiling water for 2 minutes. Drain in a colander then place in a small bowl. Toss the zucchini with olive oil, lemon juice, garlic, and cumin. Taste and add salt if desired. May be served warm or chilled.

SALADS

RASPBERRY COLESLAW

SERVES 6 TO 8

Delicately colored and fragrant, Raspberry Coleslaw gives the traditional cabbage salad a whole new dimension. The raspberries add a complexity and intensity that other versions lack, and the ground cumin adds just the subtlest hint of something more exotic. Try this Sonoma-style coleslaw with Frank's Crêpes, page 175.

   1 medium cabbage, shredded
   1 small red onion, minced
  ¼ cup chopped Italian parsley
   1 cup Raspberry Mayonnaise, page 210
  ½ cup crème fraîche or sour cream
  ¼ cup black raspberry vinegar
   2 tablespoons lemon juice or more,
       to taste
  ¼ cup sugar
   1 tablespoon ground cumin
      Salt to taste

   1 pint fresh raspberries, black if available
      Sprig of Italian parsley

Toss the cabbage, onion, and parsley together in a large bowl. In a smaller mixing bowl, whisk together the Mayonnaise, crème fraîche, vinegar, lemon juice, sugar, and cumin. Taste and correct seasonings. Pour over the cabbage mixture and toss until well coated. Taste and add a little salt, if desired. Set a few raspberries aside and toss the rest with the coleslaw. Place on a serving platter, garnish with raspberries and a sprig of Italian parsley, and serve.

VARIATION ▾ This coleslaw made with blueberries is especially good served with duck or venison. Use a blueberry vinegar in the mayonnaise and in the slaw dressing. Substitute blueberries for raspberries, omit the cumin, and add ¼ teaspoon ground cloves. Use freshly squeezed orange juice in place of the lemon juice and garnish with a fine julienne of fresh orange peel.

WINTER JEWEL SALAD

SERVES 4

One of my favorite sights in Sonoma is that of the bright plump persimmons hanging from bare trees, glowing in the early morning fog like some exotic winter jewel. For a few weeks in the fall their season coincides with that of my other favorite fall fruit, the pomegranate, and I try to pair them together several times before the pomegranate disappears for another year.

- 2 bunches watercress or arugula
- 2 persimmons
- 2 ripe avocados
- ½ cup Pomegranate Vinaigrette (page 217)
- ½ cup pomegranate seeds

Clean the watercress or arugula and arrange on individual serving plates. Cut out the leaf bases of the persimmons and halve the fruits lengthwise. Carefully slide a sharp knife between the skin and the flesh to peel the fruit. Gently cut it into slices. Divide the fruit among the servings. Cut the avocados in half, peel them, and remove the seeds. Cut into lengthwise slices and arrange on the plates, alternating with the persimmon. Drizzle the Vinaigrette over the salad and sprinkle with pomegranate seeds.

SIMPLE PASTA SALAD

SERVES 4

This salad is best served as soon as it is made, when the flavors and textures are still fresh and crisp. Some salads, including pasta salads, improve after sitting for several hours or a day, but this is not one of them. The Chicken and Raspberry Sandwich (page 108) is well complemented by this salad, with the peppery arugula acting as the perfect foil to the sweetness of the raspberry.

- ½ pound small-shaped pasta
- ¼ cup extra-virgin olive oil
- 3 cloves garlic, minced
  Juice of 1 lemon
- 3 ounces chèvre (chabis), crumbled or broken up into medium chunks
- 1 bunch arugula, cut crosswise in ¼-inch strips
  Salt and pepper to taste
  A handful or 2 of borage flowers, if available

Cook the pasta until done in plenty of salted, boiling water. Remove to a colander, rinse well in cool water, drain, and place in a salad bowl. Toss with olive oil until well coated. Add the garlic and lemon juice and toss again. Add the goat cheese and arugula, toss quickly, and taste. Add salt and pepper as desired. Arrange the pasta for serving (in the salad bowl is fine, unless you want to remove it to something more decorative) and top with borage flowers.

Pasta Salad with Golden Tomatoes

S E R V E S 4 T O 6

Pasta salad is generally a chilled dish in which pasta is the primary or dominant ingredient. Here, the tiny, seed-shaped rosemarina is not the main ingredient, but one of many in this recipe. The result is an unusual, and delicious, use of pasta in salad.

   1 pint cherry or small golden pear
        tomatoes
   ¼ cup minced red onion
        Several cloves garlic, minced
        About 1 tablespoon snipped chives
   ½ cup sliced Kalamata olives
   ⅓ pound rosemarina pasta
   1 tablespoon marinated, dried tomatoes,
        finely chopped, oil reserved
   ¼ cup extra virgin olive oil + more as
        needed
        Juice of 1 or 2 lemons
   ½ cup grated Tome cheese
   1 quart mixed salad greens

Cut the cherry tomatoes in half and toss with the onion, garlic, chives, and olives. Cook the pasta according to the directions on the package, drain, rinse well in cool water, drain again, and toss with enough of the oil from the marinated tomatoes to coat the pasta. Add the cherry tomato mixture to the pasta and toss lightly.

   Add the dried tomatoes and toss again. Drizzle about ¼ cup olive oil over the mixture, followed by the juice of 1 lemon. Taste and adjust the amounts of oil and lemon juice as desired. Add the Tome, toss again, taste, and add salt as desired. Divide the salad greens among 4 to 6 plates, top each with several large spoonsful of the pasta salad, and serve.

Autumn Rice Salad

S E R V E S 6

One of the best things about the arrival of fall is making this gorgeous salad. The pomegranates sparkle like little jewels, and the reds, golds, and greens make the salad look like an enchanted, edible treasure chest. The combinations of flavors and textures make it every bit as delightful to eat as it is to look at; it is even fun to make, especially if you welcome the chance to get your hands into a pomegranate, one of my favorite fall activities.

   1 cup rice, uncooked
   1 tablespoon Cranberry Vinegar (page 215)
   ½ cup Cranberry Vinaigrette (page 217)
   1 red, 1 yellow, and 1 green bell pepper,
        seeded and diced
   1 small red onion, diced
   ½ cup fresh pomegranate seeds
   ½ cup fresh cranberries, finely chopped
   2 tablespoons Italian parsley, chopped
   2 tablespoons chopped chives
   ½ cup Lemon Vinaigrette (page 216)

Cook the rice in water to which you have added the Cranberry Vinegar. Place the cooked rice in a mixing bowl and toss well with the Cranberry Vinaigrette. Chill for at least 2 hours. Just before serving, toss the rice with the fruit and vegetables. Add the parsley, 1 tablespoon of the chives, and the Lemon Vinaigrette and toss again. Sprinkle with the remaining chopped chives and serve.

Wild Rice Salad

SERVES 4 TO 6

Though it is not traditional, I always think of wild rice as a particularly festive food to serve at the holidays, which must be why I so frequently pair it with cranberries.

   1 cup wild rice
   1 cup chicken broth
   2 cups water
   2 teaspoons minced garlic
   1 tablespoon chives, snipped
   2 tablespoons chopped Italian parsley
   ½ cup chopped cranberries (optional; use when in season)
   ½ cup extra-virgin olive oil
   3 tablespoons sherry vinegar
      Salt and pepper to taste
   ½ cup pine nuts, toasted

Cook the wild rice in the chicken broth and water until all the liquid has been absorbed, about 40 minutes or possibly longer. Turn into a large salad bowl and fluff with a fork. Set aside to cool.

When cool, toss with the chives, parsley, and cranberries. Drizzle the olive oil over and then the vinegar. Toss again. Season with salt and pepper to taste. Sprinkle the pine nuts over and toss lightly. Garnish with a couple of sprigs of Italian parsley and several whole cranberries. Serve at once or chill, removing from the refrigerator about 20 minutes before serving.

VARIATION ▾ On 4 serving plates place a generous serving of Wild Rice Salad. Top with several slices of smoked duck and drizzle with a little Cranberry Vinaigrette (page 217). Garnish with a slice of orange and serve.

Hearts of Butter Lettuce

with Lemon and Chive Vinaigrette

SERVES 4

I love this salad. It is one of my particular favorites, especially when I have the sweet Meyer lemons available. Try the variation of this delicious salad (see next page) with a substantial pizza, such as the Ratatouille Pizza on page 119. It is a great combination.

   1 or 2 Meyer lemons
      1 clove garlic
      1 tablespoon snipped fresh chives
      ¼ teaspoon salt

½ cup extra-virgin olive oil
3 or 4 heads Butter lettuce, depending on size
1 very small torpedo onion
Fresh, cracked black pepper

If the lemons are small, use 2; if they are medium or large, 1 will be sufficient. Peel and cut away any white rind remaining. Cut in half and remove the seeds. Place the pieces of lemon in a food processor along with the garlic, chives, and salt. Pulse until the lemon is well chopped. Add the olive oil and blend together briefly. Set the dressing aside.

Remove all the large leaves from the lettuces. Break apart the remaining leaves and place them in a bowl that is large enough to allow you to toss the salad well. Peel and slice the onion very thinly. Separate the round slices into rings and add a handful to the bowl of lettuce.

Pour the vinaigrette over the lettuce and toss until all the leaves are coated. Divide among 4 salad plates, sprinkle with plenty of fresh, cracked black pepper, and serve.

VARIATION ▾ Add ½ cup crumbled imported Gorgonzola cheese and ½ cup pecans to the salad and toss lightly.

SIMPLE GREEN SALAD

SERVES 2 TO 4

"I can recommend this dish to all who have confidence in me: salad refreshes without weakening, and comforts without irritating, and I have a habit of saying that it makes us younger."—Jean Anthelme Brillat-Savarin, from M. F. K. Fisher's translation of The Physiology of Taste.

1 quart salad greens: arugula, young Romaine, oak-leaf, nasturtium leaves, miner's lettuce, Butter lettuce, etc.
⅓ cup extra-virgin olive oil
2 tablespoons lemon juice
½ teaspoon dry mustard
1 clove garlic, minced
Pinch of cayenne pepper
Pinch of salt

Rinse and dry the greens. Mix the olive oil, lemon juice, and seasonings until well blended. In a large bowl, toss the greens with the vinaigrette and serve immediately.

GREEN SALAD WITH PEARS

and Pear Vinaigrette

SERVES 4 TO 6

Pears and hazelnuts are happy companions and they appear here in two forms: each in their natural state, and each, with their essence preserved, in hazelnut oil and in pear vinegar.

  1 quart mesclun, or other salad greens
2 to 3 tablespoons + ¾ cup extra-virgin
       olive oil
     Several spears Belgian endive
  2 ripe red pears
  1 small round of goat cheese per serving,
       cabecou or Calistogan, about 2
       ounces each
  ½ cup fresh, shelled hazelnuts
  2 tablespoons hazelnut oil
  4 tablespoons pear vinegar
     Sprig of fresh thyme
     Salt and pepper to taste

Mix the mesclun with enough olive oil to coat and arrange on serving plates. Arrange 4 or 5 spears of endive in a circle on top of the greens. Cut the pears in half, core them, and slice about ⅛-inch thick. Arrange the slices in between the spears of endive. Place a round of goat cheese in the center of each salad. *Very* coarsely crush the hazelnuts, so that you have large pieces. Scatter the pieces over the salads.

  Mix together ¾ cup olive oil, the hazel-nut oil, and the pear vinegar. Taste and add more vinegar if you prefer. Add the leaves of the thyme and salt and pepper to taste. Drizzle the dressing over salad and serve immediately.

GREEN SALAD

with Apples and Roquefort Cheese

SERVES 4 TO 6

Here we have apples and Roquefort cheese in a combination that would be delicious served after the Pork Tenderloin in Red Wine Marinade on page 169.

  1 quart salad greens
  1 apple, cored and very thinly sliced
  ⅓ cup extra-virgin olive oil
  1 tablespoon lemon juice
  1 tablespoon heavy cream
  2 tablespoons Roquefort cheese
     Fresh black pepper

Prepare the greens for salad. Prepare the apple and hold in cold water with a little lemon juice. Mix together the olive oil and lemon juice. Add the cream and stir well. Crumble the cheese and add it to the dressing, mixing, but not overmixing. Season with plenty of freshly ground black pepper. Drain the apples well. Toss all the ingredients together in a large bowl and serve.

SONOMA-STYLE CAESAR SALAD

SERVES 4 TO 6

This version varies little from the traditional Caesar Salad I've always loved, though I omit the customary coddled egg unless I am making a larger quantity, using two or three heads of Romaine. I suspect my way of making this salad developed in response to my young daughters' protests about "raw" eggs, and if you prefer it with the egg included, you should be sure to do so. Also, I frequently use Vella's Dry Jack cheese instead of the traditional Parmesan.

- ¾ cup extra-virgin olive oil
- 4 cloves garlic
- 1½ cups cubes of fresh sourdough bread
- 1 anchovy fillet
  Dash of Worcestershire sauce
- 1 cup grated dry Jack or Parmesan cheese
- 1 large or 2 small heads Romaine lettuce, leaves separated, washed, and dried
- 2 tablespoons champagne vinegar
  Juice of 1 lemon
  Salt to taste
  Fresh, cracked black pepper

Place about ⅓ cup of the olive oil in a quart jar or other container that has a lid. Press 2 cloves of garlic into the oil. Add the bread cubes and shake until the bread has absorbed all the oil. Place the bread cubes on a sheet pan and bake in 250-degree oven until the croutons are dry and golden.

In a large salad bowl, preferably wooden, place the remaining olive oil. Press in the remaining garlic cloves and add the anchovy fillet and Worcestershire sauce. Mix with fork, mashing the anchovy. Add about ¼ cup of the cheese. Tear the leaves of the Romaine into the bowl. Toss well until all of the lettuce is well coated with the olive oil mixture. Sprinkle the vinegar over the salad and toss. Repeat with the lemon juice. Add ½ cup of the remaining cheese, salt as desired, and at least 1 teaspoon of black pepper. Toss well. Add the croutons and toss again. Sprinkle the remaining cheese and more black pepper on top of the salad and serve.

SPINACH SALAD LA PROVINCE

SERVES 4

This is the salad that the chef, Josef Heller, serves as part of his Taste of Sonoma dinner.

- 3 cups La Province House Dressing (page 218)
- 2 tablespoons honey
- ¼ pound mushrooms, sliced
- 4 strips bacon, sautéed until crisp, drained, and crumbled
- 2 bunches spinach, washed and drained
- 2 hard-boiled eggs
- 4 ounces chèvre

Heat the dressing with the honey, mush-rooms, and bacon. Arrange the spinach on individual serving plates and pour the dressing over. Garnish with chopped hard-boiled egg and crumbled goat cheese. Serve immediately.

LAMB AND WHITE BEAN SALAD

with Garlic-Mint Dressing and Mint Relish

SERVES 4

The flavor combinations in this salad are enough to make you swoon. Serve it as a main course, with a medium-bodied red wine, or a good ale, such as Sierra Nevada Pale Ale, an outstanding beer from Chico, California.

    16 thin slices of raw or roasted lamb,
        trimmed of fat
     1 cup Garlic-Mint Dressing
        (recipe follows)
     1 cup small white beans, rinsed
     1 ham hock
     1 small red onion
        Mint Relish (page 218)
        Sprigs of mint and cilantro, for garnish

Place the lamb in a glass dish and pour ½ cup Garlic-Mint Dressing over. Refrigerate for 8 hours or overnight.

Soak the beans overnight and drain, or bring beans to a boil in a heavy pan, remove from the heat, and let sit for 1 hour. Place the rinsed beans in a heavy pot, cover with plenty of water, add the ham hock, and simmer until tender, about 40 minutes. Remove the ham hock and drain the beans. Chop the meat from the ham hock into small pieces, toss with the beans and the remaining ½ cup dressing, and set aside.

Quickly grill or broil the lamb slices, if you are using raw meat. Chop the onion, toss it with the beans, and arrange the beans on serving plates. Top each serving with 4 slices of lamb and top lamb with a spoonful of Mint Relish. Garnish with sprigs of mint and cilantro and serve more Mint Relish on the side.

GARLIC-MINT DRESSING

MAKES ABOUT 1 CUP

     4 cloves garlic, minced
     4 tablespoons fresh lime juice
     1 teaspoon Dijon-style mustard
     ¼ cup fresh mint leaves, chopped
     ¼ teaspoon sugar
     ½ teaspoon salt
     1 teaspoon freshly ground black pepper
     ¾ cup olive oil

Combine all the ingredients except the olive oil in a small bowl or in a food processor.

Slowly add the oil and beat vigorously or process until emulsified. Taste and correct seasonings.

▼▼▼▼▼▼▼▼▼▼▼▼▼▼▼▼▼▼▼▼▼▼▼▼▼▼▼▼▼▼▼▼▼▼▼

THAI LIME BEEF SALAD

with Black Chanterelles and Fresh Ginger

SERVES 4

The first time I tasted this combination of garlic, lime, mint, cilantro, and beef was in a tiny restaurant in Ashland, Oregon. Without doubt, it is one of the most compelling combinations of flavors I have ever come across. Two weeks after the first taste, I drove the eight hundred miles it took to have this incredible salad again and to imprint it firmly in my culinary imagination. I had to be able to recreate it and had never worked with Thai ingredients before. I was extremely motivated, though, and it did not take long for me to come up with this version, which has never failed to render my guests speechless with delight as they eat.

If the chanterelle mushrooms are unavailable, omit them. They were not part of the original recipe, but represent my attempt to do something wonderful with the black chanterelles I had been given by Malcolm Clark, the president of Gourmet Mushroom. They add a great dimension to the salad, but are not at all essential to its success.

  1 quart mesclun or fall salad mix
  ¼ cup mint leaves

  ¼ cup cilantro leaves
  ¼ pound black chanterelle mushrooms
     1-inch piece fresh ginger
     Peanut oil
     Soy sauce
     Thai fish sauce
  1 New York steak, about 8 to 10 ounces, trimmed of fat
  4 sprigs fresh mint
  1 lime, quartered

DRESSING
  5 cloves garlic, chopped
  5 serrano chilies, seeded
  1 tablespoon Thai fish sauce
  2 tablespoons lime juice
  2 teaspoons granulated sugar

Start the grill or turn on the broiler. Arrange the greens on 4 serving plates and sprinkle the mint and cilantro over.

If you are using them, brush or wipe the chanterelles free of any dirt that may cling to them. Cut the fresh, peeled ginger into small matchsticks. Add a small amount of oil to a wok or small sauté pan. Add the ginger, a splash of fish sauce, and a splash of soy sauce. Heat the pan, add the chanterelles, and sauté quickly until just limp. Remove from the heat and set aside.

Place the meat on the grill or under the broiler and cook for about 5 minutes on each side. It should be very rare. While the meat is cooking, make the dressing. Pound the garlic and chilies together in a mortar and pestle or use a food processor. Add the fish sauce, lime juice, and sugar. Slice the meat very thinly. Arrange the slices on top of the greens. Divide the sautéed chanterelles among the servings, placing them on top of the meat. Pour the dressing over and garnish with mint sprigs and lime. Serve immediately.

▼▼▼▼▼▼▼▼▼▼▼▼▼▼▼▼▼▼▼▼▼▼▼▼▼▼▼▼▼▼▼

SPRING CHICKEN SALAD

SERVES 4 TO 6 AS MAIN COURSE SALAD

This sweet salad is another example of the wonderful marriage between chicken and asparagus, united with the evocative flavor of raspberries.

1½ pounds thin asparagus
    Meat from 1 small roasted free-range chicken (about 3 to 4 pounds)
2 cups Black Raspberry Vinaigrette (page 216)
1 small red onion, cut in thin slices
1 quart salad greens, mesclun
    Fresh raspberries, if available

Steam or parboil the asparagus quickly until just barely tender. Remove from the boiling water to a cold water bath. Drain. Set aside about one-quarter of the asparagus and cut the remainder into 1½-inch pieces. Place the reserved asparagus into a glass or ceramic dish. Top with the chopped asparagus and drizzle with ½ cup Raspberry Vinaigrette. Refrigerate for at least 1 hour or overnight.

Cut chicken into a medium julienne. Toss with enough Raspberry Vinaigrette to

coat thoroughly. Refrigerate for at least 1 hour or overnight. Remove from the refrigerator 1 hour before ready to serve.

To serve, toss the chilled salad greens with enough Vinaigrette to coat and arrange on a large serving platter or on individual serving plates. Arrange several rings of onion on top of the greens. Toss the chicken and cut asparagus pieces together lightly and arrange on top of the greens. Sprinkle a handful of raspberries, if they are available, over each salad. Garnish with the stalks of asparagus. Spoon a little Raspberry Vinaigrette over the salad and serve.

▼▼▼▼▼▼▼▼▼▼▼▼▼▼▼▼▼▼▼▼▼▼▼▼▼▼▼▼▼▼▼

SONOMA CHEESE AND CHICKEN SALAD

with Walnut-Dill Vinaigrette

SERVES 4

The Sonoma Cheese Factory offers this recipe as part of their promotional recipe pamphlet.

1 cup halved walnuts
2 large chicken breasts, halved
1 cup shredded Jack cheese
1 medium red bell pepper, chopped fine
2 tablespoons scallions, minced
2 tablespoons butter
2 tablespoons vegetable oil
2 whole cloves garlic

Salt and pepper to taste

2 quarts mixed greens, including arugula, chicory, endive, and radicchio

Walnut-Dill Vinaigrette (recipe follows)

To toast the walnuts, place them on a cookie sheet in a 400-degree oven. Bake until slightly brown, about 10 minutes. Reduce the oven heat to 350 degrees.

Cut a pocket in each chicken breast with a sharp knife, working horizontally from the thickest part of the breast down. Mix together the cheese, pepper, and scallions, and stuff each breast with the mixture. Heat the butter and oil in heavy skillet and sauté the garlic until just golden. Remove from the skillet. Brown the chicken breasts on each side over medium heat, remove from the pan, season with salt and pepper, place on a baking sheet, and bake for 20 minutes. Let them rest for 15 minutes before slicing.

Cut each breast diagonally into 8 slices. Divide the greens among 4 plates. Carefully lift the chicken with a spatula and arrange on the greens. Drizzle vinaigrette on each plate and garnish with walnuts.

WALNUT-DILL VINAIGRETTE

MAKES ABOUT 1 CUP

2 cloves garlic

1-inch piece peeled fresh ginger

1 tablespoon Dijon-style mustard

¼ cup rice vinegar

½ teaspoon white sugar

Salt and pepper to taste

1 teaspoon dill weed

¼ cup walnut oil

½ cup olive oil

In a food processor, finely chop the garlic and ginger. Add the mustard, vinegar, sugar, salt, pepper, and dill. With the machine running, slowly add the walnut oil and then the olive oil in a steady stream until emulsified.

SONOMA RANCH SALAD

SERVES 4 TO 6

This salad, based upon the traditional Salade Niçoise, has evolved over the years into one of The Jaded Palate's most popular items.

1 pound roasted free-range chicken meat

Raspberry Vinaigrette (page 216)

1 pound new red potatoes, yellow fin potatoes, or fingerling potatoes

Lemon Vinaigrette (page 216)

1 pound Blue Lake green beans

½ cup Kalamata olives

1 pound fresh, thin asparagus, if in season; if not, omit

1 medium red onion, cut in thin slices

3 or 4 medium, ripe tomatoes, home-grown, in season, cut in wedges; omit if good tomatoes are not available

4 hard-boiled free-range eggs, shelled, and cut in wedges

4 anchovy fillets (optional)

Cut the chicken into thin strips and toss with enough Raspberry Vinaigrette to coat well. Set aside or refrigerate overnight. If you do prepare the chicken in advance, be sure to remove it from refrigerator 30 minutes before assembling the salad.

Cut the potatoes into 1-inch pieces and cook in rapidly boiling water until *just done*. Toss with a little Lemon Vinaigrette and set aside. Trim the green beans and cut into 1½-inch pieces. Cook until just tender, rinse, drain, and toss with the potatoes. Add the olives and toss again. Cook the trimmed asparagus until just done and toss with a little Raspberry Vinaigrette.

To assemble the salad, place a mound of the potato mixture in the center of each serving plate. Surround with several spears of asparagus. Top with rings of red onion. Add a wedge of tomato between each stalk of asparagus. Top the potatoes with wedges of egg, leaving room in the center for the chicken. Divide chicken among the servings. Top each serving of chicken with a single anchovy fillet, wound into a circle. Drizzle each salad with a little Lemon Vinaigrette, followed by a little Raspberry Vinaigrette. Serve.

VARIATION ▾ On a large, decorative platter, arrange the various items in the salad in separate groups, displaying them attractively. Drizzle a small amount of each dressing over the salad and serve the remaining dressing on the side.

SMOKED CHICKEN AND FENNEL SALAD
SERVES 4

Mary Evely's Winter Luncheon salad is a delicious combination of flavors and a great way to highlight the smoked chicken. See her menu on page 66.

1 whole smoked chicken breast
2 medium fennel bulbs
8 marinated sun-dried tomato halves
1 yellow bell pepper
3 cups thinly sliced red cabbage (approximately ½ head)
   Mustard Vinaigrette (page 217)
   Escarole leaves

Skin and bone the chicken and cut it into slivers. Thinly slice the fennel bulbs horizontally, discarding the tough central core. Cut the yellow pepper into a medium julienne. Toss the chicken, fennel, and pepper together with the cabbage and the Mustard Vinaigrette. Mound onto escarole leaves and serve.

RED-LEAF LETTUCES WITH SMOKED CHICKEN

SERVES 4

Although this delicious salad is presented as one course of several in the Russian River Vineyards Fall Menu, page 65, it is substantial enough to serve as a main course luncheon salad.

2 or 3 heads mixed red lettuces: curly red-leaf, radicchio, red oak-leaf, red Butter, etc.
  ½ cup light vegetable oil
1½ teaspoons roasted sesame oil (available in the Asian foods section of many markets; be sure not to get hot sesame chili oil)
  ¼ cup raspberry vinegar
  2 teaspoons honey
  ½ teaspoon salt or a dash of soy sauce
    Pinch of white pepper
4 to 6 ounces smoked chicken or smoked turkey, diced
    A few fresh raspberries, if available, for garnish or use slivered scallions and toasted sesame seeds

Wash and dry the lettuce leaves. Whisk together the vegetable oil, sesame oil, vinegar, honey, salt or soy sauce, and pepper. Cut the lettuce in a fine julienne and make nests of it on each serving plate. Top each nest with diced chicken or turkey, and drizzle with a generous quantity of dressing. Garnish and serve immediately.

BLUEBERRY AND CHICKEN LIVER SALAD

with Blueberry Vinaigrette

SERVES 4

The appetizer version of this recipe received a Gold Medal at the 1987 Sonoma County Harvest Fair, in the same year that it appeared in Women Chefs, *by Jim Burns and Betty Ann Brown (Reading, Mass.: Addison-Wesley, 1987). The chicken livers, which are chopped fine, are wrapped in wilted spinach leaves and each little package is then garnished with a slice of quail's egg and drizzled with warm blueberry vinaigrette. Garnished with berries from Sepastopol's Green Valley Blueberry Farm, they make a perfect Sonoma appetizer.*

  ½ cup + 3 tablespoons olive oil
  6 tablespoons blueberry vinegar
1½ teaspoons ground cloves
    Salt
    Fresh, cracked black pepper
  ¾ pound chicken livers
  1 large or 2 small bunches young spinach
  3 shallots, minced
  1 cup fresh blueberries
8 to 10 soft-boiled quails' eggs or 4 soft-boiled eggs

To the ½ cup olive oil, add 3 tablespoons blueberry vinegar, 1 teaspoon cloves, and salt and pepper to taste. Set aside.

Trim, rinse, and dry the livers. Set aside.

Rinse and dry the spinach and toss with a small amount of olive oil until each leaf is coated. Arrange on a serving platter or individual serving plates.

Cut each liver into 4 pieces and toss with salt, pepper, and the remaining ½ teaspoon cloves. Sauté the minced shallots in the remaining 3 tablespoons olive oil until they are just transparent. Add the livers and sauté quickly, for about 1½ minutes on each side. Remove the livers from the pan with a slotted spoon and place them in a mixing bowl.

Deglaze the pan with the remaining 3 tablespoons blueberry vinegar. Pour the liquid over the chicken livers and toss well. Arrange the warm livers on top of the spinach and drizzle with the warm pan drippings and juice from the livers combined.

Sprinkle the blueberries decoratively over the salad and garnish with the quails' eggs, each cut in half through the shell (do not attempt to shell them). Serve with the blueberry vinaigrette on the side.

SALAD OF PETALUMA SMOKED DUCK BREASTS

with Dried Cherries, Oranges, and Hazelnuts

SERVES 8

This hearty yet light main course salad is from the Late Summer Luncheon, page 64, planned by Bea Beasley, who is a caterer.

8 cups mixed baby lettuce leaves; choose a combination of shapes and colors, with mild, spicy, and delicate flavors
1 cup whole hazelnuts
1 cup pitted dried cherries
½ cup freshly squeezed orange juice
2 large navel oranges, peeled and segmented
3 smoked duck breasts, about 12 ounces each, skinned and cut in julienne
¾ cup Orange-Hazelnut Vinaigrette (recipe follows)
Edible flowers, for garnish

Preheat the oven to 350 degrees. Wash the lettuce leaves thoroughly, dry them, wrap in a cloth towel, and chill. Spread the hazelnuts in a single layer on a baking sheet and toast in the oven for about 15 minutes. Remove the skins by rubbing the nuts in a kitchen towel. Chop the nuts coarsely and set aside.

Place the cherries in a small bowl with the orange juice to soften while you are making the vinaigrette. Drain the cherries, reserve liquid, and set both aside.

To assemble the salads, toss the lettuces in a large bowl with the vinaigrette to coat lightly and arrange on 8 plates. Place the duck on top of the lettuces. Arrange the orange segments around the duck and sprinkle with the nuts and cherries. Garnish the salads with edible flowers.

ORANGE-HAZELNUT VINAIGRETTE

MAKES ABOUT ¾ CUP

1 teaspoon Dijon-style mustard
1 teaspoon grated orange zest
2 teaspoons orange honey
2 tablespoons red wine vinegar
4 tablespoons orange juice reserved from the soaked cherries
Salt
Freshly ground black pepper
¼ cup hazelnut oil
¼ cup olive oil

Combine the mustard, orange zest, honey, vinegar, orange juice, and salt and pepper to taste in a small bowl; whisk in the oils until well blended.

PEAR, AVOCADO, AND SHRIMP SALAD

SERVES 4

This salad, in any of its versions is especially festive, perfect for a celebration or holiday brunch.

2 avocados, ripe but firm
2 pears, flavorful but firm
1 lime
¼ pound small-shaped dried pasta
½ pound cooked bay shrimp
Curry Dressing (recipe follows)
1 head Butter lettuce

Cut the avocados in half, remove the seed, and peel. Cut 3 of the halves into 1-inch chunks and place in large salad bowl. Repeat process with the pears, adding the pear chunks to the bowl with the avocado. Squeeze a little lime juice over the pears and avocados and over remaining halves, too. Set aside.

Cook the pasta according to the directions on the package and rinse well under cool water. Add it to the bowl of avocados and pears, along with the bay shrimp. Add about ½ cup of the Curry Dressing and toss lightly.

On 4 salad plates, place 2 or 3 leaves of Butter lettuce. Top with a portion of the salad. Cut the remaining pear and avocado halves in lengthwise slices and garnish the salads. Top each with another tablespoon or two of dressing. Serve immediately.

CURRY DRESSING

MAKES ABOUT 1½ CUPS

1 egg yolk
⅓ cup lemon juice
¼ teaspoon cayenne pepper
1½ teaspoons curry powder
1 teaspoon minced fresh garlic
1 cup olive oil
Salt to taste

Whisk together the egg yolk, lemon juice, cayenne, curry powder, and garlic. Slowly beat in the olive oil. Add salt to taste if desired. Refrigerate until ready to use.

VARIATIONS ▾ Instead of serving atop Butter lettuce, serve the salad on top of half an avocado or papaya. If in season, garnish with a handful of pomegranate seeds. ▾ Steam 4 artichokes and chill. Remove inner leaves and choke so that you have a clear center space surrounded by a nice set of leaves. Fill with the salad and spoon dressing over. Garnish each serving with the edible leaves removed from the center and with the slices of pear and avocado. Serve with Curry Mayonnaise (page 211) as a dip for the leaves.

▾▾▾▾▾▾▾▾▾▾▾▾▾▾▾▾▾▾▾▾▾▾▾▾▾▾▾▾▾▾▾

SALADE NIÇOISE WITH FRESH TUNA

SERVES 4

Once you have had this traditional Provençal salad with fresh tuna, you will not want to go back to the canned tuna version.

- 1½ pounds small red potatoes, quartered
- 2 tablespoons chopped Italian parsley
- ½ teaspoon Herbs de Provence
  (see Glossary)
  Lemon Vinaigrette (page 216)
- 1 pound Blue Lake green beans
- ½ cup Kalamata olives
- 1 small red onion, thinly sliced
- 4 hard-boiled eggs, peeled and quartered
  or 1 dozen quails' eggs, soft-boiled
- 4 ripe, home-grown tomatoes, quartered
- 1 pound fresh tuna steaks
- 4 anchovy fillets, packed in oil (optional)

Cook the potatoes until just tender. Rinse in cool water and drain. Toss with parsley, Herbs de Provence, and about ¼ cup Lemon Vinaigrette. Set aside.

Trim the green beans and cook in boiling water until just tender. Rinse in cool water and drain.

Toss together the potatoes, green beans, and olives. Arrange in mounds on individual serving plates. Surround with rings of red onion, eggs, and tomatoes. If using the quails' eggs, crack each egg in half, in its shell, before adding it to the salad.

Grill quickly or broil the tuna steaks, for about 3 to 5 minutes on each side. The tuna should be very rare. Cut the fish into chunks and divide among the servings, placing it on top of the potatoes and green beans. Garnish each serving with a single anchovy fillet. Drizzle Lemon Vinaigrette over the salads and serve.

ENSALADA DES ELOTES

SERVES 4 TO 6

Jim Gibbons, the chef and owner of Jacob Horner restaurant in Healdsburg, recommends this salad as an accompaniment to his Tortilla Espagñol (see page 125). When the onions and corn are grilled over coals the complex, smoky flavor that is added to their natural sweetness is memorable and delicious.

  1 red onion, peeled and cut in half
      horizontally
  6 ears fresh, sweet corn, shucked and silk
      removed
    Juice of half a lemon
  ¼ teaspoon cayenne pepper
  ¼ teaspoon salt
  2 Roma tomatoes, seeded and diced
  1 yellow tomato, seeded and diced
  2 tablespoons minced cilantro
  1 tablespoon minced Italian parsley
  1 whole Anaheim chile, roasted, peeled,
      and diced
  1 quart salad greens
  1 avocado, halved and peeled
    Sprigs of cilantro

DRESSING
  ¼ cup olive oil
  6 tablespoons red wine vinegar
  1 tablespoon chili powder
    Juice of half a lemon
  1 teaspoon garlic, ground to a paste
  1 serrano chile, minced with seeds
      (optional)
    Salt to taste

On a charcoal grill, roast the red onion until cooked through. Set aside to cool and, when cooled, dice. While the onion is cooling, roast the corn, turning frequently. Mix together the lemon juice, cayenne, and salt and use this mixture to baste the corn. Continue to roast and turn until the kernels begin to brown; a slight bit of charring is fine. Set aside to cool and, when easy to handle, cut the kernels from the cob.

Mix together the onion, corn, tomatoes, cilantro, parsley, and chile.

Combine all the ingredients for the dressing and mix well. Pour over the vegetables, toss, and let the salad sit for 20 minutes before serving. To serve, place the greens on a platter and spread the salad across the greens. Cut the avocado halves into fans and use as garnish, along with sprigs of cilantro.

FARM MARKET SALAD

VERSION 1 SERVES 4 TO 6;
VERSION 2 SERVES 6 TO 10

This salad can be simple and informal, perfect for taking on a picnic, or elegant and formal, a centerpiece in a grand buffet. It all has to do wih presentation and with the variety of tomatoes used. For taste, use the best local tomatoes you can find. For presentation, try to find a wide variety, both in color and in shape. I love this salad in August and September, when there is an abundance of varieties, from the beautiful bright yellow tomatoes that are perfect for slicing, to the smaller, delicate peach tomato with its slightly fuzzy skin and pale blush color, to the small pear-shaped orange and yellow Toy Box tomatoes, and the tiny jewel-like red currant tomatoes. Occasionally, it is even possible to find white tomatoes that have just a hint of pink and ripe green tomatoes that are intensely sweet and slightly spicy.

VERSION 1

1 quart small plum or cherry tomatoes, sliced in half
2 small torpedo onions, thinly sliced
8 cloves garlic, peeled and thinly sliced
½ cup extra-virgin olive oil
Freshly ground black pepper
Salt to taste
¼ cup fresh basil leaves, cut in thin strips

Toss the tomatoes, onions, and garlic together. Add the olive oil, salt, and pepper and toss again. Sprinkle the basil leaves over and serve.

VERSION 2

6 to 8 medium-sized golden slicing tomatoes
2 small torpedo onions, thinly sliced
1 Armenian cucumber, thinly sliced
4 cloves garlic, peeled
½ cup extra-virgin olive oil
½ cup grated dry Jack cheese
Freshly ground black pepper
Coarse salt
½ cup fresh purple basil leaves, cut in thin strips

2 sprigs fresh purple basil, with flowers if possible
Several sprigs red currant tomatoes

Cut the golden tomatoes into rounds and arrange them in a ring on a large serving platter. Next arrange a ring of onions, followed by one of cucumbers. Repeat until all the tomatoes, onions, and cucumbers are used. Cut the garlic into very thin strips and sprinkle them over the vegetables. Drizzle with olive oil. Sprinkle the cheese and freshly ground pepper over the salad. Sprinkle with small amount of coarse salt. Sprinkle the basil leaves over. Garnish with the sprigs of basil and red currant tomatoes.

GOAT CHEESE AND SUN-DRIED TOMATO SALAD

SERVES 6

This delicious way to use Laura Chenel's Chèvre comes to us from Timber Crest Farms.

2 cups crumbled goat cheese
2 tablespoons drained capers
6 halved marinated dried tomatoes, slivered
2 tablespoons favorite vinegar
2 teaspoons Dijon-style mustard
¼ cup olive oil (you may use the oil that covers the dried tomatoes)
Ground pepper to taste
2 heads Butter lettuce

In a large bowl, toss together the cheese, capers, and slivered tomatoes. Set aside.

Blend together the vinegar and mustard. Gradually add the oil, beating briskly with a whisk. Pour the dressing over the cheese mixture.

Place the washed and drained lettuce on serving plates, spoon the cheese mixture over the lettuce, and serve.

SONOMA-STYLE GREEK SALAD

SERVES 6 TO 8

Make this salad in the middle of summer, when tomatoes are at their peak. This is a great salad to take on a picnic and an excellent accompaniment for Greek Lamb Loaf, page 167.

5	medium-large tomatoes, cut in wedges
3	lemon cucumbers, cut in wedges
1	medium red onion, sliced in rings
1	small green bell pepper, seeded and sliced in rings
1	each red and yellow bell peppers, seeded and sliced in rings
	Several cloves of garlic, minced
8	ounces feta cheese, cut into ½-inch cubes
1	cup Kalamata olives
	Extra-virgin olive oil
2 or 3	anchovies, diced

Red wine vinegar
1 teaspoon Greek oregano
Fresh basil leaves
Salt and pepper to taste

Prepare all the vegetables and toss them together in a large salad bowl. Add the cheese and olives and toss lightly. Drizzle with ½ to ¾ cup olive oil. Add the anchovies. Add about ⅓ cup vinegar and toss lightly. Add the oregano. Cut about 10 basil leaves into thin strips, add them to the salad, and toss lightly. Season with salt and pepper as desired. Garnish with sprigs of basil and serve.

ROASTED PEPPER AND FETA CHEESE SALAD

SERVES 4 TO 8

Be sure to use plenty of French bread to soak up the juice that collects on the serving dish. It is one of the best parts of this recipe. Failing fresh peppers, you could use 1 jar (15 ounces) of Mezzetta brand roasted peppers.

2	cups (4 to 6 peppers) fresh roasted peppers (see glossary page 279)
5	cloves garlic, thinly sliced
2	tablespoons capers
⅓	cup best-quality red wine vinegar or Balsamic vinegar
8	ounces Feta cheese, cut into ½-inch cubes
1	loaf crusty French bread

Cut the peppers into a medium julienne and toss with the garlic, capers, and vinegar. Arrange cubes of feta cheese in the center of a serving platter and place the peppers in a circle around the cheese. Heat the bread and serve it with the salad.

WARM RED CABBAGE SALAD WITH GOAT CHEESE AND BACON

SERVES 6 TO 8

John Ash has offered a warm, robust salad as part of his Spring menu on page 62. The bacon vinaigrette is the perfect complement to the creamy chèvre.

- 1 pound red cabbage
- 1 pound best quality bacon or pancetta
- 1 teaspoon garlic, peeled and minced
- ½ cup fruity extra-virgin olive oil
- 1 teaspoon wild honey
- ⅓ cup red wine vinegar
- ½ teaspoon each sea salt and freshly ground black pepper
  Baby frisée and mâche, or watercress, for garnish
- 5 ounces goat cheese (chabis)
  Nasturtium flowers

Core and finely shred the cabbage; set aside. Cook the bacon until it is lightly browned and just crisp. Drain (reserving fat), chop

roughly, and set aside. Combine ¼ cup of the bacon fat in a bowl with the garlic, olive oil, honey, vinegar, salt, and pepper. Taste and correct the seasoning.

In a large sauté pan over moderate high heat, briefly warm the olive oil mixture, add the cabbage, and toss quickly for a minute or 2 just to warm through. Add the chopped bacon and place the salad on warm plates garnished with *frisée* and *mâche*. Thinly slice the goat cheese and arrange it attractively on top. Garnish with nasturtium flowers and serve.

ROOT SALAD TRICOLOR

SERVES 4

The cool crunch and sweetness of this salad make it a perfect accompaniment for many of the spicy recipes included in this book. Try it with the Chipotle Pork on page 170.

- 4 or 5 small golden beets
- 5 small red potatoes
- 6 ounces jícama, in one piece, peeled
- 2 medium carrots
- 8 or 10 medium radishes
- 1 teaspoon chili powder
- 2 oranges, peeled

Boil the beets until they are *just* tender. Remove to cool water. Peel the raw potatoes and cut into matchsticks. Plunge them into rapidly boiling water for about 3 minutes. Remove to cool water. Drain the beets, peel, and cut them into matchsticks. Drain the potatoes. Cut the jícama, carrots, and radishes into matchsticks, toss all the vegetables together with the chili powder, and set aside.

Cut the ends off the oranges. Squeeze the juice from these ends over the vegetables. Slice the oranges into thin rounds and arrange them on a serving platter. Top with the vegetables. Chill before serving.

SAUCES AND CONDIMENTS

RASPBERRY MAYONNAISE

MAKES 1½ CUPS

Raspberry Mayonnaise (which I make with Kozlowski Farms mustard and vinegar) is one of The Jaded Palate's signature sauces, and I receive frequent requests to sell it by the quart, which I have yet to do. It is wonderful on a chicken sandwich and is a perfect dip for raw or lightly steamed vegetables.

1 egg
1 egg yolk
2 cloves garlic, peeled
2 teaspoons raspberry mustard (optional)
¼ cup extra-virgin olive oil
1 cup olive oil
4 tablespoons black raspberry vinegar
1 teaspoon sugar
Dash salt

Place the egg, egg yolk, garlic, mustard and extra-virgin olive oil in a blender and blend at top speed for about 15 seconds. Slowly drizzle in ½ cup of the olive oil. Slowly add the raspberry vinegar. Add the sugar and salt. Continue to blend at high speed and slowly drizzle in the remaining olive oil.

VARIATIONS ▾ Vary the principal flavors with fruit vinegars, made according to the recipe on page 215, used instead of the raspberry vinegar here. The recipe will work, otherwise unchanged, for Cranberry Mayonnaise and Pomegranate Mayonnaise. To make Blueberry Mayonnaise, use a blueberry vinegar and add ½ teaspoon ground cloves. For all variations substitute ½ teaspoon dried mustard for the raspberry mustard.

Curry Mayonnaise

M A K E S   1¼   C U P S

The flavor of curry will add spark to a salad, a sandwich, or a soup. This mayonnaise is wonderful with leftover lamb and makes an interesting dipping sauce for prawns or scallops.

> 1 tablespoon finely minced yellow onion
> 2 tablespoons olive oil
> 1 tablespoon curry powder
> 1 teaspoon cumin
> 1 teaspoon ground ginger
> ½ teaspoon turmeric
> 1 cup homemade mayonnaise or a good
>   quality commercial brand

Sauté the onion in the olive oil until it is transparent. Add the curry powder and spices and stir well over low heat for about 2 minutes. Remove from the heat, cool, and stir into the mayonnaise until well blended. Refrigerate until ready to use.

Aïoli

M A K E S   1½   C U P S

It is the traditional belief that the best aïoli is made with a mortar and pestle and the olive oil added a drop or two at a time, obviously a lengthy process. Perhaps because the aïoli I first tasted was made from this recipe, I have always loved it and never felt that I was eating an inferior product because it had been made in a blender. I learned the recipe from a cooking teacher long ago when I was studying French. She told us that, on Twelfth Night, this sauce was made with one clove of garlic per guest and one for good luck. I made the sauce that year for my first Twelfth Night celebration and followed her instructions, even though one clove for each of my twenty-three guests seemed a little excessive. It was.

> 1 egg
> 2 egg yolks
> 1 teaspoon powdered mustard
> 6 or 8 large cloves of garlic, peeled
> ½ teaspoon salt
> ¼ cup extra-virgin olive oil
> 1 cup olive oil
> 2 tablespoons lemon juice and more
>   to taste
> **Pinch of cayenne pepper**

Place the egg, egg yolks, mustard, garlic, salt, and the extra-virgin olive oil in a food processor or blender and process until the garlic is pulverized. With the machine operating, slowly drizzle in ½ cup of the remaining olive oil. Add the 2 tablespoons lemon juice, followed by the remainder of the olive oil. Remove to a bowl or container. Add the cayenne, taste, and adjust seasonings as desired by adding more lemon juice, salt, or cayenne to taste. Refrigerate for at least 2 hours before serving.

JALAPEÑO AÏOLI

M A K E S   A B O U T   1½   C U P S

How can you possibly go wrong with this velvety combination of garlic, citrus, and hot peppers? This was a big success at the Second Annual Great Garlic Cook-Off in Cotati in 1988.

 2 jalapeño peppers, seeds and stems removed
 1 egg
 1 egg yolk
 6 cloves garlic
 1¼ cups extra-virgin olive oil
 ¼ cup lime juice
 ½ teaspoon salt

Coarsely chop the *jalapeños* and place them in a blender along with the egg, egg yolk, garlic, and ¼ cup of the olive oil. Blend at top speed for 30 seconds. Slowly drizzle in ½ cup olive oil. Add the lime juice and salt. With blender still running on high, add the remaining olive oil.

VARIATION ▾ Add ½ cup cilantro leaves along with the lime juice and use as a topping for Tomato-Cilantro Soup (page 100).

RASPBERRY-BASIL BUTTER

M A K E S   A B O U T   1¾   C U P S

This luscious combination of ingredients was created by Bea Beasley and completes her Summer Luncheon menu (page 64). Bea recommends that this delicious condiment be served with sweet baguette slices and a creamy, soft-textured, full-flavored cheese and paired with a medium-bodied Zinfandel.

 ¾ cup fresh raspberries
 2 tablespoons raspberry jam
 2 tablespoons Zinfandel wine
 8 fresh basil leaves, chopped
 1 cup unsalted butter, at room temperature and cut into pieces

Blend all the ingredients in a food processor or blender until just combined. Store, covered, in the refrigerator, and remove 30 minutes before serving.

RASPBERRY HOLLANDAISE

M A K E S   1¼   C U P S

This hollandaise sauce is made in a blender and produces excellent, reliable results each time. I use Kozlowski Farms Black Raspberry Vinegar, which has an acidity of 4.5 percent; some imported vinegars have as much as 7 percent acidity, so check the label and add the vinegar in increments, tasting as you go. A pinch of powdered sugar may correct the balance if you find your sauce overly acidic.

3 egg yolks
2 tablespoons raspberry vinegar
1 teaspoon fresh lemon juice
¼ teaspoon salt
   Pinch of sugar
½ cup butter

Place the egg yolks, vinegar, lemon juice, salt, and sugar in a blender. Heat the butter until it is bubbling. Cover the blender and blend at top speed for 5 seconds. With the blender still operating, remove the lid and pour in the butter in a steady stream over the egg mixture. By the time all the butter has been poured, about 30 seconds, the sauce should be finished. To hold the sauce, immerse the blender container in warm water. Should the sauce become too cool, it can be warmed over a double boiler.

▼▼▼▼▼▼▼▼▼▼▼▼▼▼▼▼▼▼▼▼▼▼▼▼▼▼▼▼▼▼▼▼▼▼▼▼

LOBSTER AND GINGER BEURRE BLANC

M A K E S   A B O U T   1¼   C U P S

A velvety beurre blanc, fragrant with the aroma of fresh ginger, is one of the most delightful gastronomic experiences in the world. In John Ash's version, it is combined with the evocative flavor of lobster, resulting in a rich, heavenly sauce. It is so good with

John's Fresh Halibut Wrapped in Chard (page 152), that you will want to use it elsewhere as well.

3 tablespoons chopped shallots
½ cup chopped mushrooms
¼ pound unsalted butter, at room
   temperature
2 cups rich lobster stock or a rich fish
   stock in which you have simmered
   shrimp shells
¾ cup dry white wine
1 tablespoon white wine vinegar
1 tablespoon fresh lemon juice
4 tablespoons fresh ginger, crushed or
   roughly chopped
¾ cup heavy cream
   Salt and freshly ground white pepper

Sauté the shallots and mushrooms in a heavy 2-quart saucepan with 1 tablespoon of the butter until lightly golden brown. Add the stock, wine, vinegar, lemon juice, and ginger, and reduce over high heat to approximately 1 cup.

Add the cream and reduce again by approximately one-half or until a medium sauce consistency is achieved. Remove from the heat, and whisk in the remaining softened butter in bits. Strain and correct the seasoning. Keep warm (not over 100 degrees) until ready to serve.

▼▼▼▼▼▼▼▼▼▼▼▼▼▼▼▼▼▼▼▼▼▼▼▼▼▼▼▼▼▼▼▼

CHÈVRE SAUCE

MAKES 2½ CUPS

A simple cream sauce is the perfect way to showcase the lovely taste of chèvre.

- 1 tablespoon butter
- 3 shallots
- 2 cups heavy cream (substitute half-and-half for a lighter sauce)
- 6 ounces chèvre (chabis, pyramid, or log)
- ¼ cup chopped Italian parsley
- ¼ teaspoon salt
- 1 teaspoon fresh, cracked black pepper

Melt the butter in a heavy saucepan. Chop the shallots and sauté them until transparent. Add the cream and reduce it over medium-high heat for 5 minutes. Add the goat cheese and stir until well blended. Add the parsley, salt, and pepper. Taste and adjust seasonings as necessary. Serve hot. This sauce is excellent with mushrooms and with pasta. Try it with the Wild Mushroom Triangles on page 95. It is featured with Sonoma Cannelloni on page 134.

▼▼▼▼▼▼▼▼▼▼▼▼▼▼▼▼▼▼▼▼▼▼▼▼▼▼▼▼▼▼▼▼

GARLIC AND CILANTRO SAUCE

MAKES ABOUT 1¼ CUPS

This sauce is extremely versatile. Omit the peppers for a milder version, and use it on tacos, quesadillas, *omelettes, and as an extra touch in soups, such as Tomato-Cilantro (page 100) and Pepper and Potato (page 104). It is also wonderful on Seafood Stew (page 156).*

- 1 head garlic, peeled and minced
- 2 jalapeño peppers, seeded and finely chopped
- 2 bunches cilantro, finely chopped
- ½ cup lime juice
- ¼ cup extra-virgin olive oil
- 1 teaspoon salt

Toss all the ingredients together. Serve as a soup topping or spoon over freshly grilled or sautéed fish. The sauce will keep, refrigerated, for 3 or 4 days.

▼▼▼▼▼▼▼▼▼▼▼▼▼▼▼▼▼▼▼▼▼▼▼▼▼▼▼▼▼▼▼▼

ROASTED GARLIC CREAM SAUCE

with Fresh Thyme

SERVES 4 TO 6

In one of my more brazen moments, I developed this recipe before a live audience at Macy's during a cooking demonstration. Of course, I did not reveal that I was inventing it before their very eyes, and they all loved it and wanted to know how I usually served it. Only on special occasions, I informed them.

- 3 cups heavy cream
  Several sprigs fresh thyme

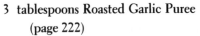
3 tablespoons Roasted Garlic Puree
   (page 222)
2 teaspoons fresh, cracked black pepper

Place the cream and all but one sprig of thyme in a heavy saucepan. Over medium heat, reduce the cream by half. Off the heat, remove the thyme and stir in the garlic. Return to the heat and stir until the sauce is evenly blended and hot. Add about 1 teaspoon of black pepper. This sauce is excellent tossed with pasta and sprinkled with remaining black pepper and fresh thyme leaves and over grilled chicken or fish, topped with chopped fresh tomatoes and chives. Serve immediately.

RASPBERRY MIGNONETTE SAUCE

MAKES 1 CUP

This recipe is from Lisa Jang who, with her husband, Jorge Rebagliati, raises the wonderful Preston Point oysters at Bay Bottom Beds.

1 cup red raspberry vinegar
1 shallot, minced
   Juice of 1 lemon
   Salt and pepper

Mix the vinegar, shallot, and lemon juice together. Add a small amount of salt and pepper and chill. Serve over chilled oysters on the half shell.

FRUIT VINEGARS

There are two reasons to make fruit vinegars, other than the delicious flavor they add to a variety of dishes. If good commercial brands are not available in your area, there is no reason to go without; they are simple to make. If you have access to quantities of good fruit and need to preserve some of it, you might consider distilling its essence into a fruit vinegar. As a base, I use a good champagne vinegar such as Le Vinaigre brand from France. Fruit vinegars, in decorative bottles, make excellent gifts, especially if you attach a few recipes suggesting how to use a particular flavor.

2 parts finely chopped fruit (pomegranate, cranberry, pear, raspberry, blackberry, peach) to 1 part vinegar

Most fruit, with the exception of pomegranates, of which one uses the individual seeds, will need to be finely chopped before being mixed with the vinegar. Place the chopped fruit in a glass jar or crock and pour the vinegar over. Refrigerate for at least 2 days, or up to 1 week. Strain through several layers of cheesecloth until the liquid is clear, bottle, and store.

Some recipes recommend the addition of sugar, in the form of a sugar syrup, but I prefer to use only the fruit, adding sugar to a recipe if it is needed.

▼▼▼▼▼▼▼▼▼▼▼▼▼▼▼▼▼▼▼▼▼▼▼▼▼▼▼▼

SPICY MIGNONETTE

M A K E S   1¼   C U P S

I first tried this sauce at a party given by the Hog Island Farm Shellfish Company in Marin, just to the south of Sonoma. In spite of the unseasonable heavy rains and cool temperatures, it was an utterly wonderful party, primarily because of the unending supply of raw oysters. The menu from that party is included on page 64.

> 1   cup unseasoned rice vinegar
>   Juice of 2 limes
> 1   shallot, finely chopped
> 1   jalapeño pepper, very finely chopped, with seeds
> 2   tablespoons chopped cilantro leaves
> ¼   teaspoon salt

Combine all the ingredients and chill. Serve with oysters on the half shell.

▼▼▼▼▼▼▼▼▼▼▼▼▼▼▼▼▼▼▼▼▼▼▼▼▼▼▼▼

BLACK RASPBERRY VINAIGRETTE

M A K E S   2¼   C U P S

For certain recipes, marinades, for example, any good brand of raspberry vinegar will do; for others, such as this one, superior vinegars will give superior results. The berry vinegars made by Kozlowski Farms are simply unsurpassed.

> ⅔   cup black raspberry vinegar
> 1½ cups extra-virgin olive oil
> 2   cloves garlic, minced
> ¾   teaspoon dry mustard
> 1   teaspoon fresh, cracked black pepper
> ½   teaspoon sugar
> ¼   teaspoon salt

Whisk the raspberry vinegar into the olive oil. Add all the other ingredients and mix together well.

▼▼▼▼▼▼▼▼▼▼▼▼▼▼▼▼▼▼▼▼▼▼▼▼▼▼▼▼

LEMON VINAIGRETTE

M A K E S   A B O U T   1¼   C U P S

Lemon Vinaigrette is a simple and versatile salad dressing, my favorite for everyday use. If I am serving it with a main course that is particularly spicy, I sometimes use the lime variation given at the end of the recipe.

> ⅓   cup fresh lemon juice
> 2 or 3 cloves garlic, minced finely
> 1   teaspoon dry mustard
> 1   tablespoon chopped fresh herbs:
>   thyme, oregano, marjoram, and Italian parsley
> ½   teaspoon salt

½ teaspoon freshly ground black
     pepper
¾ cup extra-virgin olive oil

Combine all the ingredients except the olive oil and blend well. Slowly whisk in the oil. Taste and correct seasoning as desired. Use immediately or refrigerate until ready for use.

VARIATION ▾ Use fresh lime juice instead of lemon juice and add 1 tablespoon chopped cilantro and ½ teaspoon cayenne pepper.

▼▼▼▼▼▼▼▼▼▼▼▼▼▼▼▼▼▼▼▼▼▼▼▼▼▼▼▼▼▼▼▼

CRANBERRY VINAIGRETTE

MAKES 1⅓ CUPS

The beautiful color of this dressing is reason enough to make it: it shines like liquid rubies. It is also delicious, so you should definitely do more than just look at it.

⅓ cup Cranberry Vinegar (page 215)
½ cup hazelnut oil
½ cup olive oil
1 teaspoon thinly sliced orange peel, all
     rind removed, cut into ½-inch pieces
Pinch of ground allspice
Pinch of salt

Blend all the ingredients together and shake well before using.

VARIATION ▾ To make Pomegranate Vinaigrette, use Pomegranate Vinegar (page 215) and omit the orange peel.

▼▼▼▼▼▼▼▼▼▼▼▼▼▼▼▼▼▼▼▼▼▼▼▼▼▼▼▼▼▼▼▼▼▼

MUSTARD VINAIGRETTE

MAKES 1½ CUPS

Standing before a display of the huge panorama of specialty mustards, one can get awfully confused. To complicate matters further, many wineries are now offering their own brands of flavored blends. I solve the problem by being fairly traditional in my taste for mustard; I love those from Dijon, and have never tasted a specialty mustard that improved upon the versions from the region in France that started the whole thing so long ago.

2 tablespoons Dijon-style mustard
1 shallot, minced
2 cloves garlic, minced
1 teaspoon fresh thyme leaves
1 teaspoon minced Italian parsley
½ teaspoon freshly ground black pepper
½ teaspoon salt
4 tablespoons champagne vinegar
2 tablespoons fresh lemon juice
1 cup olive oil

Place the mustard, shallot, garlic, and herbs into a mixing bowl and whisk together. Add pepper and salt and blend. Whisk in the vinegar and lemon juice. Slowly whisk in the olive oil. Taste and adjust seasonings as desired.

La Province House Dressing

MAKES ABOUT 5½ CUPS

Josef Heller, the chef of La Province Restaurant in Santa Rosa, has generously offered the recipe for his house dressing.

  4 tablespoons chopped Italian parsley
    Half a medium onion, minced
  ½ cup green olives, minced
  1 egg, beaten
  2 tablespoons Dijon-style mustard
  1 teaspoon Worcestershire sauce
  1 teaspoon soy sauce
  ¾ teaspoon each dried tarragon, oregano,
      marjoram, thyme, and paprika
    Pinch of curry powder
  3 cups peanut oil
  1 cup olive oil
  1 cup red wine vinegar

Mix together the parsley, onion, and olives. Add the egg, mustard, Worcestershire and soy sauces, dried herbs, paprika, and curry powder. Slowly mix in the oils. Add the vinegar. Allow the dressing to stand at room temperature for 2 or 3 hours before using, so that the flavors can blend well. This dressing will keep, refrigerated, for 2 weeks.

Yogurt-Mint Sauce

MAKES 2½ CUPS

Unsweetened, dried coconut may be substituted for the fresh coconut in this recipe: soak ¼ cup coconut in 3 tablespoons hot water for 15 minutes. Try making this sauce with one of the delicious goat's milk yogurts if they are available. Locally, Redwood Hill Farm Goat Dairy in Graton produces an excellent version.

  ¼ cup chopped fresh coconut
  ½ cup fresh mint leaves
  ½ cup cilantro leaves
  2 serrano peppers, with seeds
  1 tablespoon minced fresh dill
    Juice of 1 lime
  1 teaspoon sugar
  1 cup unflavored yogurt, made of cow's or
      goat's milk

Place the coconut, mint, cilantro, peppers, and dill in a food processor and process until finely chopped. Add the lime juice and sugar and process again. Add the yogurt and process until smooth. Chill until ready to serve. Serve with Thai Dolmas (page 81) or Thai Beef Rolls (page 93).

Mint Relish

MAKES ABOUT ½ TO ¾ CUP

The combination of the freshness of mint with the heat of the peppers and garlic is hard to beat. Try this with roasted meats and chicken.

1½ to 2   cups mint leaves
1   cup cilantro leaves
3   serrano or jalapeño peppers, with seeds
1   tablespoon lemon juice
5   cloves garlic
1   teaspoon salt

Combine all the ingredients in a blender or processor, adding a small amount of water if necessary. Blend until smooth. This relish will keep for several days.

▼▼▼▼▼▼▼▼▼▼▼▼▼▼▼▼▼▼▼▼▼▼▼▼▼▼▼▼▼▼▼

AVOCADO SALSA

MAKES ABOUT 2 CUPS

This is a dazzling salsa; somehow the crispness and freshness provided by the radishes surprises your palate with each bite, making this sauce rather addictive. Perhaps you should eat it with restraint.

10   small radishes, finely chopped
    Half a red onion, minced
3   jalapeño peppers, seeded and diced
1   large, or 2 small-to-medium, very ripe avocados, peeled
    Juice of 2 limes
1   tomato, peeled, seeded, and diced
3   tablespoons extra-virgin olive oil
1   bunch cilantro, chopped, large stems removed and discarded
    Salt to taste

Toss together the finely chopped radish, onion, and *jalapeños*, and set aside. Cut the

avocado into chunks and place them in a food processor with a steel blade. Add the lime juice and process until the avocado is smooth, stopping as necessary to push down the mixture. Transfer to a mixing bowl, add the radish mixture and the tomato, mixing them together quickly. Stir in the olive oil and cilantro. Taste and add salt as desired.

This salsa is outstanding with a seafood tostada or taco, and is also excellent just served with chips.

▼▼▼▼▼▼▼▼▼▼▼▼▼▼▼▼▼▼▼▼▼▼▼▼▼▼▼▼▼▼▼

CORN SALSA

MAKES 3 TO 4 CUPS

For a fast, delicious snack, melt some St. George cheese on a corn tortilla, add several spoonsful of this salsa, and roll it up. Also try Corn Salsa with grilled meats and grilled fish.

3   ears very fresh corn
2   medium, ripe tomatoes
1   small red onion
2   jalapeño peppers, with seeds
1   sweet red pepper
1   sweet golden pepper
    Juice of 2 limes
⅓   cup extra-virgin olive oil
½   cup cilantro leaves

Remove the husks and silk from the corn and plunge the ears into a large pot of rapidly boiling water for 2 or 3 minutes. Remove and rinse in cool water. Cut the kernels from the cob and place them in a mixing bowl. Dice the tomatoes and add them to the corn. Dice the onion; remove stem and mince the *jalapeños*. Add both to the corn. Remove the stems and seeds from the sweet peppers, cut them into medium dice, and add to the corn mixture. Add the lime juice, olive oil, and cilantro leaves.

Taste and adjust seasoning if desired, adding more lime juice for a more acidic salsa, more olive oil for a milder taste.

SMOKY SWEET SALSA

MAKES ABOUT 1½ CUPS

This salsa is compellingly delicious, fresh and sweet and smoky all at the same time. Be careful when adding the chipotle *peppers; they are extremely hot, so use only one if you have a tender palate. I like to serve this salsa with grilled fish, such as the Smoky Sweet Salmon on page 153. Try it with simple seafood tacos, too. Just put some grilled, peeled prawns in a hot corn tortilla and top with plenty of Smoky Sweet Salsa.*

> 4 small tomatillos, about 2½ inches across
> 1 to 3 chipotle peppers in adobo sauce, with 1 tablespoon of the sauce
> 1 large clove garlic
> ½ cup cilantro leaves
> One-quarter of a fresh pineapple
> ¼ cup chopped red onion

> ½ teaspoon salt
> 2 tablespoons extra-virgin olive oil

Remove the husks and cut the *tomatillos* into quarters. Place them in a food processor with the *chipotle* peppers and sauce, garlic, and cilantro. Process until well chopped. Peel the pineapple, cut off one slice and set it aside, chop rest in large chunks, and add them to the processor. Process until the pineapple is well incorporated with the other ingredients, but do not purée too finely. Remove mixture to a bowl. Chop the remaining pineapple into small dice, about the same size as the red onion. Add the pineapple, onion, salt, and olive oil to the tomatillo mixture and stir quickly. Taste and correct seasoning as desired.

YELLOW TOMATO SALSA

MAKES 1½ CUPS

Lisa Hemenway's version of a summer salsa makes use of beautiful yellow tomatoes.

> 1 cup small, yellow, pear or cherry tomatoes
> 1 small torpedo onion, chopped
> 4 cloves garlic, minced
> Several leaves purple basil and green basil, shredded
> ¼ cup extra-virgin olive oil
> Juice of half a lemon
> Salt and black pepper

Coarsely chop the tomatoes and toss them with the onion, garlic, and basil. Add the olive oil and lemon juice. Add salt and black pepper to taste.

▼▼▼▼▼▼▼▼▼▼▼▼▼▼▼▼▼▼▼▼▼▼▼▼▼▼▼▼▼▼▼

PESTO

MAKES ENOUGH FOR ABOUT 10 SERVINGS OF PASTA

No cook should be without a favorite recipe for pesto. I have a friend who loves this stuff so much, she dreams about it. You should find this version a particularly dreamy one.

- 3 cups, packed, fresh basil leaves
- ¾ cup extra-virgin olive oil
- 8 cloves garlic, peeled
- ¾ cup freshly grated imported Parmesan cheese
- 4 tablespoons freshly grated Romano Pecorino cheese
- 5 tablespoons softened butter
- ½ cup pine nuts

Place the basil, olive oil, and garlic in a food processor. Mix at high speed, stopping from time to time to scrape the sides of the container. When well blended, transfer the ingredients to a bowl. Beat in the softened butter. Add the 2 cheeses and blend well. Add the whole pine nuts.

This pesto is also excellent when served over simply grilled fish. Thin it with a little hot water and spoon it over the fish just before serving.

To make pesto to be frozen, process the basil, olive oil, and garlic. Store in small containers, topping each container of pesto with a coating of olive oil before freezing it. Thaw overnight in the refrigerator and then add the cheese, butter, and pine nuts, as above.

▼▼▼▼▼▼▼▼▼▼▼▼▼▼▼▼▼▼▼▼▼▼▼▼▼▼▼▼▼▼▼▼▼

BAGNA CAUDA

SERVES 6 TO 8

Bagna cauda *literally translated means "hot bath" and is a traditional and wonderful Italian dip for raw vegetables: a delicious, garlicky sauce served with hot, crusty bread (Costeaux French Bakery's pull-apart loaves are perfect) and mounds of raw vegetables. The sauce is outstanding when served in other ways: as a topping for the Farm Market Salad (page 205) or spooned over barbecued oysters. Be sure to keep it warm during the entire time of serving.*

- 1 large, firm head of garlic
- ½ pound butter
- 1 cup extra-virgin olive oil
- 2 anchovy fillets, packed in oil

Separate and peel the cloves of garlic and mince them. Heat the butter in a heavy saucepan until it is bubbly. Add the olive oil. Add the garlic and cook, over low heat, until it is softened, about 5 minutes. Chop the anchovies, stir them in, and simmer for another 3 or 4 minutes. Remove from heat.

To serve as a dip for bread and vegetables, keep the sauce warm over a candle warmer. Serve with crusty French bread, steamed artichokes, mushrooms, strips of baked eggplant, and almost any other raw or lightly steamed vegetables you choose.

HUMMUS

MAKES ABOUT 3 CUPS

Hummus *is wonderful served with chips, raw vegetables, or triangles of pita bread. It is also excellent used as a sandwich spread. Try it with leftover roast leg of lamb and sliced red onion on a hot sourdough roll. This version deviates from traditional hummus in its use of* chipotle *peppers, which add a hot and smoky element that blends perfectly with the flavor of the beans.*

1½ cups garbanzo beans (chick-peas), canned or cooked until tender (reserve about ½ cup of the cooking liquid or the liquid in the can)
6 cloves garlic
2 or 3 chipotle peppers in adobo sauce
¾ cup raw sesame tahini
Juice of 1 or 2 lemons
1 tablespoon ground cumin
2 tablespoons extra-virgin olive oil
Salt to taste

In a food processor or blender, place the garbanzo beans, ¼ cup liquid, garlic, and peppers. Process until smooth. Add the tahini and the juice of 1 lemon and process until well blended. Transfer the mixture to a mixing bowl, add the cumin, and taste. Add the juice of the second lemon if desired. Stir in the olive oil and add salt to taste. If the mixture is too thick for your purposes, stir in a little of the remaining canning or cooking liquid. This will keep, refrigerated, for 7 days.

ROASTED GARLIC PURÉE

MAKES ⅓ TO ½ CUP

Use this essence of roasted garlic as a substitute for butter, to liven up a soup, or as an addition to gravies and sauces. It will add a nutty, deep flavor, more subtle than raw garlic, complex and wonderful.

3 heads roasted garlic (page 78)
1 tablespoon oil from roasting the garlic
1 teaspoon fresh chopped herbs
Salt and pepper to taste

On a cutting board, carefully remove the root from the heads of garlic. It may be necessary to separate it clove by clove from the head, which is fine. If the heads are still basically intact, use heel of your hand to press down on each head, slowly, to squeeze out the roasted garlic pulp. If necessary, remove pulp clove by clove by squeezing the tip end. After removing all the pulp from the garlic heads, scrape it off the cutting board and into a small mixing bowl. Mash the roasted garlic until it is smooth. If you want a slightly thinner consistency, add a tablespoon of the oil in which it cooked. Stir in the chopped herbs and add salt and pepper to taste.

▼▼▼▼▼▼▼▼▼▼▼▼▼▼▼▼▼▼▼▼▼▼▼▼▼▼▼▼▼▼▼▼

WINE COUNTRY APPLESAUCE

M A K E S   A B O U T   1   Q U A R T

The addition of red wine adds a subtle, spicy depth to traditional applesauce.

> 5 pounds apples, Gravensteins, if available; if not, use a firm tart type
> 1½ cups red wine (choose a *big,* fruity wine, such as a Zinfandel or Cabernet Sauvignon)
> 5 whole cloves
> ½ to 1 cup sugar
> 1 teaspoon nutmeg
> ¼ teaspoon cinnamon
> Pinch of ground allspice
> Pinch of cayenne pepper (optional)

Cut the apples into quarters and core. Chop them very coarsely and place in large, nonreactive saucepan. Add the wine and cook, stirring every few minutes, until the apples are tender. Remove from the heat and press the apples through a potato ricer. Discard the skins and any pulp that does not go through the ricer. Return the puréed apples to the saucepan, stir in ½ cup sugar, and re-

turn to heat. Taste and add more sugar as desired. Add the spices and simmer over low heat for another 5 minutes. Serve warm or chill. This applesauce is excellent served with the Pork Tenderloin in Red Wine Marinade on page 169.

VARIATION ▼ For a chunkier applesauce, peel the apples before cooking them. When they are tender, mash them with a fork or potato masher to desired consistency.

▼▼▼▼▼▼▼▼▼▼▼▼▼▼▼▼▼▼▼▼▼▼▼▼▼▼▼▼▼▼▼▼▼▼

APRICOT CHUTNEY

M A K E S   A B O U T   3   Q U A R T S

Chutneys make wonderful gifts. Make plenty of this chutney during apricot season, and you will find yourself well ahead of the game at the holidays. Just remember to keep plenty for yourself.

> 5 pounds apricots, halved and stoned
> 3 pounds sugar
> 1 pound currants
> 3 heads garlic, cloves separated, peeled, and chopped
> 5 jalapeño peppers, seeded and cut into a very thin julienne
> 5 ounces fresh ginger, peeled and grated or chopped
> 1 ounce dried hot chilies
> 3 cups apple cider vinegar
> 1 to 2 tablespoons salt

In a large, heavy pot combine the apricots and sugar over medium heat. Stir well until sugar is dissolved. Add all other ingredients, stir well, and simmer for about 1 hour. Pour into sterilized pint or half-pint jars and process in a water bath for 15 minutes.

VARIATION ▾ You may substitute peaches or persimmons in this recipe with excellent results. When I make it with persimmons, I use golden raisins in place of the currants.

▼▼▼▼▼▼▼▼▼▼▼▼▼▼▼▼▼▼▼▼▼▼▼▼▼▼▼▼▼▼▼▼▼

GRAVENSTEIN CHUTNEY

MAKES APPROXIMATELY 1 QUART

Because the cooking process is stopped after the addition of half of the strawberries, their fresh, bright taste is captured in the chutney.

> 3 cups Cabernet Sauvignon or any full-bodied red wine
> 1 cup sugar
> 4 whole cloves
> ½ teaspoon nutmeg
>   Juice of 1 lemon

> 4 Gravenstein apples
> ½ cup red raspberry vinegar
> 4 cloves garlic, peeled
>   1½-inch piece fresh ginger, peeled
> 1 jalapeño pepper, stem removed
> 1 quart strawberries, stems removed
> 1 teaspoon crushed dried chili peppers
> ½ cup fresh cilantro leaves

Place the wine, ½ cup of the sugar, the cloves, nutmeg, and lemon juice in heavy, nonreactive saucepan over medium heat and stir until the sugar is dissolved. Peel and core the apples and add them to the liquid. Simmer for 15 to 20 minutes, until the apples are soft but not falling apart. Remove from the heat and let the apples cool in poaching liquid. When cool, remove the apples and drain them on paper towels. Reserve the liquid to use as a marinade.

Coarsely chop the apples and place in heavy pot with the remainder of the sugar and the raspberry vinegar. Stir and simmer over medium heat for 5 minutes. By hand or in a processor, finely chop the garlic, ginger and *jalapeño* and add to apple mixture. Coarsely chop the strawberries. Add the dried chilies and half of the strawberries to the apple mixture and simmer for 10 minutes, stirring occasionally. Add the remaining strawberries, stir well, and remove from the heat. Stir in the cilantro leaves, cool, and chill. Will keep, refrigerated, for several weeks.

MARINATED GRAPES

MAKES 1½ QUARTS

This recipe was such a hit at one of my tasting parties that I now have a number of friends who head straight for my refrigerator whenever they stop by, knowing that I generally have a supply of these wonderful crisp and spicy grapes available for snacking. They make excellent gifts as well.

Here, in the heart of the wine country, it is easy to get good, organically grown table grapes produced on a small scale by friends or neighbors. Thus we avoid using commercial table grapes that are contaminated by a multitude of dangerous pesticides. We are also expecting the first crop from Saralee Vineyards, which Sonoma Grapevines Inc. recently planted with twenty-two varieties of table grapes, along with nearly 100 acres of wine grapes. Production may begin as early as 1992.

- 2 pounds seedless, organic grapes, all stems removed
- 2 cups red wine
- 2 cups red wine vinegar
- 1 cup sugar
  Several whole cloves
- ½ teaspoon nutmeg
  Several whole allspice berries
- 5 or 6 cardamom seeds, crushed
  A 1-inch long cinnamon stick for each jar of grapes

Rinse the grapes and discard any bad ones. Fill pint and/or quart jars with the grapes; there should be enough for 1½ quarts. Place the remaining ingredients in a heavy saucepan, heat, and stir until the sugar is dissolved. Cool slightly, pour over the grapes, and add a cinnamon stick to each jar. Close the lids, label with the date, and refrigerate.

Allow the grapes to marinate for at least 2 days before using. They will keep several months.

MARINATED ONIONS

MAKES ABOUT 6 PINTS

This is an extremely versatile condiment, both in execution and use. Simple to prepare, it makes an attractive holiday gift and is delicious, too. I have given amounts to make about 6 pints. You can vary that to suit your needs; just keep proportions of the marinade approximately the same as those in the recipe and it will work out fine.

- 3 pounds medium, red onions
- 2 cups raspberry vinegar or a good red wine vinegar
- 2 cups red wine
- ⅔ cup sugar or more to taste
  Several gratings nutmeg
- 8 whole allspice berries, crushed
- 5 whole cloves, crushed
  A 1-inch piece of cinnamon
- 4 or 5 whole cardamom seeds
  Salt and pepper

Peel and slice the red onions very thin. Fill pint jars full with the onions, being sure not to pack them too tightly. Place all the remaining ingredients in a heavy, nonreactive saucepan, heat, and stir until the sugar is melted. Taste and add more sugar if a sweeter marinade is desired. Cool, and cover the onions with the marinade. Close the jars and let them sit for at least 2 hours before using. These onions may be kept in the refrigerator for up to 2 weeks.

Use on sandwiches, or as a side dish with roast meats.

VARIATION ▾ Prepare the onions in the same way and place in pint jars. To each jar, add 1½ teaspoons sugar, ½ teaspoon each salt and pepper, a sprig of fresh thyme, and a lemon wedge cut in pieces. Cover with white wine.

MARINATED ONIONS AND GRAPES

Use 1¾ to 2 pounds onions and approximately 1 pound small, seedless, organic, grapes. Toss the sliced onions and whole grapes together and place in pint jars. Make the marinade, using red wine and red or raspberry vinegar if the grapes are red and white wine, champagne vinegar, and the juice of two lemons if the grapes are white. Add the sugar to taste, but omit the spices and substitute fresh thyme, fresh oregano, fresh marjoram, and salt and white pepper.

DESSERTS

FRESH FRUIT EXTRAVAGANZA

ALLOW ABOUT A DOZEN PIECES OF FRUIT PER PERSON AND SEVERAL BISCOTTI, IF YOU ARE USING THEM.

My dessert of choice has always been fresh fruit. As a child I waited eagerly for the first watermelons of the summer to appear at the farm stand where my mother took me on special occasions. In addition to my beloved watermelon, we would leave with peaches, nectarines, deep purple plums, golden plums, honeydew melons, and berries of all kinds. Though I am not particularly impressed by the year-round availability of most fruits—hunger makes the best sauce, says a close friend, unknowingly paraphrasing Cervantes—this is still the dessert I always prefer, and I find it difficult to be enthusiastic about transforming fruit into some other form. I designed this fruit and sauce tray to appease guests with a sweet tooth, while still managing to leave the luscious fruit in its natural state. I vary the fruit seasonally, regardless of what might be available in the supermarket, finding as many local farm sources as I can. The possibilities of this beautiful fruit display are limited only by your sources and your imagination.

FRUIT

Strawberries, with stems
Melons: Crane, Honeydew, Crenshaw, Casaba, Cantaloupe
California kiwi fruit
Peaches
Nectarines
Plums
Figs
Apples
Pineapple
Red bananas

SAUCES FOR DIPPING

White Chocolate Buttercream Sauce, page 242

Dark Chocolate Buttercream Sauce,
   page 243
Fruit Creams: Nectarine (page 232), Peach,
   Papaya, or Mango
Berry Sauces: Raspberry, Blueberry (page
   242), Strawberry (page 233)
Biscotti

Use a large, attractive serving platter or flat basket for your display. Prepare the fruit by cutting it into 1- or 2-bite pieces (not too small) appropriate to the type of fruit you are working with: round, center-pitted fruits such as peaches and apple work well when cut into wedges; melons should be cut in lengthwise wedges and then cut in half, or in square chunks; strawberries should not be cut at all. Use your best judgement and prepare your fruit attractively. You can make several spears of fruit, or place wooden skewers in an attractive holder and set them nearby. Arrange the fruit on the serving platter, leaving space for *biscotti* and for the bowls of sauces.

Choose one sauce, or a variety of sauces. Everyone loves chocolate and the contrast between the white and the dark is lovely. The addition of a fruit sauce to the selection will provide a wonderful contrast of texture and taste and will please those who worry about calories or cholesterol. Add some biscotti to your fruit display, garnish with fresh flowers and sprigs of mint, and serve. Your guests should be dazzled.

FRESH BERRIES WITH FROMAGE BLANC AND CHOCOLATE SAUCE

SERVES 6

This is a variation of a recipe I discovered in Laura Chenel's first cookbook, Chèvre! The Goat Cheese Cookbook, *written with Linda Siegfried (Reading, Mass.: Addison-Wesley, 1990). I was preparing a menu that featured her cheese in every course and wanted to do something other than a standard fruit and cheese plate for dessert. The result has an interesting interplay of flavor, texture, and temperature contrasts.*

1 quart fresh berries: raspberries, blackberries, strawberries, or a combination
   (if you are using more than one kind,
   keep them separate)
1 lemon
   Sugar
   Chocolate Buttercream Sauce (page 242)
8 ounces fromage blanc
½ teaspoon lemon zest
½ teaspoon vanilla extract
¼ cup + 1 teaspoon sugar
2 egg whites
   Pinch cream of tartar
   Pinch salt
   Several perfect berries, small sprigs of
      mint, or some shaved chocolate for
      garnish

Toss the cleaned berries with the juice of the lemon and a little sugar. Chill for at least

1 hour before serving. Have the Chocolate Buttercream Sauce at room temperature in the top section of a double boiler. Beat the *fromage blanc* with the lemon zest, vanilla, and sugar until all the ingredients are well incorporated. Beat the egg whites with an electric mixer or wire whisk until foamy, add the cream of tartar, and beat to soft peaks. Add the remaining teaspoon of sugar and a pinch of salt and beat until stiff but not dry. Place the Chocolate Sauce over medium heat and stir occasionally until it is warmed through. Carefully fold the egg whites into the *fromage blanc*.

To serve, place a pool of chocolate sauce on individual serving plates. Divide the berries among the plates, placing them on top of the chocolate. Top each mound of berries with a large spoonful of *fromage blanc*. Garnish and serve immediately.

▼▼▼▼▼▼▼▼▼▼▼▼▼▼▼▼▼▼▼▼▼▼▼▼▼▼▼▼▼▼▼▼

APPLES POACHED IN PORT WINE

with Castello Blue Cheese and Walnuts

SERVES 6

Apples and wine are two of the main agricultural products in Sonoma County and here are joined in a happy marriage, a union that is enhanced by the flavors of the cheese and the walnuts. If you cannot find the Castello cheese, Oregon Blue or even an imported Gorgonzola would be wonderful. Brie may be used to great effect in this recipe, although the result will lack the dramatic contrasts in flavor.

6	apples
2	cups port
1	cup water
⅔	cup sugar
5	whole cloves
	A 1-inch cinnamon stick
5	whole allspice berries
	Several gratings of whole nutmeg
4 to 6	ounces Castello Blue cheese or other blue-veined cheese
6	walnut halves
2 to 3	tablespoons unsalted butter
	Chopped walnuts (optional)

Cut a slice off the stem end of each apple, fairly close to the top. With a vegetable peeler, remove the apple cores, leaving a small open space in the center of each apple.

Simmer the port, water, sugar, and spices in a heavy saucepan, stirring until the sugar is dissolved. Add the apples and simmer over medium heat for 10 to 15 minutes, until they have just begun to soften.

With a slotted spoon transfer the apples from the poaching liquid to a baking dish. Fill the cavity of each apple with some of the cheese and top with a walnut half. Cover tightly with aluminum foil and bake in 325-degree oven for 20 to 25 minutes. Meanwhile, strain the spices out of the poaching liquid, return it to the heat, and reduce it by two-thirds. When reduced, stir in the butter, a tablespoon at a time.

Remove the apples from the oven, place on individual serving plates, spoon a generous amount of sauce over the apples, and serve.

PEARS POACHED IN RED WINE

SERVES 8

These pears, which are best made a day in advance of serving, are part of Josef Heller's Taste of Sonoma Dinner *(menu on page 62) served at his La Province restaurant. Try them with vanilla bean ice cream if you can find it, or French vanilla ice cream.*

- 4 pears
- 1 quart Zinfandel wine
- 1 cup sugar
- 1 tablespoon honey
- ½ teaspoon cinammon
  Juice of half a lemon
- 1 teaspoon vanilla extract
- 1 whole clove
  Dash of Triple Sec liqueur
  French vanilla ice cream
  Toasted almonds

Peel, core, and halve the pears. Combine the Zinfandel, sugar, honey, cinnamon, lemon juice, vanilla, and clove in a medium saucepan. Place the pears in the liquid and simmer over medium heat until the pears are tender but not mushy. With a slotted spoon, remove the pears from the poaching liquid. Over high heat reduce the wine mixture by half. Add the liqueur, remove from the heat, and add the pears. Allow to cool and refrigerate until ready to serve.

To serve, place a scoop of vanilla ice cream in each of 8 serving dishes. Top with half a pear and several spoonsful of the wine mixture. Garnish with toasted almonds.

FRESH RED RASPBERRY CAKE

MAKES 8 TO 10 SERVINGS

Carol Kozlowski Every, who is Carmen's daughter and the publicist for the family farm, developed this dessert with its interesting and delicious use of French bread as the "cake."

- 3 pounds (6 cups) fresh red raspberries
- 2¾ cups sugar
- 3 loaves sweet French bread
- 1 pound butter
  Heavy cream

Butter a 9-inch springform pan and sprinkle ⅛ cup of the sugar on the bottom and sides of the pan. Blend the raspberries with 2½ cups of the sugar and set aside. Remove the crust from the bread and slice in ½-inch slices. Butter both sides of each slice of bread. Line the bottom and sides of the pan with the bread, making sure not to leave any holes. Place 3 cups of the berries in the pan. Add another layer of bread using the same process as above. Add the remaining 3 cups of berries and top with another layer of buttered bread. Sprinkle the top with the remaining ⅛ cup sugar.

Place a piece of plastic wrap on top of the

cake, a weighted plate on top of that, and refrigerate overnight.

Unmold the cake onto a serving dish, loosening the sides and bottom of the pan with a sharp knife. Serve with fresh whipped cream.

MINIATURE PEAR CRÊPES

MAKES 40 CRÊPES, EACH ABOUT 3-INCHES ACROSS

Serve these luscious little crêpes as an appetizer at an evening gathering, accompanied by a sparkling wine, such as Piper Sonoma's Blanc de Noir.

2 or 3	unbruised red pears
2	cups Black Muscat wine
¼	cup sugar
¼	cup butter
½	teaspoon cinnamon
	Pinch of ground cloves
40	small crêpes (recipe follows)

Cut the pears into quarters and core. Slice them lengthwise, about ¼-inch thick. Cover with water until ready to use.

In a heavy skillet, place the wine, sugar, butter, cinnamon and cloves. Drain the water from the pears and add them to the skillet. Over medium heat, simmer the pears for about 4 to 5 minutes. With a slotted spoon remove to a warm plate and set aside. Turn the heat to high and reduce the wine sauce until it thickens into a syrup. Remove from the heat.

Wrap a crêpe around each slice of pear. Arrange them on an attractive platter, and drizzle the reduced sauce over them. Serve immediately.

CRÊPES

1¼	cups all-purpose flour
4	eggs
1	cup milk
1¼	cups cold water
¼	cup unsalted butter, melted
½	teaspoon salt

In a blender or food processor, mix all the ingredients until well blended, about 30 to 45 seconds. Pour into a container and chill for at least 1 hour.

To make the crêpes, use a large, flat skillet or a grill. Brush with butter and use 2 tablespoons batter for each crêpe. Cook over medium-high heat until the surface is bubbly. Flip the crêpe and cook for about 30 seconds until it is golden brown. Set aside, between layers of waxed paper, until ready to use.

NECTARINE CRÊPES

with Strawberry Sauce

SERVES 6

Make these crêpes during nectarine season, when the fruit available to you is local and tree-ripened. Few things are as seductive as a naturally sweet nectarine, something many of us have forgotten because it has been so long since they were grown properly on a large scale. This may be naively idealistic, but if we decided to eat only locally grown fruit and only when it is in season, we might do much to encourage the production of fruit with its true, natural flavor. When you do have an abundance of fresh, tree-ripened fruit, fruit creams are a wonderfully simple way of preserving their flavor a bit longer.

3 eggs
2 tablespoons all-purpose flour
1 tablespoon milk
1 tablespoon water
   Butter
   Strawberry Sauce, chilled (recipe follows)
   Nectarine Cream, chilled (recipe follows)
3 nectarines, peeled and sliced
   Several strawberries with stems
   Fresh nasturtium flowers, if available

Place the eggs in a mixing bowl and beat until just foamy. Add the flour, milk, and water and beat until well blended, about 2 or 3 minutes. Refrigerate overnight or for at least 2 hours. This quantity of batter will make about six crêpes, each 6 inches in diameter; one per serving.

To make the crêpes, melt a small amount of butter, just enough to coat the bottom of the pan, in a 6-inch crêpe pan, nonstick pan, or skillet. Pour in 3 tablespoons of batter and rotate the pan quickly to spread the batter over the bottom of the pan. Cook for about 1 minute, until the crêpe is set. Using a spatula, carefully loosen the crêpe from the sides of the pan and quickly transfer it to a piece of waxed paper. Repeat the process for the rest of the batter. You may stack the crêpes on top of one another, with a piece of waxed paper between each one.

To assemble the crêpes, pour a pool of Strawberry Sauce on individual serving plates and agitate the plates to spread the sauce evenly.

Transfer one crêpe, with its waxed paper, to your preparation area. Place four or five slices of nectarine down the center and top with 3 or 4 tablespoons Nectarine Cream. Carefully fold the crêpe, using the waxed paper to help if necessary. Place the crêpe in the center of the serving plate, on top of the Strawberry Sauce. Spoon another two tablespoons of Nectarine Cream down the center of the crêpe. Top with a slice of nectarine and a spoonful of Strawberry Sauce. Garnish the plate with 2 strawberries and a fresh nasturtium flower.

NECTARINE CREAM

MAKES ABOUT 2 CUPS

1½ pounds nectarines
⅛ cup sugar
   Juice of 1 lemon
1 egg

Seed and slice the nectarines. Place them in a blender or food processor with the sugar and lemon juice. Blend on high until smooth. Pour the nectarine purée into a saucepan and simmer over medium heat for 10 minutes, stirring constantly. Remove from the heat and cool to room temperature. Beat the egg well and add it to the cooled nectarine purée. Return to low heat for a few minutes, stirring constantly until well blended. Do not allow to boil. Cool and pour through strainer or sieve. Place in covered container and chill.

STRAWBERRY SAUCE

MAKES ABOUT 1½ CUPS

- 1 pint strawberries, rinsed and stems removed
- 1 tablespoon sugar
  Juice of half a lemon

Place all the ingredients in a blender or processor. Blend on high until smooth. Chill.

▼▼▼▼▼▼▼▼▼▼▼▼▼▼▼▼▼▼▼▼▼▼▼▼▼▼▼▼▼▼▼

LEMON VERBENA SORBET

SERVES 4 TO 6

In the summer of 1989, Truffles Restaurant in Sebastopol was the location of a dinner celebrating Sonoma County's first annual "Organically Grown Week," a series of events and lectures designed to increase awareness of the importance and local availability of organically grown foods.

Mark Malicki, the chef at Truffles at the time, delighted the guests with this simple sorbet that is delicious served on a hot summer afternoon.

- 1 cup water
- 2 cups apple juice
- 1 bunch lemon verbena, with a few small sprigs set aside for garnish

Bring the water and apple juice to a boil. Place the lemon verbena in a bowl and pour the boiling liquid on top. Steep for 30 minutes. Let the mixture cool, strain it into an ice cream maker and freeze according to the manufacturer's instructions.

Serve on chilled plates and garnish with a small sprig of verbena.

▼▼▼▼▼▼▼▼▼▼▼▼▼▼▼▼▼▼▼▼▼▼▼▼▼▼▼▼▼▼▼

STRAWBERRY-RHUBARB TART

SERVES 6 TO 8

As a recent arrival in Sonoma County, Charles Saunders, executive chef at Sonoma Mission Inn, has been busy exploring the bounty of his new home. The delicious strawberries of the Sonoma Valley were the inspiration for this tart, which Charles claims as one of his signature dishes, but it is a recipe that lends itself well to any region of the country where good berries can be found.

CRUST

    1 cup all-purpose flour

    ½ teaspoon salt

    6 tablespoons unsalted butter, cold

    3½ tablespoons water, very cold

    ¼ teaspoon lemon zest, finely chopped

STREUSEL TOPPING

    ¼ **pound butter**

    ¼ **pound sugar**

    ¼ **pound cake flour**

    1½ **teaspoons cinnamon**

    1½ **teaspoons orange rind, minced**

    ½ **teaspoon ginger, minced**

STRAWBERRY-RHUBARB FILLING

    4 cups fresh rhubarb, trimmed and cut in
        medium dice

    2 cups strawberries, quartered

    ¾ cup sugar

    ½ teaspoon ginger, minced

    ½ teaspoon orange zest, minced

    3 tablespoons tapioca

    3 tablespoons all-purpose flour
       Pinch of salt

To make the tart shell, sift the salt and flour together in a large bowl. Cut the butter into small squares and work it into the flour with a fork or a pastry blender. Make a well in the center of the mixture and add the water and lemon zest. Using your fingers, quickly blend the water and the flour mixture to form a dough, adding a small amount of cold water if necessary for the dough to come together. Place the mixture on your work surface, form it into a small rectangle, and wrap it in plastic. Refrigerate the dough for several hours or overnight.

Remove the dough from the refrigerator and roll it out as you would a pie crust. Line a 10-inch tart pan with the dough, prick it with a fork, and refrigerate for 30 minutes. Bake the shell at 325 degrees until it is just golden, about 6 to 8 minutes. Remove the shell from the oven and allow it to cool.

To make the topping, blend together the sugar and butter. Add the flour and spices to the butter mixture to form a crumbly mixture. Cover the streusel and refrigerate until ready to use.

Combine all the ingredients for the filling in a large bowl and toss together well. Place the mixture into the prebaked tart shell and spread 1 cup of the streusel over the top. Bake the tart at 350 degrees for 45 minutes or until the fruit is tender. Serve warm or chilled.

WHITE CHOCOLATE MOUSSE

with Golden Raspberry and Red Raspberry Sauces

SERVES 4 TO 6

This dessert is as delicious as it is beautiful, pleasing to the eye as well as the palate. During fall and winter, try substituting fresh cranberries cooked with a little sugar for the raspberry sauces.

    5 ounces white chocolate

    ¼ cup unsalted butter

3 eggs, separated
½ cup confectioner's sugar, sifted
¼ cup Grand Marnier liqueur
1 cup heavy cream
1 teaspoon vanilla extract
1 teaspoon tangerine zest
½ pint golden raspberries
½ pint red raspberries
¼ cup granulated sugar
Juice of 1 lemon

Melt the white chocolate and butter together over low heat, stirring constantly. Set aside.

Beat the egg yolks, confectioner's sugar, and liqueur until the mixture forms a slow, dissolving ribbon when the beaters are lifted. Place the mixture in the top of a double boiler and cook, whisking constantly, until it thickens, about 3 or 4 minutes. Remove to a large mixing bowl, whisk in the white chocolate mixture, and stir until smooth and cool.

Beat the cream until it forms stiff peaks. Add the vanilla and tangerine zest. In a separate bowl, beat the egg whites until stiff but not dry. Fold the egg whites into chocolate mixture and then fold in the whipped cream. Refrigerate, covered, for at least 3 hours, until set and well chilled.

Set aside several whole raspberries for garnish. Purée the golden raspberries in a blender or food processor with ⅛ cup of the granulated sugar. Place in a small container and refrigerate until ready to use. Purée the red raspberries with the remaining sugar and the juice of half the lemon. Taste and add juice from remaining half lemon if desired. Chill until ready to use.

To serve, fill individual, glass serving dishes half full with the mousse. Spoon over a thin layer of red raspberry sauce. Fill to the top with the mouse, top with golden raspberry sauce, and garnish with a few whole raspberries. Serve immediately.

BAKED VANILLA CREAMS

with Orange Caramel Sauce

MAKES 6 SERVINGS

In Santa Rosa, Michael Hirschberg offers this creamy dessert at his Restaurant Matisse, which was voted Outstanding Restaurant in the Celebrate Sonoma 1989 Art Awards.

3 cups heavy cream
1 vanilla bean
   Pinch salt
6 egg yolks
½ cup sugar

Place the cream in a heavy saucepan, add the vanilla bean and salt, and bring to a simmer. Stir the egg yolks and sugar together until well blended and pour into the hot cream in a slow stream, whisking constantly to avoid lumps. Do not whisk so vigorously that the mixture turns foamy. Split the vanilla bean and scrape the seeds into the mixture. Strain the custard into a pitcher and skim off any bubbles. Place six ½-cup ramekins in a baking dish and fill with the cream mixture. Place the baking dish in 300-degree oven, and carefully add hot water to half the height of the ramekins. Cover loosely with foil and bake until firm around the edges, about 1 hour. Remove from the oven, cool, and chill for at least 3 hours before serving.

ORANGE CARAMEL SAUCE

2 cups sugar
1¾ cups hot water
¼ cup Grand Marnier liqueur

Caramelize the sugar by placing it in a heavy saucepan over very low heat. Stir constantly with a long-handled, wooden spoon for about 8 minutes, until the sugar is completely melted and turns golden. Remove from heat and *very slowly and carefully* add the ½ cup of the water, just a bit at a time, stirring after each addition until the mixture is smooth. Return to low heat and slowly stir in the hot water. Remove from the heat and stir in the liqueur.

To serve, cover the surface of a dessert plate with Orange Caramel Sauce, and unmold a Vanilla Cream onto the sauce.

CHRISTINE'S CHEESECAKE

MAKES 10 TO 12 SERVINGS

This spectacular version would, according to Christine Topolos, who is the chef at Russian River Vineyards, "be Frank Sinatra's favorite cheesecake, if he had ever tasted it."

1¼ cups crushed graham crackers
1 cup + 2 tablespoons sugar
½ cup butter, melted
12 ounces softened cream cheese
4 large eggs, beaten
3 teaspoons vanilla extract
1½ cups sour cream

Combine the cracker crumbs, ½ cup of the sugar, and the butter and press the mixture firmly into the bottom and sides of an 8- or 9-inch, springform pan with a removable base. Bake in a 350-degree oven for ten minutes and allow to cool.

Mix together the softened cream cheese, eggs, ½ cup sugar, and 2 teaspoons of the vanilla. Pour into the crumb crust. Bake in 350-degree oven for 40 minutes, or until the center is just set.

Combine the sour cream with the remaining 2 tablespoons sugar and 1 teaspoon vanilla, and spread over the cake. Bake for an additional 10 minutes. Chill before serving.

CALIFORNIA FOUR-NUT TORTE

MAKES 6 TO 8 SERVINGS

This dessert completes John Ash's Spring Menu on page 62.

CRUST

½ cup ground almonds
½ cup ground filberts

3 tablespoons flour

2 tablespoons sugar

⅓ cup unsalted butter, chilled, and cut into ¼-inch bits

FILLING

1 cup + 1½ tablespoons brown sugar

3 whole eggs

1 teaspoon baking powder

½ cup chopped peanuts or pine nuts

1 cup chopped walnuts

1 cup shredded, sweetened coconut

½ cup flour

Preheat the oven to 350 degrees.

Carefully mix all the ingredients for the crust till they are well combined and no lumps of butter are visible. Work quickly so that butter does not melt. The mixture should be slightly crumbly. Butter an 8-inch-round and 2-inch-deep cake pan and press in the crust mixture evenly. Crust should go up about two-thirds of the side of the pan. Set aside.

To make the filling, beat the brown sugar, eggs, and baking powder together until well mixed. Beat in remaining ingredients and pour the mixture into the prepared crust.

Bake in the preheated oven for approximately 25 minutes. Do not overbake; the cake should be soft and caramel-like in the center. To serve, dust with powdered sugar and accompany with a lemon-scented *crème anglaise* and slices of seasonal fresh fruits.

▼▼▼▼▼▼▼▼▼▼▼▼▼▼▼▼▼▼▼▼▼▼▼▼▼▼▼▼▼▼▼

SUMMER CHOCOLATE ROLL

SERVES 8 TO 10

The fromage blanc *in this cake creates a richly flavored but light dessert, not as heavy as those that feature cream.*

CAKE

4 eggs, separated

½ cup powdered sugar

1 teaspoon vanilla extract

4 tablespoons cocoa

1 teaspoon instant espresso powder

1 tablespoon cake flour

4 egg whites

¼ teaspoon cream of tartar

FILLING AND SAUCE

8 ounces (1 cup) fromage blanc

1 teaspoon vanilla extract

4 tablespoons granulated sugar

1 pint fresh raspberries

2 white nectarines

Juice of 1 lemon

Nasturtium and borage blossoms

To make the cake, prepare a 9- by 13-inch cake pan and preheat the oven to 325 degrees.

Beat the egg yolks until they are light and lemony. Gradually sift in the sugar and beat until creamy. Beat in the vanilla. Sift in the cocoa and blend well. Add the espresso and blend. Add the cake flour and blend again.

Beat the egg whites until they reach stiff peaks, adding cream of tartar when they reach the soft peak.

Gently and quickly fold the egg whites into the batter and spread it in the prepared pan. Bake for 20 to 25 minutes. Remove from the oven and let the cake rest for 5 minutes.

Remove the cake from the pan to tea towel on which you have sprinkled a couple of tablespoons of granulated sugar to help prevent it sticking.

To make the filling, blend the fromage blanc with the vanilla and 2 tablespoons of the sugar. Fold in about ¾ cup of the raspberries and set the mixture aside. Peel and slice the nectarines. Spread the fromage blanc mixture over the surface of the cake. Place a layer of nectarine over the top of the cheese. Carefully, using the tea towel to help you, roll the cake lengthwise.

To make the sauce, purée the remaining raspberries with 2 tablespoons sugar and the lemon juice. Refrigerate the cake and the sauce until ready to serve.

To serve, cut slices of the cake ¾-inch thick. In the center of the serving plates, place 2 or 3 tablespoons of raspberry sauce and agitate the plates to spread the sauce evenly. Place a slice of cake in the center of the sauce and top with a small quantity of the sauce. Garnish each serving with 1 nasturtium blossom and 3 or 4 borage blossoms. Serve immediately.

LEMON CURD

M A K E S   A B O U T   1   P I N T

If you make Lemon Curd and plan to have it around for any length of time at all, you should try to forget that it is there. It is awfully easy to convince yourself that "just one more" finger-scoopful will be your last.

- 5 whole eggs
- 3 egg yolks
- 1 cup sugar
- 1 cup fresh lemon juice
  Lemon zest (grated outer peel) from 5 lemons
- 1 cup unsalted butter, melted

Beat the eggs and egg yolks together well. Add the sugar and lemon juice. Beat in the lemon zest. Slowly beat in the melted butter. Place the mixture in a double boiler over medium-low heat. Stir until the mixture begins to thicken, about 10 minutes. Remove the pan containing the mixture from the base and set it aside to cool. The mixture will continue to thicken as it cools. Lemon curd will keep for about 3 weeks in the refrigerator.

RASPBERRY CURD

M A K E S   A B O U T   1   P I N T

Raspberry curd can be used as a filling for cakes and other pastries. Recently, I served this with a variety of shortbread cookies. *Everyone dipped the shortbread in it and thought the combination sinfully good. I have also used it as a sauce for fresh kiwi fruit.*

    3 cups raspberries
    ¼ cup lemon juice
    ¼ cup sugar (if the berries are not sweet
        enough)
    1 cup unsalted butter
    3 egg yolks

Purée the raspberries, combine them with the lemon juice and sugar, if needed. Place in saucepan, simmer for about 5 minutes, and strain through a mesh sieve.

Place the strained raspberries in a blender or food processor. Melt the butter in a saucepan until it is just bubbly. With the machine running, slowly drizzle in the butter. Return the mixture to the saucepan. In a mixing bowl, beat the egg yolks. Add 3 or 4 tablespoons of the raspberry mixture to the egg yolks and blend well. Pour the egg yolk and raspberry mixture into the saucepan with the rest of the raspberry mixture. Over very low heat, stir until the mixture thickens, about 10 to 15 minutes. Cool and refrigerate.

Raspberry curd will keep up to 10 days in the refrigerator.

RASPBERRY AND LEMON CURD TART

SERVES 8

Fruit curds, especially lemon curd, are among the most incredibly delicious things man has ever figured out how to make. The only problem is that it takes will power to get to the end of a recipe without devouring the entire production in the process.

    1 baked 9- or 10-inch tart shell (use Blood
        Peach recipe on page 240, substituting
        all white flour for the whole wheat)
    1 recipe Lemon Curd (page 238)
    1 pint raspberries, as perfect as possible

Fill the tart shell almost to the top with lemon curd. Arrange the raspberries over the surface and refrigerate until ready to serve.

VARIATIONS ▾ A touch of chocolate goes wonderfully with this tart. Melt 2 or 3 ounces of bittersweet chocolate and thin with a tablespoon of cream. Drizzle a small amount of chocolate over the tart in a loose, open pattern. Chill until ready to serve. ▾ For a double shot of raspberry, use Raspberry Curd (page 238) in place of the Lemon Curd, or use both, marbling the 2 together in the tart shell.

APPLE TART WITH POLENTA CRUST

SERVES 6 TO 8

Mary Evely of Simi Winery uses our local apples to complete her Winter Luncheon Menu (page 66). The polenta crust is a delicious variation.

- 4 pounds cooking apples, preferably the first crop of Gravensteins
- 4 tablespoons sugar
- 2 tablespoons butter
- 1 partially baked Polenta Crust in a 10-inch tart tin (recipe follows)

Peel, core, and halve the apples. Cut enough of the apples into thin, horizontal slices to make up about 3 cups. Toss with half the sugar and reserve for the top of the tart. Roughly chop the remaining apples and cook them, covered, in a heavy saucepan, stirring occasionally, until tender, about 20 minutes. Add the remaining sugar and the butter and continue to cook until the sauce thickens enough to hold its shape in the spoon. Purée in food processor for a finer texture, if desired. Cover the tart shell with the sauce and cover that with the apple slices, arranged in an overlapping spiral pattern. Bake at 375 degrees for about 30 minutes or until the apple slices have browned slightly. Serve warm.

POLENTA CRUST

- ½ cup softened butter
- ½ cup sugar
- 1 cup polenta
- 2 eggs, at room temperature
- ½ teaspoon salt
- 1½ cups all-purpose flour

Blend the butter and sugar together. Add the polenta, eggs, and salt, beat until smooth, and stir in the flour. Knead the dough very lightly on a floured board and divide into 2. Wrap the pieces and chill them in the refrigerator for at least 15 minutes. Roll out and line a buttered, 10-inch tart tin and pre-bake at 350 degrees for 8 to 9 minutes. This recipe makes enough dough for 2 tarts, so half the dough can be used for another purpose, or frozen for future use.

BLOOD PEACH TART

SERVES 6 TO 8

The reappearance of the blood peach puts a whole new perspective on the question, "Do I dare to eat a peach?" Yes, yes, yes, you will be compelled to answer if you allow yourself even one bite. And there is no reason not to; since they've attracted the attention of the more quality conscious farmers, they are frequently grown organically.

CRUST

- ½ cup whole wheat flour
- ½ cup white flour
- ¼ pound well-chilled unsalted butter
- ½ teaspoon salt
- 4 tablespoons cold water

FILLING

   5 or 6 blood peaches
      3 egg yolks
      1 teaspoon vanilla extract
     ½ cup sugar
      5 tablespoons unsalted butter

In a food processor, place both flours, the butter, and the salt. Process quickly until well blended. Transfer to a bowl, make a hole in the center of the flour mixture, pour in the water, and mix well with your fingers. The dough should hold together but not be sticky. Form it into a ball and refrigerate for 1 to 2 hours. Roll out the dough and line a 10-inch tart pan. Place the pan in the refrigerator while you prepare the peaches.

Bring a large pot of water to a boil. Plunge in the peaches for about 10 seconds, remove, and drain. Remove the skin, which should come off very easily. Cut the peaches in half and remove the stones. Cut into even, lengthwise slices and set them aside. Beat the egg yolks until light and lemony in color. Beat in the vanilla and sugar. Melt the butter and beat it into the mixture. Remove the tart shell from the refrigerator and arrange the peaches on it in even circles, beginning at the outside edge of the shell. Pour the egg mixture over the peaches and place in 400-degree oven. After 10 minutes, reduce the heat to 350 degrees and bake for another 25 to 30 minutes. Remove from the oven and let the tart stand for 15 minutes before serving.

VARIATION ▾ After rolling out the crust, melt 1 to 1½ ounces of bittersweet chocolate in a double boiler. Using a pastry brush, paint a thin coating of the chocolate on the bottom of the tart shell. Refrigerate as above. Add another 1 to 1½ ounces of chocolate to the melting butter and add to egg mixture. Continue as above.

WILD RICE PUDDING

SERVES 8

At one of the final tasting parties, this dish was the unanimous favorite. It is comfort food at its finest, and the cranberries add a festive element that makes it a perfect winter holiday dessert.

    2 cups cooked wild rice (recipe follows)
   ¾ cup cranberries, finely chopped
   ½ cup golden raisins
    1 cup half-and-half
    1 cup heavy cream
   ½ cup maple syrup
    2 eggs, beaten
    1 teaspoon vanilla extract
    2 teaspoons cinnamon
   ¼ teaspoon nutmeg
    1 tablespoon sugar

Heat the oven to 350 degrees. Toss together the wild rice, cranberries, and raisins. Combine the half-and-half and cream, heat, and add the maple syrup, eggs, and vanilla. Add ½ teaspoon of the cinnamon and the nutmeg. Pour over the rice mixture and blend well. Combine the remaining 1½ teaspoons cinnamon with the sugar and sprinkle over the pudding. Bake for 1 hour, or until the pudding is set. Serve warm or chilled.

VARIATION ▾ When cranberries are not in season, substitute ½ cup chopped pecans. Garnish the pudding, before baking, with several pecan halves.

WILD RICE

MAKES 2 CUPS COOKED RICE

½ cup wild rice
2 cups water
  Salt

Wash the rice thoroughly. Bring the lightly salted water to a boil, add the rice, cover, and simmer over medium heat for 40 minutes, or until rice has puffed open and most of the liquid has been absorbed. Drain off any excess liquid, fluff the rice with a fork, cover, and let sit for 5 to 10 minutes.

▼▼▼▼▼▼▼▼▼▼▼▼▼▼▼▼▼▼▼▼▼▼▼▼▼▼▼▼▼▼▼

BLUEBERRY SAUCE

MAKES ABOUT 3 CUPS

The intensity of flavor in this sauce may be varied by the choice of wine: an Orange Muscat will give a lighter sauce, a Black Muscat, a deeper, more complex sauce.

2 cups fresh blueberries
¼ cup orange juice
½ teaspoon ground cloves
¾ cup dessert wine

Purée the blueberries with the orange juice in blender or processor. Add the cloves. Re-

move to a bowl, stir in the wine, taste, and adjust the flavor if desired, adding more cloves, a little more orange juice, or more wine.

Use as a sauce to pour over ice cream, as a dipping sauce with a platter of fresh fruit (try it with sliced bananas), or as a sauce for the Summer Chocolate Roll (page 237).

▼▼▼▼▼▼▼▼▼▼▼▼▼▼▼▼▼▼▼▼▼▼▼▼▼▼▼▼▼▼▼

WHITE CHOCOLATE BUTTERCREAM SAUCE

MAKES ABOUT 3 CUPS

These buttercream sauces are sinfully delicious and will probably be outlawed if the word gets out. Indulge at your own risk. I have included them as sauces for the Fresh Fruit Extravaganza on page 227, but I'm sure any chocolate lover will be able to devise many, many other uses.

Vanilla schnapps is not easy to find, and you can substitute a variety of other liqueurs. Add calvados for the subtle infusion of apple it will offer; Grand Marnier would be delicious; a raspberry liqueur would accent the berries you might serve with the sauce.

1⅓ cups granulated sugar
⅓ cup water
3 egg whites, at room temperature
  Pinch of salt
¼ teaspoon cream of tartar
12 ounces white chocolate

1   teaspoon vanilla extract
¼   cup vanilla schnapps or other liqueur
½   pound unsalted butter
½   cup half-and-half

In this recipe you begin by making a meringue and a sugar syrup. Place the egg whites in the bowl of a mixer and beat at medium speed until they begin to foam. Add the salt and cream of tartar and turn the mixer to high. Beat the eggs until they form stiff, but not dry, peaks.

If at all possible, make the sugar syrup *while* the eggs are being beaten. Place the sugar in a heavy saucepan, add the water, but do not stir. Place the pan over high heat and swirl it around until the liquid is clear. Cover and allow the sugar and water to boil rapidly for 2 minutes. Uncover the pan and continue to boil until the syrup reaches the soft-ball stage, 238 degrees.

With the mixer beating at a medium speed pour the sugar syrup very carefully into the egg whites in a slow, steady stream. After all the sugar syrup has been incorporated, beat on high speed for at least 5 minutes, until the mixture is cool and smooth.

While meringue is being beaten, melt the white chocolate in a double boiler. When it is almost melted, add the vanilla and the liqueur, and stir briefly to blend. When the meringue mixture has cooled, add the melted white chocolate, a bit at a time, beating well after each addition. When it is fully incorporated, add the butter, softened, a tablespoon or 2 at a time. After the final addition, turn the mixer to high and beat well until the meringue, chocolate, and butter are completely blended.

Reduce the speed to slow and add the half-and-half to thin the buttercream to the desired consistency. The buttercream, before thinning, can be used as a frosting for cakes or cookies.

VARIATIONS ▾ To make a Dark Chocolate Buttercream, substitute 12 ounces of dark (bittersweet) chocolate for the white chocolate, and 1 tablespoon strong coffee and 4 tablespoons Grand Marnier liqueur for the vanilla schnapps. You can thin with half-and-half or with ¼ cup strong coffee. ▾ You can also make both White Chocolate Buttercream and Dark Chocolate Buttercream from 1 recipe of meringue. After making the meringue, divide it in half, setting one half aside. Proceed according to directions, halving all the remaining ingredients. Continue with the second portion of meringue, using the second type of chocolate

To make the variation I call Transylvanian Chocolate Cake, begin by making a two-layer chocolate cake using your favorite recipe. Make a full recipe of Dark Chocolate Buttercream (see first variation above) and set it aside. Separate the cloves of two heads of garlic, peel them, and slice very thinly. Melt two tablespoons of butter in a heavy ovenproof pan. Add 1 tablespoon of sugar and the garlic and toss until the garlic is well coated. Bake uncovered at 275 degrees for about 1 hour, or until the garlic is tender. Remove the garlic from the oven and let it cool. Combine the cooled garlic with about ¾ cup of the chocolate buttercream. Spread a thin coating of the plain buttercream over the bottom layer of the cake. Top with half of the garlic buttercream. Place the top layer on the bottom layer, and repeat the process of frosting. Frost the sides of the cake with the plain frosting. Serve this cake with a rich red wine or a sparkling wine; it's particularly dazzling on Halloween.

▼▼▼▼▼▼▼▼▼▼▼▼▼▼▼▼▼▼▼▼▼▼▼▼▼▼▼▼▼▼▼▼▼▼▼▼▼▼

RASPBERRY CHOCOLATE TRUFFLES

MAKES APPROXIMATELY 30 TRUFFLES

Kimberly Every, at the age of eleven, won a Blue Ribbon for these delicious truffles at the 1987 Jumbleberry Jubilee in Santa Rosa.

- ½ pound semisweet chocolate chips
- 4 tablespoons raspberry liqueur
- 6 egg yolks
- ½ cup butter
- 1½ cups powdered sugar
- 6 tablespoons cocoa
- 30 perfect raspberries

Melt the chocolate in a doubler boiler with the raspberry liqueur. Beat in the egg yolks, one at a time. Stir in the butter. Remove from the heat, add the powdered sugar, and blend thoroughly. Refrigerate the mixture until firm. Roll into small balls about 1 inch in diameter. Roll in cocoa to coat. Make a slight indentation in the top of each truffle and place a single, perfect raspberry in it. Keep chilled until ready to serve.

RESOURCES

The small farm cannot be "developed" like a product or a program. Like a household, it is a human organism, and has its origin in both nature and culture. Its justification is not only agricultural, but is a part of an ancient pattern of values, ideas, aspirations, attitudes, faiths, knowledges, and skills that propose and support the sound establishment of a people on the land. To defend the small farm is to defend a large part, and the best part, of our cultural inheritance.

WENDELL BERRY,
The Gift of Good Land
(San Francisco: North Point Press, 1981).

PRESERVING AGRICULTURE IN SONOMA

Agriculture provides twenty-five percent of Sonoma County's entire economy. The farms, of which there are more than three thousand, are valued at nearly two billion dollars by the Department of Agriculture and represent close to six hundred thousand agricultural acres in an area with slightly more than a million acres of land. Our agricultural products, before any form of manufacturing, are worth 250 million dollars a year to the industry, with wine grapes being the leader and milk close behind. Another 1.8 billion dollars per year is generated by products manufactured from crops, a figure that represents our wine, cheese, and apple industries, as well as the sausages, pastas, vinegars, dried tomatoes, roasted peppers, jams, jellies, breads, and other products discussed throughout this book.

Our agricultural community influences economic growth in other areas, such as tourism and food service, as Sonoma's rolling hills and beautiful farmlands become an increasingly popular attraction to visitors from out of the area. As we become well known for the delicious foods we produce here, we also become well known for the ways in which our wonderful local chefs transform our raw materials into menus that are characteristic of the county. It has only been recently, however, that the word about our natural wonders has really spread and, without continued, effective marketing, these natural wonders will be endangered. Sonoma products might be the most wonderful ever grown, the most delicious ever coaxed from the earth. Luther Burbank might have discovered thousands of new species, and our soil might continue to offer its delightful bounty in ever evolving abundance, yet, if the essential link in the chain of agriculture, the consumer, is not informed, no one would ever know. Ignored and invisible, the fertility of the rich land would be stillborn, silent, and dead before it had the chance to offer up its nourishing gifts.

Several decades ago, the problem was not so serious, things could move along at a much slower pace. Land could lie fallow for a time, without sprouting condominiums or shopping centers, or business parks. That is no longer true. In the last forty years, one hundred ninety thousand acres of farmland have been bulldozed for development. Urban sprawl is moving north and Sonoma has been discovered by developers; land is quickly gobbled up and turned into corporate profit, at the expense of open space and agricultural acreage. Organizations such as The Farmlands Group and the Sonoma County Agricultural Marketing Program (SCAMP), are working hard to insure that the public, the consumer, will continue to be made aware of the value of what Sonoma's rich soil and mild climate have to offer. They are also working hard in other less visible ways to preserve our irreplaceable farmlands. Once lost to us, they will be lost forever, and no one who loves Sonoma County can bear the thought of that loss.

THE RESTAURANT CONNECTION

Several organizations have worked together, sometimes unknowingly, to support So-

noma agriculture from a variety of vantage points. In 1984, Carol Klesow and her partner, Greg Neilsen, started Wine Country Cuisine as the missing link between farmer and chef, thus beginning what has proven to be a revolution in the wholesale produce market. When Carol and Greg first started, they worked with four restaurants: John Ash and Company, Madrona Manor, Hemenway & Fleissner, and Matisse Restaurant, and two specialty growers, Bob Cannard and The Farallones Institute Gardens. Together they formed a very intimate group. Bob Cannard, who soon went on to be the specialty grower for Chez Panisse, had been concentrating on the Farm Markets and was thrilled to have this link with local chefs, as was the Farallones. Carol would find out what the chefs wanted, search for the seeds, and have the farmers grow them according to the chefs' requests. It was not long before new growers were on the scene, and again, the influence of Chez Panisse proved pivotal. Thérèse Shere, the daughter of Lindsey Shere, the pastry chef at Chez Panisse restaurant, began growing peppers, tomatoes, and greens for the restaurant at her grandfather's farm in Healdsburg, and began providing some of the produce to Wine Country Cuisine. She introduced *mesclun*, the delicious mix of young, field-picked greens, to Sonoma. It was an entirely new idea, and people were delighted. It was not long before Wine Country Cuisine was making its own mix to keep up with the ever-increasing demand. That was how it all began, and now eighty percent of Wine Country Cuisine's sales of local products are made outside of Sonoma, thirty-three percent out of state. They are currently in the process of developing specialty distribution connections, the first of which is supplying a distributor in New York City with several thousand dollars worth of Sonoma produce a month. It is becoming increasingly common to see the description, Sonoma Grown, on menus throughout the country. Locally, the relationship between grower and chef has blossomed, and many chefs work directly with the specialty farms that have started appearing in the last few years. There are new, small distributors that fulfill the intimate connection that Wine Country Cuisine began, before it assumed the role of taking Sonoma County's abundance out beyond our borders. And, perhaps best of all, the consumer in Sonoma County has been educated to want locally grown products.

SCAMP

For Sonoma County agriculture to continue to prosper, its products must be in demand by more than just fine restaurant chefs. Restaurants play a crucial role, not only in the income their use of local products generates, but also in the ways in which they can create an informed public. A delicious smoked duck salad, eaten in a restaurant, might encourage many home cooks to recreate that dish in their own kitchens. A delicious free-range chicken may serve as inspiration the next time a shopper comes across "Rocky" in the local market. But exposure through restaurants is not enough. Many people never make it to a restaurant that features anything more than a Big Mac, but they cook at home; they make choices when they go to the market, and

they care about providing themselves and their families with good food. The Sonoma County Agricultural Marketing Program, or SCAMP, is dedicated to reaching this market, to educating consumers about the quality and freshness of Sonoma County products, primarily through the use of their "Sonoma County Select" logo, which appears on members' products in the form of an eye-catching sticker. SCAMP was launched after considerable research commissioned by the board of supervisors on the feasibility of large-scale marketing of Sonoma County agriculture. In addition to the labeling campaign, SCAMP plans continuing public relations and advertising in the form of brochures, product tastings and demonstrations, in-store displays, trade shows, and special events. Four times a year—once each season—SCAMP sponsors a farm tour, on which people from out of the area, as well as local residents, take chartered buses for a tour of our specialty farms. Saralee McClelland Kunde, the vice-president of SCAMP, organizes the tours and encourages local farmers to participate, not only by showing their farms, but also by taking the tours themselves. It is surprising, she comments, how many farmers have never had the opportunity to see anyone else's farm; usually there just is not time in the busy life of a farmer for such a luxury. Thus, the SCAMP farm tours not only educate the consumer, but also promote understanding and interaction among farmers. What a great way to get to know your neighbors!

THE SONOMA COUNTY FARMLANDS GROUP

The Farmlands Group is dedicated to the preservation of our precious farmlands and attacks the problem with a number of highly effective strategies. Perhaps most visible is the Wine and Food Series, seasonal tastings of varietal wines paired with appropriate local foods. The event began with a Chardonnay tasting in 1981 at Dry Creek Vineyards and now takes place at various local wineries. Many restaurants and caterers offer their delights, all in support of local farm land. Several hundred people attend each tasting, many traveling from throughout Northern California for the opportunity. All the food and wine is donated, and the money raised from the ticket sales funds the many other projects of The Farmlands Group. One such project was the production in 1989, in association with Sonoma Video Productions, of "Vanishing Farmlands: Saving Sonoma County Agriculture," a thirty-minute broadcast-quality video that focuses on the importance of our farmlands and the current threat to them by development. The Farmlands Group sells the video at cost to encourage widespread viewing, and it has been shown on our local PBS station, KRCB-Channel 22 in Rohnert Park.

The Farmlands Group works in a variety of other, less visible ways to protect our land. This organization of concerned and active citizens sponsors conferences and helps to educate the public about the importance of strong agricultural zoning. The members are active in the public sector, knowing that participation in our various agricultural and county organizations is key to the success. The group also actively, through promotional events, encourages local residents to support our farmers by buying local products. In 1989, the tenth year of The Farmlands Group, they launched their special recognition awards, including the Sonoma County Agricultural Preservationist of the Year Award, which went to Saralee McClelland Kunde of Sonoma Grapevines, Inc.

SONOMA COUNTY FARM TRAILS

One of the most appealing ways to see Sonoma County farm land is by following the Farm Trails map. The Farm Trails organization is described on pages 4 through 6 and its address may be found in the listing that begins on page 269.

THE FARM MARKET

Perhaps that aspect of Sonoma County's self-promotion that is most visible and most effective is The Sonoma County Farm Market, a series of state-certified farmers' markets that takes place year-round throughout the county. All one has to do is walk, bike, or drive to the site of the nearest farm market, and a huge panorama of locally grown products opens up before you like a dream, especially if you are used to shopping only in supermarkets. This is local food at its homegrown best. Nearly every day of the week, especially during the peak season, growers are up before dawn gathering their fresh fruits and vegetables to bring to the market, where local residents gather enthusiastically to see what treats the morning, or evening, shopping will reveal. The farm market is where you can find vine-ripened tomatoes, berries still warm from the morning sun, potatoes that just a few hours before nestled under ground. The farm market provides, in addition to inexpensive high-quality food, a sense of community that is vanishing perhaps even more quickly than our country's vast open spaces. Strangers smile and, if you attend regularly, do not stay strangers for long. A farmer may offer you a story about the garlic you are taking home, or a slice of a variety of antique apple you have never seen before. At the farm market, you are part of an intimate circle of growing, selling, and consuming that encourages agriculture at its best. This is not corporate agribusiness, with its transporters, advertisers, pesticide companies, wholesalers, and retailers. This is food that has been nourished by loving hands, going directly from farm into the hands of those it will nourish. This is how life should be lived.

In May of 1989, the Thursday Night Market began in downtown Santa Rosa and became a huge surprising success. Its popularity continued to grow during the first season, from May through September, 1989. There was some lack in the community, some need that had not been met, that simply blossomed with the availability of the Thursday Night Market. Local restaurants set up booths, musicians played, children laughed, people flirted with one another under the evening sky, and everyone had a marvelous time, including the farmers, who were thrilled at the numbers that turned out. I think it is safe to say that a new tradition has been established in Sonoma.

Hilda Swartz is the force behind the current success of the Sonoma County Farm Market, and it was her efforts that led to *Season by Season, The Sonoma County Farmers Market Cookbook*.

SONOMA COUNTY FARM MARKET SCHEDULE

HEALDSBURG ▾
Tuesday, 4:00 P.M.–6:00 P.M. and Saturdays, 9:00 A.M.–12:00 noon, from the end of June until the Tuesday before Thanksgiving; in the Town Plaza.

PETALUMA ▾
Saturday, 2:00–5:00 P.M., June through October; "A" parking lot.

SANTA ROSA ▾
Wednesday and Saturday, 9:00 A.M.–12:00 noon, year-round; Veteran's Building parking lot.

Thursday Night Downtown Market, 5:30 P.M.–8:30 P.M., first weekend in May until the end of September; Fourth Street at Courthouse Square.

SEBASTOPOL ▾
Sunday, 11:00 A.M.–2:00 P.M., from June through October; Week's Way parking lot.

SONOMA ▾
Tuesday, 9:00 A.M.–12:00 noon, from May or June until the Tuesday before Thanksgiving; Arnold Fields at First Street West. Friday, 9:00 A.M.–12:00 noon; year-round; same location.

Sonoma County Addresses

PRIMARY RESOURCES

*Restaurants ▾ Farms ▾ Caterers ▾
Producers ▾ Bakeries ▾ Cheese
Factories ▾ Etcetera*

Alvarado Street Bakery
500 Martin Avenue
Rohnert Park, CA 94928
(707) 585-3293
Ernie Stires, Sales Manager

Angelo's Meats FT#515
2700 Adobe Road
Petaluma, CA 94952
(707) 763-9586
Angelo and Frances Ibleto

Apple Tree-Christmas Tree FT#437
10055 Bodega Highway
Sebastopol, CA 95472
(707) 823-3605
Lloyd and Barbara Roberts

Batemon Meat Center and Seafoods
3695 Petaluma Boulevard North
Petaluma, CA 94952
(707) 762-7253

Bay Bottom Beds
966 Borden Villa Drive
Santa Rosa, CA 95401
(707) 578-6049
Lisa Jang and Jorge Rebagliati
Limited mail order

Bea Beasley & Company
906 Morgan Street
Santa Rosa, CA 95401
(707) 544-3059

Bengs-Best Ranch FT#380
4600 Todd Road
Sebastopol, CA 95472
(707) 823-9395
Stanley and Helen Bengtson

Bill's Farm Basket
10315 Bodega Highway
Sebastopol, CA 95472
(707) 829-1777

Brother Juniper's Bakery
6450 First Street
Forestville, CA 95436
(707) 887-9288
Peter Reinhardt, master baker

Buona Pasta
550 Gravenstein Highway North
Sebastopol, CA 95473
(707) 829-0776
Larry Urmini

California Cooperative Dairy Creamery Store
   FT#599
711 Western Avenue
Petaluma, CA 94952
(707) 778-1234

Canfield Tree Farm FT#396
4104 Canfield Road
Sebastopol, CA 95473
(707) 823-8147

Cannard Farms
1994 Sobre Vista
Sonoma, CA 95476
(707) 938-8424
Bob Cannard

Caswell Winter Creek Farm & Vineyard
   FT#414
13207 Dupont Road
Sebastopol, CA 95472
(707) 874-2517

Costeaux French Bakery
421 Healdsburg Avenue
Healdsburg, CA 95448
(707) 433-1913
and
2751 Fourth Street
Santa Rosa, CA 95404
(707) 542-1913

Cost Plus Imports
2685 Santa Rosa Avenue
Santa Rosa, CA 95404
(707) 526-0600

Crane Melon Barn
1649 Crane Canyon Road
Santa Rosa, CA 95404
(707) 584-5141

Downtown Bakery & Creamery
308A Center Street
Healdsburg, CA 95448
(707) 431-2719
Lindsey Shere

Dry Creek General Store
3495 Dry Creek Road
Healdsburg, CA 95448
(707) 433-4171

Elaine Bell Catering Company
682 West Napa Street
Sonoma, CA 95476
Elaine Bell, owner
Yong Suk Willendrup, executive chef

Farallones Institute Gardens
15290 Coleman Valley Road
Occidental, CA 95465
(707) 874-2885

Fiesta Market
550 Gravenstein Highway North
Sebastopol, CA 95472
(707) 823-9736

Fisher Farm FT#395
2870 Canfield Road
Sebastopol, CA 95472
(707) 823-4817

Forever Yours Living Trees FT#397
5815 Blank Road
Sebastopol, CA 95472
(707) 829-5643

Formica's Berry Farm FT#373
6314 Lone Pine Road
Sebastopol, CA 95472
(707) 829-2110
Ernest and Shirley Formica

Garden Valley Ranch FT#540
498 Pepper Road
Petaluma, CA 94952
(707) 795-0919

Gerhard's Napa Valley Sausages
6525 Washington
Yountville, CA
(707) 944-1593
Mail order

Good's Holiday Tree Ranch FT#331
1220 Gravenstein Highway North
Sebastopol, CA 95472
(707) 823-0831
Marv and Jeanne Good

Gourmet Mushrooms, Inc.
P.O. Box 391
Sebastopol, CA 95472
(707) 823-1743
Malcolm Clark

Grandpa's Workshop
920 Shiloh Road
Windsor, CA 95492
(707) 838-6724
(707) 528-4705
Ralph Evans

Green Valley Blueberry Farm
9345 Ross Station Road
Sebastopol, CA 95472
(707) 887-7496

Green Valley Kiwifruit Farm FT#305
11397 Green Valley Road
Sebastopol, CA 95472
(707) 823-0156

Happy Haven Ranch FT#910
1480 Sperring Road
Sonoma, CA 95476
(707) 996-0375

Hoogland's Farm FT#765
1722 Willowside Road
Santa Rosa, CA 95401
(707) 523-4360

Imwalle Gardens FT#800
685 West 3rd St.
Santa Rosa, CA 95401
(707) 546-0279

Inn at Valley Ford
14395 Highway One
Valley Ford, CA 94972
(707) 876-3182

Jacob Horner
106 Matheson Street
Healdsburg, CA 95448
(707) 433-3939
Jim Gibbons, owner and executive chef

Jaded Palate, The
P.O. Box 1552
Sebastopol, CA 95473
Michele Anna Jordan, owner

Joe Matos Cheese Factory FT#725
3669 Llano Road
Santa Rosa, CA 95407
(707) 584-5283
Mail order

John Ash & Co.
4330 Barnes Road
Santa Rosa, CA 95401
(707) 527-7687

Johnson's Oysters & Seafood Company
    FT#595
253 North McDowell Boulevard
Petaluma, CA 94952
(707) 763-4161

Kenwood Restaurant & Bar
9900 Sonoma Highway
Kenwood, CA 95442
(707) 833-6326

Kozlowski's Raspberry Farms FT#304
5566 Gravenstein Highway North
Forestville, CA 95436
(707) 887-1587
Mail order

Laguna Farms
1764 Cooper Road
Sebastopol, CA 95472
(707) 823-0823
Scott Mathieson and Jennifer Joell

Lainie's Cuisine To Go
682 West Napa Street
Sonoma, CA 95476
Elaine Bell, owner

La Province
521 College Avenue
Santa Rosa, CA 95401
(707) 526-6233
Josef Heller, owner and executive chef

Larson's Keneko Farm FT#305
8500 Templeman Road
Forestville, CA 95436
(707) 887-1014

Last Record Store, The
739 Fourth Street
Santa Rosa, CA 95404
(707) 525-1963

Laura Chenel's Chèvre FT#795
1550 Ridley Avenue
Santa Rosa, CA 95401
(707) 575-8888
Mail order

Lisa Hemenway's
714 Village Court
Montgomery Village
Santa Rosa, CA 95405
(707) 526-5111

McCoy's Cookware
2759 Fourth Street
Santa Rosa, CA 95405
(707) 526-3856
Louise McCoy

Madrona Manor
1001 Westside Road
Healdsburg, CA 95448
(707) 433-4231
Todd Muir, executive chef

Marin County Farmer's Market
1114 Irwin Street
San Rafael, CA 94901
(415) 456-3276

Marin French Cheese Company
7500 Red Hill Road
Petaluma, CA 94952
(707) 762-6001
Mail order

Mary Mary's
3464 Gravenstein Highway South
Sebastopol, CA 95472
(707) 823-2902

Ma Stokeld's Old Vic
731 Fourth Street
Santa Rosa, CA 95404
(707) 571-7555

Matt Sikora FT#585
747 Marshall Avenue
Petaluma, CA 94952
(707) 762-1315

Matthew's Mustard
3695 Petaluma Boulevard North
Petaluma, CA 94952
(707) 762-5762

Maxi Flowers à la Carte
1015 Martin Lane
Sebastopol, CA 95472
(707) 829-0592

Me Gusta Farms FT#335
(Rachel's Goat Cheese of Sonoma)
965 Martin Lane
Sebastopol, CA 95472
(707) 823-1322
Mail order

Mendocino Pasta Co.
6819 Redwood Drive
Cotati, CA 94931
(707) 795-5859
Don Luber, owner

Mezzaluna Bakery
3279 Dutton Avenue
Santa Rosa, CA 95407
Michael Hirschberg

G. L. Mezzetta, Inc.
1201 East MacArthur
Sonoma, CA 95476
(707) 938-8388

Middleton Gardens FT#148
2651 Westside Road
Healdsburg, CA 95448
(707) 433-4755
Wylie and Edna Middleton

Occidental Bakery & Café
3688 Bohemian Highway
Occidental, CA 95465
(707) 874-2894

Organic Grocery
2481 Guerneville Road
Santa Rosa, CA 95401
(707) 528-3663

P&G Art Ranch FT#419
16125 Bittner Road
Occidental, CA 95465
(707) 874-1405
Peter and Gerrie Lu

Pack Jack Bar-B-Que Inn
3963 Gravenstein Highway South
Sebastopol, CA 95472
(707) 823-9929

Pasta Etc.
2759 Fourth Street
Santa Rosa, CA 95405
(707) 579-2278
Bernard and Maria Soltes

Pastorale FT#444
12779 Bodega Highway
Freestone, CA 95472
(707) 823-0640

Pelikan Spring Farms FT#435
320 Furlong Road
Sebastopol, CA 95472
(707) 829-1495
Ellyn Pelikan

Pet-a-Llama Ranch FT#385
5505 Lone Pine Road
Sebastopol, CA 95472
(707) 823-9395

Petaluma Market
210 Western Avenue
Petaluma, CA 94952
(707) 762-8452 (general)
(707) 762-5464 (meat and wine)

Petaluma Mushroom Farm FT#575
782 Thompson Lane
Petaluma, CA 94952
(707) 762-1280

Petrini's Market
2751 Fourth Street
Santa Rosa, CA 95405
(707) 526-2080

Pimentel Family Farm FT#625
6245 Roblar Road
Petaluma, CA 94952
(707) 795-5034

Pine Ridge Farms
P.O. Box 1817
Sebastopol, CA 95473
(707) 829-5432
Pat and Bart Ehman, owners

Piotrkowski Smoked Poultry
1285 Skillman Lane
Petaluma, CA 94952
(707) 778-8482

Raven Theater
115 North Street
Healdsburg, CA 95448
(707) 433-5448

Redwood Hill Farm Goat Dairy
10855 Occidental Road
Sebastopol, CA 95472
(707) 823-8250
Steven Schack and Jennifer Lynn Bice

Reichardt Duck Farm
3770 Middle Two Rock Road
Petaluma, CA 94952
(707) 762-6314

Restaurant Matisse
620 Fifth Street
Santa Rosa, CA 95404
(707) 527-9797

Ristorante Siena
1229 North Dutton Avenue
Santa Rosa, CA 95401
(707) 578-4511
Michael Hirschberg, owner

Rocco's Freestone Corners
12750 Bodega Highway
Freestone, CA 95465
(707) 823-7756

Rocking Heart Ranch FT#676
2016 Fallon Road
Petaluma, CA 94952
(707) 778-8647

Rocky Creek Gardens
10540 Rocky Creek Road
(P.O. Box 1649)
Lower Lake, CA 95457
Schuyler Hoyt and Paula Mune

Russian River Vineyards Restaurant
5700 Gravenstein Highway North
Forestville, CA 95436
(707) 887-1562

S. E. Rykoff and Company
P.O. Box 21467
Los Angeles, CA 90021
(800) 421-9873

Salame Tree Deli
304 Center Street
Healdsburg, CA 95448
(707) 433-7224

Sawyer's News
733 Fourth Street
Santa Rosa, CA 95404
(707) 542-1311

Scott's Bay Grill
2001 Highway One
Bodega Bay, CA 94923
(707) 876-3260

Shoosh International, Inc.
San Francisco, CA 94107
(415) 626-2781

Sizzling Tandoor
409 Mendocino Avenue
Santa Rosa, CA 95404
(707) 579-5999

Sonoma Antique Apple Nursery FT#146
4395 Westside Road
Healdsburg, CA 95448
(707) 433-6420
Mail order

Sonoma Cheese Factory FT#920
2 Spain Street
Sonoma, CA 95476
(707) 996-1931
Mail order

Sonoma French Bakery
468 First Street East
Sonoma, CA 95476
(707) 938-3232

Sonoma Mission Inn & Spa
18140 Sonoma Highway
Sonoma, CA 95476
(707) 938-9000
Charles Saunders, executive chef

Sonoma Museum
425 Seventh Street
Santa Rosa, CA 95404
(707) 579-1500

Sonoma Sausage Factory
453 First Street West (retail)
(707) 938-8200
865 West Napa Street (wholesale)
(707) 996-5211
Sonoma, CA 95476
Herb Hoeser, owner
Mail order

Studio Kafe
418 Mendocino Avenue
Santa Rosa, CA 95404
(707) 545-1971

Timber Crest Farms FT#154
4791 Dry Creek Road
Healdsburg, CA 95448
(707) 433-8251
Ruth and Ronald Waltenspiel
Mail order

Toyon Books
104 Matheson Street
Healdsburg, CA 95448
(707) 433-9270

Traverso's Gourmet Foods & Wine
Third and B Streets
Santa Rosa, CA 95404
(707) 542-2530

Treehorn Books
625 Fourth Street
Santa Rosa, CA 95448
(707) 525-1782

Tre Scalini
241 Healdsburg Avenue
Healdsburg, CA 95448
(707) 433-1772

Truffles Restaurant
234 South Main Street
Sebastopol, CA 95472
(707) 823-8448
(For sale at press time)

Twin Hill Ranch FT#352
1689 Pleasant Hill Road
Sebastopol, CA 95472
(707) 823-2815

Urmini & Sons' Herb Farm FT#336
1292 Hurlbut Avenue
Sebastopol, CA 95472
(707) 829-0185
Larry Urmini

Vella Cheese Factory FT#922
315 Second Street East
(P.O. Box 191)
Sonoma, CA 95476
(707) 938-3232
Mail order

Volpi's Italian Market, Deli & Speakeasy
124 Washington
Petaluma, CA 94952
(707) 762-2371

Walker Apples FT#408
P.O. Box 220
Graton, CA 95444
(707) 823-4310
Lee and Shirley Walker

Western Hills Rare Plants Nursery
16250 Coleman Valley Road
Occidental, CA 95465
(707) 874-3731

Westside Farms FT#144
7097 Westside Road
Healdsburg, CA 95448
(707) 431-1432
Pam and Ron Kaiser

Wild Distributors
P.O. Box 14204
Santa Rosa, CA 95402
(707) 544-9453
Wayne and Susan Toress
Mail order

Williams-Sonoma
Mail Order Department
P.O. Box 7456
San Francisco, CA 94120-7456
(415) 421-4242

Willie Bird Turkeys FT#745
5350 Highway Twelve
Santa Rosa, CA 95404
(707) 545-2832

Willowside Meats & Sausage Factory
3421 Guerneville Road
Santa Rosa, CA 95401
(707) 546-8404

Wine Country Cuisine
P.O. Box 7366
Santa Rosa, CA 95407
(707) 526-9434
Greg Nielsen

Wishing Well Nursery
306 Bohemian Highway
Freestone, CA 95465
(707) 823-3710

WINERIES

Adler Fels
5325 Corrick Road
Santa Rosa, CA 95405
(707) 539-3123

Alderbrook Vineyards
2306 Magnolia Drive
Healdsburg, CA 95448
(707) 433-9154

Alexander Valley Fruit & Trading Company
5110 Highway 128
Geyserville, CA 95441
(707) 433-1944

Alexander Valley Vineyards
8644 Highway 128
Healdsburg, CA 95448
(707) 433-7209

Angel Vintners (Mariposa Wines)
18700 Geyserville Avenue
Geyserville, CA 95441
(707) 398-4144

Balverne Winery & Vineyards
10810 Hillview Road
Windsor, CA 95492
(707) 433-6913

Bandiera Winery
555 South Cloverdale Boulevard (Highway 101)
Cloverdale, CA 95425
(707) 894-4295

Bazzano Vineyards
P.O. Box 383
Fulton, CA 95439
(707) 526-1714

Bellerose Vineyard
435 West Dry Creek Road
Healdsburg, CA 95448
(707) 433-1637

Belvedere Winery
4035 Westside Road
Healdsburg, CA 95448
(707) 433-8236

Black Mountain Vineyard
101 Grant Avenue
Healdsburg, CA 95448
(707) 431-7015

Braren Pauli Winery
1161 Spring Hill Rd.
Petaluma, CA 94952
(707) 778-0721

Brenner Cellars
35 Executive Avenue, #4
Rohnert Park, CA 94928
(707) 584-5522

Buena Vista Winery
18000 Old Winery Road
Sonoma, CA 95476
(707) 252-7117

Davis Bynum Winery
8075 Westside Road
Healdsburg, CA 95448
(707) 433-5852

Carmenet Vineyard
1700 Moon Mountain Road
Sonoma, CA 95476
(707) 996-5870

Caswell Vineyards
13207 Dupont Road
Sebastopol, CA 95472
(707) 874-2517

Cecchetti Sebastiani Cellar
710 West Napa Street, #4
Sonoma, CA 95476
(707) 996-8463

Chalk Hill Winery
10300 Chalk Hill Road
Healdsburg, CA 95448
(707) 838-4306

Charis Vineyards
7850 Dry Creek Road
Geyserville, CA 95441
(707) 433-3533

Chateau DeBaun
1160 Hopper Avenue
(P.O. Box 11483)
Santa Rosa, CA 95401
(707) 544-1600

Chateau Diana
6195 Dry Creek Road
(P.O. Box 1013)
Healdsburg, CA 95448
(707) 433-6992

Chateau St. Jean
8555 Sonoma Highway
(P.O. Box 293)
Kenwood, CA 95452
(707) 833-4134

Chateau Souverain
Independence Lane at Highway 101
(P.O. Box 528)
Geyserville, CA 95441
(707) 433-8281

Clos Du Bois
5 Fitch Street
(P.O. Box 339)
Healdsburg, CA 95448
(707) 433-5576

B. R. Cohn
15000 Sonoma Highway (Highway Twelve)
Glen Ellen, CA 95442
(707) 938-4064

H. Coturri & Sons
6725 Enterprise Road
(P.O. Box 396)
Glen Ellen, CA 95442
(707) 525-9126

Dehlinger Winery
6300 Guerneville Road
Sebastopol, CA 95472
(707) 823-2378

De Loach Vineyards
1791 Olivet Road
Santa Rosa, CA 95401
(707) 526-9111

De Lorimier Winery
2001 Highway 128
P.O. Box 726
Geyserville, CA 95441
(707) 433-7718

Diamond Oaks Vineyard
26900 Dutcher Creek Road
Cloverdale, CA 95425
(707) 894-3191

Domaine Laurier
8075 Martinelli Road
Forestville, CA 95436
(707) 887-9791

Domaine Michel
4155 Wine Creek Road
Healdsburg, CA 95448
(707) 433-7427

Domaine St. George Winery
1141 Grant Avenue
(P.O. Box 548)
Healdsburg, CA 95448
(707) 433-5508

Dry Creek Vineyard, Inc.
3770 Lambert Bridge Road
(P.O. Box T)
Healdsburg, CA 95448
(707) 433-1000

Eagle Ridge Winery
111 Goodwin Avenue
Penngrove, CA 94951
(707) 664-9463

Ferrari-Carano Vineyards & Winery
8761 Dry Creek Road
Healdsburg, CA 95448
(707) 433-6700

Field Stone Winery
10075 Highway 128
Healdsburg, CA 95448
(707) 433-7266

Fisher Vineyards
6200 St. Helena Road
Santa Rosa, CA 95404
(707) 539-7511

Foppiano Vineyards
12707 Old Redwood Highway
Healdsburg, CA 95448
(707) 433-7272

Fritz Cellars
24691 Dutcher Creek Road
Cloverdale, CA 95425
(707) 894-3389

Fulton Valley Winery
875 River Road
Fulton, CA 95439
(707) 578-1744

Gan Eden
4950 Ross Road
Sebastopol, CA 95472
(707) 829-5586

Gary Farrell Wines
P.O. Box 342
Forestville, CA 95436
(707) 433-6616

Gauer Estate Winery and Vineyards
18700 Geyserville Avenue
Geyserville, CA 95441
(707) 433-4402

Geyser Peak Winery
22281 Chianti Avenue
(P.O. Box 25)
Geyserville, CA 95441
(707) 433-6585

Glen Ellen Winery
1883 London Ranch Road
Glen Ellen, CA 95442
(707) 935-3000

Gloria Ferrer Champagne Caves
23555 Highway 121
(P.O. Box 1427)
Sonoma, CA 95476
(707) 996-7256

Golden Creek Vineyard
4480 Wallace Road
Santa Rosa, CA 95404
(707) 538-2350

Grand Cru Vineyards
1 Vintage Lane
Glen Ellen, CA 95442
(707) 996-8100

Gundlach-Bundschu Winery
2000 Denmark Street
Sonoma, CA 95476
(707) 938-5277

Hacienda Winery
1000 Vineyard Lane
Sonoma, CA 95476
(707) 938-3220

Hafner Vineyard
4280 Pine Flat Road
(P.O. Box 1038)
Healdsburg, CA 95448
(707) 433-4675

Hanna Winery
5345 Occidental Road
Santa Rosa, CA 95401
(707) 575-3330

Hanzell Vineyards
18596 Lomita Avenue
Sonoma, CA 95476
(707) 996-3860

Haywood Winery
18701 Gehricke Road
Sonoma, CA 95476
(707) 996-3860

Hop Kiln Winery
6050 Westside Road
Healdsburg, CA 95448
(707) 433-6491

Robert Hunter Winery
15655 Arnold Drive
Sonoma, CA 95476
(707) 996-3056

Huttgren and Samperton
P.O. Box 1026
Healdsburg, CA 95448
(707) 433-5102

Iron Horse Vineyards
9786 Ross Station Road
Sebastopol, CA 95472
(707) 887-1507

Jimark Winery
602 Limerick Lane
Healdsburg, CA 95448
(707) 433-3118

Johnson's Alexander Valley Wines
8333 Highway 128
Healdsburg, CA 95448
(707) 433-2319

Jordan Vineyard & Winery
1474 Alexander Valley Road
Healdsburg, CA 95448
(707) 433-6955

Joseph Swan Vineyards
2916 Laguna Road
Forestville, CA 95436
(707) 546-7711

Kenwood Vineyards
9592 Sonoma Highway
(P.O. Box 447)
Kenwood, CA 95452
(707) 833-5891

Kistler Vineyards
Nelligan Road
Glen Ellen, CA 95442
(707) 996-5117

Korbel Champagne Cellars
13250 River Road
Guerneville, CA 95446
(707) 887-2294

La Crema Vinera
971 Transport Way
(P.O. Box 976)
Petaluma, CA 94952
(707) 762-0393

Lake Sonoma Winery
9990 Dry Creek Road
Geyserville, CA 95441
(707) 433-8534

Lambert Bridge Winery
4085 West Dry Creek Road
Healdsburg, CA 95448
(707) 433-5855

Landmark Vineyards
9150 Los Amigos Road
Windsor, CA 95492
(707) 838-9466

Las Montanas
4400 Cavedale Road
Glen Ellen, CA 95442
(707) 996-2448

Laurel Glen Vineyard
P.O. Box 548
Glen Ellen, CA 95442
(707) 526-3914

Limerick Lane Vineyards
1023 Limerick Lane
Healdsburg, CA 95448
(707) 433-9211

Lyeth Vineyard & Winery
24625 Chianti Road
(P.O. Box 558)
Geyserville, CA 95441
(707) 857-3562

Lytton Springs Winery
650 Lytton Springs Road
Healdsburg, CA 95448
(707) 483-7721

Marietta Cellars
P.O. Box 1260
Healdsburg, CA 95448
(707) 433-7721

Mark West Vineyards
7000 Trenton–Healdsburg Road
Forestville, CA 95436
(707) 544-4813

Martinelli Vineyards
3362 River Road
Fulton, CA 95439
(707) 525-0570

Martini & Prati Wines, Inc.
2191 Laguna Road
Santa Rosa, CA 95401
(707) 823-2404

Matanzas Creek Winery
6079 Bennett Valley Road
Santa Rosa, CA 95404
(707) 528-6464

Matrose Wines
25510 River Road
Cloverdale, CA 95425
(707) 894-3197

Mazzocco Vineyards
1400 Lytton Springs Road
(P.O. Box 49)
Healdsburg, CA 95448
(707) 433-9035

Meeker Vineyards
9711 West Dry Creek Road
Healdsburg, CA 95448
(707) 431-2148

Melim Vineyard
1500 Chalkhill Road
Healdsburg, CA 95448
(707) 431-7479

Merry Vintners, The
3339 Hartman Road
Santa Rosa, CA 95401
(707) 526-4441

Mill Creek Vineyards
1401 Westside Road
(P.O. Box 758)
Healdsburg, CA 95448
(707) 431-2121

J. W. Morris Winery
101 Grant Avenue
(P.O. Box 921)
Healdsburg, CA 95448
(707) 431-7015

Robert Mueller Cellars
P.O. Box 1392
Healdsburg, CA 95448
(707) 433-5576

Murphy-Goode Vineyards
4001 Highway 128
Geyserville, CA 95441
(707) 431-7644

Nervo Winery
19550 Geyserville Avenue
Geyserville, CA 95441
(707) 857-3417

Pastori Winery
23189 Geyserville Avenue
Cloverdale, CA 95425
(707) 857-3418

Pat Paulsen Vineyards
25510 River Road
(P.O. Box 565)
Cloverdale, CA 95425
(707) 894-2969

J. Pedroncelli Winery
1220 Canyon Road
Geyserville, CA 95441
(707) 857-3531

Piper Sonoma Cellars
11447 Old Redwood Highway
Healdsburg, CA 95448
(707) 433-8843

Pommeraie Vineyards
10541 Cherry Ridge Road
Sebastopol, CA 95472
(707) 823-9463

Porter Creek Vineyards
8735 Westside Road
Healdsburg, CA 95448
(707) 887-1150

Preston Vineyards
9282 West Dry Creek Road
Healdsburg, CA 95448
(707) 433-3372

Quivera Vineyards
4900 West Dry Creek Road
Healdsburg, CA 95448
(707) 431-8333

Rabbit Ridge Vineyards
3291 Westside Road
Healdsburg, CA 95448
(707) 431-7128

A. Rafanelli Winery
4685 West Dry Creek Road
Healdsburg, CA 95448
(707) 433-1385

Ravenswood Winery
21415 Broadway
Sonoma, CA 95476
(707) 938-1960

Richardson Vineyards
2711 Knob Hill Road
Sonoma, CA 95476
(707) 938-2610

J. Rochioli Vineyards & Winery
6192 Westside Road
Healdsburg, CA 95448
(707) 433-2305

Rodney Strong/Sonoma Vineyards
11455 Old Redwood Highway
Windsor, CA 95492
(707) 433-6511

Rose Family Winery
3260 River Road
Windsor, CA 95492
(707) 575-3160

St. Francis Winery & Vineyards
8450 Sonoma Highway (Highway Twelve)
Kenwood, CA 95452
(707) 833-4666

Sausal Winery
7370 Highway 128
Healdsburg, CA 95448
(707) 433-2285

Sea Ridge Winery
935 Highway One
Bodega Bay, CA 94923
(707) 875-3329

Sebastiani Vineyards
389 Fourth Street East
(P.O. Box AA)
Sonoma, CA 95476
(707) 938-5532

Seghesio Winery
14730 Grove Street
Healdsburg, CA 95448
(707) 433-3579

Sellards Winery
6400 Sequoia Circle
Sebastopol, CA 95472
(707) 823-8293

Simi Winery, Inc.
16275 Healdsburg Avenue
(P.O. Box 946)
Healdsburg, CA 95448
(707) 433-6981

Smothers Brothers Tasting Room
9575 Highway Twelve
(P.O. Box 789)
Kenwood, CA 95452
(707) 833-1010

Sonoma-Cutrer Vineyards
4401 Slusser Road
Windsor, CA 95492
(707) 528-1181

Sonoma Hills
4850 Peracca Road
Santa Rosa, CA 95404
(707) 523-3415

Sotoyome Winery
641 Limerick Lane
Healdsburg, CA 95448
(707) 433-2001

Robert Stemmler Winery
3805 Lambert Bridge Road
Healdsburg, CA 95448
(707) 433-6334

Taft Street Winery
6450 First Street
Forestville, CA 95436
(707) 887-2801

Topolos at Russian River Vineyards Winery
5700 Gravenstein Highway
Forestville, CA 95436
(707) 887-2956

Toyon Winery & Vineyards
9643 Highway 128
Healdsburg, CA 95448
(707) 433-6847

Trentadue Winery
19170 Redwood Highway
Geyserville, CA 95441
(707) 433-3104

M. G. Vallejo
1883 London Ranch Road
Spain Street at Second Street West
(P.O. Box 477)
Sonoma, CA 95477
(707) 935-3000

Valley of the Moon Winery
777 Madrone Road
Glen Ellen, CA 95442
(707) 996-6941

Van der Kamp Champagne Cellars
307 Warm Springs Road
(P.O. Box 609)
Kenwood, CA 95452
(707) 833-1883

Viansa Winery
24926 Arnold Drive
(P.O. Box 1849)
Sonoma, CA 95476
(707) 996-4448

Vina Vista Vineyards
24401 Chianti Road
Geyserville, CA 95441
(707) 857-3722

Weinstock Cellars
231 Center Street
(P.O. Box 947)
Healdsburg, CA 95448
(707) 433-3186

White Oak Vineyard
208 Haydon Street
Healdsburg, CA 95448
(707) 433-8429

William Wheeler Winery
130 Plaza Street
(P.O. Box 881)
Healdsburg, CA 95448
(707) 443-8786

Williams-Selyem
850 River Road
Fulton, CA 95439
(707) 887-7480

Winery at Asti, The
26150 Asti Road
(P.O. Box 1)
Asti, CA 95413
(707) 433-2333

Z Moore
3364 River Road
Windsor, CA 95492
(707) 544-3555

Stephen Zellerbach Vineyard
4611 Thomas Road
Healdsburg, CA 95448
(707) 433-9463

FOOD, WINE, & VISITORS ORGANIZATIONS

Convention and Visitors Bureau, The Sonoma
   County
10 Fourth Street
Santa Rosa, CA 95401
(707) 575-1191

Culinary Guild, Sonoma County
% Flavors Gourmet Adventure
1008 Hopper Lane
Santa Rosa, CA 95403

Fair Association, Sonoma County
1350 Bennett Valley Road
(P.O. Box 1536)
Santa Rosa, CA 95402
(707) 545-4200

Farm Bureau, Sonoma County
920 Piner Road
Santa Rosa, CA 95401
(707) 544-5575

Farmlands Group, Sonoma County
P.O. Box 3515
Santa Rosa, CA 95402
(707) 576-0162
Marty Roberts, director

Farm Markets, Sonoma County
110 Valley Oakes Drive
Santa Rosa, CA 95409
(707) 538-7023
Hilda Swartz, manager

Farm Trails, Sonoma County
P.O. Box 6032
Santa Rosa, CA 95406
(707) 544-4728
Betsy Timm, publicist

Grape Growers Association, Sonoma County
850 Second Street, Suite B
Santa Rosa, CA 95404
(707) 576-3110

Harvest Fair, Sonoma County
1350 Bennett Valley Road
(P.O. Box 1536)
Santa Rosa, CA 95402
(707) 545-4203

Luther Burbank Center for the Performing Arts
50 Mark West Springs Road
Santa Rosa, CA 95401
(707) 527-7006

Luther Burbank Home & Gardens
Santa Rosa Avenue at Sonoma Avenue
(P.O. Box 1678)
Santa Rosa, CA 95402

Museum, The Sonoma County
425 Seventh Street
Santa Rosa, CA 95401
(707) 579-1500

Russian River Wine Road
P.O. Box 46
Healdsburg, CA 95448
(707) 433-6935
(800) 648-9922 (in California only)

SCAMP (Sonoma County Agricultural
 Marketing Program)
1055 West College Avenue, South, #194
Santa Rosa, CA 95401
Dan Benedetti, president

Sonoma Valley Visitors Bureau
453 First Street East
Sonoma, CA 95476
(707) 996-1090

Sonoma Vintners Club
347 Healdsburg Avenue
Healdsburg, CA 95448
(707) 433-2337

Stage-a-Picnic Dilworth-Geyserville Stage Line
P.O. Box 536
Geyserville, CA 95441
(707) 857-3619

Vintners Association, Sonoma County
453 First Street East
(P.O. Box 238)
Sonoma, CA 95476
(707) 935-0803

Vintners Cooperative, Inc., Sonoma County
7675 Conde Lane
Windsor, CA 95492
(707) 838-6678

Wine Country Inns
P.O. Box 51
Geyserville, CA 95441
(707) 433-4667

Wine Growers Association, Sonoma County
50 Mark West Springs Road
Santa Rosa, CA 95401
(707) 527-7701

Wine Library, Sonoma County
 at Healdsburg Regional Library
139 Piper Street
Healdsburg, CA 95448
(707) 433-3772

Wine Library Association, Sonoma County
P.O. Box 15225
Santa Rosa, CA 95402

Wine Showcase & Auction, Sonoma County
50 Mark West Springs Road
Santa Rosa, CA 95404
(707) 579-0577

CHAMBERS OF COMMERCE

BODEGA BAY
555 Highway One
(P.O. Box 146)
Bodega Bay, CA 94923
(707) 875-3422

CLOVERDALE
220 North Cloverdale Boulevard
(P.O. Box 476)
Cloverdale, CA 95425
(707) 894-2507

COTATI
8000 Old Redwood Highway
Cotati, CA 94931
(707) 795-5508

GEYSERVILLE
P.O. Box 276
Geyserville, CA 95441
(707) 857-3745
Jean Dix

GUERNEVILLE
Russian River Chamber of Commerce
14034 Armstrong Woods Road
(P.O. Box 331)
Guerneville, CA 95446
(707) 869-9009

HEALDSBURG
217 Healdsburg Avenue
Healdsburg, CA 95448
(707) 433-6935

MONTE RIO
P.O. Box 220
Monte Rio, CA 95462

OCCIDENTAL
P.O. Box 159
Occidental, CA 95476
(707) 874-3090

PETALUMA
215 Howard Street
Petaluma, CA 94952
(707) 762-2785

ROHNERT PARK
5550 State Farm Drive, Suite E
Rohnert Park, CA 94928
(707) 584-1415

SANTA ROSA
637 First Street
Santa Rosa, CA 95404
(707) 545-1414

SANTA ROSA HISPANIC
P.O. Box 11392
Santa Rosa, CA 95406
(707) 578-2309

SEBASTOPOL
265 Main Street
(P.O. Box 178)
Sebastopol, CA 95473
(707) 823-3032

SONOMA VALLEY
453 First Street East
Sonoma, CA 95476
(707) 996-1033

WINDSOR
8987 Windsor Road
(P.O. Box 367)
Windsor, CA 95492
(707) 838-7285

GLOSSARY OF INGREDIENTS

Many of these ingredients are available by mail order ▼ see Addresses, beginning on page 252.

ACHIOTE ▼ A spice blend from Mexico made from ground annatto seeds, cumin, vinegar, garlic, and other spices; provides a richness and depth of flavor that is difficult to duplicate. Available in Mexico (bring plenty back with you; the packages are small) and Hispanic markets. In Sonoma County, it is available at the Mexicanita Market in Petaluma and La Luna Market in Healdsburg.

ANDOUILLE SAUSAGE, FRESH ▼ Thick Cajun sausage made with pork, pork fat, and lots of garlic. There is no substitute for the particular flavor of *andouille*; if it is unavailable, simply use your favorite sausage.

ANDOUILLE SAUSAGE, SMOKED ▼ A smoked version of the above; sold fully cooked, they do not require heating or cooking, though they are excellent when grilled or in a variety of dishes.

ARBORIO RICE ▼ The classic risotto rice, this plump, large-grained rice is by far the most plentifully produced of the Italian premium rices. It yields more in proportion to its original volume and, because of its size, takes longer to cook than other rice varieties.

ARMENIAN CRACKER BREAD ▼ A Middle Eastern bread available in many markets. Though the large rounds of the bread are most traditional, the square version produced by Ak-Mak Bakeries is easier to use and produces a better, more uniform, *lavosh* sandwich.

ARMENIAN CUCUMBER ▼ A long, 10- to 18-inch, pale green cucumber with edible skin, ridges that give the slices a slightly scalloped edge, and a bright, fresh taste. Also called English cucumber.

ARUGULA ▼ (also called rocket, or roquette) A dark, leafy green with a peppery, slightly bitter flavor that is very appealing. It is becoming increasingly available in this country, and is generally available at the Farm Markets in Sonoma County.

BLACK RASPBERRY VINEGAR ▾ A rich, full-flavored vinegar, more intensely raspberry than the red version, and the best choice for raspberry mayonnaise and raspberry vinaigrette. Kozlowski Farms makes a good one. I know of no other commercial brand that is comparable to the quality they achieve. If you have a supply of black raspberries, try making some of your own (page 215). Available by mail order.

BLOOD PEACH ▾ Deeply colored, vibrant red-purple peaches, with a mild hint of spiciness in their flavor. Blood peaches are excellent with chocolate. The skins are tough and should not be eaten; plunge the fruit into boiling water for 10 seconds, remove, and cool. The skin should peel off easily. Grown by specialty farmers and occasionally available in better markets; ask the produce manager of your favorite store. Substitute a standard peach, though certainly with a loss of eye appeal and lack of the subtle flavors.

BLUEBERRY VINEGAR ▾ Produced in Sonoma County by Kozlowski Farms; a full-bodied vinegar with lots of berry flavor. Excellent with liver, duck, some game, and with fruit salad. Some national distribution and available by mail order.

BORAGE AND BORAGE FLOWERS ▾ A hearty, fast-growing herb, young leaves and flowers of which are excellent in salads. The flowers also make a beautiful garnish, though they wilt fairly quickly (within several hours), making them unsuitable for commercial sale.

CABECOU CHEESE ▾ The smallest of the goat cheeses made by Laura Chenel, the 1½-ounce buttons are marinated in olive oil and herbs. Available by mail order.

CALISTOGAN CHEESE ▾ A slightly aged, very creamy, dense textured chèvre made by Laura Chenel; weighs 2½ ounces. Available by mail order.

CHABIS CHEESE ▾ The most common, popular fresh goat cheese; it is light and delicate, with a creamy texture, and perfect for Chèvre Sauce. Available by mail order from Laura Chenel, and from Rachel's Goat Cheese in Sebastopol, where four types are produced: dill, herb/garlic, black pepper, and plain.

CHANTERELLE, BLACK ▾ A fungus also known as *trompettes des morts*, or trumpets of death, so-called for their shape and their color. One of the more delicious of the wild mushrooms, with a lighter, silkier texture than that of the golden chanterelle, but harder to find. Malcolm Clark of Gourmet Mushrooms, Inc., feels that the flavor is improved with drying.

CHANTERELLE, GOLDEN ▾ Easier to find than its darker cousin, the golden or yellow chanterelle grows throughout the world, but is impossible to cultivate. Although its shape varies a great deal, those chanterelles that resemble an umbrella turned inside out are the most readily recognized. The chanterelle is nearly as much a joy to look at as it is to eat, but not quite; it is delicious. Never hunt wild mushrooms without an expert to guide you; ask the produce manager of your favorite market to try to find a source. Available from fall through early spring, if there has been enough rain.

CHAURICE SAUSAGE ▾ A pork sausage flavored with chile peppers; outstanding grilled, with red beans, or in ratatouille; great on a French roll with onions and sweet peppers.

CHÈVRE ▾ Cheese made from goat's milk. With many producers throughout the country now, it is becoming more and more widely available.

Laura Chenel's Chèvre, which started the whole thing, is available by mail order. See also Goat Cheese.

CHICKEN-APPLE SAUSAGE, EAST INDIAN-STYLE ▼ A family-owned operation in our neighboring county, Gerhard's Napa Valley Sausages offers outstanding products without unpleasant and harmful preservatives. All their products are of top quality; this particular sausage is outstanding. Praised by Margaret Fox of Cafe Beaujolais and Marion Burros of the *New York Times*, these are sausages to remember and to make an effort to get. Available by mail order.

CHIPOTLE PEPPERS ▼ Ripened and smoked *jalapeño* peppers that are very hot but delicious. Some Hispanic markets have them dried, but they are more readily available canned, in adobo sauce; all of the recipes in this book call for that style. There is no substitute for their unusual, smoky flavor.

CHORIZO ▼ A very spicy, Mexican-style sausage, that is available from Sonoma Sausage Factory and, in bulk, from Sebastopol's Fiesta Market. There is no perfect substitute, but *linguiça* will provide a delicious intensity of flavor when *chorizo* is not available. Both should be drained of their fat after cooking and before using.

CHUTNEY ▼ Traditionally a fresh relish served with Indian curries, chutney has come to refer most often to the very sweet, and frequently spicy, preserved fruit mixtures that go wonderfully with a variety of meats, in addition to standard curries. Many types are available; several are made locally. Chutney is also easy to make in your own kitchen and worth the effort. One large batch, using up extra peaches, apricots, persimmons, or green tomatoes, can provide wonderful holiday gifts and keep you in chutney for a year or more.

COCONUT MILK ▼ The liquid in which the grated flesh of mature coconuts is steeped. Acceptable canned versions are available in Asian markets; be sure to get the unsweetened type.

To make at home, place 2 cups grated or finely chopped fresh coconut in 3 cups of scalded milk. Stir and let stand until the mixture cools to room temperature. Strain the mixture through several layers of cheesecloth, using a wooden spoon to press out the liquid.

CRÈME FRAÎCHE ▼ Not unlike sour cream, common in Europe, and just becoming popular here. Hard to find and expensive when you do, it can be made at home in either of two ways. Add 1 tablespoon of buttermilk to heavy cream; place in very clean crock, cover, and keep in warm place until the mixture thickens, up to twenty-four hours. The second method is more reliable, but the results are slightly inferior. Combine one cup sour cream and one cup heavy cream in a very clean jar. Blend well, shake for two minutes, and place in warm, dark area for twenty-four hours. Crème fraîche will keep in the refrigerator for about ten days.

CRIMINI MUSHROOM ▼ (also called portobello, golden crimini, and brown mushrooms) Similar to the commercial white mushroom but, according to several growers, with a greater depth of flavor, a longer shelf life, and more resistance to disease. Commercial producers have scorned criminis until recently because the white give a higher yield. Currently, golden criminis are grown organically by Donald B. Mills, Inc., of Healdsburg. If you can choose between commercial white mushrooms and criminis, take the latter.

CRUDITÉS ▼ Bite-sized servings of vegetables, generally uncooked, sometimes lightly blanched, served as an appetizer with sauces for dipping.

DEMI GLACE ▼ A *sauce espagñole*, or classic brown sauce, to which *glace de viande* has been added and the mixture simmered to reduce by one half.

DRIED TOMATOES (AIR DRIED) ▼ Roma tomatoes air-dried and sold in various forms.

Bits Dried tomatoes ground up. Use in recipes that include plenty of liquid or soften for two minutes in boiling water. Excellent in polenta.

Marinated Halves of dried tomatoes packed in olive oil.

Tapenade A condiment of pureed dried tomatoes and garlic in olive oil.

Timber Crest Farms produces all three varieties under the Sonoma brand; they are available by mail order.

DRIED TOMATOES (SUN DRIED) ▼ Most dried tomatoes are air-dried these days, a faster process more practical for keeping up with the growing demand. Mezzetta, Inc., does distribute an authentic sun-dried version that is very good. The actual drying technique is less important than the quality of the raw materials used.

DRY JACK CHEESE ▼ An excellent hard cheese, aged for seven to ten months, and perfect for grating and slicing. "California Gold" is a version of this cheese that has been aged for a minimum of two years and acquires a crumbly texture similar to that of aged Parmesan. Both are available by mail order from the Vella Cheese Company, the Dry Jack in whole or half wheels, the Gold in whole wheels only.

FROMAGE BLANC (CHEESE) ▼ Fresh, day-old curds, with some of the whey whipped back in; similar, but lighter in texture to ricotta, with a more delicate flavor. It is available by mail order from Laura Chenel, who offers it plain, or flavored with dried tomato, garlic, and basil, fresh herbs, or apricot honey. Rachel's Goat Cheese offers it plain, flavored with dill, or with herbs

and garlic, and, occasionally, smoked salmon with chives; hers are also available by mail order, at Marin County Farm Markets, or at her farm.

GARLIC JACK CHEESE ▼ The traditional Sonoma County-style Jack cheese, with the addition of garlic. Sonoma Cheese Factory's version is somewhat milder than that of Vella's Bear Flag brand, so choose according to your own taste for garlic.

GLACE DE VIANDE ▼ A rich, concentrated reduction of beef stock.

GOAT CHEESE (CHÈVRE) ▼ Cheese made from goat's milk; lower in fat than other cheeses; many varieties, from the day-old curds called *fromage blanc*, to the hard, dry aged Tome, similar in texture to Parmesan. See the listings of specific types. Most goat cheeses have a delicate, light, and slightly earthy flavor. Laura Chenel's Chèvre, the first and best-known of the domestic brands, is outstanding and is available by mail order. Rachel's Goat Cheese, made in Sebastopol, is also excellent and available by mail.

GOLDEN RASPBERRIES ▼ As delicious as they are beautiful, these delicate members of the berry family are in great demand by fine chefs everywhere. Frequently sweeter and more delicate than their more robustly colored relatives, they are always a special treat. They are offered by a number of local berry farms and are frequently available in local markets and at the Farm Market. Kozlowski Farms is always a reliable source.

GORGONZOLA CHEESE ▼ A blue-veined Italian cheese, creamy and delicious. Its American counterpart is a good cheese, but not a substitute for the wonderful imported version.

GRAVENSTEIN APPLE ▼ An early ripening apple originally planted by the Russians who settled in Fort Ross in the early 1800s. Sebastopol's climate of hot days and frequently cool, foggy nights is the perfect growing environment for

Gravensteins, and most of those grown in this country are produced there. This apple ripens quickly and must be used soon after picking, so it is unsuitable for extensive shipping.

GROUND CHERRY ▼ (*Physalis peruviana*; also known as the strawberry tomato, husk tomato, husk cherry, cape gooseberry and, in Hawaii, *poha*) Sweeter than a tomato and generally only a little bigger than currant tomatoes, ground cherries are used as are their more common nightshade cousins, the tomatoes, raw or cooked. They make a novel addition to a salad or vegetable platter and are becoming increasingly popular and available. Occasionally available at the Farm Market in Sonoma County and at some grocers.

HAZELNUT OIL ▼ A lightly textured oil full of the rich essence of hazelnut. Expensive, but a little goes a long way. Available in specialty markets.

HERBS DE PROVENCE ▼ A mixture of dried herbs, including thyme, rosemary, savory, sage, lavender, basil, and sometimes fennel seed. Provides a distinct aroma to dishes and is used to flavor fish, poultry, meat, and breads. Many versions are available, including one by mail order from Williams-Sonoma.

HOT CREOLE SAUSAGE ▼ A fresh sausage with a smoky flavor that makes it perfect in gumbos and jambalayas. It is also excellent grilled and with ratatouille.

JALAPEÑO JACK CHEESE ▼ A vibrant, delicious cheese full of fresh *jalapeño* peppers. Produced by Vella Cheese Factory and available by mail order.

JÍCAMA ▼ Though it grows underground like a tuber, it is part of the legume family. Beneath the thick brown skin which must be removed and discarded, the flesh is creamy white and sweet. It is crunchy and delicious on its own,

drizzled with lime juice or sprinkled with cayenne pepper or chili powder, and is excellent as an addition to salads, especially those in which other vegetables of similar texture but different taste are used.

KALAMATA OLIVE ▼ An almond-shaped, intensely flavored Greek olive, purple to purple-black in color, packed in brine. Imported and distributed by Sonoma's G.L. Mezzetta, Inc., in Sonoma.

KUMAMOTO OYSTER ▼ A small Pacific oyster originally from Japan; highly prized for its delicious, delicate flavor. It is increasingly hard to find true kumamotos because of inbreeding with the *miyagi*. Bay Bottom Beds has some stock, but no longer produces quantities sufficient for sale.

MESCLUN ▼ (also known as *mesclum, mesculum*, spring mix, fall mix) A traditional French mixture of tiny lettuces, including Romaine, curly endive, red lettuce, oak-leaf, Butter lettuce, rocket, and, increasingly, flower petals and leaves, wild greens such as miner's lettuce, herb flowers, and whatever else the grower wants to add to create a signature mixture. Increasingly available in markets throughout the West and very easy for a home gardener to produce.

MINER'S LETTUCE ▼ A wild, flat-leafed green with tiny white flowers that grows from fall through late spring near redwood groves. Not available commercially, but worth the effort to gather it if you live where it grows.

NASTURTIUM FLOWERS ▼ Sweet and peppery flowers, in yellow, orange, red, and purple; one of the most common edible flowers, delicious in salads, and beautiful as a garnish. Limited commercial availability, but very easy to grow in most climates.

NASTURTIUM LEAVES ▾ The leaves of the nasturtium plant have the same peppery flavor as the flowers, but with a crisp, fresh element and without the sweetness. Best when young and no larger than 3 inches across, they make a great salad or addition to a salad, and are excellent as a small appetizer, spread with about ½ teaspoon of one of the cream cheese mixtures on page 85 and wrapped around one of their own flowers. The cheese should keep the leaf securely wrapped. Those exposed to too much sun will become tough.

OLD-FASHIONED CREAM CHEESE ▾ Cream cheese without any gums or stabilizers added to make it easier to spread. The Gina Marie brand, made by Leprino Cheese Co., in Newman, California, and distributed locally in Sonoma by Clover-Stornetta, has a slightly crumbly texture and is far superior to the spreadable brands.

OREGANATO BREAD ▾ A coarse-textured bread from Brother Juniper's Bakery in Forestville, fragrant with plenty of oregano. I cannot imagine a substitute.

PANCETTA ▾ Unsmoked, Italian bacon. If unavailable, use a high-quality, thinly sliced domestic bacon.

PASILLA PEPPERS ▾ If the peppers are named accurately, the *pasilla* will be long, narrow, and very dark green, a characteristic that gives it the name *chile negro* when dried, when it looks almost black. I like to use this pepper for stuffing because of its heat, which is greater than that of many other peppers used for that purpose, the Anaheim in particular.

PASTA, DRIED ▾ Dried pasta has been seen, for reasons that have absolutely nothing to do with taste and everything to do with trend, as the inferior cousin of fresh pasta. Nothing could be further from the truth. Fresh pasta has its place, especially for cannelloni, pasta rolls, homemade ravioli, and so on, but if you eat only fresh pasta, you are limiting yourself foolishly and unnecessarily. When buying dried pasta, look for one of the Italian brands; they are still far better than anything produced domestically.

PASTA, FLAVORED ▾ Originally the domain of fresh pasta only, now available dried. The fresh types have the strongest flavors, for which a variety of herbs and spices and such ingredients as puréed red pepper, pumpkin, sun-dried tomato, and wild mushroom are used. Locally, Pasta Etc. and Buona Pasta sell the best fresh pastas. For the dried variety, Mendocino Pasta Co.'s products are available by mail order through S. E. Rykoff.

PASTA, FRESH ▾ Popularized in the late 70s, there are now many commercial brands available, some of them distributed to major markets, some of them sold only locally. In Sonoma, you can find Pasta Etc.'s fine products in Santa Rosa and Buona Pasta's in Sebastopol.

It is simple to make at home, too, and I recommend the Atlas pasta machine.

Most food experts and chefs will tell you to use flour for your fresh pasta, I find I prefer it made with semolina. Experiment until you find your favorite style.

However, if you have a fresh pasta store in your area and like their product, then it is probably best to leave the work to them; they are the experts, and if they are doing a good job, you probably will not be able to improve on it.

PASTA, FRESH DRIED ▾ This is pasta made according to the technique for fresh pasta and then air dried with the same technique that is used for drying fruit and tomatoes. Obtainable from Mendocino Pasta Co., in Sonoma County by mail order.

PASTA, JALAPEÑO-TOMATO ▾ A freshly made dried pasta made by Mendocino Pasta Co. of Cotati and distributed at many Safeway stores in California, gourmet shops and fine markets in the Bay Area, and by mail order from S. E. Rykoff, P.O. Box 21467, Los Angeles, CA 94021 (800) 421-9873.

PEACH TOMATOES ▾ Pale, blush yellow tomatoes with a slightly fuzzy skin and a mild, subtle flavor. The fruit tends to be about two inches in diameter. Sometimes available at the Farm Market in Sonoma County.

PEAR VINEGAR ▾ A champagne vinegar in which fresh pears have been marinated. Just slightly sweet and subtly evocative of the flavor of pears, this vinegar makes an excellent, light vinaigrette. Le Vinaigre, a French brand, is excellent, and I have seen an increasing number of specialty brands. Currently, it is not produced commercially in Sonoma County. To make your own, cover several peeled, seeded, and sliced pears with one quart champagne vinegar. Refrigerate for at least two days or up to one week. Strain through several layers of cheesecloth and place in one-pint jars. In decorative bottles it makes a nice gift.

POBLANO PEPPERS ▾ Frequently confused with the *pasilla* pepper, the *poblano* is the fresh pepper that is known as *ancho* when dried, though *ancho*, the name, is also correct for the pepper in its fresh state. When fresh, it is a shiny, smooth deep green, and its mild to moderate flavor makes a perfect stuffing pepper.

POLENTA ▾ Very coarsely ground corn meal, available in specialty stores and many major markets. Substitute yellow corn meal if necessary, but it is worth the effort to find authentic polenta which has a much better texture.

POMEGRANATE CONCENTRATE ▾ Pure, concentrated pomegranate juice produced and distributed by Shoosh. Excellent with game duck, and lamb. Available in some specialty markets or by mail order from Shoosh International, Inc. (415) 626-2781.

PORCINI MUSHROOMS ▾ (also called cèpes and king boletus) Considered by many to be the most delicious fungus in the world, this mushroom does not lend itself to commercial cultivation. Widely popular and available in Europe, it is hard to find fresh in this country. Gourmet Mushrooms, Inc., distributes a small quantity domestically, but most of what they collect goes to Europe. Dried porcini are outstanding, and a small quantity (half an ounce), reconstituted in a little hot water, will add a great depth of flavor to any dish. The water should be used as well, or may be reserved for use in another soup or sauce.

POTATOES, PURPLE ▾ (also called blue) Originally from South America, they are becoming increasingly popular here. Because they are farmed in smaller quantities, attention to quality is high, and frequently they are organically grown. The fingerlings make wonderful additions to vegetable platters and there is nothing quite like purple mashed potatoes to tickle the young imagination. Locally the Farallones Institute Gardens and Laguna Farms are producing excellent purple potatoes and they are sometimes available at the Farm Markets in Sonoma County and frequently at the Fiesta Market in Sebastopol.

POTATOES, FINGERLING ▾ Small, oblong potatoes; delicate in flavor and texture.

PRESTON POINT OYSTERS ▾ (also known as *miyagi* oysters) Pacific oysters grown by Bay Bottom Beds in Tomales Bay near Preston Point; delicious and perfect for serving as oysters on the half shell.

PROSCIUTTO ▼ An Italian, salt-cured, pressed, air-dried ham that is neither cooked nor smoked. Those from around Parma are legendary for their wonderful flavor. Best when thinly sliced.

RASPBERRY SYRUP ▼ A sweet concentrate of raspberries. An excellent version is produced by Kozlowski Farms.

RED RASPBERRY VINEGAR ▼ A light and delicious berry vinegar. The intensity of the berry flavor varies greatly from brand to brand, so sample to find your favorite. Le Vinaigre from France does an excellent job for a reasonable price; Kozlowski Farms' version is state of the art.

ROASTED PEPPERS ▼ Generally the term describes red, green, or golden bell peppers that have been blackened over coals or under a broiler, held in a bag to steam for 20 minutes, then peeled, stemmed, and seeded. Though it is never possible, with a canned version, to achieve the quality of fresh peppers, Mezzetta comes close with their excellent product. They have plans for mail order soon.

ROCKY THE RANGE CHICKEN ▼ A free-range chicken produced in Petaluma by Pine Ridge Farms, the producer and distributor of Sonoma Baby Lamb (which goes to restaurant chefs). The happy birds are fed organically, allowed to run and peck, and grow into more muscular birds with a deeper, richer flavor. Rocky Junior is the smaller, younger brother. Available widely throughout the North Bay and California in general; no mail order for obvious reasons. The name has been registered with the U.S. Department of Agriculture after some controversy over the degree of freedom implied in the word, "range." Rocky is in compliance. Consult your Farm Bureau or local specialty markets for an equivalent type of chicken in your area.

SERRANO CHILE ▼ A small, hot pepper with a bright, delicious taste. Serranos vary in size from half an inch to two inches long and in color from bright orange to very dark green. The meatier *jalapeños* may be substituted, but with some change in flavor since the serrano is generally a hotter pepper.

SHIITAKE MUSHROOM ▼ A medium-sized, highly flavored mushroom common in Japan and China for many generations, and popularized in this country by Malcolm Clark of Gourmet Mushrooms, Inc. in Sebastopol. Once available only dried, the fresh are increasingly easy to find throughout the country, from more than a thousand domestic producers. If you cannot find them, talk to the produce manager of your favorite market.

SONOMA JACK ▼ The official brand name of the high-moisture Jack cheeses produced by Sonoma Cheese Factory. Several styles are produced, including the traditional with no additional seasonings, Onion Jack, Garlic Jack, Caraway Jack, Hot Pepper Jack, No Salt Added, and Sonoma Lite (made with part-skim milk). All are available in various sizes as well as in gift pack combinations from Sonoma Cheese Factory.

SOPRASSATTA ▼ An Italian salami-style sausage, but much more flavorful.

ST. GEORGE CHEESE ▼ A semisoft Portuguese-style cheese, named for St. George in the Azores where the producers, Joe Matos and his family, are from. A rich, full-bodied cheese, it is made entirely from the milk of their own herd of cattle. Suitable substitutes include fontina, gruyere, and Jack, though with some loss of character.

TAUPINIÈRE ▼ An aged goat cheese with a white surface bloom; complex, and slightly piquant. A compellingly delicious cheese available from Laura Chenel by mail order.

THAI FISH SAUCE ▾ A thin, salty, translucent brown sauce that forms the base of most Thai sauces. Available in Asian markets; there is no acceptable substitute.

TOMATILLOS ▾ Husk tomatoes; small, light green fruit with a tart, citrus-like flavor. The tan parchment must be removed and they must be rinsed in warm water before they are used. They may be eaten raw or cooked.

TOME ▾ A dry, aged goat cheese, with a hard texture suitable for grating; produced by Laura Chenel and available by mail order.

WILD RICE ▾ Not a rice at all, but a grain purportedly native to America, though China grows a variety. Once prohibitively expensive, the increased availability of and interest in wild rice have reduced the cost considerably. Naturally Wild Wild Rice, harvested from northern Clear Lake and distributed throughout northern California by Wild Distributing in Santa Rosa is an excellent product; also available by mail order.

INDEX